Theatre Through the Camera Eye

Edinburgh Studies in Film and Intermediality

Series editors: Martine Beugnet and Kriss Ravetto
Founding editor: John Orr

A series of scholarly research intended to challenge and expand on the various approaches to film studies, bringing together film theory and film aesthetics with the emerging intermedial aspects of the field. The volumes combine critical theoretical interventions with a consideration of specific contexts, aesthetic qualities, and a strong sense of the medium's ability to appropriate current technological developments in its practice and form as well as in its distribution.

Advisory board
Duncan Petrie (University of Auckland)
John Caughie (University of Glasgow)
Dina Iordanova (University of St Andrews)
Elizabeth Ezra (University of Stirling)
Gina Marchetti (University of Hong Kong)
Jolyon Mitchell (University of Edinburgh)
Judith Mayne (The Ohio State University)
Dominique Bluher (Harvard University)

Titles in the series include:

Romantics and Modernists in British Cinema
John Orr

Framing Pictures: Film and the Visual Arts
Steven Jacobs

The Sense of Film Narration
Ian Garwood

The Feel-Bad Film
Nikolaj Lübecker

American Independent Cinema: Rites of Passage and the Crisis Image
Anna Backman Rogers

The Incurable-Image: Curating Post-Mexican Film and Media Arts
Tarek Elhaik

Screen Presence: Cinema Culture and the Art of Warhol, Rauschenberg, Hatoum and Gordon
Stephen Monteiro

Indefinite Visions: Cinema and the Attractions of Uncertainty
Martine Beugnet, Allan Cameron and Arild Fetveit (eds)

Screening Statues: Sculpture and Cinema
Steven Jacobs, Susan Felleman, Vito Adriaensens and Lisa Colpaert (eds)

Drawn From Life: Issues and Themes in Animated Documentary Cinema
Jonathan Murray and Nea Ehrlich (eds)

Intermedial Dialogues: The French New Wave and the Other Arts
Marion Schmid

The Museum as a Cinematic Space: The Display of Moving Images in Exhibitions
Elisa Mandelli

Theatre Through the Camera Eye: The Poetics of an Intermedial Encounter
Laura Sava

edinburghuniversitypress.com/series/esif

Theatre Through the Camera Eye
The Poetics of an Intermedial Encounter

Laura Sava

EDINBURGH
University Press

Edinburgh University Press is one of the leading university presses in the UK. We publish academic books and journals in our selected subject areas across the humanities and social sciences, combining cutting-edge scholarship with high editorial and production values to produce academic works of lasting importance. For more information visit our website: edinburghuniversitypress.com

© Laura Sava, 2019, 2021

Edinburgh University Press Ltd
The Tun – Holyrood Road
12 (2f) Jackson's Entry
Edinburgh EH8 8PJ

First published in hardback by Edinburgh University Press 2019

Typeset in Garamond MT Pro by
Servis Filmsetting Ltd, Stockport, Cheshire

A CIP record for this book is available from the British Library

ISBN 978 0 7486 9747 2 (hardback)
ISBN 978 0 4744 8428 2 (paperback)
ISBN 978 0 7486 9748 9 (webready PDF)
ISBN 978 1 4744 4590 0 (epub)

The right of Laura Sava to be identified as author of this work has been asserted in accordance with the Copyright, Designs and Patents Act 1988 and the Copyright and Related Rights Regulations 2003 (SI No. 2498).

Contents

List of Figures vii
Acknowledgements viii

Introduction
Accommodating Difference: The Filmic Representation of Theatre 1

Part I Theatre, Interrupted: Strategies of Intermedial Embedment

1. No Strings Attached: Framing Puppets in Movement 23
   The Double Life of Véronique and the Theatrical *Mise en Abyme* 27
   Dolls: Theatrical Bracketing and Filmic Distortion 39

2. Theatre, Memory and the Framing Voice 53
   The Jester: Competing Voices in Alternating Scenes 57
   All About My Mother: Filmic and Theatrical Repetitions 71

3. The Making and Unmaking of Theatre Rehearsals on Screen 84
   Theatre in Multiple Frames: *L'Amour fou* and the Self-defeating Rehearsal 87
   Synecdoche, New York: Film and Theatre as Mutually Contaminating Worlds 100

Part II Divided Attention: Intermedial Performers and their Split Audience

4. Spectatorship by Proxy meets Multimodal Performance 119
   Subversive Performances and Sonic Perspectives in *Opening Night* 122
   Conspicuous Camera and Utopian Spectatorship in *A Tale of Winter* 134
   Exit the Actor: Restrained Performances and the View from the Wings in *I'm Going Home* 145

5. Cinematic Monologues and their Spectatorial Address 157
   The Travelling Players and the Historical Monologue 160
   'Something to Do with Living': *My Dinner with André* and the Ekphrastic Duologue 171
   Spalding Gray and the Autobiographical Monologue 182
   The Arbor and the Unreliable Monologue 194

Epilogue 209

Bibliography 214
Index 233

Figures

All figures, image composites made by the author, fall within the provisions of fair use.

1.1	Bruce Schwartz's 'enormous paws' and his rod puppets – *The Double Life of Véronique*	37
1.2	The gaze of the Bunraku dolls – *Dolls*	40
2.1	Theatrical narration in *The Jester*	69
2.2	Layered beginnings – *All About My Mother*	77
3.1	Theatre imitating life – *Synecdoche, New York*	111
4.1	Vision obstructed – *Opening Night*	129
4.2	Human statues – *A Tale of Winter*	141
4.3	Viewers from the wings – *I'm Going Home*	149
5.1	The three monologues in *The Travelling Players*	167
5.2	The ekphrasis of paratheatre – *My Dinner with André*	179
5.3	Pull and counter-pull – *Swimming to Cambodia*	187
5.4	The monologue at the window – *The Arbor*	201

Acknowledgements

First of all, I would like to thank the series editors, Martine Beugnet and Kriss Ravetto, for their support at the book proposal stage and their insightful comments during the editing process, and the EUP team, Richard Strachan, Eddie Clark, Gillian Leslie and Rebecca Mackenzie, for their patience and assistance. I am also grateful to the anonymous readers employed by EUP for their valuable feedback, which helped refine and focus the book proposal, and to Michael Ayton, the copy editor of the book, and to Zoe Ross, the indexer commissioned by EUP, for their exemplary thoroughness.

This book started its journey to print as a doctoral research project, completed at the University of Warwick. The project was funded through a Warwick Postgraduate Research Scholarship, sponsored by a Warwick alumnus, Mr Chris Rees, to whom I am very grateful, and later through an Early Career Fellowship at Warwick's Institute of Advanced Study. Beyond Warwick, I received financial support from the university where I currently work, Xi'an Jiaotong-Liverpool, in the form of a Research Development Fund.

The book benefited from the input, tutelage and assistance of many academics and library staff. I am first of all profoundly indebted to my PhD supervisor, Jon Burrows, for his unwavering support, intellectual guidance and trust, and to Alastair Phillips, the internal examiner of my doctoral dissertation, for his much-appreciated encouragement. I would also like to acknowledge Werner Wolf, who kindly sent me copies of his articles to which I did not have access, and Adrian Martin, who oversaw the publication of one of my early pieces on film theatre intermediality in a special issue of *Screening the Past*. Thank you also to Daniel Brémaud from the Archives Françaises du Film at Bois D'Arcy for preparing the reels of *L'Amour fou* and enabling one of the best film viewing experiences I have ever had. Ideas that ended up in the book were presented and refined at a number of international conferences. Two in particular were important in the genesis of the book, the 2010 'Theatre and Film' Southeastern Theatre Conference at Agnes Scott College in Decatur and the 2012 colloquium *Théâtre au cinéma, cinéma au théâtre* at the New York University in Paris, and I would like to thank the conference organisers for facilitating intellectually rewarding discussions and encounters.

In the Department of Film and Television Studies at the University of Warwick, I was privileged to study with and alongside many inspiring staff members and colleagues. When I first came to Warwick for an MA, I was initiated into film studies by a triumvirate of wonderful professors, Erica Carter, Richard Dyer and Victor Perkins, the latter unfortunately no longer with us. I could not have wished for a better induction into the discipline, nor for better examples of rigour and intellectual insight. The Warwick experience was also made better by José Arroyo's kindness, good humour and friendship, and by Catherine Constable's generosity. Thanks are also due to Helen Wheatley, Douglas Morrey, Rachel Moseley, Stella Bruzzi, Stephen Gundle, Charlotte Brunsdon, Martin Pumphrey and Ed Gallafent.

The University of Warwick is an intellectually stimulating place and, in addition to the academic staff I already mentioned, there are many former colleagues who made it so for me. I would especially like to acknowledge Michael Pigott, Tom Steward, Pete Falconer, Tom Hughes, David McGowan, Anna Cooper, Paul Cuff, Malini Guha, Chris Meir and Wujung Ju. Particularly generous was James Zborowski, to whom I am grateful for many acts of kindness. My former fellow postgraduate Jason Simpkins passed away in his twenties while working on his PhD and I would like to add his name to the Warwick roll call of gratitude. Warwick is also where I met my former husband, Brian Haman, who offered a lot of assistance and support, especially in the early stages of writing the book, for which I am truly grateful. Ours was a momentous encounter and I learned much from being with him. Thank you also to my Warwick friends from outside the film studies department, Jeanine Tuschling and Knut Langewand, Arina Lungu and Remus Cârstea, Rebecca Mahay, Andrew Ferguson, Yamen Rahwan, Martin Sauter, Stephen Soanes, and to my Warwick university library family, Amy Townsend, Nadežda Jočić-Parry, Chris Godfree-Morrell, Ianis Matsoukas, Martha Michaud, Pinar Dönmez, Rachel Falconer, Victoria Mier and Barclay Lane.

Post-PhD, I found an institutional home at Xi'an Jiaotong-Liverpool University, initially working for the Department of English, Culture and Communication and currently in the School of Film and Television Arts. At XJTLU, as successive heads of departments, Zhoulin Ruan, Nick Cope, Holger Briel and Adam McIlwaine supported me in ways both administrative and collegial. Thank you also to the university VP David Goodman and to all my XJTLU colleagues and students. A special thank you to my lovely student Danni Zhao and her classmates for organising the most affectionate and magical farewell party I have ever had. I would also like to single out Tom Duggett, Paul Cheung, Tabe Bergman, Diana Garrisi and Xianwen Kuang for always managing to find time for a friendly chat amid our busy schedules. Special thanks are also due to Chris Berry and Yannis Tzioumakis for personal and intellectual encouragement.

The friends who stood by me the longest are Bogdan Tănase, Ruxandra Olaru, Nicoleta Bălan, Cristina Sava, Irina Cărăbaș, Ada Hajdu, Ioana Măgureanu, Ciprian Buzilă, Alice Bardan, Andra Moise, Claudia Dragostin, Mihaela Hagea, Alex Radu, Vlad Bedros and Adriana Oprea. The Department of Art History at the National University of Arts in Bucharest, where I met several of them and where several of them now work, was the place where we came of age intellectually and where we were mentored by great professors. I would especially like to thank Anca Oroveanu, who has had a great impact on my intellectual development and who remains a prodigious source of inspiration.

This book was completed at a difficult time in my life. My friend Louis Bayman supported me the most during this time, both emotionally and intellectually, and our conversations brought me much comfort and renewed confidence. In many ways, our dialogue was life-restoring, and I thank him for his trust, patience and profound empathy. I draw much strength from my family and to them I would like to turn now with a grateful heart. Thank you to my brother Ștefan Sava and his partner Magda Radu for their hospitality, care and steadfast support. Thank you most of all to my extraordinarily generous and loving parents Doina and Ștefan Sava, to whom I owe so much. This book is dedicated to my awe-inspiring grandmother Victoria Omoreanu, who is dearly missed.

In loving memory of my grandmother, Victoria Omoreanu

INTRODUCTION

Accommodating Difference:
The Filmic Representation of Theatre

> You are an actor and you take up this terrible chair [demonstrating] and you put it up here on the table, and then you tell the audience: 'My dear friends, you may think this chair looks terrible but you are mistaken. This is the most expensive and the most beautiful diamond-encrusted gold chair ever created. It was made for a small Chinese empress six thousand years ago; she died sitting on it, and it was buried with her. Now it's here – and it is very, very fragile. But now take care of it, for I must leave you for a few moments.' Then you come back as a scoundrel, and you begin to knock the chair around – and the entire audience will hate that scoundrel. They will become anxious because they have accepted the suggestion and have developed feelings about the chair. And *that* is theater. (Marker and Marker 1982: 20–1)

It is through this simple but suggestive set-up described in a 1979 interview that Ingmar Bergman explained, with enviable self-assurance, what he understood by the theatre experience. The passage went on to form the basis of a scene in the television version of the 1982 film *Fanny and Alexander*, a film which was promoted as Bergman's farewell to cinema and subsequently hailed by critics as 'a Rosetta stone to his entire oeuvre' (Kakutani 2007: 156). In what follows, I shall take a closer look at this scene in order to introduce the key theoretical concerns of this book, which aims to explore filmic representations of theatre in arthouse films through an intermedial lens.

In the slightly modified version offered in the film, Bergman's basic theatrical experiment becomes a bedtime story told by Oscar Ekdahl (Allan Edwall), the head of an Uppsala-based theatre family, to his children, the film's eponymous Fanny (Pernilla Allwin) and Alexander (Bertil Guve). The scene is immediately preceded by a magic lantern show narrated by Alexander to his sister and two younger cousins, a ghost story featuring a lonesome girl named Arabella who, in the dead of night, receives the unexpected visit of her mother's ghost. The girls are spooked by the story, and their terrified shrieks together with the smell of the paraffin lamp used for the projection give away the children's wakefulness. Oscar enters the nursery where the four children are feigning to be asleep in their beds and thus starts his performance when he, in his turn, feigns a moment of surprise. 'That's odd. Very odd', he says as he picks up a small, timeworn chair from the nursery, visually appraising it. The deictic expression instantly captures the children's interest and they begin to stir in their beds, curious about the unnamed object of marvel. It is at this point that Oscar starts weaving the fanciful story which prefaced this introduction around the modest, forgotten chair of the nursery. As in Bergman's account, he places it on a table under the dim light of a lamp, which gives the chair a faint glow, and sitting on one of the beds amid the children, who huddle around him in delighted anticipation, he points and nods in its direction as he tells the story. The children's attention is maintained through a series of teasing questions uttered in a slow, calculated cadence ('Do you see the mysterious light radiating from the chair?', 'Why is the chair luminous?'), followed by an accumulation of ever more incredible details, revealed after the children are sworn to secrecy. Oscar teases them further, by bringing over the chair and asking them to gently touch it. He briefly goes away, only to reappear shortly thereafter, his robe over his head in a thin disguise as the scoundrel mentioned by Bergman. He sits on the chair and comically pretends to be bitten by it, but when he tries to enact his revenge, violently shaking the wooden chair, Fanny intervenes to stop him. Bergman's beautiful demonstration of theatrical effect proceeds like clockwork, hitting all the right notes.

Critics have justly observed that what is at stake in this scene is a process of 'activation of belief' that confirms the 'power' and 'danger' of stories (Kalin 2003: 173–4). The interpretation makes sense because the film will later require a considerable leap of faith from its viewer, a leap of faith onto which hinges the film's entire narrative edifice. However, I want to complicate and broaden the scope of this reading, by taking up and elaborating on Bergman's bold claim that the scene shows us what theatre is. As Bert O. States has noted, the words 'performance' and 'theatre' are 'hyperactive as metaphors' (1996: 26), which is why my goal here is not to propose via Bergman a definitive definition of theatre. What I would like to suggest instead is that filmic representations of theatre contribute to a never settled, constantly evolving experiential understanding of the mechanisms of the two media. It is telling in this respect that the scene I have just described, which, if we are to believe Bergman, illustrates what the medium of theatre at its most minimal can achieve, follows and inevitably challenges the representation of a magic lantern show, a forerunner of cinema and as such, a simplified, 'primitive' version of film's own capabilities.

STRANDS OF ENQUIRY AND THEORETICAL ASSUMPTIONS

Several ideas are worth drawing out from the story of the empress of China chair, ideas that tie it to influential notions of theatricality and launch themes of reflection that will be continued throughout the book. The first thing to note regarding the way in which theatre is represented in the extract is the scene's very distinct spatial arrangement, the way in which it literally takes place. Oscar needs a stage and he improvises one, by placing the chair high up on a table under a light. The camera supports this act of spatial organisation by showing in one shot the chair and the table in splendid isolation, fairly well-lit and ready for Oscar's performance. The notion of a physical arrangement being integral to what we understand by theatre has been proposed numerous times. Josette Féral, for instance, remarks that theatricality

> recognizes subjects in process; it is a process of looking at or being looked at. It is an act initiated in one of two possible spaces: either that of the actor or that of the spectator. In both cases, this act creates a cleft in the quotidian that becomes the space of the other, the space in which the other has a place. Without such a cleft, the quotidian remains intact, precluding the possibility of theatricality, much less of theater itself. (2002: 98)

The 'cleft in the quotidian' that Bergman's scene vividly illustrates is established by a separation between those who watch and those who are being watched, between spectators and performers. According to Féral, this separation, or to use a different formulation, this 'portable proscenium arch' (States 1996: 16), can be the initiative either of an actor 'seizing control of the quotidian and turning it into theatrical space' or of a spectator, whose gaze can render the space theatrical (Féral 2002: 97). In Bergman's scene, the onus is on the actor to constitute the space that shapes the theatrical encounter but he does it with the willing complicity of his audience.

Féral is not the only author who has linked theatre as a medium with spatiality. Samuel Weber associates theatricality with a process of 'situating' and 'framing' (2004: 315) and the military use of the term ('theatre of operations') leads him to conceptualise theatre as 'a medium in which conflicting forces strive to secure the perimeter of a place in dispute' (ibid.). In his book *Acting in Cinema*, James Naremore has similarly used the idea of a 'force field' to address the process of theatricalisation, noting that 'when art theatricalizes contingency' what it does is to put 'a conceptual bracket around a force field of sensations' (1988: 23). According to Naremore, while both film and theatre are characterised by 'a physical arrangement that arrays spectacle for persons in an audience role' (ibid.), what distinguishes the two is that in theatre the physical arrangement allows the actor and the audience to have a 'provisional', open exchange, whereas in cinema, 'the physical arrangement is permanently closed' (ibid.: 29).[1] One can hardly refer to the ideas of 'framing' and 'arrangement' without in the same breath mentioning the work of Erving Goffman, an author that Naremore himself acknowledges. Thanks to Goffman (1986) and

Richard Schechner [1988] (2005) and their notions of 'framed behaviour' and 'restored behaviour', the concept of frame is part and parcel of how we think about performance activities in general. Framing is also central to the first half of the book, which looks at how film frames diegetic theatre for the film spectator. The second half of the book will consider the relation between actors and spectators as it is articulated in films which represent or evoke theatre and so both sections trace their lineage to this spatial understanding of theatricality.

The second idea that Bergman's scene enables us to reflect on, corresponding to yet another important conceptual strand that runs through the book, is theatricality as emanating from the actor. Oscar is the one who effects, through techniques of verbal compensation and enhancement, the transfiguration of the nursery chair into the precious seat belonging to the fictional empress of China. To quote Bert O. States, in theatre *'everything* happens through the actor' (1987: 153–4) and it is this mediation together with the actor's actual presence or bodily facticity that for some scholars constitutes the fundamental characteristic of theatre. To give but one example, Eli Rozik's understanding of theatricality privileges acting, which he defines as a 'deflection of reference', an 'evocative device' whereby the actor produces 'indexes of actions' belonging to somebody else, this somebody else being the character (2002: 112). Films about theatre often involve in some shape or form a reflection on this phenomenon and the present study will discuss some of the ways in which this occurs.[2] Rozik extends the function of acting to all stage objects, in a move which echoes Peter Handke's assertion that in theatre 'a chair is a chair pretending to be another chair' (cited in States 1987: 20). This 'deflection of reference' is straightforwardly epitomised by Bergman's scene, in which the humble nursery chair, by standing in for another, more illustrious chair, serves to re-enchant the space it occupies. To use Catherine Ailloud-Nicolas's wording, we could argue that the chair is rescued from its 'semiological exhaustion' and aesthetically 're-motivated' (2003: 251, my translation). It is significant that Bergman has chosen as a starting point for his fiction one of the most frequently used stage objects. In his book on theatrical props, Andrew Sofer (2003) has singled out four representative objects (the bloody handkerchief for the Elizabethan stage, the skull for the Jacobean stage, the fan in the Restoration period and the gun in modern theatre), tracing their so-called 'stage life', their steady accumulation of meanings. To his compelling list one could legitimately add the chair, important for both the nineteenth-century realist drama and for modern theatrical experiments. Bert O. States has spelled out the chair's connotative richness, by noting that while it was initially associated with and indicative of 'the gradual atrophy of verbal scenery' in theatre, functioning primarily as the *'locus operandi* of the chat', it then went on to serve a variety of purposes:

> In the modern theater the chair (or such derivatives as Edward Albee's park bench and Beckett's urns) becomes: territorial preserve, weapon and shield (Ibsen and Pinter); the curse of the material world (Ionesco); the seat of anxiety, of time and place as enemy, of the problematical nature of existence among 'the things' (Chekhov and Beckett). (1987: 46)

One could safely assume that, as a consummate theatre practitioner, Bergman was not only aware of this prestigious pedigree, but also indirectly alluded to it and to the way in which objects can be invested with theatricality. Bergman's story, ostensibly a mere illustration of how belief in fiction may be engendered, belies therefore a more complex interplay of ideas about the mediality of theatre which will have echoes throughout the present study.

In this book, similar filmic moments of embedded theatre will constantly stand out, a 'reading situation' that Mary Ann Caws would describe as positively 'stressful'. In her work, stress is taken to mean, on the one hand, an 'anxiety relating to the projects both of comparison and of the expression of that comparison' and, on the other hand, an 'accent placed on certain details in particular' (1989: 3). Caws is concerned with the relation between visual and verbal texts and the interpretive stress is generated in her case by the thought of having to 'translate perception' and by the need to develop 'a translating sort of perception' (ibid.: 13). Fundamentally, her anxiety of comparison is not very different from the 'stress' of my analysis, which seeks to explain how film 'translates' theatre and to render communicable through language the mechanisms of two media, film and theatre, whose arsenal of modes of expression far exceeds the verbal. This theme of the irreducibility of one thing to another, one language to another, one medium to another, is a well-trodden path. Jacques Derrida has written of 'the necessary and impossible task of translation' (cited in Hawker 2009: 274), John Mullarkey of the 'recalcitrance' of film to 'various theories of film' (2009: 189), Carol Chillington Rutter of the problematic conversion of 'the 'thisness' of performance into the 'thatness' of analysis' (2001: xiii) and the list could continue. This theoretical conundrum lies at the heart of the present study as well, but like my more distinguished predecessors, rather than worry about the inbuilt risk of fallibility, I take comfort in the knowledge that translating (inter)medial experiences into analysis is a necessary exercise, which brings us closer to understanding how media reflect on themselves and on each other. As a final caveat, this act of translation challenges one to develop, as Lesley Stern and George Kouvaros have argued, 'a more ostensive and demonstrative mode of description': 'in order to turn the film into writing, in order to convey movement, corporeal presence, performative modalities and affective inflections, a certain refiguring is required, an attentiveness to the fictional impulse at the heart of any ekphrastic endeavour' (1999: 17).

Another set of tacit assumptions that underlies such a study has to do with the way in which we engage with films when we analyse them, often through technologies that, as Laura Mulvey eloquently put it, afford us the 'possibility of returning to and repeating a specific film fragment' and thus 'interrupting the flow of film, delaying its progress', allowing 'dormant details [. . .] to be noticed' (2006: 8). When this type of persistent attention is brought to bear specifically on moments of film performance, what happens is that, as James Naremore observes, 'The same machinery that fetishizes performance also permits it to be deconstructed or replayed in ways that run counter to its original intentions', allowing us, the spectators, 'to become postmodernists, alienating the spectacle, producing a heightened awareness of the artificiality in all acting' (1988: 31). At the same time, as William Uricchio reminds us, 'projects of close formal analysis', as this book aspires to be, are informed by a 'perception of textual stability' and by a commitment to "restoring' textual perfection, archiving it, defending it', habits of mind that are increasingly challenged by the digital culture in which we are immersed (2004: 165). For all these reasons, the act of interpretation itself is an intervention in the filmic text, pausing and slowing it down at chosen moments, directing and amplifying attention to certain aspects of it while at the same time reasserting the stability and integrity of the film as a whole.

INTERMEDIALITY AS A GENERAL FRAMEWORK OF ANALYSIS

Bergman's films will not be discussed in the remainder of this book, but I chose to open with an example drawn from his extensive filmic output, not only because his films abound in theatre representations and, as such, are an unavoidable landmark, but also because recent critical estimates of his oeuvre have increasingly concentrated on the filmmaker's practical espousal of intermediality, a concept that I would like to introduce next. Active in several media (film, theatre, opera, television), Bergman was not only versatile in his engagement with them, but also, it would seem, flexible about the prospect of working in several formats, at one point writing 'scores for the media in general' and subtitling one of his projects 'Nine dialogues for an optional medium' (Törnqvist 2003: 12–13). According to Ulla-Britta Lagerroth, in addition to this ease of movement between media, Bergman also exploited the 'possibilities of intermedialising them': 'he theatricalised his films, as well as cinematised his theatre productions' and more than once resorted to 'pictorialisation' and 'musicalisation' (2008: 35).

Ever since it was embraced by academia, the concept of intermediality has undergone a process of taxonomic proliferation, a fact which does not make it especially tractable from a methodological point of view. What complicates matters further is that intermediality is a cross-disciplinary project, or a 'research axis', as Jürgen Müller labelled it (2010: 237). The very term 'intermediality' points to the existence of a state of in-between-ness that needs to be accounted for. In a narrow sense,[3] this in-between-ness may refer to 'a specific quality of individual artefacts or texts in which more than one medium participates in their signification' (Wolf 2002: 15). In the case of film, Ágnes Pethő finds that this quality whereby more than one medium participate in the process of filmic signification is tantamount to a 'kind of excess, a surplus in the cinematic image' (2011: 6), which is then taken as an object of analysis. However, there is no consensus on how this analysis ought to be conducted and intermediality often encompasses diverse approaches. As Pethő notes:

> We have seen semiotic interpretations of intermediality (whereas media have been defined as complex sign systems), we have seen intertextual approaches to intermediality (extending a pre-existing vocabulary and methodology over inter-art relationships), and we have seen philosophical theorizing of intermedial relations based on ideas originating in the works of Deleuze and Guattari, Derrida, Lyotard. (ibid.: 69)

Pethő has singled out the works of Joachim Paech and Yvonne Spielmann as exemplary for what she calls a 'historical poetics of intermediality', focused on cataloguing and analysing intermedial figures and relations, such as the layered image or the 'cluster' in Peter Greenaway's films and the widespread technique of the *tableau vivant*, both of which allow us to observe the nexus of film and other media (ibid.: 43–4). Pethő's own methodological inclinations take her in an altogether different direction and she calls for an understanding of intermediality that would be 'entirely divorced from models of "text", "texture" and "reading"' (ibid.: 67), advocating instead for a 'phenomenology of intermediality' that would take into account the experience of the 'embodied spectator' and would seek to do it justice in analyses of intermedial relations (ibid.: 69). Phenomenology does indeed enable a heightened attention to the formal properties of the medium, which is fundamental to any avowed intermedial project, and this book will resort to phenomenological theory in the readings of several of its case studies.

The fact that intermediality often results in an approach with a strong formal component raises the issue of the well-known 'rift' between formal approaches and cultural/contextual ones, a rift which has been intelligently discussed by Kamilla Elliott (2014) with respect to adaptation studies, a sub-field, some may argue, of intermediality studies. Commenting on this divide, Elliott has emphasised the need for 'hybrid methodologies' that would avoid the danger of a 'culturally irrelevant formalism' (ibid.: 584–5) and Lúcia Nagib has issued a similar warning regarding 'formalist intermedial analyses of cinema' that run the risk of 'becoming purely narcissistic exercises' (2014:

21). While not overtly political in nature and of a mostly formalist bent, this book will take into account issues of cultural context for each of the case studies, because in the absence of such an awareness of cultural variations, the very term 'theatre' becomes unusable.

Intermediality has proven especially fertile as a concept in understanding the genesis of the film medium, out of extensive borrowings from and reworkings of other media. According to André Gaudreault and Philippe Marion, the period surrounding the birth of a medium is characterised by a 'spontaneous intermediality', an intermediality which is subsequently replaced by a 'negotiated intermediality' (2005: 94). The medium in their view is not a static formation, but a fluid one, subject to reconfigurations, and the metaphors they use to refer to it (prism, constellation) are indicative precisely of this dynamic media environment in which intermediality represents a sort of breeding ground for media, old and new (ibid.: 88–90). It must be said that, while the discourse of intermediality *needs* the medium to be able to analyse how it is destabilised and violated, not all theoreticians are still willing to work with a paradigm that distinguishes between various media. In the 1990s, the art historian Rosalind Krauss declared the medium 'obsolete', in need of re-invention, fuelling a discussion which continues to this day about the 'post-medium condition' (Krauss 1999, Kim 2009), but also interestingly resuscitating, if only to question it, the medium specificity debate, which seeks to differentiate between media in ways that have been read as essentialist (Doane 2007: 129). In the first chapter of his book *Engaging Cinema*, Noël Carroll, one of the most astute critics of the medium specificity thesis, has famously urged us to 'Forget the Medium!', challenging the view that 'each and every artform must correlate to a single medium that is distinctively and uniquely its own' (2003: 5) and proposing that we replace the notion of film as a medium with the notion of 'moving image' (ibid.: 9). In response to what he saw as Carroll's 'medium eliminativism', Murray Smith has suggested instead a position of 'medium deflationism' that would treat both 'medium' and 'medium specificity' as historical notions which artists and theoreticians alike continue to explore and which are thus still informing the thought process that goes into an art work (2006: 140–1, 145). This position bears some similarity with the treatment of media as 'conventionally distinct' in intermediality scholarship (Wolf 2005: 252).

For a long time, the prevalent definitions of the word 'medium' have been the 'semiotic definition' (the medium as a 'technical means of expression') and the so-called 'transmissive definition' (the medium as a 'conduit') (Ryan 2005: 289), but soon after intermediality as a concept started gaining momentum, it was recognised that a more 'flexible' definition of the medium was needed, one that would somehow reconcile the previously distinct definitions and encompass semiotic, technical and cultural aspects (Wolf 2008: 18). Recent interventions (Elleström 2010) have therefore called for a 'multimodal' understanding of media that would be more amenable to intermediality studies. In the multimodal framework, media are seen to possess several modalities (material, sensorial, spatiotemporal, semiotic) which are variously pedalled when one analyses the relations between media.[4]

Intermediality itself is a very capacious term and this book is not going to consider all forms of film–theatre intermediality.[5] What I shall be concerned with primarily is the explicit representation of theatre in film and films in which theatre has a diegetic presence. By certain standards, this is a mild form of intermediality and there are scholars who would even dispute that it is an actual form of intermediality. For instance, Jens Schröter classifies 'the representation of one medium by another' under 'transformational intermediality' and remarks that

> it is questionable whether we can talk here of intermediality since the artifact of a certain medium (e.g. a film) does not contain another medium (e.g. a painting) as another but instead, represents it. A painting in a film or a building on a photograph are no longer paintings or buildings but are integral parts of the medium representing them: they are simply being represented. (2011: 5)

However, he also adds that in the process of referentially pointing to another medium, the representing medium can comment not only on the medium it represents, but also on its own 'self-conception', and that the representation can be done in such a way as to 'defamiliarise' and 'transform' the representing medium (ibid.). Schröter allows therefore that this type of representation has intermedial implications and it is the latter part of his argument that I want to underscore here. In an alternative classification, Ágnes Pethő subsumes the category of 'embedded representations of one art within the other' (note the shift from 'medium' to 'art') under comparative analyses of cinema and the other arts (interartiality) and expresses her own set of reservations regarding this body of work, in so far as they often do not openly explore aspects of mediality (2011: 34–5). Pethő's concern is justified and, in response, this study intends not only to offer an examination of how the embedding of diegetic theatre is achieved from a narrative and formal point of view but also to explore what it reveals about the mediality of the arts involved.

THE RELATIONSHIP BETWEEN FILM AND THEATRE IN ACADEMIC SCHOLARSHIP

Film and theatre are both considered to be composite media. Despite their different medial articulations, performance and staging are nonetheless common denominators, so much so that theorists such as Eli Rozik have gone so far as to claim that cinema is 'a kind of (moving) photography, characterized by a particular kind of object: performed drama' (2005: 170), that, in other words, 'a feature film is a recording of a fictional world formulated in the medium of theatre' (ibid.: 169). A similar position was previously voiced by Richard Allen who, in the context of discussing the 'projective illusion' of cinema, argued that 'The cinema inherits the fictional incompetence of the photograph. It has the ability to convey or enhance dramatic fiction, but it is not a medium of fiction' (1993: 40). These scholars and others of a similar persuasion seem to suggest that film already incorporates theatre in its makeup. Performance is seen not only as a bridging element between the two media but also as a category in relation to which theatre and film function as 'sub-practices', leading Charles Musser to propose that one 'might profitably seek to write an integrated history of theatrical entertainment which includes both live stage performance and the cinema' (2004: 4).

However, film and theatre are media with different 'automatisms', different 'affordances', to use two words that often crop up in media theory. At the opposite end of the views expressed by Allen and Rozik, Stanley Cavell once remarked that 'the general answer to the common question, "In what ways do movies differ from novels or from theater?" ought to be: "In every way"' (1979: 73). Even when the contamination between theatre and film is at its most effective, there are still ineludible differences that will manifest themselves. Some of these dissimilarities have been pointed out by Ben Brewster and Lea Jacobs in their study on the influence of theatrical pictorialism in early cinema, where they compare the theatrical and the cinematic stage in terms of scalar fixity, width and depth of composition (1997: 148–51). Another important distinction is to be found in drama theory and involves the presence or absence of what has been termed a 'mediating communication system', namely 'the selective, accentuating and structuring medium of the camera or narrator' (Pfister [1977] 1993: 24–5). In his latest book on narrative film, George M. Wilson alerts the reader to this very difference, when he states that, despite there being ample reason to classify film alongside theatre among the forms of 'mimetic storytelling', the fact that the 'dramatic materials are displayed to spectators through a mediating chain of edited photographic shots gives film an additionally discursive character' (2011: 21). These are just some of the more recent contributions to a complex and long-standing debate about the differences between film and theatre, a debate which is impossible to rehearse here in all its intricacies and modulations.[6]

The main entries in this vast literature on the differences and relationship between theatre and film have been discussed and anthologised several times with varying emphases (Nicoll 1936; Hurt 1974; Knopf 2005; Cardullo 2012;

Jackson 2013) and they testify to an enduring interest in the pairing of the two media. The topic of cinematic theatricality was recently brought back into the spotlight by an English language collection of essays, which judiciously differentiates theatricality as it is understood in theatre theory from theatricality in film, defining the latter as self-conscious artificiality and, following Judith Butler, as an 'agent of *exposure*, which reveals the performativity of performed conventions' (Loiselle and Maron 2012: 4–5, 9). In the editors' view, theatricality admits of many forms, ranging from 'obvious devices like ostentatious performances, formal staging, and fragmentary montage to more subtle techniques of dialogue delivery and movement carried out to challenge film's realist claims' (ibid.: 5). The French language scholarship has been equally productive, with at least three collective volumes on topics such as theatricality and cinema and the so-called 'film de théâtre'/'theatre film' (Hamon-Sirejols et al. 1994; Prédal 1999; Picon-Vallin 2001a) constituting important precedents for the problems I am exploring in this book. All of them pre-date the 'intermedial turn' and, as such, do not frame the issues they address in intermedial terms.

FOCUS AND STRUCTURE OF THE BOOK

In contradistinction to the approaches reviewed thus far, this book aims to be a more focused study, concerned solely with films that feature theatre performances, rehearsals or monologues, and structured around two main problems of representation (the embedding of theatre in film and modes of spectatorial address in filmic representations of theatre). My hope is that what is lost in breadth is gained in depth and sustained attention. Had I cast my net wider, I would not have been able to deliver the close textual analysis that is fundamental to my book and that is all too often sidestepped in writings which amass examples in order to provide an inventory of as many forms of theatricality in cinema as possible. This book's focus roughly corresponds to what Jacques Gerstenkorn, in the introduction to the volume *Cinéma et théâtralité*, identifies as one of the main manifestations of theatricality in cinema, namely the 'explicit reference to theatre' achieved through the 'partial or complete diegetisation of the theatrical *dispositif*' or through 'citation and allusion' which can similarly 'inject' theatre in the film's diegesis (1994: 16, my translation). One of the aims will be to analyse how the diegetisation of theatre in film can be accompanied by more implicit forms of theatricality. The book situates itself at the intersection of different theoretical concerns, combining textual/formalist analysis with insights derived from drama theory, narratology, performance philosophy and film and theatre phenomenology, in a way that I believe is sanctioned and even encouraged by the intermedial framework, which represents, to quote Rebecca Schneider, a 'scholarship on the slip' (2006: 253).

In designing the structure of this book, I was interested in assembling a class of films that would communicate inside and across chapters. The films form tighter alliances within each chapter, as they contribute, in sub-groups, to the foregrounding of specific issues. The book is organised in two main parts: the first part is dedicated to different forms of embedment of diegetic theatre in film, while the second part focuses on various modes of spectatorial engagement at play in films which either represent theatre or incorporate theatrical monologues. Chapter 1 introduces the first two forms of embedment (*mise en abyme* and bracketing) alongside an interest in filmic and theatrical illusion, explored with the help of two films which feature fragments of puppet theatre: *The Double Life of Véronique* (Krzysztof Kieślowski, 1991) and *Dolls* (Takeshi Kitano, 2002). Chapter 2 proposes yet another pair of films (José Álvaro Morais' 1987 *The Jester* and Pedro Almodóvar's 1999 *All About My Mother*) through which a shift of emphasis is proposed from visual framing to aural framing. The films share an interest in memory and voice-over and, in their representation of theatre, they use patterns of alternation and repetition which draw attention to this alliance between theatre, voice and memory. Chapter 3 carries forward the concern with how film formally 'contains' theatre, by examining more complex forms of embedment (multiple framings and infinite regress structures) as they are deployed in two films revolving around theatre rehearsals: Jacques Rivette's 1969 *L'Amour fou* and Charlie Kaufman's 2008 *Synecdoche, New York*.

Although issues of formal embedment continue to be important in the second part of the book, Chapter 4 switches gears towards considering how the representation of theatre in film often articulates a dual address, by assigning various positions to the diegetic theatre audience in relation to the film spectator. The case studies which shine a spotlight on this issue are *Opening Night* (John Cassavetes, 1977), *A Tale of Winter* (Eric Rohmer, 1992) and *I'm Going Home* (Manoel de Oliveira, 2001). Chapter 5 extends the scope of this enquiry by focusing on the spectatorial experience afforded by the use of monologues in *The Travelling Players* (Theo Angelopoulos, 1975), *My Dinner with André* (Louis Malle, 1981), *The Arbor* (Clio Barnard, 2010) and two of Spalding Gray's filmed monologues (*Swimming to Cambodia* and *Monster in a Box*).

Notes

1. Not only is the medium of theatre associated with spatiality, but its distinct use of space is often invoked in discussions that aim to identify the differences between

film and theatre. For André Bazin, the two media involve different 'dramaturgical systems' (1967: 106): the '*locus dramaticus*' in theatre is 'an area materially enclosed, limited, circumscribed' (ibid.: 104), whereas the principle that governs cinema is 'the denial of any frontiers to action' (ibid.: 105) and, as a result, the actor is differently positioned in each of these two media. For Susan Sontag, the difference lies in the issue of the continuity of space, theatre being confined in her view to 'a logical or *continuous* use of space', whereas cinema has the possibility, through editing, of using space in an 'alogical or discontinuous' manner (1966: 29).
2. Ariane Mnouchkine's *Molière, ou la vie d'un honnête homme* (France, 1978) is an example of a film that vividly foregrounds this understanding of theatricality (Sava 2011).
3. Intermediality can also be used in a broader sense, in which case the in-between-ness covers a whole spectrum of relations between media, including adaptation and the transmedial traffic of artistic conventions (Wolf 2005; Mariniello 2011), relations that automatically arise in the ever-changing media ecology to which every medium belongs. In other words, the very fact that media exist alongside one another means that they inevitably 'intermedialise', or, to quote Jay Bolter and Richard Grusin, 'Media are continually commenting on, reproducing, and replacing each other, and this process is integral to media. Media need each other in order to function as media at all' (2000: 55). In a similar vein, Lars Ellestrӧm sees intermediality 'as a general condition for understanding communicative and aesthetic mechanisms, events and devices, rather than as a peripheral exception to "regular" mediality' (2010: 12) and his position is not without antecedents, especially among historians of the media, who similarly define intermediality as 'a mixing of mediums in cultural production' (Gaudreault 2000: 12).
4. For Ellestrӧm, who proposed this highly ramified framework, media manifest themselves: (a) materially, through their distinct 'corporeal interface' (such as the flat surface of the screen in the case of cinema); (b) sensorially, through the specific way in which they engage the senses in the act of perception; (c) spatio-temporally, via the experience of space and time they afford; and (d) semiotically, by enabling meaning-making through signs, representations, symbolic forms (2010: 17–24). This layered, multimodal view of mediality is complicated by an additional distinction between 'basic', 'qualified' and 'technical' media (ibid.: 12). Theatre and film are not only multimodal, but also plurimedial, in the sense of being the result of a combination of basic media. According to Ellestrӧm, theatre 'normally combines and integrates, to varying degrees, basic media such as auditory text, still image and body performance' (ibid.: 28), while film is 'primarily based on moving images, auditory text and non-verbal sounds' (ibid.: 27). Theatre and film are both qualified in the sense that they are each associated with a set of 'historical and cultural conventions and aesthetic standards' (Ellestrӧm 2010: 29) that have sedimented in time and they involve different technical media. In Ellestrӧm's model, theatre entails technical media such as the performing body, whereas historically film has relied on the technical medium of photography and consists of a complex technological apparatus, made up of techniques of recording and projecting.

5. An influential contribution to intermediality studies is the discussion of intermedial references by Irina O. Rajewsky and Werner Wolf. In slightly different but compatible formulations, both postulate that there are various possible scenarios of interaction between two media involved in a process of referencing: a medium can thematise, partially quote, evoke or imitate another medium (Rajewsky 2005; Wolf 2005). Examples of the last two types may include literary, musical, painterly and theatrical effects in film, but not the explicit representation of theatre in film, which would technically fall under 'thematisation' or 'partial quotation', as the case may be. To describe the instances in which a given medium evokes or formally imitates another medium, Rajewsky points to their 'as if' quality and claims that 'an intermedial reference can only generate an *illusion* of another medium's specific practices' (Rajewsky 2005: 55, emphasis in the original). Wolf further contributes to the elucidation of this particular situation by noting that the referenced medium has 'a conceptual rather than a physical presence' within the referencing medium and that, therefore, when we discuss intermedial references we are not dealing with an actual case of medial heterogeneity (Wolf 2005: 254). The formal imitation of another medium is also Andrew Shail's category of predilection, which prompts him to define intermediality 'as merely formal' (2010: 5). For scholars strictly following the Wolf/Rajewsky model, the formal imitation of theatre in film would cover what is sometimes elusively called 'stagey' films but not diegetic moments of represented theatre. I believe, however, that intermediality needs to be more than an exercise in matching categories to examples and that the case studies discussed in this book often straddle the divide between thematisation, partial quotation, evocation and formal imitation. Wolf himself has issued a caveat about 'borderline cases and multiple labellings of one and the same phenomenon' (ibid.: 255), which is one of the reasons why this stringent classification will not be used in this book.

6. In its beginnings, film theory has engaged almost obsessively with theatre, a medium that represented for film both the closest kin and the most feared influence. Gregory A. Waller (1983) has provided a pertinent and detailed analysis of the historical arguments around theatre and cinema (the stage screen debate), suggesting that before 1940 the two media were aesthetically pitted against one another because there was a perceived economic rivalry between them. Waller reviewed both positions articulated by film theoreticians and their mirror developments in the contemporaneous popular press, and what he saw at work, beyond outmoded disagreements over the ranking of the two media, were two principal attitudes: either a purist, 'Lessing-esque' approach, exemplified by theoreticians such as Hugo Münsterberg, Allardyce Nicoll, Rudolf Arnheim and Siegfried Kracauer (ibid.: 27–9), or an attempt to identify affinities and to trace a historical dialogue between the two media, as illustrated by Sergei Eisenstein, A. Nicholas Vardac and Raymond Williams, to name but a few (ibid.: 30).

Part I

*Theatre, Interrupted:
Strategies of Intermedial Embedment*

Theatre represented in film is theatre interrupted, theatre affected by intermittence, by inconstancy of attention. In this first section of the book, I seek to unravel the logic of this fragmentariness, taking into account matters such as spread, duration and rate of occurrence. By examining irregularly interspersed representations of theatre of varying lengths that are sometimes offered with barely any narrative warning, the first section makes of this diversity of scale and arrangement its very *raison d'être*. The duration of the theatre segments and the points at which they intersect the narrative of the films impinge upon the imagination of the viewer in ways which, I argue, are well worth exploring. While an initial impulse might be to sift and to demarcate in order to isolate the moments of represented theatre, the first three chapters that make up this section question whether the presence of theatre in film can and should be quarantined, whether the separate assessment of diegetic theatre as different from a more diffuse theatricality might, under certain circumstances, be considered a prosaic and limiting choice. The explicit representation of theatre can operate alongside miscellaneous nods to theatre that need to be acknowledged as well and that can magnify the effects of the representation. The questions that I shall therefore ask are: What assumptions do we mobilise when we distinguish the theatre inserts in a film from the rest? How is theatre embedded in film, how is it introduced and how is it 'turned off'? To what extent can we mark off the explicit moments of theatre when a film is saturated with intermedial references?

The phenomenon of embedding has been examined mostly from a narratological angle, with a focus on framed narratives, and, via this route, it has found its way into intermediality studies (see e.g. Wolf 2006). One of the underlying assumptions of the narratological approach to embedding is that in fictional texts showcasing such a feature, there are 'hierarchically discontinuous levels', separated by boundaries (Füredy 1989: 749), or, in a different formulation, narrative levels in 'syntactic subordination' (Coste and Pier 2009: 297). Applied to the case of theatre embedded in film, this amounts to postulating that embedded theatre occupies a different (onto) logical level than the film framing it. Implicit in the narratological paradigm is the idea that, in order to understand the structural relation between the two, it is essential to consider how salient and how functional the border between them is.

For the purpose of fleshing out this point, I shall briefly pause to illustrate how the notion of borders and levels may be understood with reference to a recent film that incorporates theatre. Alain Resnais's 2012 *Vous n'avez encore rien vu/You Ain't Seen Nothin' Yet* is a film in which frames of various kinds are put in place, unhinged, restored and dissolved again in a complex metafictional game. The film draws on two plays by Jean Anouilh, *Eurydice* and *Cher Antoine/Dear Antoine*, to construct a narrative about a fictional playwright (Antoine d'Anthac, a character invented by and serving as an alter ego of Anouilh), who orchestrates an unusual, pluri-voiced performance of his best known play *Eurydice*. A group of friends (acclaimed French actors playing themselves) are summoned to his house, under the pretext of attending the reading of his will, but are instead asked to watch and evaluate a recorded rehearsal of *Eurydice*, performed by a young theatre company, Compagnie de la Colombe. After the playwright has staged his own death, this is his second ruse, designed to get the actors to re-immerse themselves in their former roles, which begins to happen almost instantly as the recording runs in the background. Having all been involved in stagings of the play in the past, the main actors, two distinct generations with two different approaches to performing the text, are moved to re-enact it, and this re-enactment soon engulfs the rest of the film, generating a performative echo chamber in which a line is heard twice or three times, with different inflections. The recorded rehearsal is explicitly framed as being on a different level from the one occupied by the actors asked to assess it. It is watched in a home theatre, on a screen initially concealed by remote-controlled panels and placed above a pink marble railing, which functions like a physical barrier of sorts, keeping the projected performance from 'spilling' into the outer world at the same time as barring entry from the outside. The enclosure is rendered futile and the border revealed to be porous when at one point during this multi-sited performance the actors in the inner play seem to respond to lines coming from the outer level re-enactment. This transgression of boundary becomes even more forceful once the split screen technique is introduced, allowing one of the actors (Mathieu Amalric) to be present in two scenes simultaneously.

A go-between the two outer-level Orpheus/Eyridice pairs (Pierre Arditi/Sabine Azéma, Lambert Wilson/Anne Consigny), Amalric is granted a flexible positionality which makes him the obvious choice for the film's most radical violation of narrative borders, occurring towards the end of the performance. In a quadruple split screen that divides the visual field into co-ordinated, boxed-in perimeters of action, one of which is suggestively vacated of any human presence, standing for Orpheus and Eurydice's disappearance from one another, Amalric is seen exchanging lines with an actor in the rehearsal video (the inner level performance) at the same time as he is watching himself perform from the auditorium seats. He is both within and without, actor and spectator. The edges of the grid formed by the four frames would suggest a neatly segregated world of discernible and logical connectedness, but what is in fact visualised is a passage between levels and a simultaneous cohabitation of worlds. The overall ambivalence and mixing of the reality/fictionality frames in the film is further exemplified by Resnais's choice of using actors who are playing themselves to engage with a fictional playwright, and of embedding in the film a theatre segment produced and recorded elsewhere and by someone else (the play was staged by the Compagnie de la Colombe and filmed by Bruno Podalydès).

The notion of levels in embedding has been challenged by Paisley Livingston, who operates with an alternative term ('nesting') and who focuses his attention on instances where a work of art (which he calls 'matrix work') nests another work of art, either in its entirety or partially (2003: 233). The condition for such a relation to exist is that the structure of the nested work be 'perceptible or *observable-in* the structure of the nesting work' (Livingston's emphasis) (ibid.: 233). This raises for Livingston the problem of 'cross-media nesting', namely the extent to which a work realised in a particular medium can be effectively nested in a work realised in a different medium. The matrix work would need to provide some measure of perceptual access to the sensorial experience of the nested work and, according to Livingston, this involves a form of display, of 'ostension' (ibid.: 236). In terms of representational ambit, film can semiotically accommodate and capture theatre (although not without distorting it, as we will see later on), offering the visual and aural access to it that Livingston recommends. Similarly, Murray Smith uses the term 'perceptual prompt' to refer to film's ability to approximate the sensory experience of what it represents (1995: 119). In my own analyses of embedded fictional theatre, I shall be interested in the kind of 'ostensive strategies' and 'perceptual prompts' that film employs in its representation of theatre and I shall unpack the implications of these displays.

Several functions of artistic nesting have also been proposed, chief among them being 'reflexivity', 'entrapment' and 'voyages' (Livingston 2003: 242–3). Reflexivity is generally held to be one of the main stakes in representing or referencing a work realised in another medium. In her book on the representation of visual arts in cinema, Susan Felleman writes:

> When a film undertakes the representation of 'art' as a theme or engages an artwork as motif, it is, whatever else it is doing, also more or less openly and

more or less knowingly entering into a contemplation of its own nature and at some level positing its own unwritten theory of cinema as art. (2006: 2)

This may well be the case with the examples discussed by Felleman, but there are conceptual risks attached to treating reflexivity as the default explanation for all manner of embedded representations, be they artistic ones. Writing about films that foreground their mediality, Robert Stam has proposed that we test their professed self-reflexivity by asking: 'Are they truly reflexive or do they merely exploit the filmmaking milieu as a decor in which to set a conventional comedy or a dramatic realist film?' (1992: 81). In so doing, he has drawn attention to a problem that could be raised, with equal impact, in relation to films about theatre. Do these films truly orchestrate a reflexive encounter of media or are they using theatre as just another backdrop?

Returning to the functions delineated by Livingston, 'entrapment' refers to instances where the nested work 'reinforces' the effects of the matrix work, by closely matching its style and its overriding thematic concerns (2003: 242). This appears to be in line with one of the most persistent tendencies in the interpretation of diegetic theatre in film, namely the analogy between the story and meanings of the play within the film and the story of the film itself, encapsulated in the concept of *mise en abyme*. This congruence, however faintly sketched, seems to function for many films that incorporate theatre as a binding narrative contract and it will be addressed head-on in the first case study. Indeed, evidence of such a thematic parallelism can be found in most, if not all, of the case studies in this book. However, the discovery and description of such a parallelism is not the be-all and end-all of theatre in film. The limitation of this otherwise valid approach is that it prematurely tames the presence of theatre in film, disproportionately concentrating the discussion on narrative and thematic considerations to the detriment of an analysis of form.

Finally, what Livingston means by 'voyages' is the potential of the nested work to productively disrupt the 'routine' of the matrix work by offering something excitingly different, a release from textual '*ennui*' (ibid.: 243). The alterity of the embedded work is thus equated with the ability to break, suspend, interfere with the unfolding of the embedding narrative in ways that are formally stimulating, in some sense spectacular. In my own analysis, I aim to show that when the representation of theatre is introduced in film with a certain degree of attention paid to its mechanisms, what is obtained is not only a narrative zoning of sorts but a complex attempt to evoke the experience of another medium. In other words, I seek to emphasise how eventful the representation of another medium can be for its embedding medium and to analyse the formal 'switch' that occurs.

Taking his cue from Ludwig Wittgenstein, Edward Branigan (2006) has provided a systematic overview of the notion of frame, situating it in a variety of 'language games', most of which will be variously activated throughout this book. Noting the centrality of the word to 'our vocabulary of viewing', its polysemy and its inseparability from the ways in which we think of cinema (Branigan 2006: 100), he identifies no fewer than fifteen understandings, running the gamut from definitions which draw attention to the array of decision-making in film that produces the framing to definitions which are geared towards acknowledging the role of the spectator. In a selective enumeration, these understandings include seeing the frame as a 'real edge' and a 'subjective contour' (ibid.: 103), but equally as the '*gestalt form* of an image', its 'overall composition' and the 'shape of an object or group of objects' inside an image (ibid.: 104). In terms of anchoring the act of looking itself, the frame can refer to both the 'implicit rationale' for seeing something (ibid.: 105) and the '*view* that is given on a fictive action from within the diegesis' (ibid.: 108). Importantly also, the spectator's 'disposition' (ibid.: 112) and the 'world knowledge' (ibid.: 113) that is both inscribed in and projected onto a film are also frames in this hermeneutic web that informs and complicates the activity of interpreting a film.

The notion of 'frame' is also invoked in another recent attempt to systematise decades of theoretical speculation on the nature of film and its mechanisms. Thomas Elsaesser and Malte Hagener have placed at the heart of their system the 'relation between the (body of the) spectator and the (properties of the) image on screen' (2010: 4) and have used the various articulations of this relation to organise a dauntingly complex set of theories developed in time. The first of seven conceptual pairs they single out is the 'window-frame' metaphor. What characterises, in their words, this '*mode of being (in the cinema/world)*' (emphasis in the original text) is the fact that it is 'ocular-specular (i.e. conditioned by optical access), transitive (one looks at something) and disembodied (the spectator maintains a safe distance)' (ibid.: 14). The ocular-centrism of this metaphor is counterbalanced by paradigms which shift the emphasis away from vision to the other senses (two of the other conceptual pairs are ear/space and skin/touch). What I take from Elsaesser and Hagener's work is an attention to the multiple sensorial modalities which are implicated in the cinematic framing of theatre. In recognition of these multiple ways of approaching film, while at all times considering the multi-track nature of film, the two case studies discussed in the first chapter will tip the scales somewhat in favour of visual framing, while the second chapter will redress the balance by favouring sound and the third chapter will attempt to bring the two dimensions together. This first part also inaugurates an engagement with phenomenological thought, one of the main paradigms that inform my understanding of intermediality.

The case studies I shall be discussing in this section were also chosen to illustrate different representational patterns: *The Double Life of Véronique* offers an example of a solitary, compact theatrical performance which then reverberates through the whole film. By comparison, *Dolls* symmetrically places the explicitly theatrical at the beginning and end of the film, throwing into question the status of everything in between. *The Jester* operates with a model of alternation, whereby the theatre rehearsals are intertwined with the characters' interactions outside theatre in a mutually illuminating way. In *All About My Mother* the explicit theatrical moments, which, taken separately, never exceed a few minutes, achieve a sense of range through sheer persistence. *L'Amour fou* complicates the model of alternation, by filming with two different cameras and by incorporating fragments of interviews which verbally frame the rehearsals we witness on screen. *Synecdoche, New York* trades on the illusion of infinite regress, by imagining an endlessly self-reflexive theatre piece. In each of these case studies, the integration of the theatrical moments demonstrates a high degree of technical finesse and of conceptual complexity. The analysis of this integration needs, therefore, to be an equally involved procedure.

CHAPTER ONE

No Strings Attached: Filming Puppets in Movement

The two case studies that will be analysed in this chapter, Krzysztof Kieślowski's *The Double Life of Véronique* (1991) and Takeshi Kitano's *Dolls* (2002), feature fragments of puppet shows which occupy key positions within the films' narrative. In addition to facilitating a close examination of ways of embedding theatre (*mise en abyme* and bracketing), these films will also enable me to address the way in which the concept of illusion has been deployed in film and theatre theory and, by extension, also in the discourse on intermediality. Why then choose two films featuring puppet theatre to foreground this concern with illusion, why is illusion an important concept to consider in the context of this book, and how will the variations of the idea found at work in these films be analysed?

Puppet theatre makes unique demands on the spectator, in that often it does not conceal the evidence that the puppet is handled by a puppeteer. Depending on the particular type of puppetry, this may mean that the puppeteer is partially or fully visible to the audience and the audience is expected to engage in an imaginative exercise of mentally removing the presence of the puppeteer as it interferes with the illusion of puppets in movement. There veritable 'mental acrobatics' required from the spectator often also entail perceiving the puppet as 'concomitantly alive and dead, serious and ironic, adult and childlike, mechanical and spontaneous, enthralling and uncanny' (Posner 2014: 225). A similar variety of response is assumed with respect to the puppeteer, who can be seen as 'an impartial observer, an aspect of the puppet's personality, or invisible altogether' (ibid.: 226). The 'mental acrobatics' that Dassia Posner describes are conceptualised by Paul Piris as a productive tension between imagination and perception: 'The puppet maintains a distancing effect because imagination never fully takes over perception. Perception confirms the puppet as a real object, while imagination displays the puppet as an apparent subject' (2014: 40). The 'distancing effect' that Piris mentions amounts to a move towards curbing full immersion (or illusion, if we use the unreconstructed term).

As Posner goes on to argue, thanks to this type of complex spectatorial address, puppet theatre is eminently suited to illustrate theatre's 'double vision' (2014: 225). What the notion of 'double vision' or 'double consciousness' (Julia Walker cited in McConachie 2008: 41; Collard 2014: 268) attempts to capture is a sense of theatre being simultaneously immersive and contrived, and demanding of spectators a similarly paradoxical dual ability to become imaginatively invested in the fictional world of theatre at the same time as retaining awareness of the theatrical skill involved in the articulation of this fictional world. Bruce McConachie situates this double consciousness in a cognitive framework, relating it to the mind's ability to perform 'conceptual blending' (2008: 42). One example of such a conceptual blend is 'the actor/character', a composite entity born out of the ability of spectators to combine 'general knowledge of the basic-level concepts of actor and character with specific information about which actor and what character, taken from the performance they are watching as well as from memory' (ibid.). Elaborating on McConachie's ideas, Andrew Kimbrough explains:

> Grasping blends is neither troubling nor schizophrenic for the audience; rather blending provides an incredibly rich experience of performance given that individuals may shift effortlessly and at no loss of comprehension between the various modes of the performance event. (2011: 110)

The concept of illusion is pertinent to a study that uses intermediality as a framework of analysis partly because of the claim, advanced by scholars such as Ágnes Pethő, that the use of 'techniques of poetic (inter-media) reflexivity' ruptures 'the transparency of the filmic image', drawing attention to 'the apparatus that produces the illusion we call cinema' (2011: 65). Pethő clarifies that by 'transparency' she means instances when we do not perceive the medium 'as a "medium", but we perceive something else that is communicated by it (i.e. the represented world itself), we have the illusion of the immediacy of the object, and we do not have a sense of any mediation taking place' (ibid.: 96). However, as I shall explain in what follows, illusion is a highly contested term in both film and theatre theory and the debate surrounding it has to be acknowledged in order to qualify the use of the term. That being said, my purpose in this chapter is not to arbitrate the dispute between these various theories but rather to give a sense of its complexity as a lead-in to an exploration of the ways in which films representing theatre can reactivate a debate which has had parallel ramifications in film and theatre theory and which has only recently been recast as a transmedial issue.

One of the most recent discussions of the concept of illusion comes from Richard Rushton, who has challenged the highly entrenched logic of representation opposing illusion to reality, transparency to reflexivity, logic which also underlies Ágnes Pethő's argument. Revisiting writings by André Bazin, Christian Metz, Stanley Cavell and Gilles Deleuze, Rushton has carved out a theoretical space for Deleuze's proposal of a 'new Real', a new order of experience enabled by and embodied in films, refusing 'to automatically presume that films are illusions in the face of a "real" reality that exceeds them' (2011: 15).

This is by no means the first or the only time the concept of 'illusion' has been contested in film studies. Starting in 1995 and continuing in 1998, the *Journal of Aesthetics and Art Criticism* hosted a polemic between Richard Allen and Murray Smith on this very notion, occasioned by Allen's publication of a book-length re-evaluation of the concept's standing in film theory (Smith 1995; Allen 1998; Murray Smith 1998). Seeking to account for the impression of reality in cinema, Allen argued for the centrality of illusion in our engagement with media and redefined it as a 'benign disavowal where spectators entertain in thought that what they see is real in a manner akin to the experience of a conscious fantasy' (1995: 5). Reviewing a number of texts, including the influential apparatus/subject positioning theory where illusion features prominently, Allen retained from these earlier writings the idea of a 'movement in and out of medium awareness' fostered by cinema (ibid.: 38), irrespective of whether the films were openly reflexive or not (a more nuanced position on the matter than the assumption that transparent films preclude medium awareness, which seems to be what Pethő upholds). This led him to theorise a specific form of illusion operating in cinema, which he termed 'projective illusion' and which he then distinguished from other forms of pictorial and dramatic illusion, by defining it as 'a predisposition to see the image as a fully realized world' (ibid.: 139). For Allen, projective illusion was a sensory, but not epistemic, form of illusion (ibid.: 100), in other words an intense response to representational cues unaccompanied by cognitive deception, allowing for 'our knowledge about what we are seeing' to 'break the hold of illusion' at any point (ibid.).

Arguing against Allen's revival of the concept of illusion, Murray Smith proposed retiring the concept, on the grounds that it entailed a problematic loss of consciousness, and replacing it with a conceptualisation of spectatorship and of the film experience, which would privilege notions such as 'attention, imagination, perception, and sensation' (Smith 1995: 113). Incidentally, two of the processes mentioned by Smith are also part of how Paul Piris, previously quoted in this introduction, conceptualises the spectatorial dynamic in puppet theatre. The corollary of this line of argument according to Smith is that even highly emotional responses to media artefacts are deemed to be rooted in an understanding rather than a repression of medium awareness and the gap between so-called transparent films and reflexive films is considerably narrowed, in that both types are now seen as forthright about their artificiality, albeit in different degrees and in different ways (ibid.: 121).

The concept of illusion is just as contentious and multifaceted a concept in theatre theory. In his 1948 *Short Organum for Theatre*, Bertolt Brecht famously opposed his epic theatre to the bourgeois theatre of illusions. In this particular context, the term is more or less coterminous with the idea of a naturalistic style in both acting and stage design and, as in film theory, it is intertwined with the notion of spectatorial identification. As James Hamilton remarked, for Brecht, 'the *way* in which the stories were told (the means by which they were presented) helped to obscure the falsity of the assumptions on which they were based' (1982: 41, emphasis in the original). In other words, the cumulative illusion of acting, set design, costume and lighting was deployed in order to shore up ideological illusions and it was these latter illusions that Brecht was interested in dismantling.

Without explicitly referencing any of these positions, a recent attempt to map out the meanings of and features contributing to 'aesthetic illusion' in the Rodopi series 'Studies in Intermediality' seems to respond to echoes of this debate and reconcile what is perhaps not so easily reconcilable. 'Aesthetic illusion' is defined in this recent work as a 'transmedial reception effect' (Wolf 2013: 4) consisting of 'an *activation of the imagination*' (ibid.: 7, emphasis in the original), generating 'quasi-experiences' (ibid.: 12) while preserving 'a residual rational awareness of our true situation' (ibid.: 15).

In the analysis of the first two case studies, in addition to exploring the narrative, visual and aural conditions under which we are diegetically experiencing moments of theatrical 'illusion', I shall also focus on the implications of introducing the film camera into the complex puppeteers–puppets–audience equation. The two films I have chosen for this chapter have more in common than an incorporation of puppet theatre. Upon their release, both were seen as atypical products of their directors: *The Double Life of Véronique* was the first of the French–Polish co-productions made by Kieślowski in the 1990s, inaugurating an unabashedly formalist phase in his oeuvre, while *Dolls* has been described as an 'anti-Kitano' film, stylistically far less 'restrained' than his previous output (Abe Kashō cited in Gerow 2007: 190). Both films have been taken to task for their gender politics and, more generally, for their ideological underpinnings. The Polish critic Maria Kornatowska writes about Kieślowski's French-language films that they are populated by 'psychologically trembling heroines living inauthentic lives in a diminished reality' (Kornatowska cited in Haltof 2004: 112), while Sean Redmond notes that in Kitano's films (of which *Dolls* in this case is no exception) the women often 'stand-by, do or say little', while the men 'fill the space' and drive the narrative (2013: 60). While constituting viable avenues of research, these issues lie outside the scope of this chapter; they do, however, allude to the existence of other patterns of representation that the two films share, which further justifies their pairing.

THE DOUBLE LIFE OF VÉRONIQUE AND THE THEATRICAL MISE EN ABYME

The first case study in this chapter is going to assist me in discussing the *mise en abyme* of fictional theatre in film, one of the most frequently encountered forms of embedment in cinematic representations of theatre, a form that I shall then connect with Steve Tillis's concept of 'figurative occlusion', which is akin to the notion of illusion, but is unencumbered by its history of contestation. *The Double Life of Véronique* (Krzysztof Kieślowski, 1991) is, ostensibly at least, the story of two young women, a Polish piano student and singer (Weronika) and a French music teacher (Véronique), who are each other's double. Suffering from what we presume to be the same heart condition and having an identical appearance and similar musical tastes, Weronika and Véronique, both played by Irène Jacob, lead separate lives, oblivious of each other's existence, but experiencing a confounding sense of ontological rapport. The connection between the two is exacerbated after Weronika's sudden death, supported by a series of mysterious events, including Véronique's sudden decision to abandon hopes of a singing career and her late realisation that she had briefly and fatally crossed paths with her double. In an alternative reading, the film has been seen as focusing on a single young woman who navigates the time–space continuum forwards and backwards, being thus given the chance to remake a choice that previously proved deadly (Žižek 2001: 83). The film broadly situates itself in the 'poetic art cinema tradition' (Romney 2011). Because art films often entail a loose and tenuous connection with existing genres, a more precise pigeonholing of the film is neither entirely possible nor imperative. One word that has been used several times to describe the film, in no small measure due to the *Doppelgänger* motif, is 'metaphysical'. Joseph Kickasola has prefaced his analysis of the film by remarking that it exemplifies Kieślowski's 'metaphysically aimed formalism' (2004: 242) and the film's producer, Leonardo de la Fuente, referred to it as a 'metaphysical thriller' (de la Fuente cited in Maurer 2000: 73). While I generally concur with the view that the film is probably best experienced at a 'sensual, emotional or even – if we are so inclined – spiritual level' (Romney 2011), my entry point into the film is through an examination of its use of theatre, which means that I maintain a general interest in the film's formalism.

The explicit occurrence of theatre happens approximately thirty-three minutes into the film in the guise of a puppet show that only lasts three minutes and a half. The character of the puppeteer introduced in this sequence, Alexandre Fabbri (Philippe Volter), is developed beyond the three minutes, further linking Weronika and Véronique and functioning as a stand-in for the director himself, aspects which are generally picked up by the film's exegetes (e.g. Parshall 2012: 218). The ways in which the puppet show in *The Double Life of Véronique* has been read manifest the deep-seated philosophical fascination with the puppet motif. Slavoj Žižek (2001) has produced an interpretation in a German idealist key, while Emma Wilson (2000) has channelled both Freud and Deleuze in her own reading.

In my analysis, I shall treat the puppet show as a *mise en abyme* with an intermedial complication, aiming to show that the way in which the moment of puppetry is framed in the film mobilises a specific understanding of the relation between the puppeteer and his 'performing objects' which carefully curates the viewer's imaginative engagement with the theatrical offering and with the film as a whole. Because of the striking parallel between Weronika's death during a concert and the apparent demise of a puppet ballerina during the puppet show, the latter is customarily labelled a *mise en abyme* (Mannone 1999: 210; Wilson 2000: 25; Nagler 2003: 15) but beyond referring to it as such, there is precious little attention paid to how this actually works in the film.

Isolating a three-minute extract and elevating it to a position of privilege in the interpretation of the entire film is liable to appear reductive, but constructions of the *mise en abyme* type come with just such a proviso. Borrowed from heraldry, the term is generally understood to refer to a section or aspect of a work that mirrors and foregrounds the mechanisms, meanings and form of the work as a whole (Dällenbach [1977] 1989: 8). The writer André Gide is credited with bringing *mise en abyme* to scholarly attention in a diary entry from 1893 and his comments have since been reprised and scrutinised countless times. In terms of the relation between *mise en abyme* and the broader work that contains and is reflected in it, Gide has been influential in proposing that the device, through its reduced yet strikingly compressed scale, dutifully 'establishes the proportions of the whole' (Gide cited in Ron 1987: 418). For a theoretician such as Moshe Ron, this raises an interesting problem, in that the structural relation between the reflecting component and the 'whole work' implies a rather intractable sense of 'closure and totality' (ibid.: 422–3). In her analysis of Lautréamont's use of *mise en abyme*, Patricia Lawlor, building on Lucien Dällenbach's conceptualisation of the term, prefers to envision the device as opening up a 'vertiginous perspective', a 'whirlwind' ('tourbillon') within the work which draws the reader in by promising a head-twisting revelation about the content of the work the device is mirroring (1985: 829–33). Different interpretative inclinations notwithstanding, *mise en abyme* tends to place itself in relationship with the framing narrative in ways that make questions of size matter less than they usually do or matter differently from usual.

To all intents and purposes, the *mise en abyme* section of a work declares its size but at the same time transcends it.

In an interview with Danusia Stok, Krzysztof Kieślowski has recounted in some detail the production background of the puppet show, beginning with the recollection of seeing the American puppeteer Bruce Schwartz in a series hosted by Jim Henson and broadcast on Polish television (Stok 1993: 180–2), in all likelihood the 1985 series *Jim Henson Presents the World of Puppetry*, which featured Schwartz in one of its six episodes. Schwartz gained critical recognition in the 1980s on Off-Off-Broadway, at a time when puppetry was especially flourishing, alongside other innovative puppeteers such as Theodora Skipitares, Paul Zaloom and Julie Taymor (Gussow 2000: 214). His puppet shows were a one-man operation, the puppets being designed and manipulated by Schwartz alone. In 1988, after a professional hiatus, Schwartz received a MacArthur Fellowship, but the award did not have the long-term effect of returning him to puppetry, as had been hoped. When Schwartz was offered a part in Kieślowski's film, the commission took the form of a short-lived artistic comeback of sorts. The puppet show, recorded several times, with different camera set-ups, lasted ten minutes, but only three of them ended up in the film. A group of some two hundred schoolchildren from Clermont-Ferrand was featured as an audience, a much larger audience than Schwartz was apparently accustomed to. Combined with the fact that Schwartz usually performed for adults, this caused him to approach the performance with a degree of apprehension, but his initial fears of being misunderstood or rejected by the young audience were quickly dispelled by what Kieślowski described as the children's 'wonderful' and 'moving' reactions (Stok 1993: 181–2). The film channelled some of this live emotion, leaving out the post-performance discussions. Despite the fact that, for the strict purposes of the film, the performance need not be composed in full, nor performed as such, the account seems to suggest that the puppet show enjoyed a certain autonomy in relation to the film hosting it and that the film medium recorded what ended up being a genuine theatrical event, rather than a mere persuasive arrangement of pro-filmic material.

The fictional puppeteer in *The Double Life of Véronique* belongs to a series of 'agents' traditionally associated with the inauguration of a *mise en abyme*, a series ranging 'from wise old men through artists and novelists to dreamers and madmen' (Ron 1987: 428). In his pursuit of stories to tell, Fabbri appears prone to manipulative mind games and Véronique, an ideal target for his artful experiments, plays right into his hands, in more ways than one (in a beautiful shot towards the end of the film we see Fabbri manipulating Véronique manipulating in her turn a puppet in her likeness). The puppet show is itinerant, but the moment of arrival is elided and the puppeteer's presence is initially unassuming. After the performance, as Véronique looks on from a classroom, the puppeteer packs things up in a van on the side of which a painted, eye-catching winged puppet advertises the content of the travelling show. The perimeters of the event seem to be firmly in place. Even if the arrival per se is not depicted, we are prepared for the puppet show by one of Véronique's colleagues mentioning the interruption of the regular schedule ('we're finishing early today'). The issue of the kind of narrative interruption that a *mise en abyme* brings about in its 'syntagmatic chain' has been addressed by theoreticians of the device, with Moshe Ron making a point of asking whether what we are dealing with is in fact a 'diegetic downshift' (ibid.: 427) and Mieke Bal noting that the *mise en abyme* is 'hypodiegetic', 'the object of a second degree narration' (Bal cited in Ron 1987: 428). Ron's choice example is that of a 'certain class of *objects*' in literary texts that broker the *mise en abyme*, such as 'a picture or a piece of music' (ibid.: 428). The key aspect for Ron is that the painting or the musical piece that are cast in abyss are only 'mentioned or described' in the text, and thus not genuinely interruptive. This leaves the question open for a class of objects (such as theatre performances in film) that are actually figured in the framing narrative, not just mentioned, and to which we are given extensive audio-visual access.

On screen, the event takes Véronique by surprise. She enters the school carrying a set of chimes and makes her way towards the classroom where she finds the puppeteer preparing his equipment. The encounter seems to be just as much a chance meeting between two people as it is a meeting of instruments and tools: with each step and each word, Véronique's tubular bells produce jangling sounds, whereas the puppeteer is surrounded by unopened boxes and lighting equipment with which he fiddles. These objects both stand between Fabbri and Véronique, screening the future lovers from each other, and align the two with their *métier*, allowing them to appear defined, engaged and purpose-oriented. It is also worth noting that the puppet show will happen in Véronique's classroom, in 'her' space from which she has been temporarily displaced, an early indication that the performance will be primarily directed at her and that the puppeteer is there to unsettle the semblance of a routine, to disarrange and re-anchor her very existence (Véronique is in many respects powerless and this is undoubtedly problematic). Exiting from the classroom in a cloud of confused jingles, Véronique crosses paths with a colleague, of whose advances she takes no notice and who informs her about the marionettes. A cut then takes us to the moment and place of the performance, the classroom now transfigured, showing in close-up a revolving closed box, moved slowly by a hand ensconced in darkness that barely touches its edges. The box is framed such that it seems, in its rotating movement, to hover weightlessly above the ground. A conventional pattern is then introduced, whereby shots of the diminutive stage are made to alternate with reaction shots of the audience, consisting mostly of schoolchildren in the midst of whom Véronique is clearly visible. As the lid of the box is lifted, a puppet ballerina is revealed lifelessly positioned inside it. The moment the hand reaches out to touch it, the puppet appears reanimated, slowly emerging from the box as she is made to look timidly around her. In their turn, the children, immediately enthralled, stand up and crane their necks to get a better view. The puppet's performed demureness and curiosity are met with genuine excitement and the rest of the show unfolds in this mode of mutual calibration of feeling and tone between the performance and the audience. The scene is in line with the cinematography of the entire film, in that it uses the yellow-green filters favoured by Sławomir Idziak, the film's director of photography. For Paul Coates, these filters 'laminate Kieślowski's film with a single colour' (2008: 19), with the exception of the striking red that accompanies Weronika's anamorphic image in one of the film's later, more enigmatic moments. The effect produced by the use of filters has also been described as the 'sometimes stifling golden glow of amniotic well-being, as if Veronicas' lives were enclosed in a protective bubble that can only be shattered by the viewer's eye' (Romney 1992: 43). In this respect, the scene of the puppet show does not mark a departure from the formal tenor of the rest of the film and does not shatter the protective bubble, but rather, by creating a bubble within the bubble, engenders increased attention to the ways in which levels of fiction fluidly communicate as if separated and cushioned by only the thinnest of pellicles. The puppet ballerina collapses after she 'performs' a series of approximate ballet steps and moves, including a pas de bourrée couru, a grand battement devant and an arabesque, and is then shrouded and miraculously resurrected in the form of a winged puppet/butterfly with the 'help' of an elderly female puppet.

Despite being referred to in the film as a 'marionette', the ballerina is not technically speaking a marionette, but a rod puppet, the difference being that, according to Stephen Kaplin, 'marionettes use a more tenuous mechanical linkage', suspended as they are from above via strings and controlled 'through a precise play of gravity against the shortening and lengthening of the strings in relation to each other' (1999: 34), whereas the rod puppet is more of a 'human appendage' (ibid.: 33). As we witness it on screen, the only visible indication that there is a mechanism to the puppet's movements is constituted by the arm rod manipulated by the puppeteer, the rest being a refined exercise in stagecraft, in finding ways of communion between the adroit hand and the puppet. The point of contact between the two is, throughout the show, the fragile neck of the ballerina, steered by the nimble hand. In her silence and gracefulness, in being acted upon, the dancer functions as a quintessence of the French Véronique, prone, like the other heroines of Kieślowski's French films, to 'tiny dumb shows and gestural *études*' (Helman 1999: 127).

Writing about the play within the play of the *mise en abyme* variety, Carol Replogle remarked that in Shakespeare's time it was often introduced by 'the arrival of a company of actors at a court or great house' and at its most successful, the device succeeded in 'converting actors of the main action into spectators, bound for the moment with the real audience' (1969: 153). For the duration of the play within the play, the actors of the outer play watching the actors of the inset play are almost on the same footing as the audience who is watching them all: 'These actors thus acquire a kind of *new actuality* as, together with the audience, they inspect a performance which is equally remote from both' (ibid.: 153, my emphasis). By the same token, *The Double Life of Véronique* could be said to bring closer together two audiences (the film viewer and the puppet show's spectators), but it also engineers a mixed reception effect. In his *Sight and Sound* review of the film, Jonathan Romney rightfully notes that the 'texture and energy' of the film epitomised by Jacob's performance (and one might add, by the exquisite charm of Schwartz's puppetry) manage to offset the conventionality of the 'ontological tricks' and 'metafictional paradoxes' that the film employs (1992: 43). The most conspicuous of these tricks and paradoxes listed by Romney are the partial duplication of the film's title in the new puppet show Fabbri mentions he is preparing at the end of the film and the tape received by Véronique which functions as both a 'recording of earlier events' and a 'pre-recording, a prediction of things she will witness in Paris' (ibid.). Together with the *mise en abyme* of the puppet show and the many motivic reiterations and mirror images that punctuate the story, these 'tricks' partake in the film's metafictionality, insofar as they lay bare the internal organisation of the film's narrative and thus exemplify what Linda Hutcheon would call a form of 'textual self-awareness' (1980: 1).

Interestingly enough, the 'new actuality' mentioned by Replogle could be seen in this case as both a by-product of the *mise en abyme* arrangement and something that detracts from its underlying artificiality. For Hutcheon, the *mise en abyme* is a device which can be used to achieve a type of 'overt diegetic narcissism', through a 'thematization' of the 'storytelling concerns' within the story itself (ibid.: 53). As such, it shares with other metaphenomena a complex conceptual undertaking, aptly described by Werner Wolf as a 'movement from a first cognitive or communicative level to a higher one on which the first level thoughts and utterances, and above all the means and media used for such utterances, self-reflexively become objects of reflection and communication in their own right' (2009: 3). This abstract, introverted operation of exposing the work's fictionality and mediality has the potential of undercutting its immersiveness, its 'illusion'. However, the puppet show *mise en abyme* in *The Double Life of Véronique* manages to not only function metafictionally but to also hold its own as a riveting theatrical set piece with origins independent of the film, inspiring the main character to act as enraptured spectator, on a par with the film audience. This reflects the bifurcated way in which *mise en abyme* is sometimes conceptualised. Bruce Morrissette has argued that historically the function of the *mise en abyme* has oscillated between leading 'from fiction to life' and leading 'back into the work, away from the referential "outside"' (1975: 259–60). He charted the development of the device from a literary technique initially reinforcing 'the psychological or referential meaning of the work by causing the characters to become themselves aware of some import that the author wished the reader to derive from the work' to the way it came to be understood and used at a later stage by postmodern theoreticians like Jean Ricardou, namely 'broadened in conception to include formal as well as thematic duplications' and 'cutting the work off from any lines or anchors' that could link it to 'real life' and 'daily world' towards greater self-containment (ibid.: 259–60). In the wake of such arguments, one could see the film's Véronique as caught between the different agendas of the *mise en abyme*, psychologically confronted with a constellation of feelings and impressions generated by the superordinary possibility of a double and with a character (Fabbri) who, for a while at least, appears to understand her better than she understands herself, but also turned into a pawn of sorts in a formal interlude. During the scene of the puppet show, she is rendered more 'actual' in the sense proposed by Replogle and less fictitious if we favour the psychological, referential understanding of *mise en abyme*, and more fictitious, less 'actual' if we privilege the formal, metareferential character of the *mise en abyme* and of the film as a whole. In other words, we can respond to the mise *en abyme* in one of two ways. We can choose to focus on how Véronique's fortuitous aesthetic experience triggers an intuition of a world beyond and plays a role in the character's subsequent mental reckoning with coincidences and unexplained phenomena. In this reading, Véronique is a baffled epistemologist of her own condition, akin to the film spectator not only because she is positioned as a spectator herself but also because, like us, she is trying to piece together highly inconclusive and perplexing evidence. Or, we can choose a response that privileges the abstract, intensely duplicated narrative design of the film, in which the figure of Véronique is but one element in a self-generating structure, no more substantial than the puppet ballerina. It is the productive tension between these two readings which sustains the film and makes it compelling.

More often than not, a *mise en abyme* is realised in the same medium as the one enunciating the larger narrative of which it is a miniature replica. Even if it is sometimes marked off by a change in style (Replogle 1969: 153), the play within the play, for instance, involves, as its very name suggests, keeping within the parameters of the medium to then cast it in abyss. What is reflected therefore is not just a story or a theme, but also a medium. The *mise en abyme* in *The Double Life of Véronique* comes with an intermedial twist. In this regard, it is useful to consider the intriguing spatial arrangement of the puppet show. During the performance, one slightly lateral shot of the stage taken from the back of the room reveals that on its left-hand side a parallel show is taking place: a reflection of what happens on the stage in the mirror covering one of the walls. We are seeing in this shot at once the audience of the puppet show, the puppet show in the distance and its reflection in the mirror at an equal distance only in a different direction from us, the edges of this compositional triangle meeting in a vertex roughly where the camera itself is positioned. The children and schoolteachers forming the audience are interposed both between us and the puppet show and between us and the reflection of the puppet show, making the reflection look very much like a projection on a screen that the audience has curiously lost interest in. The use of mirrors and of various reflective surfaces throughout the movie and their potential to foreground 'the act of mediated vision and [its] consequent derealization' have been discussed persuasively by Emma Wilson (2000: 13), who makes a general observation about the film when she remarks that 'Kieślowski sets up a mirror to his own filmmaking' (ibid.: 7). In the shot I have just described this is literally the case, with the amendment that the reflection contributes to an intermedial effect. Theatre and film appear to be evoked side by side, in a relation of mutual reinforcement, as staging and projection. To put it differently, I would argue that what is at stake in this shot is a variation of the idea put forth by David Roberts in relation to the play within the play, namely the 'paradox of self-implication', the manner in which the device of the play within the play (in this case, the theatrical *mise en abyme* in film) renders 'the space of play visible by redoubling it in order to stage the *form* of representation' (2007: 39). Roberts goes on to explain that what he means by the form of representation in this case is the relation between 'a visible scene and an invisible audience but also the in/visible distinction between actor and role' (ibid.). In other words, what the paradox of self-implication means for the film is that both the invisible audience (the film spectator) and the invisible distinction between actor and role (Jacob as Véronique, Volter and Schwartz as Fabbri) are made visible through their fictional duplication (the visual presence of the theatre audience and the mechanics of the puppet show).

A brief comparison with pictorial antecedents of *mise en abyme* can further elucidate the importance of the shot and the way in which it foregrounds the 'form of representation'. In his oft-quoted study dedicated to the *mise en abyme*, Lucien Dällenbach describes one of the effects of the use of mirrors and reflections in Vélazquez's painting *Las Meninas* as a 'reciprocity of contemplation, that creates an oscillation between the interior and the exterior, making the image "come out of the frame", while inviting the visitors to enter the picture' ([1977] 1989: 11). Without intending to reduce the *mise en abyme* in *The Double Life of Véronique* to the use of mirror reflections, I would submit that a *mise en abyme* used in the context of a cinematic representation of theatre similarly challenges the constraints of the frame, understood here both as the edge of the screen and the edge of the stage. However, not having to deal with the restrictions of the canvas means that exceeding the frame possesses a different type of appeal for films. Happening on a stage in front of an audience, the puppet show is also reflected by a mirror and presented to us in a brief instant as if on an adjacent screen, and all of this through the mediation of the film camera. The brief shot offers no clear view of the stage. Instead, it takes in most of the audience but from an angle that does not allow us to feel placed in the midst of this audience. We are asked to observe a combination of circumstances, a medial set-up in which film gives rise to a theatrical experience that is then superseded by an effective reminder of the film apparatus.

The effect is strengthened when, at a certain point during the performance, Véronique diverts her gaze from the actual puppet show to its reflection, a moment which is doubly significant because, after an interval devoid of music, in which the only sounds are the noises of the audience, it is at this moment that we begin to hear the haunting music of the fictional Van den Budenmayer (in actuality composed by Zbigniew Preisner), music associated up to this point with the dead Weronika (the music she was performing when she died). Once Véronique's attention shifts, her gaze will remain glued to the puppeteer's image, but right before we see Véronique turning her gaze towards the reflection, the camera performs a similar transfer of attention through a pan that moves away from the stage and to the left to show the mirrored, blurred glimpse of the puppeteer's half-concealed body. Véronique's pivot immediately follows the camera's, which creates the impression that the movement is not self-willed and that Véronique herself is handled, manoeuvred by the film's invisible force, obeying its muted command. The fact that, while she is looking at the blurry reflection, we are still occasionally getting clear views of the stage encourages us to separate the camera's vision from Véronique's point of view, which is also offered.

Michel Chion has suggested that one of the effects of *mise en abyme* (which he defines broadly as embedded performance) is to create 'a "real-time" reference, a temporal frame, that of a performance, a temporality that supposedly unfolds according to its own rhythm, independent of the constraints of filmic narration', but also 'an anempathic situation because the embedded performance can follow its own path entirely indifferent to the drama of the film's characters' (2009: 274). This independence of path and rhythm is manifested in the shots I am analysing as well, because we are not only made aware of Véronique's discordant viewing experience, but are also given visual access to the performance from an angle that we know the character is no longer sharing. However, the camera is never indifferent to Véronique and it subtly registers her awakening to something she does not quite comprehend but which nonetheless exerts a magnetic appeal. It is telling, for instance, that at the end of the performance, when Véronique and Fabbri lock eyes, the shot of the winged puppet is intercalated between the shots of these two characters looking in each other's direction. Theirs will be a romance that will be tied to an absent young woman, briefly brought back through the puppet show, both as voice (a recording of Weronika's last performance) and as re-imagined character (the puppet ballerina). Schwartz himself has conveyed a predilection for all things past and a desire to re-create with his puppets 'the feeling of something that has vanished' (Schwartz et al. 1983: 105). It is entirely plausible therefore that the film's Véronique is reacting to the inbuilt nostalgia of Schwartz's work with her own as yet unspecified sense of loss. Loss is thus both externalised and unformulated and this is befittingly rendered in a medium which is also profoundly marked by loss, since 'In cinema, everything we hear and everything we see isn't *there* anymore. It is an echo and a reflection' (Lawrence 1991: 2).

As Steve Tillis has pointed out, while in most forms of theatre, the actor is both the 'producer and the site of performance', in puppetry 'the operator's corporeal being produces the signs of character', but those signs are ultimately 'sited on the puppet' (1996: 110). What arises from this split, Tillis goes on to argue, is a situation where the operator is occluded, either literally or figuratively. By '"figurative" occlusion' Tillis understands the process whereby 'Puppet operators are comfortable in the knowledge that, despite their physical presence, they will remain in the shadow, as it were, of the puppets on which they site their performance' (1996: 114). The occlusion in *The Double Life of Véronique* belongs somewhere in between the two ends of this spectrum (Tillis would call it a 'mixed occlusion'), as the puppeteer is neither fully concealed nor fully revealed. Entirely clad in black and conveniently cloaked in the darkness of the performing space, the puppeteer is reduced to a pair of hands which are nonetheless emphatically visible. Kieślowski was himself aware of the occlusion which lies at the heart of puppet theatre. For him, Bruce Schwartz was

> exceptional in that unlike most puppeteers, who usually hide their hands in gloves, or use strings, sticks or whatever, he does the opposite; he shows

you his hands. And, after a second or two, you forget that those hands exist, because the doll lives its own life, even though you can see his enormous paws all the time. Yet you don't notice them; you only see the dancing, the puppet dancing beautifully. (Stok 1993: 181)

Schwartz's 'enormous paws' find an expressive correlative in the elongated fingers of the puppets themselves and during the performance the puppets' hand gestures are often either the most eloquent element of the performance or in beautiful, parallel articulation with the puppeteer's own hand movements, and this further conjoins them. Schwartz has described the intended effect of his uncamouflaged hands as 'keeping the mechanics out in the open' and 'asking people to come *into* my fantasies with me by cutting me *out*' (Schwartz et al. 1983: 106). In other words, for Schwartz, the puppeteer both implicates and obliterates himself in giving shape to his vision and siting it on the puppet.

For most of the performance, Bruce Schwartz occupies the space between the figure of the ballerina and the background puppet of an elderly woman

Figure 1.1 Bruce Schwartz's 'enormous paws' and his rod puppets – *The Double Life of Véronique* (Krzysztof Kieślowski, 1991, France, Poland)

in a rocking chair. Prior to her appearance on stage after the ballerina's collapse, the rocking chair puppet is to be presumed hardly visible from most corners of the room, but the camera favours a tighter framing and angles from which she is allowed to accompany the ballerina's dance with her undisturbed swaying movement under a minor spotlight. In the context of a discussion about the differences but also the convergence between sculpture, theatre and performance art, Silvio Gaggi has referred to Samuel Beckett's one-woman play *Rockaby*, whose physical action consists solely of the eerie motion of a rocking chair, as offering, through the chair's mechanised movement, evidence of a 'rapprochement between theater and a sculpture that moves' (1986: 47). Similarly, the rocking chair puppet could be said to initially function as a 'kinetic sculpture', minimally animated before the puppeteer's intervention. The occlusion in this case is both enhanced and rectified. We see more of the puppeteer, including a revelation of his face in the mirror (Philippe Volter taking over from Bruce Schwartz), but we also see more of what his dark silhouette could have partially concealed. For Tillis, the 'exposure in the face of occlusion' ultimately raises the question of whether the audience is thus cued for a 'particular *frisson*' (1996: 117), one that results from the way in which the puppeteer's own corporeality interferes with the process of animating the puppet.

As I have noted in the introduction to this piece, the fact that the puppet show is only three minutes and a half in length does not make it less eligible for qualifying as a fragment capable of reflecting the whole film, as *mise en abyme* is often defined as 'a rebellion against scale in the quantitative sense', a 'small part carrying "as much" significance as the whole that contains it' (Ron 1987: 430). This feat of dense encapsulation, or to use Peter Lunenfeld's expression, of 'nano-thinking' (2001: 52–3), is achieved not only through analogies and duplication, but also through a particular type of temporality, which can be 'prospective', 'retrospective' or 'retroprospective', depending on whether the *mise en abyme* reflects events that have yet to happen, events that have happened or events which are both anterior and posterior to the moment in time when the *mise en abyme* is introduced (Ron 1987: 432). In the case of Kieślowski's film, the puppet show seems to be both forward and backward looking, as it reflects the past (Weronika's death dramatised through the collapse of the puppet ballerina) and anticipates the future: Véronique takes life-altering decisions, as a lesson learnt from her dead double (the spreading of the wings in the puppet show). Both Annete Insdorf and Karen Mann have commented on this complicated relationship that develops between Véronique and Weronika. Insdorf interprets the film in metaphysical terms, proposing as its central question the notion of whether there could be 'a double who prepares us for survival', a 'double who is setting the stage for another to live more wisely' (1999: 131), while for Mann, the relationship between Weronika and Véronique is one in which 'one girl *does*, while the other gains the *consciousness of that doing* after the fact' (2002: 345, emphasis in the original). Both of them establish a relationship of anteriority of action between the two women, which is also at stake in the puppet show, as the show offers the encrypted experience of one woman for the aesthetic delight and existential discomfiture of the other.

As a *mise en abyme*, the puppet show in *The Double Life of Véronique* functions at several levels, providing a concentrated glimpse of the film's narrative development, establishing a relation of both attraction and manipulation between its protagonists and, more importantly for the purposes of this study, proposing an intense scrutiny of the mechanics of theatre through film. In the next case study, I shall explore a different form of embedment (bracketing) as I continue to examine the intermedial function of theatrical fictions in film.

Dolls: Theatrical Bracketing and Filmic Distortion

Takeshi Kitano's *Dolls* is inaugurated by an extract of a Bunraku performance of Chikamatsu Monzaemon's 1711 play *The Courier for Hell* (*Meido no hikyaku*). This outright embrace of theatricality is sustained for several minutes and suggestively flanked by the production credits of the film, which simultaneously isolate the segment and hint at its primordial, generative function in the economy of the narrative. We are reunited with the Bunraku dolls after the brief punctuation of the credits, only to find them seemingly moving of their own accord and looking straight at the camera. The absence of the puppeteers and of the stage creates the impression of a sudden emancipation of the dolls from their human operators and, equally, of a respite from the physically wrenching yet highly codified emotional turmoil witnessed during the Bunraku performance, which I shall analyse in detail later on. In a reversed act of gazing, the dolls appear to then watch and/or conjure up three tales of obsessive attachments, enacted by human actors instead of dolls but permeated by a sense of awkward, repetitive, mechanical behaviour. By inverting the dynamic between humans and puppets, Kitano calls to mind one of the core ambiguities that haunt Bunraku theatre. In the words of Roland Barthes, 'In taking up a fundamental antilogy, that of *animate/inanimate* (present, moreover, in the very structure of the Japanese language), Bunraku obscures it, dissolves it, without promoting either of its terms' (1976: 44).

The film circles back to the gazing dolls at the very end and what is thus achieved is a bracketing or bookending effect, noted in one form or another by most reviewers. For Aaron Gerow, this means that ultimately the film is 'about framing' and, more precisely still, that the 'dominant structure of *Dolls* is in fact point-of-view editing' (2007: 180). This point-of-view structure is not only used to colligate the beginning and end of the film, both of them markedly theatrical, but also interfered with and frustrated in the lengthy middle section that connects the three intersecting stories through a web of disconcerting looks that do not quite align. It is this middle section that has received the most attention in critical readings of the film. Both Gerow and Des O'Rawe remark that, despite the frequency of subjective visions and flashbacks in the three stories, they are rarely matched to an identifiable perspective. What we are dealing with instead are 'impossible acts of looking' and 'unanswered gazes' (Gerow 2007: 195) or, differently put, a 'gaze from elsewhere' (O'Rawe 2007), difficult to pin on any one character, or anchor in any one consciousness.

The stories 'imagined' by the dolls (Kitano in Ciment and Goudet 2003: 15) centre on a man and a woman who share an emotional connection that defies time and social logic and brings about their joint ruin. In the first story, on the brink of his arranged marriage to a rich woman, Matsumoto

Figure 1.2   The gaze of the Bunraku dolls – *Dolls* (Takeshi Kitano, 2002, Japan)

(Hidetoshi Nishijima) hears that his former fiancée, Sawako (Miho Kanno), has attempted suicide and that the failed attempt has left her cognitively impaired. He decides to abandon the proceedings to reunite with her and, as if bound by an unspoken pact, together they take up vagrancy, which removes them from the realm of social interactions, into a form of detached, sublime insouciance. This peculiar state of disengagement from the world into which the characters progressively descend accords with what has been described in an interview Kitano gave to the French magazine *Positif* as an experience of '*hors-temps*' (ibid.: 19). The feeling of being outside of time is strikingly combined in the film with a vividly colourful sense of seasonal change. In the second story, Hiro (Tatsuya Mihashi), an old yakuza boss, reminisces about a former love, Ryōko (Chieko Matsubara), from whom he regretfully separated a long time ago in pursuit of success. When he visits the park where they had their last meeting decades prior and where Ryōko promised him to return every day with lunch, Hiro is surprised to discover that Ryōko has been keeping her promise, despite the fact that she is now unable to recognise the very person for whom the lunch is intended. The two forge a new bond, before Hiro is assassinated by a rival. Ryōko, stuck in a time loop of her own making, will continue to faithfully bring lunch to the park for a partner who we now know will never come. The third story is focused on the female pop idol Haruna (Kyoko Fukada) and her devoted following. When Haruna suffers a disfiguring traffic accident, an obsessed fan, Nukui (Tsutomu Takeshige), blinds himself in response. After being granted a meeting with the now recluse Haruna, Nukui is killed in a car accident.

The three stories fit comfortably within what Jonathan Romney has rightfully identified as 'conventional pathetic functions: the repenting lover, the obsessive and deluded worshipper, the old man made wise by loss' (2003: 42), but they have also inspired different intertextual readings. According to Des O'Rawe, they are 'Chikamatsu variations', reiterating narrative patterns that are common to the playwright's work, namely the 'bound beggars', 'the remorseful warrior' and the 'infatuated servant' (2007). For Aaron Gerow, each of the three stories bears a different intertextual imprint: Matsumoto and Sawako's story is influenced by *shinpa* melodrama, Hiro and Ryōko's story by the yakuza films, whereas the Nukui/Haruna story is reminiscent of a novel by Tanizaki Jun'ichirō (2007: 199). Sean Redmond notes the influence of Noh theatre, seeing Sawako as a character derived from the 'madwoman play' (2013: 59). Out of these interpretations, only Des O'Rawe pays detailed attention to the Bunraku connection, comparing *Dolls* with other Japanese films which adapt or are loosely based on Bunraku or Kabuki plays, most notably with two examples of what he calls 'meta-theatrical films', *Chikamatsu's 'Love in Osaka'* (Tomu Uchida, 1959) and *Double Suicide* (Shinoda Masahiro, 1969).

While his article is rich in contextual information and the comparison is instructive, O'Rawe's aims are different from mine and they do not include the type of close analysis of the film's strategies of accommodating theatre which constitutes the focus of this piece.

Improvidently saddled with the sobriquet the 'Japanese Shakespeare', Chikamatsu Monzaemon, the author of the play staged and fragmentarily represented in the film, is best approached not through this misnomer and the comparison it automatically invites, but within the context of the development of Bunraku theatre, of which he is a most fitting representative. Chikamatsu wrote plays for both Bunraku and Kabuki theatre, but it is mostly with Bunraku that his name is associated. Bunraku combines three forms of artistry: puppetry, the recital of a poetic text and shamisen music, produced by a three-stringed instrument played with a plectrum. By the time Chikamatsu started writing in the late seventeenth century, during the much-celebrated Tokugawa period, Bunraku already had an established, if somewhat unsophisticated, repertory (Keene 1990: 4). Ultimately it was his period that became known as the golden age of Bunraku, because of the unparalleled convergence of talent in writing, chanting and puppet handling (Hironaga 1976: 12). Chikamatsu worked within two main genres of puppet play (*ningyo jōruri*): the history play (*jidaimono*), replete with incidents and spectacular effects and offering ample scope for the use of stage machinery, and the domestic tragedy (*sewamono*), structurally much tighter and featuring mostly characters from the merchant class (Keene 1990: 5–6). Of the latter, his series of similarly titled love-suicide plays, inaugurated by *The Love Suicides at Sonezaki*, was particularly popular and started a veritable vogue for suicides (ibid.: 17). The love-suicide plays rework the same narrative template, pairing a young man, usually a townsman, with a prostitute he falls in love with and whose freedom he unsuccessfully tries to buy. According to Steven Heine, the characters of the love-suicide plays are social misfits whose fates

> hang precariously in the balance between sin and redemption, hell and heaven, against the background of the floating world, which functions not so much as an actual place as a conceptual arena that represents a form of decadence, corruption, and most of all, estrangement that stands in polarity with the mainstream. (1994: 370)

The love-suicide plays also typically include the trope of the lovers' journey (*michiyuki*), a poetic 'prelude to the climax' in which the doomed lovers travel to 'a place of death or hiding' (McDonald 1994: 121). The journey was often used by playwrights as an opportunity to engage in showy displays of their literary craft: Chikamatsu, for instance, devised exquisite puns around the names of the places dotted along the journey (Keene 1990: 24). A refined literary exercise, the journey has also been likened to a spiritual pilgrimage, driven by the hope of a rebirth and connected to the Buddhist themes of 'impermanence' and 'causality' (Heine 1994: 375–6). After Chikamatsu's death, Bunraku theatre developed in a direction which fundamentally altered the manner in which his plays were performed and received: the distinction between history plays and domestic plays became less pronounced, the number of puppeteers was increased from one to three, and the literary quality of the text was de-emphasised in favour of the handling technique and an overwrought style of chanting (Keene 1990: 7).

The Courier for Hell bears a strong resemblance to the love-suicide plays, but the version translated by Donald Keene, which will be referenced throughout this analysis, ends with the capture and punishment of the two lovers, instead of a suicide. The fragment of the play performed in the beginning of the film belongs to Act Two of the *Courier for Hell* and contains one of the most emotionally charged scenes of the play, building on a subtle chain of deceptions in which the characters become irreparably trapped. Skipped in the film, Act One introduces the young courier Chūbei, who, we are told, is usually reliable, but has of late neglected his duties, prompting several of his customers, including his friend Hachiemon, to enquire about delayed remittances. The source of this change in comportment is soon revealed to be his infatuation with a courtesan of low rank, a so-called 'teahouse girl' by the name of Umegawa (transliterated 'Umekawa' in the Artificial Eye DVD version of the film), whom Chūbei tries to free from sexual servitude. His income, however, is no match for the exorbitant ransom needed and Chūbei starts embezzling money from his clients. As is already apparent from the outline of the play provided thus far, at its core, *The Courier for Hell*, like all domestic tragedies, is a morality play, staging a clash between *giri* (social obligation) and *ninjō* (personal feelings) (Keene 1990: 33). Confronted by Hachiemon, Chūbei is forced to admit his moral failing and finds a sympathetic creditor in his friend. However, the arrival of a sizeable commission proves too much of a temptation. In Donald Keene's powerfully evocative translation, Chūbei feels as if 'bewitched by a fox' (Keene 1990: 171) and, under this spell, finds himself once again diverted from the straight path of rehabilitation, rushing to meet Umegawa and spend money that is not his.

Act Two changes locale to the pleasure quarters in Osaka and introduces the other half of the ill-fated pair, as well as refining the theme of deception. Hachiemon unexpectedly arrives at the teahouse and Umegawa goes into hiding, hoping to avoid him. Soon afterwards, Chūbei also shows up but chooses not to make his presence known, curious about the conversation he overhears between Hachiemon and the courtesans. The episode is skilfully designed: as Hachiemon discloses Chūbei's financial recklessness, both

Umegawa and Chūbei from their respective hiding places listen in as the prospect of a happy ending for their love story is taken apart, one unforgiving fact at a time, by the pragmatically minded Hachiemon. Spatially separated, Umegawa and Chūbei are united in their mounting trepidation, their bodies strung in an act of pained attention, each realising that their love is doomed. Chūbei soon goes into a state of utter denial: he comes out of hiding and challenges Hachiemon's version of the story, even if he knows full well that his friend's verdict is accurate. Umegawa also reveals herself and begs him not to jeopardise his career for her sake. Her heart-rending entreaty is the segment of the play that the Bunraku performance at the beginning of the film shows, together with the commencement of the ensuing journey, as the two lovers decide to flee from justice, after Chūbei squanders the money he was supposed to deliver. Act Three, from which Kitano selects a final segment for inclusion in the film, is devoted to the lovers' hopeless three-week journey, which takes them to the village where Chūbei's father resides, in what turns out to be both a farewell and an act of filial repentance.

In my analysis, I shall focus on the ways in which the Bunraku inserts are visually framed and on the kind of attention that the film brings to bear on these particular moments of theatre in order to argue that the film's visual framing of theatre can be used as a guide in our interpretive 'framing' of the film. According to the supplementary material included in the Artificial Eye DVD release of the film, the Bunraku excerpts used in the film are fragments of a live recording at Tokyo National Theatre. In an insightful article about the use of recording technology in theatre for documentation and archival purposes, Sarah Bay-Cheng has proposed that we think of mediated theatre as 'theatre squared', captured within a frame, evincing a 'dramaturgy of distortion'. She notes that 'the recording of performance is always a distortion of the live event, radically reorganizing space, composition and time' (2007: 40). Applying Bay-Cheng's model, I shall examine the ways in which these three aspects find themselves transformed under the gaze of the camera in *Dolls*. This is an important set of issues to consider in relation to theatre represented in film, because, to quote Bay-Cheng once again, 'The camera not only sees things we do not and cannot see by ourselves, but it also alters what we *think* we see through the change in spatial perceptions' (ibid.: 44).

The performing space of Bunraku comes with its own set of particularities, derived from the three-way split that characterises its theatrical offering. According to Roland Barthes, 'Bunraku practices in effect three separate modes of writing, which allow us to read simultaneously three areas of the spectacle: the marionette, the manipulator, the vocalizer: the effected gesture, he who effects the gesture, and the vocal gesture' (1976: 46). The separation of the reciter's vocal performance from the symbiotic physical movement of puppets and puppeteers is reflected in the architecture of the Bunraku stage by the division between the stage proper and the elevated dais (*yuka*), placed to the left of the stage, where the reciter (*tayū*) and the music accompanist sit. The stage itself is partitioned into a narrow area whose function is to hide the footlights and the stagehands, a sunken forestage called *funazako*, which screens from the audience the lower bodies of the puppet handlers and a raised platform (*hon yatai*), where sets usually depict the interior of a house (Jones 2013: 7–8). This varying relief of the Bunraku space, combining a low-lying pit with raised platforms and shallow corridors, ensures a specific circuitry of acted emotions as well as a hierarchy of theatrical labour, with the reciter set apart and ranked above the puppet manipulators. Different regimes of performance reinforce the spatial divide between stage and dais. As Susan Sontag suggested, in Bunraku theatre

> [t]he drama has a double displacement of emotion, a double scale, a double physical and emotional gait. On the stage proper the leading principle is a kind of anti-hysteria. There is the muteness of the protagonists – who, instead of being living actors, are puppets; there is the impassivity and omnipresence of the humans who make them move. To the *joruri* reciter, who is not only off-center (from the audience's point of view) but physically immobile, is given the task of maximal expressiveness. ([1983] 2013: 130)

Building on André Bazin's distinction between the 'centrifugal space' of the screen and the centripetal configuration of the stage (1967: 105), Bay-Cheng explains the spatial distortion that occurs in mediated theatre as stemming from the fundamental tension between a form of spatial extroversion (the theatre 'coming towards us') and a form of spatial introversion (the screen 'pulling away from us') (2007: 42). In the transition from live to recorded performance, the spatial dynamic tips over into its opposite: 'What was formerly intended to push toward the viewer is now pulling away. Areas of the stage that were previously expansive have become narrowly compressed' (ibid.: 43). Bay-Cheng goes on to explain that a compensatory mechanism is often needed to counteract the risk of an 'anemic' recording and this mechanism typically amounts to a repeated penetration of the stage space 'so as to make it a dynamic environment', a penetration effected through 'moving the camera into the stage space much like the camera moves through cinematic space' (ibid.: 43). A similar mechanism is deployed in *Dolls*, where the camera knows no proxemic restrictions, often insinuating itself in the immediate surroundings of the puppets.

The film starts with a pre-performance frontal line-up of propped-up Bunraku puppets, stranded in a liminal space, awaiting their reactivation. The selective lighting that picks out the two leading puppets, Chūbei and

Umekawa, leaving the others submerged in partial darkness with only occasional accents of light landing on shoulders and foreheads, is reinforced by a semi-circular dolly shot around the two dolls that further individuates them. What these initial shots depict, one could argue, is a slow 'emergence of the imagined subjectness of the puppet within its materiality' (Piris 2014: 41). The two shots both establish the unresponsive materiality of the dolls vis-à-vis the movement of interest around them and embody an act of focused attention that already begins to invest them with expressive potential. Paul Piris has suggested that, in puppet theatre, the 'subjectness of the puppet is bound to its objectness through an opposition' (ibid.: 41). The interdependency of the two opposites and the oscillation between them is epitomised by the discriminating light which gives favour to the leading puppets at the same time as it maintains them on the cusp of their stage life.

What rescues the puppets from their inertia is a move initiated in another realm: after the two shots, we cut to a view of the reciter and the shamisen player sitting on the *yuka* turntable, which is then rotated to face the audience, propelling them out of the darkness and into the spotlight. The artifice of the Bunraku narrators brought suddenly into frontal view by the revolving stage is followed by a shot of the camera spinning downward from the ceiling lights to meet the audience. The narrators and the audience are now physically and symbolically aligned, but the placement of the camera slightly below eye-level in the shot of the reciter and the accompanist and slightly above eye-level in the shot of the audience enables the former to tower over the assembly. Reflecting on the problem of the ground in theatre, Martin Puchner has discussed the philosophical implications of the 'raised stage' model, seeing it as indicative of a desire for 'full control' over the ground as well as of a positioning of theatre 'against the ground' (2014: 69). Like the other mechanical contraptions mentioned by Puchner, the turntable of the raised *yuka* may be read as a sign of a 'deracinated, ungrounded theatricality' (ibid.: 69), of theatre elevated above ground and artfully manipulating it, and it is the framing of the camera that reinforces this association.

Aside from visually establishing the basic spatial arrangement of the encounter between the audience and the performers, the shots that I have just described also amount to a spatial distortion, inasmuch as they bestow centrality on an off-centre element of the stage and of the performance. As I have already noted, in Bunraku theatre the chanter and the shamisen player are stationed to the right of the audience and to the left of the stage. Relegated to this space, the voice in Bunraku is, to quote Barthes, 'put to the side', set up as a 'counterweight' to gesture (1976: 46). In what follows, I shall turn my attention to the space of the gesture, mindful, however, of the fact that once the Bunraku performance is initiated through the first strings of the shamisen, setting in motion the puppets, the two spaces become sonorously linked. By the space of the gesture, I mean both the 'objective' space, the stage that accommodates the movement of the puppets, and, borrowing an expression from Patrice Pavis, the 'gestural space' of the performance, 'the space created by the presence, stage positions, and movements of the performers: a space "projected" and outlined by actors, induced through their corporeality, an evolving space that can be expanded or reduced' (2003: 152). This space encapsulates, according to Pavis, the ground covered by the performers but equally the "trail" left in the space in their wake' (ibid.: 152). During the supplication segment of *The Courier for Hell*, when Umekawa urges Chūbei to listen to reason, the Umekawa puppet is moved between Chūbei and Hachiemon, who are positioned symmetrically above the partition, at opposite edges of the *funazako*. This is, however, not immediately apparent, as the camera is frequently placed within close proximity of the puppets, fragmenting the space. As Umekawa turns towards one, we lose sight of the other and vice versa. However, her emotional anguish is directed at Chūbei, and, consequently, our orientation within this space is firmly on the side of the lovers, our experience structured by their exchange of looks.

Bystanders to this tumultuous scene are the courtesan dolls on the raised stage behind the *funazako*, who are moved only slightly during the performance, but in an impressively effective manner. When the chanting swells up with emotion, they are seen slowly leaning forward and bringing the large sleeves of their garments to their faces, a gestural shorthand for crying. At times, their doll eyes are also mechanically closed, as if to express the same kind of overpowering, yet discreetly contained emotion. Although they are kept on the margins of the scene, the subtle movements imparted to them through the grips and cords manipulated by the puppeteers suggest they are attuned to Umekawa, hanging on her words and physically affected by her despair. While in the supplication scene the space is crowded with dolls and their handlers in two parallel rows, the performance of the lovers' journey, divided in two separate segments, one at the beginning of the film and the other at the end, is comparatively more spatially rarefied, paring down the number of characters/performers but hiking up the energy and the commotion of the scene.

This brings into question the second distortion discussed by Bay-Cheng, the compositional distortion resulting from the camera placement and movement. In Bunraku theatre, at least as it has been practised from the mid-eighteenth century onwards, each of the main puppets is manipulated by three puppeteers, unlike the more rudimentary, one-man puppet of Chikamatsu's time. As Susan Sontag eloquently put it, 'The operators move together, as one giant body, animating the different parts of the puppet body, in a perfected division of labor' ([1983] 2013: 131). The 'perfected division of labor' referenced by Sontag has the chief operator control the head, body and right arm of the puppet, the second operator in charge of the left arm and the third operator manipulating the feet and the lower body of the puppet. The principal operator is allowed to show his face, unlike the other two puppeteers, who wear back hoods, veiling their faces. The black clothes worn by all three grant the puppeteers 'a conventional invisibility' (Bolton 2002: 752) or, to reprise a term I borrowed from Steve Tillis in the previous sub-chapter, a sense of 'figurative occlusion', on the condition that the audience 'blot out mentally the presence of the human intruders in the world of the puppets' (Keene 1990: 478). In the film, the camera assists this process of blotting out the puppeteers, by drawing close to the puppets and keeping them in focus while the immediate background is blurred. According to Sarah Bay-Cheng, the role of the camera in the 'dramaturgy of distortion' epitomised by recorded theatre is that of a 'performer-observer', assembling fragments of performance into a 'collage of action' (2007: 44). How then can we interpret the role of the camera in framing a form of theatre where, according to Paul Claudel, the 'soul of the puppet' is 'dispersed among the performers, the audience and the language of the text' (Claudel paraphrased in Bolton 2002: 754)? How can we correlate Bay-Cheng's comments about the camera of recorded theatre assembling fragments of performance with cinema's treatment of fragments?

Following on from Bay-Cheng's remarks, my contention is that the camera in *Dolls* acts as a fourth puppeteer, framing the work of the other three, bringing forth its fluidity and dexterity, but at the same time allowing, to use Shuzaburo Hironaga's words, the 'diminutive bundles of clothes' to acquire 'stature' and 'personality' against and in apparent detachment from their handlers (1976: 2). One of the fragments that are repeatedly brought into focus, a focus that conceals the traces of the manipulation, is the head of the Umekawa doll. This occurs, for instance, in several shots as she pleads with Chūbei to 'calm his heart' and assumes full responsibility for his recklessness, torn between being grateful for his love and feeling guilty for inspiring such a dire turn of events. The handling of the Umekawa puppet works equally as well in full shot as it does in tighter framings. The longer shots allow an appraisal of the range of skilfully choreographed body contortions: despite being wrapped in layers of robe, the puppet is able to cut a surprisingly graceful *figura serpentinata*. The tighter framings combined with a mobile camera foreground the sequence of micro-gestures and flashes of 'emotion' that overtake her, a feat even more remarkable considering that the expression of the face mask remains unchanged. Instead, everything is expressed kinetically, as the head turns, bows, nods and quivers. When the puppet is made to collapse to the ground in distress, the camera tilts downwards to follow her, and the same kind of reframing occurs with each dramatic gesture. As she sheds invisible tears on the golden coins Chūbei has mishandled for her sake, coins that are themselves unseen verbal props, evoked by the reciter, Umekawa is bent over, close to the partition, and the camera is right there with her, registering her despair, conveyed through a constant shaking of the wooden body. This is undoubtedly an excessive, florid style of puppetry, swinging between 'paroxysms' of emotion, as many commentators have remarked (Barthes 1976: 46; Sontag [1983] 2013: 131). By frequently isolating a puppet in close-ups or medium shots, the camera both visually dislocates it from the context of its deft manipulation and exalts the theatrical craft that animates it. At the same time, the framing of the Umekawa doll brings to mind Stephen Heath's claims about the figuration of the body in cinema:

> The body in films is also moments, intensities, outside a simple constant unity of the body as a whole, the property of a some *one*; films are full of fragments, bits of bodies, gestures, desirable traces, fetish points – if we take fetishism here as investment in a bit, a fragment, for its own sake, as the end of the accomplishment of a desire. (1981: 183)

Similarly complicated is the way in which the camera interferes with the spatial relation between the puppets and their operators. It has been argued that Japanese puppet theatre replaces the 'vertical geometry' of Western puppetry, whereby the operator stands above the puppet, with a spatial envelope of sorts, in which several operators and the reciter 'surround' the puppet (Bolton 2002: 754). The suggestion is echoed in Sontag's essay on Bunraku where she writes that the puppet is 'outnumbered, beleaguered, surrounded' ([1983] 2013: 131). In Kitano's film the puppets are often shown surrounded by their human retinue, but just as often they are freed from this encumbering trail by occupying the frame on their own. Interestingly also, for most of the Bunraku performance, with the exception of one shot in which we see the chanter sobbing, the voice is visually separated from the body which produced it. By purposefully omitting the reciter from the compass of its vision, the camera affords new possibilities for the voice to join the puppet. Allowed to float, disembodied, around the puppet, the voice imaginatively attaches itself to it, despite the lingering dissonance resulted from its none-too-convincing re-gendering (in Umekawa's case, the male reciter is vocally impersonating a woman).

The third and last distortion identified by Sarah Bay-Cheng is the distortion effected through editing. As Bay-Cheng rightfully notes, 'editing has no true visual parallel in the theatre' (2007: 46), which is why its distortions are potentially the most disruptive. In line with the previously discussed role of the camera as 'performer-observer', editing can 'construct the gaze of the viewer as being physically within the performance', a gaze which supplements the traditional audience perspective (ibid.). Used in this way, editing is meant to reassemble the pieces into which the performance has been broken by the camera, to link the fragments of bodies, spaces and action, scattered across the shots produced by the multiple camera set-ups. This process of reassembling can be variously inflected and each inflection can result in a different viewing experience. I have already analysed some of the ways in which the camera recomposes the Bunraku performance in *Dolls*, to which I am going to add a few examples of rhetorically used editing. In her book *The Musicality of Narrative Film*, Danijela Kulezic-Wilson argues that Kitano's use of editing in *Dolls* establishes 'formal rhymes' and 'visual rephrains' at both micro and macro levels (2015: 71). An alternative, Deleuzian, interpretation of Kitano's pattern of editing comes from Sean Redmond, who writes of the elliptical cutting in his films generating 'jolts' that are experienced by the viewer as 'intense blocs of sensation' (2013: 23). While one approach emphasises the frequent repetitions of visual details and segments of narrative, the other points out the inherent violence of the image. Without intending to propose an overarching interpretation of how editing functions in Kitano's film, I shall pause to consider some of the ways in which it is used to manage the film spectator's experience of the theatre performance, as well as to create the transition between the three stories in the middle and the bookending doll shots.

The supplication segment of the Bunraku performance in the introduction of the film ends with a shot of the shamisen player strumming his plectrum on the strings of his instrument in a series of concluding musical notes. The subsequent three shots, joined together through overlapping editing, resume the performance by showing the rotation of the *yuka* onto which the shamisen player and the reciter are seated next to one another. The same rotation is shown three times from the same frontal angle but in ever closer framings and inched a little further each time. By all accounts, the general function of overlapping editing is to 'stretch' time, to expand the duration of a particular event or action, and this is no doubt true of the shots I have mentioned, but what is also at stake in this prolonged moment, I would contend, is an underscoring of a ceremonial call to order, a reaffirmation of the strict principles of interaction that govern an event such as this, a reminder of the 'appointment' with theatre. Implicit in the use of the technique is also a sense that what we are seeing is the result of a process of historical sedimentation, a rotation that has occurred with exacting regularity in performances stretching back hundreds of years. As Aaron Gerow notes, the shots could also be read as indicative of the film's 'cyclical repetition', as the same technique is used later in the film in the scene of Nukui on the beach (2007: 199).

The film is indeed committed to internal reduplication of both formal strategies and visual motifs, and nowhere is this more evident that in the cross-cutting between Matsumoto and Sawako's trudge and tumble through the snow and the Bunraku dolls' laborious movement, powered by their retinue of handlers. This occurs at the very end of the film, after Matsumoto and Sawako have wandered in and out of their past and present lives and have intersected in their meanderings the other two stories. As they come upon the ski lodge where they had first publicly declared their love for one another in front of a gathering of friends, before misfortune hit them, they briefly rouse themselves from their mental stupor to wordlessly acknowledge that they both remember the significance of the place. They then loiter around the lodge, seeking comfort from the winter cold with a small fire kindled next to its walls. After a moment's respite, they are chased away by the custodian of the place and they resume their bone-weary roaming, their large, stylised costumes trailing across the snow behind them. We see them going from screen right to screen left and, as they plod uphill, we cross-cut to the Bunraku dolls in the journey segment of *The Courier for Hell*, moved in the same screen direction and in a similar formation (the man leading the way, dragging the woman along). The parallel could not be stated in a more obvious way: matching costumes, matching configuration, matching movement. As Matsumoto and Sawako suddenly stop to contemplate the precipice ahead towards which they will then helplessly fall end over end, what they are in fact contemplating is their fictional finish line. This is as far as their story will take them – the story's other two companion pieces have already reached their tragic conclusion and the journey in the Bunraku play itself is just a headlong plunge towards the inevitable end. The shot of Matsumoto and Sawako hanging from a tree with a steep drop below them is followed by the shot of the gazing dolls, who are slowly turning towards each other, as the camera starts to back-track, in a second gesture towards completion. The effect of this series of consecutive closures is consistent with the characteristics of the bracketed narrative, as outlined by Richard Neupert, who remarks that 'Using identical situations to begin and end a film can work comically or dramatically to buckle the story into a very controlled narration' and 'such bracketing proves that the narrator knew where the story was heading all along' (1995: 22). *Dolls* is indeed a highly controlled theatre-inspired formal experiment, impeccable in its logic and confidently executed from start to finish, with the discipline of the Bunraku performance setting the tone for the rest of the film and providing an elaborate set of brackets. Using the term in a different sense, to refer to instances where the camera moves towards what is of importance in a scene, filtering all else from attention, Noël Carroll points to a commonsensical understanding of how brackets work when he writes that as viewers we are compelled to 'look inside the bracket rather than outside it' (2003: 38). In his discussion of narrative frames, Jeffrey Williams notes that 'Frames presuppose their own forgetting, as if casting a spell on their audience, thus functioning as a lure or charmed path to the narrative' and that frames are 'valuable precisely because they disappear' (2004: 99), but he seems to make an exception for the bracketing or bookend frame, whose aim, he argues, is 'precisely *not* to disappear, but to give closure and thereby to shape the narrative' (ibid.: 123). The theatrical brackets in *Dolls* exceed the purpose of self-effacingly pointing to what they are framing (the stories in the middle), and while they 'signal', as Richard Neupert would have it, both 'closure as a manifest narrational strategy' and 'the film's programmatic form' (1995: 22), they also exert their own 'dramaturgy of distortion' on the film, forcing it into a most stylised straightjacket.

CHAPTER TWO

Theatre, Memory and the Framing Voice

In the previous chapter, using the concepts of 'figurative occlusion' and 'dramaturgy of distortion', I analysed how the embedded theatre performances were compositionally subsumed within the ever-shifting edges of the films' visual field. Lest this be considered a visual bias, the second chapter will consider two films in which sound plays a fundamental role in shaping the experience of embedded theatre, namely *The Jester* (José Álvaro Morais, 1987) and *All About My Mother* (Pedro Almodóvar, 1999). These case studies will introduce and help explore two additional forms of embedment of theatre in film, namely alternation and repetition, both of which, by virtue of being forms of recurrence, impart a sense of rhythm to the narrative.

As Edward Branigan cautions, 'One shouldn't think that the act of framing is confined to visible and/or visual aspects of imagery. Sound can frame' (2006: 116). Not only can sound frame but, according to Michel Chion, it also 'vectorizes or dramatizes shots, orienting them toward a future, a goal' (1994: 13) and one need not subscribe to the teleological slant of Chion's statement to acknowledge sound's sequential thrust. Its temporal capabilities and the fact that sound is a shared dimension of theatre and film, both of which unfold in time, make it an especially apt interface between the two media. The attention to temporality that subtends the interest in sound is further justified in this case because the two films with which I shall engage in this chapter give ample scope to a consideration of the workings of memory in and through theatre, in and through the framing voice.

More often than not relying on a repertoire of texts that are staged and restaged, theatre accommodates and mobilises memory. Jeanette Malkin acknowledges as much when she writes: 'Theater is the art of repetition, of memorized and reiterated texts and gestures. A temporal art, an art-through-time, theater also depends on the memoried attentiveness of its audience with whose memory (and memories) it is always in dialogue' (1999: 3). She is joined by Marvin Carlson, who, in a famous study on theatre as a 'memory machine', makes the case that theatre is centrally concerned with the 'retelling of stories already told, the reenactment of events already enacted, the re-experience of emotions already experienced' (2003: 3). Theatre's involvement with memory is not only incontrovertible but also protean, a point emphatically made by Attilio Favorini: 'theatre seems particularly thick with memory. From rehearsals to memory plays to theatrical memorabilia to theatres themselves – which constitute the exoskeleton of theatre's memory – theatre can be fruitfully contextualized as an activity of remembering' (2008: 2–3).

Memory is a function equally integral to film and their mutually binding connection has been discussed on numerous occasions. As a recording medium, film ensures a prolonged and reiterable lifespan for sounds and images, and this is precisely why the representations it generates can serve as a 'technological memory bank' (Anton Kaes cited in Kilbourn 2010: 2). In 1966, Susan Sontag claimed that the 'youngest of arts is also the one most heavily burdened with memory', as 'Films age (being objects) as no theatre-event does (being always new)' (1966: 32). Both film and theatre have thematised memory and allowed it to have a transformative effect on their aesthetic. Favorini has identified and analysed the 'memory play' as a 'play in which the intention to remember and/or forget comes prominently to the fore, with or without the aid of a remembering narrator' (2008: 128), and in a kindred move, Russell Kilbourn has written about 'memory-films', defining them as films which 'show how, in a more than metaphorical sense, both the structure of memory and processes of remembering and forgetting are provided for us now by cinema' (2010: 49).

Film is also no less prone to repetition than theatre, but, with the possible exception of rehearsals and retakes, its repetitions are of a different kind. As Raymond Bellour has astutely argued, repetition is built into the 'very body of the film', not only as a 'weave' of successive frames (1979: 66), but also as an 'ordered return' of narrative elements dictated by the principle of alternation which Bellour sees at work in serial structures such as shot-reverse-shot and point of view, but also more generally in the way in which film language works (ibid.: 67–8). Memory is implicated to such a degree and in so many forms in the mechanisms of media and is itself so inescapably mediated that art theorist Rosalind Krauss was inspired to paraphrase Marshall McLuhan's widely quoted dictum 'the medium is the message' as 'the medium is the memory' (2010: 19). This becomes especially evident when we consider film practices such as 'the memorialization of past genres' and the 'imitation of film-historical referents', discussed by Noël Carroll under the umbrella term of 'allusionism' (1982: 52), and Elena Gorfinkel's work on the similar phenomenon of filmic 'anachronism', which mobilises a 'film historical imaginary' and 'cinephile attachments' (2005: 153) in ways that equally foreground the constitutive role of memory in film.

Given the discursive elasticity of the term 'memory' and its lasting critical popularity (Radstone 2000; Radstone and Hodkin 2003; Erll 2011), some clarification of the approaches that are relevant for this chapter is in order. The narrative of both films I shall be discussing is centred around the death of a loved one, an event which not only occurs in the proximity of a theatre space, but also reveals the characters' deeper connection with the medium. This core narrative event is a wound gaping in the body of the films, and the way in which it becomes inextricably linked to theatre resonates well with Alice Rayner's phenomenological reading of theatre as a ghostly place, where 'the dead whisper to the living through repetition' (2006a: 34). Rayner is concerned with how theatre enables a perpetual cycle of appearance, disappearance and reappearance, and argues that in theatre 'the recovery of writing through the voice of the performer gives a second life to the memory buried in the text' (ibid.: p. xxxii). It is this process of recovery that accounts for the ghostliness of acting: 'the actor is ghosted by an absent text that has already produced the phantom of character, and to inhabit a character fully is to become a ghost that wears a human, living mask' (ibid.: xx).

What is perhaps even more revealing for the purposes of this chapter, going some way towards explaining the appeal of figuring the processes of memory in film through a representation of theatre, is the way in which Rayner conceptualises the theatre and the body as being alike, two apparatuses that encrypt and guard secrets of their own making and that entail a complicated relationship between what appears outwardly and what lies inside. In Rayner's words,

> the human body is also theaterlike: an inhabited space containing and exhibiting its own material and psychic history, ghosted by the continuing disappearance of its own present and presence, on a trajectory to and from nothingness, and encoded by family and cultural histories. Like the human body, the empty space of theatre is ghosted by its own history, by its family resemblances, by subjectivity and perception. Only the ghost light illuminates the fact that the space is haunted by an unknown past and by unknown others. The phenomenal appearance of the body, then, is also an encrypted space that, theaterlike, is haunted by the history of its own self-representation as well as the history of others who inhabit it. The body/theater is thus an exterior space that displays, like a hollow vessel or vaulted crypt, the surfaces of its own interiority. (ibid.: 62–3)

This conceptual rapprochement between body and theatre allows Rayner to marry phenomenology and psychoanalysis in an attempt to make sense of the lack and loss that are defining experiences for both body and theatre. Crucially, Rayner's argumentation resorts to the concept of '*appareil*'/'apparatus' to refer to their inner organisation. Defined by Rayner as a 'display of structure, a visible form that shelters an emptiness or wound' (ibid.: 64–5), the notion of apparatus is of particular interest here because of the role it also plays in intermediality studies, albeit in a different conceptual articulation. The volume *Appareil et intermédialité*, the result of a collaboration between the Center for Research on Intermediality in Montreal and a Paris-based research team co-ordinated by Jean-Louis Déotte, posits that intermediality understood in experiential terms presupposes an 'être appareillé', a being that both 'acts upon' and 'is acted upon' by her/his 'technical environment' (Froger 2007: 8, my translation). Déotte has been known to analyse things as diverse as perspective in painting and the museum as apparatuses, and in line with this terminological largesse, all media are treated as apparatuses of representation. Each apparatus amounts to and makes available a distinctive way of appearing and a distinctive way of knowing and, as we navigate a world populated by a multitude of apparatuses, we are constantly affected by the way in which we engage with them and by the extent to which we allow them to mediate our relationship with the world. In this context, the film apparatus is deemed to 'stage, configure and render visible' a series of fundamental 'relationships of projection', including the 'distinction between subject and object' and the 'psychoanalytic structure of the conscience' (ibid.: 11, my translation).

A valuable contribution to the volume *Appareil et intermédialité* comes from Johanne Villeneuve, who starts from the observation that the theory of the apparatus is dominated by a critical lexicon derived from writing (*écriture*, inscription) and who proposes as a corrective an increased attention to 'oral mediations' (2007: 210, my translation). Given this chapter's emphasis on the framing voice and on memory, both of which are also dimensions of orality, her ideas are worth a closer look. According to Villeneuve, in the process of orally preserving and relaying a text, the body turns itself into an apparatus – in French, she writes of the 'corps oralisé' as a 'corps appareillé par lui-même' (ibid.: 212, 216). The body 'retains' the oral text, acts as its only material support, through what Villeneuve calls a 'choreographic memory', an immaterial scaffold of 'faces, gestures and rhythms' (ibid.: 215, my translation). Orality therefore points to the body as the 'first manifestation' of the 'mediating function of the technique' (ibid.: 222). Villeneuve also usefully distinguishes between sight which 'isolates' and sound which 'incorporates' (ibid.: 215), and this distinction could be applied to the different approaches I am adopting in my analysis of the cinematic embedding of theatre representations. In the previous chapter, in discussing both the theatrical *mise en abyme* and the theatrical bracket primarily in visual terms, I emphasised their isolating features. The present chapter will attend to the way in which theatre and its voices could be said to 'move through' film, in keeping with the logic of what Villeneuve calls the 'double fluidity of sound', the fluidity of the 'sweeping current' and the fluidity of the 'milieu in which one finds oneself' (ibid.: 219; all translations mine). This also accords with Régis Durand's description of the voice *dispositif* as 'passage, tunnel, passing through (*traversée*)' (1997: 303). Pedro Almodóvar referred to the main character in *All About My Mother*, the second film that will be analysed in this chapter, as being 'persecuted by Tennessee Williams's *A Streetcar Named Desire* as if the streetcar were a wild, fierce animal that rips her apart and is present at all of the important moments of her life' (Montano 2004: 136). This affecting recurrence of theatre will be unpacked using phenomenological conceptualisations of memory and performance and theories of voice in cinema.

The films I have chosen for this chapter both hail from the Iberian Peninsula, but beyond this superficial geographic commonality and the fact that their directors belong to the broadly defined art cinema and to roughly the same generation (born in the 1940s, active in the post-Salazar, post-Franco period), their contexts are significantly different. Pedro Almodóvar is a prolific and much-fêted director whose films regularly feature moments of performance of various kinds. It has been argued that exposing the 'performative nature of culture' and of identity is one of his overarching aims (Ballesteros 2009: 71, 78). By contrast, José Álvaro Morais, who died in 2004, is insufficiently known and the author of only a handful of films, some of which suffered from vicissitudes of funding and unfavourable production circumstances. Despite these differences, however, both films allow for a rewarding probe into the use of memory as a bridging element between the two media.

THE JESTER: COMPETING VOICES IN ALTERNATING SCENES

Positively reviewed by Eugène Green in *Sight and Sound*'s November 2010 edition and included by Manuel Mozos in his selection of Portuguese films shown at the 2012 Viennale, José Álvaro Morais's film *O Bobo/The Jester* has yet to receive the critical attention it deserves. An esteemed representative of Portuguese cinematic late modernism, Morais studied with André Delvaux in Brussels in the first half of the 1970s and, by his own admission, adopted a theatrical approach to film under the influence of New German Cinema, in particular Hans-Jürgen Syberberg (Mendes 2011: 8). Initiated with a small budget in 1979 and shelved for a number of years because of severe underfunding, his first fictional film *The Jester* was eventually completed in 1987, when it was awarded the Golden Leopard prize at the Locarno Film Festival. Pre-released in the same year in Portugal, the film had to wait until 1991 for a limited commercial release, after which it disappeared from view until 2005, when it was made available on DVD by Atalanta Filmes (Mendes 2011: 2). In one of the DVD's special features, David Streiff, the former director of the Locarno Film Festival, gives an account of the film's final stages, suggesting that in addition to financing issues, the reason the film took several years to complete was that Morais intended to have a sophisticated sound design, for which studios in Portugal were at the time insufficiently equipped. As a result, sound editing was completed with Streiff's support in a Swiss sound studio. Although not exclusively geared towards elucidating this aspect, my analysis will attend to some of the complexities of the sound arrangement, for which the film was rightfully commended.

The action of the film takes place in Lisbon and its environs (Estoril) in the summer of 1978, four years after the overthrow of the repressive right-wing Salazar regime. The non-violent 'Carnation Revolution' of April 1974 was followed by an unstable period of discord between various political forces vying for power, compounded by the late process of decolonisation and the economic uncertainty caused by the loss of the African markets (Kaufman and Klobucka 1997: 13). Morais's social background was staunchly middle-class on both sides of the family, but, according to Jacques Lemière, his lineage also replicated a divide that was characteristic of Portuguese society at the time: on the one hand, the landed rural bourgeoisie, supportive of the idea of democracy, on the other, the Salazarist industrialist bourgeoisie, opposed to political change (2008: 137). The hopeful ousting of the right-wing dictatorship gave way to a difficult political cohabitation between the left and the centre, and between various factions on the left, with several coalitions succeeding one another in a short span of time. One such coalition forms the rather inconspicuous political background of the events recounted in *The Jester*. While contemporary politicians remain unnamed and explicit references to the political volatility of the late 1970s are similarly eschewed (the exception being a passing remark to the war in Angola), the film is nonetheless suffused with a sense of post-revolutionary disenchantment (Lemière 2008: 142), as the main characters repeatedly discuss the prospect of leaving Portugal. The momentousness of the post-Salazar transition to democracy is emphasised indirectly, by being set against or alongside another foundational period of political turmoil, Afonso Henriques's accession to the throne as the first official king of Portugal in the twelfth century, effected through the defeat of his mother, Dona Theresa, and her second consort, the Galician Count of Trava. The reference to this historical moment is introduced in the film via the rehearsal of a theatre show, based on Alexandre Herculano's 1843 novel *O Bobo* (*The Jester*). Initially inspired by Carmelo Bene's *Our Lady of the Turks*, Morais eventually settled for Herculano's novel because it represented (and thus enabled him to question) a certain romantic and 'exalted' idea of history and of national identity that had been peddled by the Salazarist regime (ibid.: 143–4). However, as Lemière argues, Morais did not relinquish the national paradigm altogether: instead of entertaining illusions of national grandeur, he went the opposite way from a discursive point of view by concentrating on what he believed to be a profoundly Portuguese malaise, which he ascribed to his main protagonists (ibid.: 147). The choice of a historical fiction consolidates and complicates the film's involvement with memory, because as Pierre Nora has argued, 'History, especially the history of national development, has constituted the oldest of our collective traditions: our quintessential *milieu de mémoire*' (Nora 1989: 9).

The film revolves around theatre actor-cum-director Francisco, also known as Chico (Fernando Heitor), his girlfriend Rita (Paula Guedes) and his childhood friend João (Luís Lucas). A seamless transition occurring midway through the film blends a song performed on stage into a radiocast, revealing that *The Jester*, the play Francisco had been rehearsing with his theatre group 'A Carroça', was planned for a July opening at the Lisbon Film Studio. However, before this planned opening, João is killed and the film retraces the events that led to it. Conveyed in an extended flashback, taking up almost the entirety of the film, the last week in João's life overlaps with the dress rehearsals for Francisco's theatre show. The attentively woven texture of this flashback is made intricate by the fact that, as he discusses with Rita the events of the fateful week, Francisco goes further back in the past by recalling earlier scenes from his childhood. These scenes set the stage for the way in which the more recent past is reconstructed but at the same time short-circuit it, as will become evident from the analysis of the opening sequence of the film.

What we learn is that before his untimely death, João was staying with Francisco and Rita in the large house owned by Francisco's mother, taking photographs of the rehearsals as a cover for shadier dealings. Unbeknownst to the family, but with Francisco's begrudging approval, João hid weapons in the house, weapons he had inherited, we are led to believe, from a stormier past, opposing the now defunct right-wing regime. To this level of secrecy is added another, as João is blackmailed by Jorge (Rogerio Samora) with compromising photos from the scene of a mutual friend's murder. The relation of João with the male victim (friend and possible lover) is yet another layer of the past which is partially and inconclusively exposed in the film. We get glimpses of it through a home movie shot during a holiday in Greece that João projects for Francisco, but this only deepens the mystery. Under the uncomfortable spotlight of a police investigation, João is forced into a pernicious arms' deal intermediated by Jorge and the unexplained sabotage of the deal costs João his life. Before his killing, João's presence in the house drives a wedge between Rita and Francisco, but his death seems to bring them back together in a stronger bond than before.

Intertwined with this narrative strand are the story of the play itself, pursued with unrelenting linearity through several fragments of interrupted rehearsals, and additional scenes showing Rita recording her part in a film and later watching the film on a television set with Francisco and a group of friends. To complicate matters further, at the end of the film an attempt is made to confuse the boundary between the film within the film and the film itself. The other embedded fiction, the theatrical rehearsals, runs parallel to the narrative of the film, which results, as Eugène Green remarks, in the 'emotions produced by both entering a common stream' (2010: 14). The play-within-the-film focuses on a pair of star-crossed lovers, Dulce (Luisa Marques), a noble orphan, who is part of Queen Theresa's entourage, and Egas (Victor Ramos), companion-in-arms to the royal heir Afonso Henriques (Luis Miguel Machado). Caught on opposite sides of the military conflict between the Queen's camp and her son's, Dulce and Egas have their loyalty put to the test and their story ends tragically with Dulce's death, made to concur in the rehearsals with João's offstage assassination. The film manages the intersection of these narrative strands by threading information and commentary through an effective use of voice-over, but, while the voice-over does offer explanations and contexts for what we see unfolding in the flashback, it conceals as much as it reveals, ultimately precluding the possibility of a full disclosure and unsettling our response to the characters.

The opening credits sequence of the film, by which I understand the first nine shots of the film, establishes its audiovisual complexity and mixed temporality, as well as the entanglement of theatre and memory. This visual and aural density warrants close textual attention, which is what I shall provide next with a view to then engaging into an exploration of the relation between theatre and memory as it is articulated in the film with the help of a phenomenological understanding of memory. In the very first shot, as wisps of dark clouds approach a distant moon, the sound of a train horn grows increasingly loud as if to compensate, with its strident immediacy and nearness, for the remoteness of the lone planet. The clouds' passing is synchronised with the train whistling by and, as the sound diminishes and the clouds floatingly march ahead, a feeling of unease, of something else being obscured or faded, is induced. João's death, mentioned a minute later, is thus visually announced beforehand, in a poignant reminder that, to quote Shelley, 'We are as clouds that veil the midnight moon', destined to be lost forever as 'night closes round' (1993: 2). The moon, the darkness, and the image or sound of the passing train will be used throughout the film, either together or independently, to distinguish between blocks of remembered content or between different levels of the past and to make the transition from domestic scenes, taking place in Francisco's house, to the site and time of the theatre rehearsals (and vice versa).

The clouded moon is not the only image suggestive of João's demise. The voice-over conversation that follows insistently comes back to a childhood memory of João disappearing through a trapdoor in the attic of Francisco's house one night a long time ago, during an improvised theatre performance initiated by Francisco's cousins from Oporto. The first thing we hear after the receding sound of the train wheels on tracks is a woman's voice, later revealed to be Rita's, enquiring about the time, as the face of the moon turns nebulous once again. As Michel Chion would put it, this is the film's first *acousmêtre*, the first bodiless voice whose source is not yet visualised, soon to be followed by a second. In Chion's account of the effects of the *acousmêtre*, once introduced, the human voice 'structures the sonic space that contains it' (1999: 5) causing our attention to 'fasten' 'onto this other *us* that is the voice of another' (ibid.: 6). The opening of the film has us suspended in time, together with this unknown voice, stranded in a moment of darkness that surrounds and eludes us at the same time. In a poetic reflection on the 'appointment with theatre' seen as a 'missed encounter', Alice Rayner writes that 'the mark of time always fails to stop time, which flows on around it' (2006a: 29). Plunged into a similarly unbounded temporal flow, we are thrown a metaphorical lifeline by the two voices that have emerged from the darkness to beckon us forward into the story. These voices are what Chion would call 'I-voices', speaking in the first person singular and enjoying, by virtue of being close-miked, 'a sense of proximity to the spectator's ear' (1999: 49).

Unanswered but oriented towards another, Rita's voice proceeds to admit that the idea of going home, where the police are still looking for the trapdoor, frightens her, to which a male voice, later attributed to Francisco, rejoins with an acknowledgement of fear related more diffusely to the trapdoor. Queried by Rita, Francisco traces back the affect to his childhood when the space behind the trapdoor served as a site of punishment for the cook's grandson, Eugenio, who would stay 'for an hour or two in the dark without crying'. Richly symbolic, the dark place behind the trapdoor is initially invoked as a place that silences, confines and separates, in other words a place of lurking death. Equally, however, as is subsequently revealed, the place behind the trapdoor functions as a place of transgression and escape, a place through which the boys would surreptitiously gain access to the maid's room. Since the adult João hides weapons behind the trapdoor, it transpires that both connotations (death and secrecy) are maintained and intensified in the narrative development.

What we are seeing during the oral account of Eugenio's unusual punishment stands in a curious relation to the content of the story, not yet converging with it, but not exactly disconnected from it either. During Rita and Francisco's first segment of conversation the shots invariably feature a character either moving into the frame or outside of it, akin to the ebb and flow of memory, gradually bringing images into relief or escorting them out of consciousness, but also suggestive of theatrical entrances and exits. While the shot of the clouded moon was conjoined with the train sounds and with an affirmation of temporal indistinctness, the shot that inaugurates the series of images accompanying Francisco's verbal recollection shows from a low angle the deck of a staircase and the walls adjoining it caught in a play of striped shadows, generated by what we assume to be moonlight streaming through the windows. The moonlight of the first shot is thus prolonged into the second, ambiguously bridging two moments, Francisco and Rita's night-time conversation and a fuzzy childhood memory, none of which is at this point explicitly identified as such.

The play of shadows and light on the walls and the floorboard is the only movement we initially perceive. Two pitchers are placed next to the balusters, such that they seem an interpolated still life, and a toy car lies discarded on the floor, remnant of some forgotten game. As the shot lingers, the changing pattern of light on the balusters heralds an approaching human figure, who slowly climbs the stairs from the right. The camera tilts to prepare for the arrival of the figure, who is shown in a medium long shot to be an adolescent, dressed as a warrior angel, holding a sword. As the adolescent comes into full view, facing the camera, flanked by two staircases and further hemmed in by the deep shadows and a pile of books, he seems at once an apparition and a participant in an enigmatic game of make-believe. In an eyeline match, the camera then cuts to a youthful female figure seated in an armchair and returning the gaze. This other space, previously off-screen, is bathed in the same blue light and similarly arranged, with piles of books on each side, a cardboard giraffe propped against the wall and the handrail of the staircase visible on our right, a space of creative refuge. As the young woman calls out 'Francisco', with a voice coming from a temporal remove and thus of a second-order compared to Francisco and Rita's, a second boy enters the frame from the right and takes a seat next to the woman. It is at this point that the images catch up with the aural content of the story, as Francisco mentions his father's younger cousins who used to come to visit every summer and stage plays with the boys. Henceforth we get a number of verbal indicators that point to the status of the images ('I remember the first time we went there' and later, about this forgotten play, 'I don't remember what it was. I remember Eugenio dressed as an angel', and later still, 'I remember him going through the trapdoor. I remember the play. I don't know why.').

Together the woman and the teen Francisco look at Eugenio, then turn their attention upwards to their left. Following the direction of their gaze, the camera cuts to a shot of a rectangular opening in the slanted ceiling of the attic roof and pans until we catch sight of a second woman with yet another boy (the young João). Gently nudged forward, João descends the stairs in front of him and, as both woman and camera stand still, we see him disappearing from view through the bottom of the frame, as if he were submerging. Graphically matched, the following shot reprises the same dynamic (appearance–disappearance), showing the young João, encased within the dark square of the trapdoor opening, while the angel-impersonating Eugenio lowers the trapdoor, sealing him off from view. The visualisation of this memory ends with a medium shot of young Francisco in the attic, stepping into the frame from the right, the background occupied by blurred family photos, while Francisco the narrator confesses that all his memories 'are connected to that house'. The shots that follow change location to the massive soundstage where the adult Francisco rehearses with his theatre group. The lowered gaze of the young Francisco in the attic is mirrored by the lowered gaze of the older Francisco in a shot which begins with João's body covered by a white sheet, being carried away on a stretcher. As police cars and an ambulance leave the inside of the soundstage in a high angle shot that allows us to take in the expanse of the red floor, suggestive of an overflowing bloodstain, its sliding metal doors are closed, echoing the lowered trapdoor of the previous shots. In addition to setting up a complex web of interconnected images, some of which will be repeated later on in the film, the sequence crucially makes the connection between theatre, place and memory. In what follows, I shall further reflect on the significance of the film's beginning, drawing on Edward Casey's phenomenological analysis of remembering.

In his nuanced discussion of mnemonic modes, Casey underscores the importance of place in remembering, noting that 'memory is naturally place-oriented or at least place-supported', thriving 'on the persistent particularities of what is properly *in place*: held fast there and made one's own' (2000: 187, emphasis in the original). This marks a significant junction in his argument, allowing him to move beyond a conceptualisation of memory as 'temporally expansive' (ibid.: 39) towards considering the spatial articulations of memory. The vocabulary that assists Casey in this conceptual move is itself spatial: 'place is a *mise en scène* for remembered events precisely to the extent that it guards and keeps these events within its self-delimiting perimeters' (ibid.: 189). The place amounts to subjective orientation and directionality and, within this framework, the body itself, both remembered and remembering, functions as 'intra-place' and 'inter-place' (ibid.: 196). According to Casey, 'we almost always remember places from the point of view of our body's own intra-place within a remembered place: *there we were*, there and nowhere else', but, as we remember, the body also 'moves us from place to place' (ibid.: 196). Casey's emphasis on the embodied and situated nature of memory chimes with Hans Belting's understanding of the body as 'a living medium that makes us *perceive*, *project*, or *remember* images and that also enables our imagination to censor or to transform them' (2005: 306, emphasis in the original), as well as with Johanne Villeneuve's notion of the body as the first mediation, an idea mentioned in the introduction to this chapter.

The body mediates the memory, shapes and structures it, before any other level of mediality intervenes. In the sequence that I described the voice of the adult Francisco summons the image of the younger Francisco in a meaningful place, the site of the character's first encounter with theatre. While the film voices, to use Casey's words, 'the self-moving soul that recollects itself in place' (ibid.: 189), the various bodies that we see on screen are isolated and positioned within scenes, moved like pawns on a chessboard, or like actors on a stage (which they incidentally are), by a will to remember. These scenes have lost much of their initial context: Eugenio's costume no longer makes dramatic sense, but it is precisely the absence of specification that renders it intensely emblematic, enabling it to resonate with other similarly decontextualised objects (the pitchers, the abandoned toy car, the books). The interaction between characters appears minimal and truncated, and, interestingly enough, the boys' actions are controlled and overseen by young women. Later in the film, Rita will describe João's relation to Francisco's mother as a 'double act', and this idea, never quite pursued or clarified, is already intimated in the pairings of the opening sequence.

In Casey's analysis of the processes of memory, it is the 'lived body' that 'traces out the arena for the remembered scenes that inhere so steadfastly in particular places: the body's maneuvers and movements, imagined as well as actual, make room for remembering placed scenes in all of their complex composition' (ibid.: 189). But how do we, as spectators, experience this sense of imagined movement in place that organises the memory from within, as it were? To stay within the phenomenological framework, we experience it through what Vivian Sobchack famously conceptualised as the film's body. Earlier in this analysis, I quoted Chion's remarks about the 'other *us* that is the voice of another' in film. By the same token, as Sobchack argues, the 'film's seeing' could be understood as 'the seeing of another who is *like* myself, but *not* myself' (1992: 136). In *The Jester*, the film's seeing is steered by the character's remembrance which re-stages a familiar place. In the more recent past that the flashback extensively covers, the attic will appear revamped, modernised, but this first memory repopulates it with objects since removed, objects of blurred contours and forgotten functionality, which bring to mind what Lesley Stern calls a 'cinematic thinginess' (2001: 323). According to Stern, in cinema, 'the *movement* of the image invests the delineation of things with a particular affectivity' (ibid.: 321, emphasis in the original), whereby the 'signifying potential of things' is often de-emphasised in favour of their sensuous and affective potential and of a certain 'indeterminacy' they carry which can function as both 'a resistance and an allure' (ibid.: 334). The opening sequence of *The Jester* brings into play precisely this indeterminacy of things and their often cryptic materiality. As we navigate from one puzzling image to another, guided by a voice which admits to partiality, we get the distinct sense of a place that is purposefully rediscovered, marshalled towards uncovering something of significance, but that significance is very much of an emotional nature. As Casey claims:

> To be implaced in memory is to know our way *around*: to know the world around us. In memories of place we remember things, pathways, horizons as these concern and encompass us. Together they constitute a structure of containment, an environment for remembering of many kinds and with many interests. (2000: 259)

One of these 'many interests' in the film, what drives, in other words, the return to these moments and to this place, is the desire to produce the emotional outline of a relationship that has been lost. João's death relegates his relationship to Francisco to the past, but this past contains enough mystery to keep the remembering effort gainfully engaged. The rehearsed play itself valorises the idea of the past as a 'treasury of passions and joys' and it is precisely the root of past passions and joys that the conversation between Rita and Francisco tries to retrospectively unearth. Consequently, the film moves between the memory of a national past acted out through fictionalised history in the play and the memory of Francisco's past as it is ghosted by both João and his father, whose tragic disappearance is revealed towards the end of the film. Francisco's past is visualised through what one might be tempted to call the private theatre of memory. To apply Christopher Bollas's terminology, theatre seems to function in the film as both a 'mnemic object' (1993: 19) that preserves and releases 'self states' and as a 'choice of representational form', a 'kind of psychic route' that provides a sense of structured 'lived experience' (ibid.: 41). According to Bollas, the object world is used by the individual as 'a lexicon' through which a private idiom is spoken (ibid.: 21). In keeping with this logic, theatre in *The Jester* constitutes a medium of self-expression for the main character in more ways than one.

The opening sequence presents the first of several early memories, scattered throughout the film, and featuring the same place (the attic of the house). In another scene, we see the two boys, Francisco and João, retrieving what looks like a cigarette case and inspecting its contents. We are not privy to what they find inside the case, but we get to glimpse the image of a jester on the case, indicative of the film's insistence on self-imbrication, on showing earlier, incipient images and versions of situations and relations that lock the characters in place. Later still, Francisco recounts and the film lets us see how, on the night of his father's suicide, he was keeping watch, ready to distract his father, while João tried to steal a rifle for a planned hunting expedition with Eugenio. As Francisco explains in the voice-over accompanying this remembrance, 'It was always like that. I entertained and João did it.' This distribution of roles, this dichotomy (doing and performing) appears to be continued through to João's last moments, with João trading arms and keeping dangerous company and Francisco only experiencing risk and peril through his character Dom Bibas, the jester in the eponymous novel and theatre show. However, in terms of duration and detailed articulation, the film privileges the virtual action of the play over João's tangled affairs, which begs the question of whether there might be a subtler dynamic at work that we are asked to consider. Francisco's words reveal a deeper logic of alternation between the characters' actions, theatrical and actual.

As Alice Rayner argues, theatre offers fertile ground for an exploration of action and its components, 'intentionality, materiality, and performativity' (1994: 12), or in a different formulation, 'praxis', 'kinesis' and rhetoric (ibid.). Following Rayner, I would argue that *The Jester* allows these aspects to play off each other in a way that highlights the theatricalisation of memory and of ordinary behaviour. João insists that he knows why he acts the way he does and even cultivates a certain air of urgency and decisiveness (he tells Francisco that he is the reason why he got involved in the arms' deal, he claims that he has no time to lose and deplores the fact that Francisco lacks the bravery to act), but at the same time the intentionality of his actions is undermined by the blackmail. The opening shots that I analysed in detail feature several actions whose intentionality is unavailable, which allows us to focus on their materiality and perceived reactivity, on motion as motion, looking as looking, and their interconnections.

For Rayner, the performative dimension consists of 'the discursive or rhetorical formulations that implicate an audience or world in the act itself and that give it qualities' (ibid.: 12). This is acting for an audience, a seductive dimension of action, a sensory overlay. The film is replete with instances where the performativity of the action is at stake, but one scene in particular vividly foregrounds it. One day, the week before João's death, Francisco comes home to find Rita packing, preparing to leave him. The characters' interaction in the scene is explicated in the commentary provided by their later-date voice-over. As Rita rushes past Francisco, going up the stairs in the flashback, Francisco's voice-over, in dialogue with Rita's, remarks: 'Seeing you so nervously pretending not to notice me gave me courage.' While Rita is seen strutting about and flicking her hair, we hear Francisco's voice-over gently mocking her 'phoney self-assurance'. While Francisco is shown throwing a shoe at her in anger, we hear Rita's voice-over admitting that, while it was happening, she was struggling to keep a straight face. The voice-over dissects, to use Elizabeth Burns's expression, 'the grammar of composed behaviour' (1972: 33) that the characters engage in as they try to upstage each other, feigning self-command and nonchalance. Their histrionic excess is decoded for us after the fact by the very participants in the charade.

The way in which the voice-over is made to interact with the image-track is consistently one of the most interesting features of the film. This is apparent not only in Rita and Francisco's voice-over conversation, but also in what I understand to be the main strategy of the embedded theatre show, the use of theatrical narration. In the theatre show he is directing, Francisco plays the part of Dom Bibas, the jester at Queen Theresa's court, who, after being flogged at the Count's orders for speaking freely, has an instrumental role in his downfall. In many respects, Dom Bibas is a typical jester. Often finding himself at the receiving end of merciless gibes and derision, traditionally the court jester had a crucial function to fulfil: not only that of entertaining the king (no small feat), but also daring to speak when and what others would not or could not. In fictional portrayals of jesters and fools, this ability to speak their mind is often coupled with unequalled verbal prowess. Situated 'on the margin of their worlds' (Janik 1998: 9), the jesters revelled in their outsider's perspective and, with a 'mind possessed of paradoxes and oppositions' (ibid.: 10), they often turned their social marginality into a source of discursive defiance, into a privilege. Their impudence was the flipside of convention, and it was welcomed and treasured as such.

Variously characterised as 'a comic king' and 'the king's symbolic twin' and 'shadow' (Hyers 1996: 113–15), the jester is a figure of enduring appeal, not only in theatre (Shakespeare's memorable fools) but also in philosophy. The jester is the one who trips up the tightrope dancer on his dangerous crossing in Friedrich Nietzsche's allegorical *Thus Spoke Zarathustra*, a reminder that 'human existence can be derailed even by a foolish joke, a random bit of bad luck, and nothing more' (Burnham and Jesinghausen 2010: 25). Poised between existential mischief and restorative humour, the figure of the jester is bound up with the reflection on the human condition itself, calling to mind its intrinsic vulnerability, folly and 'awkwardness' (Hyers 1996: 123).

The film retains the title of Alexandre Herculano's novel and in so doing affirms the centrality of the jester for both the framing and the framed narrative. In adapting Herculano, Morais has imagined a jester who generally fits well in this tradition and who functions moreover as a 'figure of freedom and equality' (Lemière 2008: 141, my translation). While Dom Bibas does not serve a king (the king, like Francisco's father, has died) and enjoys more narrative agency than jesters are usually granted, he displays many of the familiar features: he engages in witticisms and wisecracks, he is trusted by the Queen, and allowed the opportunity to creatively misbehave, until he is suddenly punished for his daring, which transforms him into an active participant in the conflict. Through most of the rehearsed show, the jester is hyper-visible, not only because of his licence to be anywhere and say anything, but also by virtue of his peculiar visual appearance. The anachronistic tuxedo coupled with the slicked-back hairstyle composes a look of utter displacement in comparison with the faux medieval garb that the other characters are wearing. It is only towards the end of the film that the jester assumes the brightly coloured, mottle-patterned attire that one has come to expect from jesters. However, the unusual feature that I am more interested in, because it aligns the theatre rehearsals with the rest of the film, is the fact that Dom Bibas appears to be a character-narrator. The jester is not only hyper-visible, but also hyper-vocal.

Theatrical narration is a relatively rare device. We have seen it at work in Bunraku theatre in the analysis of *Dolls* and it is found, in the form of addresses to the audience and various techniques of estrangement, in Brecht's epic theatre, where its function is to overturn any illusions that the audience may be lured into. Although the latter can serve as a lens through which to understand the use of theatrical narration in *The Jester*, I want to suggest an additional hermeneutic context for the device. In her analysis of voice-over in cinema, Sarah Kozloff devotes a brief passage to the similarities and differences between the two. She notes that theatrical narrators 'generally stand in sight on stage rather than wafting in as disembodied voices' like voice-over narrators do and, as far as similarities are concerned, 'theatrical narration, like voice-over, is first, intermittent; secondly, interwoven with dramatic scenes that are not mediated through that narrator; and thirdly – crucially – *spoken aloud*' (1988: 18). The emphasis in Kozloff's text on 'spoken aloud' points to a distinction that has been discussed at length by Andrew Gibson, between what Jacques Rancière calls '*la parole muette*' (the mute language) of the novel and the materiality of the voice in cinema (2001: 645–7). Drawing on Rancière and Jacques Derrida, Gibson critically engages with the work on voice in film done by Kozloff, Bordwell and Chion, arguing that 'it is precisely in the cinema that the intimate relationship between the materiality of the voice and its ghostliness – between voice and the principle of writing – may be most strikingly evident' (ibid.: 648). Within this deconstructive logic, it is not only Chion's 'acousmatic voice' that is bodiless but 'voice in film itself is *never other than bodiless*' (ibid.: 652, emphasis in the original). This view is echoed by Pamela Robertson Wojcik, who in a different context argues that 'virtually all sound is technically acousmatic in production and postproduction' (2006: 75). For Gibson, the voice in cinema is spectral and 'haunted' by writing insofar as it is scripted and 'always subject to an order that is not its own', both 'human' and 'technological', and 'canned' and iterable (2001: 648). *The Jester* can be said to foreground these issues and, tellingly, it is through the embedded representation of theatre that this is achieved.

The scriptedness of the voice and its command over the story which appears to emanate from it are flaunted throughout the rehearsals, whenever Francisco is seen and heard reading passages from the novel (usually in a microphone). This happens at various junctures: preceding, concluding, or during a scene and sometimes overlapping with the characters' dialogue. In one scene, initially camped outside the designated playing area, Francisco as Dom Bibas is shown wandering into the set, still reading from a sheet of paper, in a move that confuses the exact meaning of what we are seeing. Given that Francisco is at once the main actor, the director and the stage manager of his show, this could be interpreted as a stage manager reading from his prompt book, were it not for the extent and nature of the text being read.

Unlike what we might expect from a dramatisation of a novel, the excerpts are unmistakable residues of the source text, needlessly descriptive and unabashedly sententious. As Egas is visited in prison by Dulce, Francisco's

Figure 2.1 Theatrical narration in *The Jester* (José Álvaro Morais, 1987, Portugal)

theatrical voice-over is heard outlining the scene ('A door began to open quietly and someone entered the sinister room. It was the figure of a woman. She was dressed as for a banquet'), despite the fact that the image is self-explanatory (a shaft of light and a creaking sound are followed by a figure clad in white stepping through the door frame). Elsewhere in the rehearsals, Ana Maria, the actress playing Dulce, recites passages in which she refers to her character in the third person, sliding effortlessly into the stance of a character narrator. Her lines are later hijacked by Francisco/Dom Bibas, who reads them from a bound folder prompting the Count of Trava to address Dulce in the scene as if the words had come from her. The show being rehearsed appears therefore to be designed as a Brechtian theatre experiment in which, instead of the narration 'in the making', as Patrice Pavis (1998: 234) terms the way events are usually unfolding in theatre, we get a hybrid narrative mode whereby events are both dramatised and recounted by the amplified voice or by the characters themselves. The way in which narration is used in the film's theatre rehearsals accords with Brecht's prescriptive discussion of the 'transposition into the third person' in his 'Short Description of a New Technique That Produces a *Verfremdung* Effect':

> Using the third person and the past tense allows the actors to adopt the right attitude of detachment. In addition they will look for stage directions and remarks that comment on their lines and speak them aloud at rehearsal [. . .] Speaking the stage directions out loud in the third person results in a clash between two tones of voice, estranging the second of them, the text proper. This style of acting is further estranged by taking place on the stage after having already been outlined and announced in words. (2014: 186)

For Brecht, the actors speaking the stage directions and referring to themselves in the third person is part of a larger project of devising acting techniques that would enable them to function 'as long as possible as readers' (ibid.: 185) and to perform their parts 'like a quotation' (ibid.: 185).

The second factor in Gibson's account of the spectrality of the voice in cinema, the technological mediation of sound, is frequently divulged in the film: the voice of the theatrical narrator is at times heard resonantly, drowning all other sounds, other times fading in the background, overtaken by the voices of the other characters. When Francisco demands from Ana Maria a second attempt at a scene on account of her not hitting the right pauses, we hear a tape being rewound, which returns the actors to a moment previously surpassed. This is a film which gives voices an unusually central role in shaping our experience of the narrative and of the diegetic theatre embedded in it. The film so frequently layers voices, both in the theatre sequences and outside of them (the police detective prying around the rehearsal space, whistling a waltz, sailors being noisy in the tavern where Rita and Francisco are having their film-long conversation), that the present of the storytelling appears internally split and constantly overrun by the past, which itself takes the form of what Casey would call a 'thick memorial magma' (2000: 273). Within this entanglement of the present and the past, the various embedded representations (the theatre rehearsals within the film, the film within the film, the flashbacks) form an incomplete intermedial patchwork of competing voices. The next case study will examine yet another arrangement of voices that lends itself to an analysis of the association of theatre, film and memory.

ALL ABOUT MY MOTHER: FILMIC AND THEATRICAL REPETITIONS

Pedro Almodóvar uses the repetition of voice-over/voice-off in the embedding of theatre in *All About My Mother*, in order to draw attention to theatre as a mnemonic playground where the memory of the viewer, the memory of the characters and the memory of the text itself are interacting. The film thus broadly gestures towards some of the important ways in which the voice can situate itself between the two media that constitute the focus of this book. Each time he visually separates the voice from its source, Almodóvar devises a complex way of introducing and justifying it: superimposition, visual obstruction or lip-synching, and these stylistic choices offer important clues about the film's approach to theatre and memory.

Pedro Almodóvar's 1999 film *Todo sobre mi madre* (*All About My Mother*) focuses on Manuela (Cecilia Roth), a nurse who works in a transplant unit in Madrid, while she raises her only son Esteban (Eloy Azurin). Esteban is killed in an accident when he tries to secure an autograph from Huma Rojo (Marisa Paredes), the actress playing Blanche Dubois in the staging of *A Streetcar Named Desire* that Manuela and Esteban attend on his seventeenth birthday (incident adapted from a similar sub-plot in John Cassavetes's *Opening Night*). In the aftermath of her son's death, Manuela travels to Barcelona in search of the boy's transsexual father Esteban/Lola, and while in Barcelona she sees the show again and later ends up acting in it, as a last-minute substitute for Nina, the actress playing Stella (Candela Peña), reprising a role that she once used to perform. As Stephen Maddison convincingly argues, Esteban's death allows Manuela to 'mother' other characters (2000: 278), including her old friend, the battered yet quick-to-recover transsexual La Agrado (Antonia San Juan), Sister Rosa (Penélope Cruz), whose son, also fathered by Lola, is adopted by Manuela after Rosa's HIV-related death, and Huma herself, who struggles in a tempestuous relationship with Nina. Manuela's maternal acts are so frequent and so spontaneous that Susan Martin-Márquez has dubbed her the film's 'ur-mother' (2004: 502). In addition to these complications of melodramatic extraction, the film also employs, in a manner characteristic of much of Almodóvar's cinematic output, references not only to theatre (Tennessee Williams's *A Streetcar Named Desire*, Federico García Lorca's *Blood Wedding*) but also to literature and film (Truman Capote's *Music for Chameleons*, Joseph Mankiewicz's *All About Eve*). As José Arroyo rightfully notes, the common denominator of these references, ranging from twentieth-century classics to iconic film performances, is their affiliation to a 'broad range of queer cultures' and 'queer interpretative communities' (1999: 40). In a different reading, inspired by the film's own themes (transplants, transsexuality) and by Gérard Genette's work, Jean-Marc Lalanne (1999: 35) has seen in these references a manifestation of 'transtextuality', understood as 'the textual transcendence of text' (Genette 1997: 1). For Lalanne, this desire to go beyond textual and generic limitations shares with the idea of transsexuality an impulse to incorporate 'the signs of that which is not the self' (in the original 'absorber les signes de ce qui n'est pas soi') (Lalanne 1999: 35).

In focusing on the use of voice in Almodóvar's film, I am building on Marsha Kinder's insightful examination of the director's evolving relation to sound design. In the previous case study, the technological handicaps of the Portuguese film industry were singled out as the main cause for *The Jester*'s delayed completion and release. A similar technological lag is described by Kinder with respect to the Spanish film industry of the 1980s, a situation that many Spanish filmmakers tried to overcome by 'designing disjunctive relations between sound and image that violated the rules of Hollywood classical cinema' (2013: 282). Kinder attributes Almodóvar's early sense of experimentation with sound to this compensatory logic and remarks that the 'legacy of conceptual sound design' (ibid.) continued to be felt in his work even after the introduction of Dolby technology and the beginning of his long-term collaboration with sound engineer Miguel Rejas, which can be traced back to *All About My Mother* (ibid.: 283). In relation to this latter film, Kinder notes that Almodóvar pays attention to the 'gendering of sound-image relations' by constructing Lola as 'visually female and acoustically male' (ibid.: 296) and that it is useful to think of the film's 'hyper-plotting' using the musical metaphor of 'a series of harmonic lines' that are carefully orchestrated (ibid.: 297). Elsewhere, Kinder has suggested that Esteban's post-mortem voice-overs, 'carried' as they are by Manuela, are indicative of a 'trans-subjective collaboration' that prolongs his presence beyond death (2004: 17).

Kinder's insights are valuable but they do not exhaust the implications of studying the voice in Almodóvar's film, especially when considered in the context of film–theatre intermediality. In order to contribute to such a study, I shall examine the Streetcar fragments of performance (one in Madrid and four in Barcelona – the fourth one never shown, merely heard through the loudspeakers) in both their overlaps and their particularities. The Madrid fragment and the first two Barcelona fragments are approximate repeats of the same segment in the play, with a varying input of details. In these three fragmentary performances, Manuela, a former Stella ghosted by her role, is the privileged spectator and the way the film selects and frames details of performance is influenced by her changing situation of viewing (in the auditorium or in the wings, with or without her son). Although I shall be primarily concerned with repetition as it manifests itself across these fragments, what also needs to be acknowledged is that repetition operates more widely throughout the film, with several situations being prefigured (and thus repeated) in the narrative (e.g. the hospital simulation in relation to the actual organ donation to which Manuela agrees after Esteban's death). For Susan Martin-Márquez, it is the 'motherhood paradigm' that gets 'produced and reproduced, albeit with some variations, *ad infinitum* within the film text' (2004: 502). Leo Bersani and Ulysse Dutoit's Lacanian analysis of the film also starts from the realisation that there are numerous repetitions in the film, although nothing ever reappears in the exact same form, which for them begs the question 'What exactly is repeated when a theatrical character or situation reoccurs, differently, in reality – a reality which is of course itself the aesthetic construction of Almodóvar's film?' (2004: 98). The answer they propose towards the end of their analysis is:

> The principal realistic narrative of the film *un*seriously repeats the art it quotes. The fascination of such works as *All About Eve* and *A Streetcar Named Desire* most probably derives from the skill with which they, like so many realistic plays and films, reformulate psychological fantasy as a given, irrevocably realized world. (ibid.: 114–15)

For Dutoit and Bersani, the effect of repetition in the film is not 'certifying whatever gets repeated', but rather 'undermining' it (ibid.: 100), with identities 'dissipated as they are being repeated' (ibid.: 101) in what amounts to a 'massive deconstruction' of the film's title through an ultimately 'unlocatable' referent of 'Mother' and an uncertain 'proprietary' subject of 'my' (ibid.: 117). While I share Dutoit and Bersani's interest in the film's repetitions, I place a different emphasis, namely on the repetition of formal mechanisms of embedding theatre in film, and therefore use a different interpretive paradigm to account for the effects of repetition.

Any investigation into the nature of repetition should begin by acknowledging one of the paradoxes informing this attempt: 'beyond mentioning the fact of repetition, we can say nothing about it except through a discussion of differences' (Rimmon-Kenan 1980: 153). Bruce Kawin makes a similar point in his extended analysis of the functions and mechanisms of repetition, which he calls 'near-repetition', when he remarks that 'The aesthetics of repetition cannot really be separated from the aesthetics of change' (1972: 7). Kawin situates his reflection on repetition within a broader discussion about the incommensurability of the 'act of living' with the 'act of recording'. He explains:

> Words and frames occur singly, and accumulate into statements or movements. It is in their nature to divide experience and to present pieces of experience in sequence, trusting the act of apprehension to restore continuity. They make it necessary for us, and thus instruct us, to apprehend the present, a perfect continuum, as a series of instants. It is this act of division which distinguishes art from experience. Pure continuum remains inexpressible; while we are aware of its nature (when, for example, we experience the enormity of actual *love*, and no italicizing or adjectiving or framing or insisting will begin to express or image that transcendence which is falsified even by being called 'feeling') the act of dividing and arranging and killing into the communicable is laughable to us and horrible. (ibid.: 153–4)

In *All About My Mother*, Almodóvar appears to be profoundly aware of the effects of this 'act of dividing and arranging and killing into the communicable' and uses stylistic repetition precisely to fervently circle around an inexpressible core of love, loss and mourning. The very medium of repetition, theatre, serves him therefore not only as 'a more abstract, metaphorical mise-en-scène' (Allinson 2005: 234), but also as an arena in which, to use Alice Rayner's expression, 'a repetition is planned but still open to accident' (2006a: 29). Rayner herself is concerned with what she calls 'the trauma of the impossible present' and, in a remark that echoes Kawin's, discusses the co-presence of performers and audience in theatre as a 'kind of temporal mirror for the present in which what is passing is known while it is passing' (ibid.: 32), a mirror that tries to capture this very evanescence. Following in the footsteps of Rayner and Kawin, I argue that *All About My Mother* trades on this idea of theatre as a site of planned but never identical reiteration at the same time as it portrays it as a communal space in which the characters' feelings and experiences meaningfully bounce off each other. Almodóvar's filmic repetitions (of music, of voice-over/voice-off) bring to the fore and enhance the theatrical repetitions, revealing them to be subject to the vagaries of spectatorship.

The main theatrical reference of the film, Tennessee Williams's *A Streetcar Named Desire* (1947), is a canonical play, whose tension and tragic conclusion are often seen to arise from a meeting of opposites: Blanche Dubois, cultured, theatrical, emotionally scarred, versus Stanley Kowalski, her virile, unmannered and brutal brother-in-law, who ends up raping her. In his notebooks, Elia Kazan, who directed the play for both Broadway and the screen, phrased this opposition in terms of the confrontation between 'the emblem of a dying civilization' (Blanche as representative of the antebellum American South) and the 'basic animal cynicism of today' (Stanley) (Kazan cited in Neve 2009: 34). As Philip Kolin observes, Kazan's take on the play was Stanislavskian, naturalistic, behavioural (2000: 9–10). The social opposition identified by Kazan has since been complicated by a plethora of critical readings that have emphasised the characters' contradictions. Anne Fleche, for instance, interprets Blanche's 'raging heterosexuality' (her serial seduction of young boys) as a form of atonement for her 'deeply rooted homophobia' (the cruelty she showed towards her gay husband) (1995: 267). In her essay, she takes issue with the notion that Blanche can be seen as a 'drag role' (ibid.: 266), a notion that was in all likelihood inspired by Williams's own confessed identification with Blanche (Kolin 2000: 4). Almodóvar himself has spoken of the temptation to re-imagine the play from a queer perspective:

> I can quite see, for example, the part of Blanche Dubois being played by a man – Stella's older brother arrives, broke, perhaps just out of prison, and Kowalski, the brute who constantly makes fun of him, ends up going to bed with him. For a male Blanche, such a sexual encounter would pack a real punch. I could stage the play from that perspective. I don't know, however, whether we have the right to touch the madness of Blanche, a theatrical icon. (Strauss 1994: 191)

Resisting this temptation, Almodóvar has instead re-worked Tennessee Williams's text in *All About My Mother* in such a manner as to both engage our sense of familiarity with the play, by selecting a section which contains the much-quoted line 'I have always depended on the kindness of strangers', and introduce slight and not so slight alterations. While Tennessee Williams recommends a 'peculiarly tender blue, almost turquoise' sky (Williams 1959: 11) and has Blanche wear a Della Robbia blue jacket (ibid.: 115), Almodóvar employs a darker and more intense shade of blue to flood the theatre sets, in what Paul Julian Smith would call a 'cinema of saturation' (2000: 3). Against this backdrop of vibrant blue, of unforgiving radiance, the silhouettes and gestures are more decisively outlined to the effect that the 'emotional penumbra surrounding the events and characters' that characterises, in Mary Ann Corrigan's view (1997: 83), the atmosphere of the play is replaced by an ambiance that offers no possibility for psychological hideouts, a space without recesses. The characters in the play are no longer distinguished by their association with a specific range of colours; Blanche's 'pastels' shown in 'half-lights' (ibid.: 84) would have created a discordant note with the indiscriminate use of strong colours throughout the movie. Blanche, as played by the fictional actress Huma Rojo, is majestically taller than her sister and inflexibly statuesque, especially in the scene of the struggle. There is little about her to remind us of what a critic called the 'feeble and hysterical decorativeness' of Williams's Blanche (Clurman cited in Corrigan 1997: 90).

Almodóvar references the play even beyond the confines of the theatrical fragments he features in the film. When Manuela tells Huma about the death of her son, Huma suddenly remembers the circumstances of the evening in question and, as she remembers them, the sounds of the falling rain and of Esteban knocking on the car window are heard (and visualised), not unlike the way in which the stage directions of *A Streetcar Named Desire* and Elia Kazan's 1951 influential adaptation of the play emphasise the connection between the memory of Blanche's dead husband and the Varsouviana in what Philip Kolin has called a 'theatre of interiority' (2000: 4). Perhaps most significantly, *All About My Mother* devises an ending inspired by Kazan's film adaptation, disregarding the ambiguous ending of the play in which a sobbing Stella is consoled by Stanley after Blanche's removal and instead having Stella leave Stanley. However, if the 'penitential ending' of Kazan's film adaptation, in which Stella rejects Stanley's attempt to appease her, was the result of a complex set of negotiations with the Production Code's Breen Office, whose representatives did not want to see Blanche's rape go unpunished (Cahir 1994: 74), Almodóvar's ending, unconstrained by any such considerations, seems to have been designed to underscore Stella's understanding of herself as a mother first and a wife second. Both Manuela and Almodóvar's Stella leave their husbands in order to protect their children. As Stephen Maddison has argued, the changed ending in Almodóvar's staging also suggests that 'women have choices outside of their relations with men' (2000: 267) and one of these choices is 'female resistance' and 'bonding' (ibid.: 277, 279).

The three fragments that are picked out from the last section of the play (Blanche waiting for a fictitious Huntleigh to call, the arrival of the doctor and matron/nurse, Blanche's struggle and the alternative ending showing Stella's departure) together convey the impression of a marked preference for the final moments of the play over the rest, despite the considerable variation manifested in their treatment. The first theatrical fragment from *A Streetcar Named Desire* begins after Manuela and Esteban enter the theatre in Madrid, with an extreme close-up on a poster of Huma Rojo's face. The camera then draws back to reveal more of this overblown portrait. As the image stares at us, a voice-over transports us into the theatre performance, continuing at the same time the line of interpellation inaugurated by the gazing poster: 'Why are you looking at me? Am I horrendous?' The actual utterance is not visualised, but we get to see the stage on which these lines are spoken in a lingering superimposition with the poster that eventually gives way to a series of proximate and clear views of Blanche being chased and immobilised by the nurse and subsequently accompanied out of the house by the doctor. The congruence between the insecure, questioning voice and the incisiveness of the poster's gaze makes the voice-over initially function as the 'inner lining' of the image, to borrow an expression from Mary Ann Doane (1980: 41). As we transition from the superimposition to the series of distinct shots, the unmoored voices settle on bodies, in what Michel Chion would call the 'de-acousmatization' of the voice, a 'symbolic act' that strips the voice of some of its power (1999: 27–8).

The way in which this fragment of performance is introduced, combining the theatre poster's piercing, immovable gaze with a voice-over which begins unattached but is then anchored to a performing body, also brings to mind Alice Rayner's discussion of theatre's slippery relation to time. Rayner puzzles over the question '*when* is it theatre?' (2006a: 4) and attempts to trace its ever-elusive beginnings:

> The appointment with theatre demands that one not only witness a missed encounter but also act it out. I already know I will miss the exact time of a play's beginning. When did that event actually begin? When I stepped inside the building; when the curtain opened? It asks me to be a witness to that imaginary moment of the beginning when the curtain opens and reveals the other place in the same space, or, lacking a curtain, when the lights go down, or lacking lights, when the first word is spoken, or lacking words, when the first motion is made. (ibid.: 28)

For Rayner, theatre's complex relation with time requires that we understand it at once as an event of consciousness and a stirring of the unconscious, an experience that situates itself at the intersection of multiple regimes

Figure 2.2 Layered beginnings – *All About My Mother* (Pedro Almodóvar, 1999, Spain)

of temporality. She goes on to remark that 'in theatre we do not remember an event, an object, or even a relationship as much as we remember having forgotten and wake to our own forgetfulness' (ibid.: 30). Given Manuela's deliberate forgetting of a past life marked by the play, the performance is shown to have started already, because in a sense, for Manuela it has never ended. Her own story functions in some respects as the play's unwritten postscript. It's not that Manuela falls victim to a delusional continuum between life and theatre, but rather that she experiences theatre as what Rayner has called a 'logically impossible event, one that is both unique and a repetition, singular and double' (2006a: xxiv).

The second performance in Barcelona, by including a longer version of the conversation between Stella, Eunice and Blanche preceding the arrival of the doctor, fills the gaps of the first Madrid performance, revealing it to be a subjective and elliptical montage of images. In between Blanche's anxious enquiry about her appearance and the doctor's arrival, the second Barcelona performance shows Stella offering to help Blanche with a necklace and includes a line in which Eunice pretends to be envious of Blanche's upcoming trip, to assuage her increasing restlessness. Both moments are absent from the Madrid performance. Instead, the cumulative effect of the superimposition, the voice-over and the extradiegetic bandoneón music is that of a drifting along with the performance, the passage of time pleasantly unregistered until a scene strikes home and suddenly one feels intensely present (the series of distinct shots). In a discussion of the voice *dispositif* with particular reference to Marguerite Duras's experiments with voices, Régis Durand writes of 'the powerful currents, gusts, shudders of desire which run through the voices' and of bodies which 'seem a creation of the voices' (1997: 308). This could also be said about the theatre fragments of *All About My Mother*. The Madrid performance begins with a short dialogue of uncircumscribed voices, and before we even witness on stage the heightened drama of Blanche's resistance to her forced institutionalisation, the brief but haunting voice-over exchange allows us to hear her extreme fragility, her retreat into the beguiling comforts of a made-up alternative to reality, as well as Stella's emotional tiptoeing around Blanche's shattered self.

When at the end of the first Madrid performance Stella announces her decision never to go back to Stanley and leaves her home fondling her baby, she moves on stage in a straight line perfectly parallel to the viewer, movement which flattens the image, by contrast with the depth of space achieved in the previous scenes with Blanche. Thus Stella herself becomes a poster image of the firm resolution to leave everything behind and start life anew, a counterpoint to Blanche's tragic fixity, her inability to move on from the trauma of her past. The staging of the scene privileges the visual shorthand

and the memorable line, better to imprint its finality onto the spectator, and Manuela is shown emotionally responding to it, under the watchful gaze of her son. With regard to theatre in particular, Marie-Laure Bardèche has commented on the idea of a 'beginning which is already repetition' (1999: 10, my translation). This applies to the Madrid performance, not only in the general sense in which any theatrical performance is already a repetition of its rehearsals and of its underlying text, but also because of Manuela's prior involvement with the play and because of her own re-enactment of *Streetcar*'s mutated ending. Following Bardèche, one could say that in this first theatrical fragment 'the origin is flaunted as a lack' (ibid.: 51, my translation). The film does not show us anything from Manuela's theatrical past, playing Stella alongside Lola's Stanley, nor are we privy to her domestic misfortunes during Lola's transition, issues that are only mentioned briefly or indirectly, but Almodóvar's stylistic choices encourage us to feel they are both comprised and repeated with every new staging of *A Streetcar Named Desire* that Manuela witnesses.

There is another level of memory that the film could be said to engage with, a level that has been uncovered by Juan Carlos Ibáñez as 'the subtle intertextual play established by Almodóvar between the character of Manuela and the biography of actress Cecilia Roth' (2013: 163). It is Ibáñez's contention that during the 1970s, when Almodóvar was active in independent Madrilenian theatre groups, he was able to experience first-hand the influence of several important figures of the Argentine theatre community, such as Norman Brinski and Carlos Gandolfo, who had fled the country after the rise of an ultra-right anti-communist movement and had temporarily settled in Spain (ibid.: 164). Cecilia Roth herself was an Argentine émigré during this period and through her father and her profession had direct ties to the Argentine artistic diaspora. Traces of this background are present, Ibáñez claims, in Manuela's own displacement, but also in the incorporation of a fragment from *Haciendo Lorca/Performing Lorca*, whose original production was also associated with Argentine performers (ibid.: 166). If we concede, together with Ibáñez, that history has indeed crept into the character development, then this historical intertextuality could be said to supplement what Ernesto Acevedo-Muñoz has called the film's 'corporeal intertextuality' (2003: 27), adding to the sophistication of Almodóvar's handling of theatre.

After Esteban's death, Manuela goes to see the show again in Barcelona and, as in the first instance, we see her in the theatre vestibule, before she is shown in the audience. The shot fades from an image of Esteban's notebook to the lights at the theatre venue, letting them share the screen before the camera slides onto the play's poster, continuing its descent until it reaches Manuela's face. She stares into the distance where her gaze is met by an imagined/remembered Esteban, but this brief encounter appears neither comforting nor disturbing as Manuela's stare remains selfsame, mired in its own stoniness. As she turns her back to the camera, a rack focus brings clarity to a theatre poster in the background, a form of beginning, although Rayner's wonder at theatre's missed beginnings is as relevant as before. The rack focus also brings to mind Edward Casey's notion of 'imaginal and rememorative margins', the aura or fringe which rings around a memory and into which 'the imagined or remembered content dissolves' (2000: 77). A cut then takes us into the auditorium where our view of the stage is partially obstructed by Manuela, seated just in front of the film viewer, which results in a brief voice-off. A consequence of this obstruction is that we only get to see the theatrical characters when they move towards the right extremity of the stage; specifically, we see Stella go past the poker players, stopping to say her final lines and then continue towards the exit, at the opposite edge from that occupied by Manuela's head. I shall discuss this type of obstructive placement in more detail in my analysis of *Opening Night*, a film which makes profuse use of it and which is alluded to in *All About My Mother*. For now, suffice it to say that, heard in a voice-off, Stella's feminist battle cry 'Don't ever touch me again, bastard', an Almodóvar invention, is dislocated from Nina's body and instead resonates from the space blocked by Manuela's head, as if to suggest its boundless mental grip on her. Significantly shorter than the previous fragment, the first performance in Barcelona is reduced to the ending of the play, a decision that reinforces the film's affiliation to melodrama, a genre which operates, according to Thomas Elsaesser, with a 'foreshortening of lived time in favour of intensity' (1991: 76). This considerably abridged fragment can also be said to more generally affirm what the same author claimed as a specificity of the film medium, namely the tendency towards 'concentrated visual metaphors and dramatic acceleration', as opposed to the 'fictional techniques of dilation' privileged by the novel (ibid.).

During the second performance in Barcelona, Manuela, now working for Huma Rojo, stands in the wings of the stage, lip-synching Stella's lines while Nina utters them on stage. To paraphrase Bruce Kawin, through repetition, the role has now fully become a 'secular mantra' (1972: 170), Manuela's method for accessing and at the same time protecting herself from her memories. After it shows us Manuela's lip-synching, the film 'returns the voice' to its rightful body, at least partly because, as Mary Ann Doane has argued, the effectiveness of the voice-off 'rests on the knowledge that the character can easily be made visible by a slight reframing which would reunite the voice and its source' (1980: 41). In a sense, voice-off represents in this case the film's interference with and disturbance of theatre's image–sound integrity, an example of intermedial static. The film tampers with the sound, by taking it away from its source (Manuela lip-synching), restoring it (the camera leaves Manuela in order to pay attention to the interactions on the stage) and then removing it again (Manuela listens to the loudspeakers while she prepares coffee in the dressing room). Granting that the voice-off 'deepens the diegesis', creating the effect that 'there is a space in the fictional world which the camera does not register', a 'lost space' in Doane's phrasing (ibid.: 40), one could then proceed to argue that in *All About My Mother*, this lost space is often the theatre space. The voice-off in the theatre sequences achieves the sense of a performance that is taking place irrespective of whether the film captures and/or chooses to show it (if the reader recalls, this bears some similarity with Michel Chion's notion of the embedded performance possessing a semblance of independence, an idea I mentioned in the analysis of *The Double Life of Véronique*). Doane crucially emphasises the spatialising function of sound, noting that 'the voice has a greater command over space than the look – one can hear around corners, through walls' (ibid.: 44). This is literally exemplified in the film's most extreme use of voice-off, where the stage and the actors are not shown at all. The camera in this sequence shows Agrado listening to and trying to simultaneously recite the lines she hears through the loudspeakers. The sequence begins with the camera panning over the surface of a wall, painted in three horizontal bands of colour (perhaps a visual reminder of the parallel tracks in the film strip). While we see the wall, we also literally hear through it.

Almodóvar breaks the stylistic pattern of vocally embedding theatre once to powerful and noticeable effect: when, due to a casting emergency, Manuela resumes playing Stella after a twenty-year lapse, the fragment is not introduced by music and voice-over or voice-off like the other Streetcar fragments. From the tango sounds of the bandoneón in the Madrid fragment to the jolting, isolated piano chords in the Lorca monologue that I shall discuss in the conclusion to this case study, music is an important component in the film's representation of theatrical performances. Given that it is used without fail in all but one of the fragments, the glaring absence of extradiegetic music during Manuela's performance cannot be left unexplained. The place once occupied by music is taken by sounds amplified by the surrounding silence, the sounds in the interstices of dialogue. The moment, a fragment of the play's scene eight, is that of Blanche's birthday dinner, during which Stanley unexpectedly and indelicately gifts her a bus ticket back to her hometown. In addition to the dialogue, we hear the sounds of the envelope being opened and then dropped on the table, of Stanley pouring himself a glass, and even of Stella rumpling a napkin and tearing Stanley's shirt. Manuela sobs as Stella goes into labour and her sobbing, described by critics as a 'wail of grief' (Dutoit and Bersani 2004: 108), is loud and unmitigated. This new-found poignancy of sound gestures towards a change occurring at the level of spectatorship and, to a certain extent, also towards a change in tense. Manuela moves from the auditorium to the stage and from remembrance with its 'backward repetition' (Bardèche 1999: 165, my translation) to the present of performance. By stripping the music from the theatrical performance and by eschewing the voice-over/voice-off, the film seems to afford the film viewer the impression of a more direct experience of theatre. In its prior uses, music contributed a sense of a play whose duration was experienced each time in a different rhythm and whose text was travelled through at different speeds with different halts and different emphases. By comparison, the fragment without music appears to be comparatively more dependable and steadier in temporal trajectory and sequentiality, standing out both because it features a different section of the play from the one repeated in the other fragments and because of its more austere, cinematically less showy treatment. The camerawork is at its most inconspicuous, for the most part stationary. It pans when the characters move across the stage, but this apparent movement occurs in order to exchange one fixed position for another.

The Lorca insert is a fragment from *Haciendo Lorca/Performing Lorca*, a staging by the Catalan director Lluis Pasqual. Marvin D'Lugo has interpreted this theatrical insert as an element in an elaborate attempt at constructing a cultural genealogy:

> The importance of the Pasqual substitution of the original Lorca text stresses one of the key aspects of the entire process of genealogical transformation posed throughout the film, the mechanism of recycling of cultural identities through their successive restagings in order to produce new identities. This is the same principle we have already noted in the regeneration of the young Esteban's identity into the body of the organ recipient, and in the third Esteban's birth as the icon of a refigured cultural community. In effect, the three literary intertexts woven into Manuela's spiritual and geographic itinerary cohere as an artistic genealogy that mirrors the plot as a narrative of reformulated Spanishness. (2002)

Although it is tempting to read it in a cultural key, I shall once more consider the way in which the fragment foregrounds the voice, or orality more generally. In its original form, the dramatic excerpt belongs to Act Two, Scene Two of *Bodas de Sangre/Blood Wedding*, Federico García Lorca's 1932 play, and is spoken on the eve of a wedding during a dialogue between the Bridegroom's Mother and the Bride's Father about the hope of a new generation of men being conceived from the connubial union. As a reaction to her future in-law's remark about the expediency of hasty procreation – 'What I'd like is for it all to happen in one day. For them to have two or three men straight away' (Lorca 1997: 35) – the Bridegroom's Mother, in a rhetorically efficient and moving speech, contrasts the *longue durée* of a mother's love and suffering for her son with the implacable swiftness of his passing. The strange world of the play, featuring what Paul Julian Smith has identified as instances of 'introjection' (1998: 46), 'pathological mourning' (ibid.: 63) and a 'sadistic and desiring orality' (ibid.: 64), is on full display in this extended speech, in which the mother talks about licking the blood of her murdered son, a speech made two lines longer by the intercalation 'Animals lick their young, don't they? I'm not disgusted by my son.' The addition prolongs the theatrical moment long enough for it to succeed as a stand-alone, the traces of its separation from the body of the play concealed by the slow cadence of the utterance. The fragment as a whole powerfully conceptualises motherhood as a multisensorial experience, an experience in which the mother connects with her son, dead or alive, through any and all means afforded to her, in keeping with Manuela's continued engagement with Esteban beyond his death.

In the film, the scene opens with yet another brief voice-off. As the words of the recital begin to be heard, the actress who utters them (Huma Rojo) is kept out of view. Instead, the first image we see is that of the director of the show, Lluis Pasqual, looking intently in the direction of the voice. The camera then engages in an elegant movement, away from its initial object of attention and slightly upwards. Registering the presence of Huma Rojo, it proceeds to encircle her in what ultimately becomes a visual embrace of the kindred spaces of the stage and the auditorium. The camera swirl in the Lorca recital is part of a strategy of naturalising a fragment of dramatic dialogue as a self-contained and believable poetic monologue. The same function is performed by the instructions received by Huma Rojo during the rehearsals to keep kneading and to channel her sorrow into this absorptive activity. The almost empty rehearsal theatre, and the special resonance Lorca's words acquire when considered together with the image of a distraught mother (Rosa's mother in the immediately preceding scene) and within the more general context of a film about mourning mothers, make the Lorca recital a very private performance, one that fittingly concludes the film's engagement with theatre. In *All About My Mother*, theatre is ushered in by the voice of the performer, a voice which either accosts the spectators with a question or an unsettling remark or hooks them with the promise of a dramatic revelation. This voice is also intimately involved in reviving secrets and memories buried deep inside the text and in the characters' psyche, as well as in providing a seamless passage between two media.

CHAPTER THREE

The Making and Unmaking of Theatre Rehearsals on Screen

This chapter will prolong the concern articulated thus far with questions of intermedial framing at the same time as it will reflect on ways in which films about theatre dramatise the discourse of artistic truth in rehearsals. In selecting two films that showcase lengthy, if imploding fictional rehearsals (Jacques Rivette's 1969 *L'Amour fou* and Charlie Kaufman's 2009 *Synecdoche, New York*), I am also drawing attention to the process of rehearsal as a form that is arguably more difficult to represent and 'contain' than its comparatively more accomplished twin, the theatre performance. Partly in response to this challenge, the chosen case studies showcase more complex forms of embedding, multiple framings and infinite regress structures, in which different levels of mediation and fictionality either confound one another or bleed into each other. In *L'Amour fou*, a theatre group, led by the stage director Sébastien Gracq (Jean-Pierre Kalfon), rehearses Jean Racine's *Andromaque*, and is filmed in the process by a television crew, the result being a dual framing of the theatrical rehearsals, achieved through the use of a 16 mm camera for the television footage and a 35 mm for the rest. One of the aims of the chapter will be to parse this camera syntax. In *Synecdoche, New York*, Philip Seymour Hoffman plays Caden Cotard, a theatre director who rehearses a sprawling play based on his own life in theatre spaces which are logically impossible in their expansiveness. Given the peculiar nature of his project, theatre and film appear as communicating worlds, with acting, set design and staging functioning as veritable portals between these worlds. The theatre world depicted in the film is made up of a collection of recursive and recessive sub-worlds, which cannibalise each other for dramatic content, and in this voracious proliferation of worlds, the fictional rehearsal procedure is meant to keep everything in place.

In his insightful study on the 'meta' employment of fictional rehearsals in modern dramatic texts, Robert Baker-White argues that one of the functions of the device is to 'show theater as a disjunctive, fragmented, incoherent, contradictory, interrupted, and interruptable enterprise' (1999: 16). The dramatic introspection achieved through the incorporation of rehearsal scenes in plays exposes theatre's fundamentally conflicted identity such that it inspires

Baker-White to write of a dialectical play between 'being and becoming', 'maintenance and subversion of authority', 'imagination and practicality' for the observation of which the rehearsal constitutes a privileged vantage point (ibid.: 14–15). This dialectical premise leads him to probe the effects of folding one dimension into the other, in a series of questions that will be applicable, *mutatis mutandis*, to the present chapter as well: 'Are the freedoms of the rehearsal moment cancelled by virtue of their placement within the finished dramatic text? Or, conversely, is the ostensible stability and traditionality of the text itself upset by the presence within it of rehearsal's potentially disruptive energy?' (ibid.: 16). In other words, to what extent and to what purpose can the qualities of the theatrical rehearsal be conveyed in a form that contradicts it (a finished film or play)? A self-governed, often unruly activity that thrives on rawness and spends itself in fumbled pursuits aspiring towards a culmination that may never come, the rehearsal process does not sit easily in any context other than that of its own imperfect production. It rejects strict regimentation, and therein lies the rub: when a play or a film attempts to capture or invoke it, the unshaped or the half-formed automatically acquires contours and this fundamentally distorts the very nature of the process. According to Baker-White, the rehearsal rebels against what he calls the 'apparatus of closure', while at the same time moving inexorably towards it (ibid.: 17). The two films I have chosen for this chapter are mindful of this paradox and, while inevitably structured, and cleverly at that, they also allow themselves occasionally to appear to 'go on' for longer than expected, drifting towards the obscure or the seemingly irrelevant only to find themselves again within the intricate web they have spun around their elusive object of representation. Lasting a little more than four hours, *L'Amour fou* easily affords this distention. As for *Synecdoche, New York*, despite only lasting the standard two hours it is so packed with incident and so richly self-referential that James Ponsoldt has rightly noted that 'it has the feel of an entire lifetime, crushed like a snowball, stuffed into a glass globe and shaken madly, the bits of life allowed to gently float and drift and settle' (2008).

The rehearsal's provisionality, openness and undecidability are some of the features that have powered the discourse of truth in theatre, a word that is used by characters in both *L'Amour fou* and *Synecdoche, New York* to describe their theatrical endeavours. The characters' obsessive insistence on some form of precision, of intonation, of impersonation or of scenography, and their radical rejection of artistic compromise are consistent with Baker-White's observation that the rehearsal process has often been 'championed as the site of truth and authentic knowing' (1999: 23). Yet both Sébastien Graq and Caden Cotard are ultimately driven by this self-imposed truth injunction into an insolvable artistic deadlock. What is more interesting to consider and what I shall focus on in this chapter is how this process of grappling with theatrical projects which cave in under their own weight is given expression in film, a medium which has its own compulsions and tipping points.

In the wake of a 'spatial turn' in theatre theory, recent contributions to rehearsal studies have emphasised the importance of rehearsal space as foundational for performative work. More specifically, Andrew Filmer and Kate Rossmanith have analysed several ways in which theatrical labour can be spatialised, by questioning the 'orientational metaphors' used by theatre practitioners in professional parlance, amounting to a 'topography of self' that emerges from theatre discourses (2011: 231), as well as by discussing the role played in rehearsals by what they call the 'tactical inhabitation' of theatre spaces (ibid.: 232). In my own analysis, I shall turn to some of their insights in order to scrutinise the use of space in cinematic representations of rehearsals. The space need not be physical, although it often is in these discussions. As Antoine Vitez eloquently phrased it, theatre delineates 'an imaginary field' which functions during the rehearsal period as a 'diving bell, a kind of bubble' inside which the artists create a 'whole world of metaphors, comparisons, ideas' (Vitez cited in McAuley 2008: 285). The rehearsal, therefore, is as much a physical and imaginary space as it is a network of relations between the occupants of this jealously guarded safe zone of experimentation. Much of the tension in *L'Amour fou* arises precisely because the breach of this protected zone is shown to disturb its delicate homeostasis. The characters' dialogue in the film will be used as a barometer of sorts for the series of moods that traverse it and will be analysed for clues about how the characters relate to one another within this imaginary as well as physical space. By contrast, *Synecdoche, New York* imagines a lock-in theatrical project, an ever-expandable, self-sufficient bubble that can withstand any challenge short of the death of its participants. Its excess, or, better said, its representational zeal, invites us to question the role and limits of mimetism and the way in which media generate fictional worlds.

Partly because of the difference in their theatrical texts, the two films can also be said to fictionalise different approaches to the rehearsal, namely what we could call, following Patrice Pavis, a 'texto-centrist' approach versus a 'sceno-centrist' one (2008: 119). Jacques Rivette's film stages a seventeenth-century tragedy by Racine, and the participants in the rehearsal process are shown to agonise over words and their delivery. Charlie Kaufman on the other hand imagines a theatre director who writes the text to be performed on the go, deriving it from his own experiences, in what amounts to a solipsistic, self-searching effort of massive proportions which pays an inordinate amount of attention to minute reconstructions of spaces. While the two films are in many respects very different and are separated by no fewer than four decades, what also links them beyond their complex focus on theatre rehearsals is an interest in 'authorial self-projection', to use Linda Haverty Rugg's formulation. According to Rugg, 'The term represents a shift in vocabulary, from a focus on life story and self-representation to the use of the cinematic apparatus (actors, projector, screen, cinematography) as a means of creating the sense of an author, *and* as a means for that author to reach out, to project to spectators' (2014: 11). In *L'Amour fou*, Sébastien defends his decision to let the actors come into their own, performance-wise, by invoking his intellectual objection to the model of the 'metteur-en-scène papa', who 'feeds ideas' to the actors instead of allowing them to reach their own interpretation. His formulation not only calls to mind a similar expression, albeit used with a different meaning, namely the stance taken by the Nouvelle Vague directors against 'le cinéma de papa', but also points to a congruence of ethos between Sébastien/Kalfon and Jacques Rivette. Indeed, by Rivette's own admission, he and Kalfon 'were in complete agreement about this idea of non-interference as our guiding principle; the idea that the director must not only not be a director but must not be a father-figure' (Aumont et al. 1977: 15). As for Charlie Kaufman, he was acknowledged as an *auteur* even before his directorial debut, on the strength of his offbeat screenplays, which often feature what Gennelle Smith calls 'duplicated self-configurings' (2013: 164). These include a number of embattled artist roles, from the puppeteer Craig Schwartz in *Being John Malkovich* to the screenwriter Charlie Kaufman in *Adaptation* and *Synecdoche, New York*'s own Caden Cotard.

Theatre in Multiple Frames: *L'Amour fou* and the Self-defeating Rehearsal

In January 1969, Jacques Rivette's film *L'Amour fou/Mad Love* was shown in Paris in two different versions. It was the decision of the distributors to allow the four-hour version to be shown only in one cinema (Studio Alpha), while four other cinemas (Marais, Quartier Latin, Hollywood and Studio Raspail) screened an abridged version of two hours (Chazal 1969; Pierre 1969). As a result, many of the contemporary reviewers championed the cause of the long version, which proved to be the more successful of the two, and lamented the distributors' misreckoning. Writing for *Cahiers du Cinéma*, Sylvie Pierre criticised the practice of quickly digesting and forgetting a film, a practice encouraged by distributors butchering long films into standard two-hour versions (1968: 55), and she subsequently emphasised the role of the trade press in inviting the film viewer to resist the standardisation of the films' duration (1969: 62). Elsewhere, *L'Amour fou* was branded a 'film fleuve' and celebrated as such (Daussois 1969).

When, years later, Robin Wood analysed the length of the film, the 'conditions of consumer-capitalism' which favour an efficient use of time were highlighted as the main target of the 'act of cultural transgression' effected by the challenging duration of the film (1981: 3). By that time already a Rivettian trademark, this unusual length was read as 'somehow part of the point', as 'Rivette not only demands our time, he demands our patience' (ibid.). For James Monaco, several reasons make the length interesting and powerful for the spectator: 'the durée works to break down our resistance to the world of Rivette's characters', it enables dramatic relationships to 'build at a natural rate' and it gives us 'the freedom to work out the mystery for ourselves' (1976: 311–12). More recently, Sam Rhodie has argued that Rivette's long films, culminating in his almost thirteen-hour-long film *Out 1: Noli Me Tangere*, do not 'feel' long, but rather 'seem to be aerated, lightened as if the length is necessary for the sense of momentariness and immediacy, of buoyancy [. . .] Rivette's films fly, but to fly, they need to risk, at every moment, a possible disaster, a fall, *cadere*, a *cadenza*' (2015: 196). For Rhodie, the length of Rivette's films is experienced as a form of levity, but this lightness is a tricky act to achieve and maintain. Beyond the different explanations offered of the logic of this duration and its effects, there seems to be an agreement about the object to which it is applied. In *L'Amour fou*, the length of the film serves the idea of a process (the rehearsals, but also the downward spiral of a relationship) being recorded as it takes place. Time and again, critics have noted that 'the film is far more concerned with process than product' (Shaffer 1973: 54), showing Rivette to be a director focused on 'the reality of work' ('la réalité du travail') (Chevrie n.d.: 136), which he approaches with a mixture of 'documentary and theatrical realism' (Wexman 1980: 30).

As much as it is about theatre, *L'Amour fou* is also about the painful disintegration of a couple, Sébastien and Claire, played by Jean-Pierre Kalfon and Bulle Ogier. Both Kalfon and Ogier continued their collaboration with Rivette on 'theatre films' beyond their work in *L'Amour fou*, with Ogier playing, among others, a professor of drama in Rivette's *La Bande des quatre/Gang of Four* (1989) and Kalfon cast as the eccentric Clément Roquemaure, a playwright who devises his own sophisticated version of 'théâtre à domicile', in *L'Amour par terre/Love on the Ground* (1984). The venue of the theatre rehearsals used in the film was the Palais des Sports in Neuilly and Rivette fully entrusted Kalfon with the staging and the co-ordination of the rehearsals, knowing that he had prior theatre experience but also inspired by the experimental productions of Marc O's troupe, to which several of the film's actors belonged (Wiles 2012: 45–6). In this sub-chapter, I shall argue that in *L'Amour fou*, the theatre rehearsals are multiply framed (compositionally, by two different cameras and verbally, through the numerous conversations and interviews), but at the same time, 'de-framed' through the characters' contradictory statements.

The film begins with the sight of an empty rectangular stage surrounded on all sides by a depleted audience. Backstage, a group of anxious actors are waiting for their fellow actor and director Sébastien to arrive. Following a shot of a woman on a train, Sébastien is shown on the floor of a ravaged apartment, listening to a tape recording. The film then goes back in time to reveal the circumstances leading up to this moment. We learn that Sébastien and his partner Claire were both involved in a theatre production of Jean Racine's *Andromaque*, in which they were meant to perform as Pyrrhus and Hermione. As the play's director, Sébastien agreed to have a television crew film the rehearsals for a documentary in the series *Théâtre de notre temps*. The crew, led by André S. Labarthe playing himself, is given carte blanche to film the rehearsals and ask questions, but it soon becomes evident that its presence on set is highly disruptive. Uncomfortable with the presence of the cameras and unable to concentrate, Claire repeatedly botches the punctuation of a phrase in Racine, objects to the work conditions and quits the show. Quick to find a solution, Sébastien offers the part of Hermione to his former wife Marta (Josée Destoop). The film then settles into a formula of alternation between, on the one hand, showing the rehearsals accompanied by interviews and discussions, and, on the other, following Claire as she superficially busies herself with shopping or tidying the apartment. Initially Claire maintains a connection with the rehearsals, by visiting the set and socialising with the actors, but she increasingly withdraws from the group. In search of a new pastime, she starts recording herself on tape. She begins by reciting lines from Hermione's soliloquy, but the recorded material gradually becomes more heterogeneous, incorporating street noises, snippets of radio transmissions, telephone conversations and private messages to Sébastien. At one point, Claire speaks of the material accumulated on tape as evidence against Sébastien.

There are early signs that Claire and Sébastien's relationship is falling apart, such as the night when Claire holds a hat pin close to Sébastien's eyelids, in a mad vigil of love, a scene apparently based on an incident from Luigi Pirandello's life (Aumont et al. 1977: 24). The Pirandello connection goes even further than that, as Mary Wiles has convincingly shown. Marta confesses during an interview with Labarthe that her stage name was inspired by Pirandello's mistress Marta-Abba, which leads Wiles to suggest that Marta competes with Claire 'not only for the love of the director Sébastien-Pyrrhus but also that of dramatist Sébastien-Pirandello' (2012: 48). Increasingly estranged from Claire after she unleashes several jealousy-driven verbal attacks, Sébastien sleeps at the theatre or at Marta's, but after

Claire's attempted suicide, he returns home. During one of their more playful moments, Sébastien jokingly compares Claire to a basset hound and as a result Claire becomes obsessed with the breed, to the point where she tries to kidnap one. Later in the film, she sleeps with a fellow actor. These private scenes are constantly interwoven with scenes of rehearsals and interviews, which I shall analyse in more detail later on. Under unremitting pressure, both professional and emotional, Sébastien is also slowly unravelling. In a memorable scene, after Claire suggests a break-up, he shreds his clothes with a pair of scissors. Sébastien's close collaborator Michèle (Michèle Moretti) confronts him about his apparent lack of interest in the quality of the theatrical turn-out and urges him to deal with the personal issues which are impairing his commitment to the play. After a read-through with the actors at their apartment that marks a new low of enthusiasm for the *Andromaque* project, Sébastien and Claire temporarily cut ties with the outside world. In a frenzy of anarchic energy, they spend two days making love and destroying their apartment. After tearing apart the wallpaper, hammering down the doors and smashing their objects, they set up camp amid the domestic debris. However, when the energy subsides, Claire returns to the idea of separation and her rejection drives Sébastien back to work. When she finally leaves, the shock of her departure is such that Sébastien repudiates his theatre work and hides away in his apartment, where he plays Claire's recordings in a loop, while the telephone rings unanswered. In its broad outline, the plot would therefore seem to support one of Geneviève Sellier's claims about gender relations in French New Wave cinema. Sellier has famously argued that the representation of female characters in the French New Wave films is typically handled in one of two ways. In the prevalent type, to which *L'Amour fou* could be said to pertain, the female characters are 'the male hero's fear and desire made concrete [. . .] They embody directly or indirectly the fatality that will befall the hero, for the very reason that he has fallen in love with them. In order to exist, he must drive them away or destroy them, but he may also risk being destroyed himself' (2008: 149).

In order to establish the importance of the verbal framing of the rehearsals, of their '*mise en mots*' (Deschamps 2001: 42), I shall briefly pause to consider the thirty-four-page unpublished scenario of the film, written by Jacques Rivette and Marilù Parolini, which I consulted in the archives of the Cinémathèque Française in Paris. The scenario, which Rivette described as a 'calendar', is a selective daily breakdown of Claire and Sébastien's lives during the three-week interval covered in the film, written in a 'more literary form' (Aumont et al. 1977: 17). This rough script developed from an earlier, shorter version of only ten pages and was the result of preliminary conversations between Rivette, the co-writer and the main cast, which facilitated the use of improvisation in the film (ibid.). In Rivette's account, the atmosphere on the set was itself highly conversational:

> the original idea of the film led immediately to conversations, with Jean-Pierre, with Bulle, with Marilù, with everyone we met for one reason or another in any connection with the project [. . .] In the evenings, we stayed together – we didn't leave each other's sides for five weeks – talking, not necessarily about the film but about everything else around it, and everything fell into place; then the next day, filming, we would continue the previous night's conversation [. . .] My memory is of one long, uninterrupted conversation. What *L'Amour fou* was, was a subject of conversation between us; and not necessarily with words; with silences as well, listening to records or going to see a film . . . (ibid.: 12)

The shooting of the film is presented as part of an extended conversation, which in its turn is described as the sharing of time and experience, as the forging of interpersonal bonds. None of the talking that happens in the film in the margins of the theatre production was scripted as such. However, this preparatory stage does give a clear indication of how the directorial treatment of the play would change over time and of the general drift and substance of the conversations between Claire and Sébastien.

In the script, Sébastien embarks on the production of *Andromaque*, a pet project of his and Claire's, with the idea of conveying to the contemporary audience the 'modernity' and the underlying 'violence' of Racine's play (Rivette and Parolini n.d.: 3; all translations from this MS are mine), but after his relationship with Claire degenerates, Sébastien 'imposes on the actors a style of acting which is ever more removed from reality, ever more abstract, in line with the deadly language to which everything is ultimately subordinated, a constant icy paroxysm, which risks making all things equally unbearable'. The original reads: 'Désormais, il leur impose un jeu toujours plus irréel, plus abstrait, à l'image de ce language meurtrier auquel tout doit enfin se soumettre: un constant paroxysme glacial, au risque de tout égaliser dans l'insupportable' (ibid.: 33). The script forewarns about the clash between the director's theoretical ideas and 'the reality of the actors' bodies and voices' (ibid.: 3), but its more fine-grained description is reserved for the relationship between Claire and Sébastien and their desultory verbal exchanges, many of which were developed in the film in a manner similar to the one outlined in the script. Mostly on the offensive, Claire regularly questions Sébastien about his work and his views about the other women in the theatre company, in 'a relentlessly monotonous, even tone' (ibid.: 9), and during an awkward visit from Marta she exposes her theory about Sébastien's infidelity with 'a terrifying false ease', in a lengthy, 'calmly delirious' one-track 'improvisation' (ibid.: 11). As she isolates herself further and further, her interventions become ever more 'enigmatic', ever more 'cryptic', at times 'ironic' or 'vaguely threatening' (ibid.: 25). In response to Claire's volatility of mood and tone, Sébastien's verbal behaviour is mostly cautious or defensive. On his return home from rehearsals, after Claire's attempted suicide, he gives her a minutely detailed account of his day, and 'when he runs out of real details, he goes on, unwillingly inventing' others, seized by an imperative to talk (ibid.: 16). At other times, his tendency is to respond to her with 'flatly delivered, prefabricated phrases', a form of civility of which he is aware and to which he is averse even as he engages in it (ibid.: 28). The script explains Claire's dilemma in terms of a conflict between love and contempt and her view of Sébastien as a 'failed Don Juan, a pitiful seducer of actresses' (ibid.: 20). Throughout the script, Rivette and Parolini show an acute sensitivity to nuances of speech and behaviour, practising a hermeneutics of attitudes that is in evidence in the film as well.

In its turn, the play rehearsed in the film could be and indeed has been read as a study of mood fluctuations, often of a violent kind. First performed in 1667, *Andromaque* is built upon a tragic bind of unrequited love that ends with murder and madness: Orestes loves Hermione, who loves Pyrrhus, who loves Andromaque. The passions and desires of the Racinian characters are so devastating that they are often at the mercy of what they are feeling at any one time, although, as Jon Elster has argued, they often mistake their feelings for their opposite and engage in acts of self-deception (1999: 111–17). Alain Seznec has in fact referred to Hermione, the character initially played by Claire, as one of the 'two most impatient and moody figures in the play' (1972: 63). This violence and moodiness are, however, well regimented within the alexandrine verses of the tragedy and it is to the rhythm of the verses that Sébastien and his troupe devote most of their attention.

Staged at a time of emotional trial for Sébastien and Claire, Racine's *Andromaque*, with its portrayal of tremendous mental disquiet, conveyed in strict wording, was bound to enhance the crisis in the characters' relationship, but also offer a counterpoint to it. Critics have noted the contrast between the highly ordered language of the Racinian play and the increasing inarticulacy of the characters in their interactions outside theatre, between 'the pure physicality of Sébastien and Claire's marriage and the pure linguistics of reading' (Shaffer 1973: 55). The difficulties experienced by Sébastien in explaining and carrying out his approach to the play relate not only to his emotional troubles, but also to a particular cultural and historical moment. In other words, Sébastien has to grapple with the question of how to stage Racine for a late 1960s audience. For Hélène Deschamps, Kalfon's staging of *Andromaque* marks 'both a progress and a regression', in the sense that it appears to be informed by a modern awareness of 'the limits of speech', brought about by the theatre of the absurd, but at the same time falls back on the Racinian text (2001: 17). According to Deschamps, the discourse around theatre ('la parole autour du théâtre') functions as 'aborted speech' in direct opposition to Racine's text (ibid.: 40). Hélène Frappat reaches a similar conclusion with regard to Rivette's film *Out 1*, noting that Balzac's text serves as a repository of linguistic 'mastery' ('maîtrise') and a 'compass' guiding Jean-Pierre Léaud in his improvisations (2001: 36). According to Frappat, in *L'Amour fou*, the relationship between the play and the film similarly translates into a 'secret rapport' between performed words and words which are lost and searched (ibid.: 42; all translations mine).

At the time of its release, the film's dialogue triggered mixed critical reactions. The soundtrack as a whole attracted complaints of roughness and unintelligibility. One reviewer found it to be 'muddled' and 'exhaustingly difficult to follow, knit with irritating noises, whispering silences and missed sentences' ('son trop brouillon', 'bande sonore branquignol, épuisante à suivre, tricotée de bruits énervants, de silences qui chuchotent, de phrases perdues') (Rabine 1969), while another showed little patience for the actors' 'confidential mutter' ('murmure confidentiel') (Dupeyron 1969). Serge Daney tried to retrospectively explain this type of reaction, by observing that the public did not have 'educated ears' and were thus unaccustomed to treat sound 'as a character' (1982, my translation). In an edited collection on Rivette published by the Turin Museum of Cinema, François Thomas has argued that Rivette's use of direct sound could be understood as exposing the very impossibility of reaching any 'aural realism', since the more one makes an attempt at neutrality and objectivity in the use of a recording technology, the more technology is bound to pick up sounds which the 'more selective' human ear would not (Thomas n.d.: 165).

Amid the contemporary reviews, by far the most caustic (and indeed sexist) reaction to the extent and manner in which the actors both perform and discuss theatre in the film comes from *Le Figaro*'s Pierre Mazars, who summarises the theatre segments of the film as follows:

> Une troupe de comédiens médiocres répète *Andromaque*. Aucune des jeunes personnes en mini-jupe n'a la moindre notion de ce qu'est un vers classique, ne sait respirer ni marcher. Elles avalent la moitié de leur texte, comme s'il s'agissait de lire l'annuaire du téléphone. Quand vient l'occasion d'exprimer leurs pensées ou leurs idées, ce sont des 'Heu!', des 'Ben!', des 'Ecoutez!' et des phrases qui finissent en points de suspension. (1969)

> (A group of mediocre actors are rehearsing *Andromaque*. None of the young persons wearing a miniskirt has the faintest idea what a classical verse is. They don't know how to breathe nor walk and their pronunciation is slurred,

as if they were asked to read the telephone directory. When they have the opportunity to express their thoughts or ideas, they come up with 'Hem!', 'Well!', 'Listen!' and with unfinished sentences.)

The reviewer is equally dismissive of Sébastien's attempts at critical elucidation: 'Ten lines of one of Jouvet's lessons at the *Conservatoire* in a volume recently published by Gallimard on tragedy teach us more about Racine than the stammering of the theatre director' (ibid., my translation). The opposite side of the argument is represented by the critic from *Le Nouvel Observateur*, who finds that Jean-Pierre Kalfon delivers 'a fascinating analysis of the tragedy and of Racine's language' and a different sense of the play from the one presented by the Hachette editions of the classics (Bory 1968, my translation). It is significant to note that, although their evaluations are at variance, the two critics use the same type of comparative appraisal. They both watch the rehearsal sequences in the expectation they will be instructed about Racine and his play and they both operate with a literary yardstick, treating Sébastien's interpretive efforts on a par with pedantically put-together editions in which the paratext is carefully selected and displayed.

However, the nature of Sébastien's comments is fundamentally incommensurable with the polished Racine editions, mentioned by the reviewers. More often than not, Sébastien's remarks are unfinished either because they are cut in the editing room or because they progressively become inaudible, as the camera moves away from the site of the interview. Linguists might argue that the 'hesitation particles', invoked by the *Figaro* reviewer, fulfil a paradoxical function: they are indicative of incoherence but at the same time, by owning up to this incoherence, they offset it. In conversation analysis, they are often discussed as 'coherence-building devices' (Barnes 1995: 813). According to Betsy Barnes,

> *well* and *ben* are response markers which serve to enhance the coherence of a discourse by signalling the speaker's realization that there exists a certain lack of coherence between the preceding context and the utterance he or she is about to produce [. . .] More generally, *well* or *ben* can introduce any turn which manifests a lack of appreciation (in the sense of Goffman) of the preceding discourse, whether it be by the expression of a difference of opinion, a denial, or an otherwise inadequate response. (ibid.: 816–17)

Sébastien's involvement in the documentary is kept ambivalent in the film precisely in order to convey the fundamental indeterminacy of the rehearsals. He accepts the presence of the TV crew on the premises but at the same time he undermines the enterprise through evasiveness, diffidence, unwillingness to elaborate on difficult points. By his own account, Labarthe believes in the power of explanations to make things 'interesting' and in the capacity of a documentary to track a 'transformation', the transformation of rehearsals into a theatrical event. Sébastien, on the other hand, claims that when one tries to explain things which are not final, one inevitably goes astray. If he takes a decision, it is bound to be provisional and the scenes are only temporarily fixed. The result of this meeting of dissimilar attitudes can only be inconclusive, concessional: what we are seeing in the Sébastien–Labarthe interaction is a dialogue in which the very 'machinery' of questions is repeatedly placed under scrutiny and denied satisfaction.

Of higher frequency in Sébastien's speech than the 'ben' and 'écoutez!' mentioned by the *Figaro* reviewer is the idiom 'comme ça', mostly used as a conversation filler and, as such, needing no translation, but occasionally used to mean 'this way', 'like this', alluding to a specific way of doing things. Sébastien's habit of dropping 'comme ça's as a means of separating ideas within a verbal stream contaminates the rest of the interviews. Françoise/Cléone (Françoise Godde) tells Labarthe that Sébastien has problems with some of the actors' work, adding 'but it's always like this' ('enfin c'est toujours comme ça que ça se passe'). When asked about the progress of the rehearsals, she replies 'Not bad, see for yourself'. In a subsequent interview, Marta is asked whether she prefers playing a part like Hermione 'comme ça ou différemment' ('like this or in a different way'), to which she replies that she much prefers it 'this way'. Elsewhere, she refers to the rehearsals as 'exciting' and 'honest/truthful' ('c'est passionnant, je crois que c'est vrai'). The particularity of the method is, however, never entirely established discursively. The closest we come to an explanation of the aims of the theatrical production is when, in one of the longer interview answers he gives in the film, Sébastien likens theatre to 'a game with masks', involving characters, 'each trapped in his/her own subjectivity', who are convened in a 'waiting room' of sorts in order to 'talk and confess and empty their minds'. The desired effect, he goes on to add, is that of walls 'burst open' to reveal 'feelings' ('états d'âme'). The abstract nature of his comments and the general scarcity of explanations place the onus on the film camera to capture the specificity of the production ('see for yourself'), as if the recording technology would somehow ensure a degree of self-evidence to everything that happened under its gaze. In his analysis of nested art, briefly discussed in the introduction to Part I, Paisley Livingston remarked that 'often it is the "how" or manner rather than the propositional content that it is more important to convey' in works about art (2003: 236). However, it is precisely this manner which proves more difficult to represent:

> In the production of works of fiction about art and artists, nesting is sometimes the more risky task, as not everyone has the talent required for some feats of indexical 'elevation' [. . .] For example, it is easy enough for an author

to describe a character as a genius who has written a brilliant poem, painted a masterpiece, or composed great music, whereas ostension of this figure's brilliantly original artistic structure is another matter [. . .] (ibid.: 237)

The issue raised by Livingston is legitimate and worth keeping in mind as it shifts attention from the propositional content of the discussions about theatre to what is actually shown of the rehearsals. I want to suggest that in *L'Amour fou* what is at stake is a challenge specific to rehearsal practices in general, a challenge of which Rivette is clearly aware and which is foregrounded in the film. In her analysis of various traditions of rehearsal, Kate Rossmanith has aptly described this challenge as follows: the knowledge theatre practitioners bring with them to rehearsals 'is expressed not as a series of formal, declarative knowings about the world, but as embodied knowledge' (2008: 142). She goes on to helpfully add that 'rehearsal practices are doings, not writings' (ibid.: 145). Therefore, far from being atypical, Sébastien's incoherence is to be understood as in line with the 'messiness of rehearsal work' (ibid.). His discourse is replete with admissions of uncertainty and of difficulty and he repeatedly resorts to what is called in conversation analysis self-repair or reformulation. His changing attitudes are not always easy to reconcile: he defers to Racine, considering that the director's task is to approximate his rhythm and impart it to the public, but later in the process he seems to be advocating the primacy of the experience of the actors ('What's important is first off that we, here on stage, feel what we mean'), to the point where he doubts that the show he is preparing 'can reach or please the public' at all. Within this altered framework, the fact that the actors are not speaking loudly enough (Labarthe's observation) ceases to be a problem.

If Sébastien's remarks are inconclusive and contradictory and marked by the frustration of having to verbally (and thus inadequately) express an embodied knowledge, the next logical step is to think how, if at all, the film represents this embodied doing that emerges during the rehearsals. As I announced in the introduction to this chapter, the spatial turn in rehearsal studies has yielded valuable insights into theatrical work which can assist us in the next section of the argument. Taking their cues from Henri Lefebvre's notion of the 'bending' of the self in training, Andrew Filmer and Kate Rossmanith have discussed the 'strong individual routines' they observed at a musical rehearsal as combining to form 'highly regularized backstage choreographies or place-ballets' executed within a strictly 'segmented temporality' (2011: 234). Filmer and Rossmanith have drawn attention to the way in which the performers' bodies in certain types of rehearsal develop what they call an 'intersubjective rhythm or groove' that is meant to ensure the successful reproduction of the performance (ibid.: 236).

The development of a similar spatial and temporal automatism or 'place-ballet', to use Filmer and Rossmanith's expression, is represented in *L'Amour fou* on more than one occasion. In her study dedicated to the film, Hélène Deschamps has compared the white rectangular rehearsal stage in the film, surrounded on all sides by spectator seating, to a 'boxing' or 'circus' ring (2001: 22), but the stage could also be said to resemble a gymnastics floor, with many of the actors' movements arranged along its diagonal axis. Several times at the end of a rehearsed scene, the actors are shown resuming their positions in the corners of the square from which they are to 'launch' themselves towards one another or towards the centre of the space. Sébastien himself in one of his exchanges with Labarthe emphasises the importance of blocking and of figuring the temporal frame of the scenes, which suggests that he strives to create a physically and temporally disciplined performance in which the actors would construct and inhabit their role starting from a particular spatial position occupied in a particular segment of time as well as from their spatially predetermined interaction with the other actors.

Towards the end of the film, during the dress rehearsal, we see the actors standing in pairs at the corners of the stage, facing outwards. A set of suspended gongs is placed on the stage. The moment one of the gongs is struck, Dennis (Dennis Berry) as Pylade and Yves (Yves Beneyton) as Orestes break apart and move inwards, occupying their respective positions, Yves sitting down and Dennis making his way towards him as he recites his lines. The rest of the fragmentary performances we witness afterwards are punctuated by the sounds of a woodblock or a similar percussion instrument, which seem to coincide with the end of beats and units within the actors' speech. Gestures are often discussed in theatre semiology as 'mobile signs', elements of a flow, 'a continuum which cannot be broken down' (Pavis and Biller-Lapin 1981: 71). Although not strictly divisible, the actors' gestures in the rehearsal are nonetheless attentively scored and Sébastien is shown several times micro-managing them, acting as a conductor of sorts for the gestures, movements and corporal postures of his actors.

The interplay between the two cameras, the 16 mm of Labarthe's cinematographer Étienne Becker and the 35mm of Rivette's own director of photography, Alain Levent, supports and enhances this place-ballet, this inter-subjective groove. Jacques Rivette has explained the proxemic and attitudinal differences in the use of the two cameras:

> the 35 mm is giving a completely 'cow's eye view' of things. In a strict sense, it's the person who came in on tiptoe, the intruder who doesn't come too close because he'll get yelled at if he comes any closer, who watches from the corners, who looks down from the balcony, always hiding a bit. It has its oppressed voyeur side to it, like someone who can never come up as close

as he would like to, who doesn't even hear everything. The Mitchell and the Coutant are two opposite forms of indiscretion, a passive one and an active one, one sly and one bossy; but it's the same idea, that reality is pre-existing, when it is not being filmed, as well as when it is. (Aumont et al. 1977: 18)

Building on Rivette's own statements, Douglas Morrey and Alison Smith have argued that the 35 mm is in a position comparable to that of a distant mobile spectator 'debarred from involvement', whereas the 16 mm TV camera 'circulates among and between the actors as they rehearse' and isolates 'the developing *Andromaque* from its context' (2009: 153). According to Morrey and Smith, by combining the footage taken with the two cameras, Rivette gives shape to a paradox, in attempting at once to 'break down the division between performance and audience which exists in both theatre and cinema' and to preserve a sense of the audience's 'autonomy' (ibid.: 154). In what follows, I want to extend the discussion of the function of the two cameras by examining their contribution to the sense of embodied knowledge which I have so far argued is at stake in the film's representation of theatre rehearsals.

Building on Harry Berger's work, Rob Conkie has described the practice of 'deceleration' and 'reacceleration' of lines during rehearsals as a dialectic between 'holding still' the text in order to scrutinise it for 'discrete significances' and imagining the lines 'flying by' in order to encourage 'increasing levels of discovery and confidence' (2012: 424). This aspect of the rehearsals' embodied knowledge is also represented in the film in one of the read-throughs happening in the proximity of the stage. The read-through in question is of the conversation between Hermione and her confidante Cléone occurring in Act III, Scene 3 of *Andromaque*. After Pyrrhus deceives himself into accepting wedding Hermione on the advice of his mentor Phoenix, Hermione in her turn deceives herself into thinking that Pyrrhus, previously uninterested in her, has suddenly realised he loves her. Blinded by her feelings, she counters Cléone's mistrust with a eulogy of Pyrrhus. Although we see all the play's actors gathered around the reading table, the reading is mainly done by Marta and Françoise, under Sébastien's supervision. The 35 mm camera is positioned right behind the 16 mm camera, moving slowly from left to right and right to left, its movement punctured from time to time by shots taken with the more probing 16 mm camera which cuts in closer to the actors' faces. As Marta and Cléone read their parts, Sébastien motions for a speeding up of the rhythm, urging them to deliver the lines in a livelier manner. As Joseph Roach has eloquently put it, at the start of a rehearsal, the actor's body 'resists his will: his gestures die stillborn, words fail him, his rhythms splutter and lurch like a new machine whose parts do not quite fit' (cited in Rossmanith 2008: 148). What Sébastien is shown trying to do is fine tune this imperfect machine, break the resistance of the actor's body through an acceleration meant to build a self-regulating rhythm. He is also the one to impose a deceleration when one line in particular ('Do you know who Pyrrhus is?') misses its mark. The two cameras give us the perspective of the general set-up (the 35 mm), with different levels of concentration and distraction coming from the different actors around the table, and the perspective of the more focused poring over the text (the 16 mm), with the space between the two actresses and Sébastien appearing to suddenly contract as they turn their attention towards one another.

The two cameras are also involved in creating a sense of conversational comfort or discomfort. Although he is, in the film, a self-professed practitioner of non-interference, Sébastien is shown taking control over the interviews even when the question is not necessarily addressed to him. During one of the interviews, we initially see Dennis in a profile close-up, nodding in approval of Labarthe's suggestion that 'When you start a line, you have to see the whole context'. Dennis is more than content to concur with the statement, but his precipitated agreement is soon rectified by Sébastien, who is heard saying 'No, but we really try', to which he later adds that this has not been his approach of choice. Sébastien is so quick to intervene that Dennis's only available recourse is to turn to him for approval. The 16 mm camera lingers for a second on Dennis's embarrassed grin, then pans to the right to find Sébastien, slightly in the background but immediately brought into focus. Given the swift nature of his intervention and the ease with which he reclaims attention and takes the floor during this exchange, Sébastien sets himself up as a conversation supervisor of sorts. What makes him an interesting case is that often he asserts his authority in conversation and in rehearsals only to relinquish it soon afterwards. In this, his behaviour is similar to how Sam Rhodie has described Rivette's manner of working as 'both manipulating and not, exercising power and renouncing it' (2015: 197).

The frequent cuts which reduce the interviews to mere conversational scraps are replaced, in the case of the conversations between Michèle and Sébastien, by long takes with the 35 mm camera, which permit a relatively uninterrupted exchange. Michèle's view of Sébastien benefits from the vantage point of a long period of acquaintance and of professional collaboration. Each time, she approaches him in a prudent and discreet manner, yet with a frankness that is the privilege of their close association. Their dialogue is therefore characterised by the presence of what John Shotter would call 'moments of common reference' in which 'as two people [. . .] regard one another *and* their common situation, they know from each other's "attunements" [. . .] that they are each sensing it in the same way' (1993: 146). When the rehearsals suffer from Sébastien's emotional turmoil, Michèle knows that he knows it ('You see . . .

you know . . . you've seen it. Your rehearsals are really impossible now'), so the discussion has an unusually advanced starting point. Whether in a café or in one of the rooms at the theatre, they are seated next to one another, sharing the frame, in contradistinction to the 'tightly-insulated dialogue' (Morrey and Smith 2009: 154) of the Labarthe interviews.

If there is a truth or authenticity to the theatre rehearsals in *L'Amour fou*, as one of the actresses in the film would have it, then it is the truth of an embodied indecision, of tentative stage activities which may or may not facilitate an easing of the body into the role, and it is the multiple framing devised by Rivette that allows this sense of provisionality to never settle.

SYNECDOCHE, NEW YORK: FILM AND THEATRE AS MUTUALLY CONTAMINATING WORLDS

Thomas Pavel has remarked that media are 'not just referential paths leading to worlds: to read a text or to look at a painting means already to inhabit their worlds' (1986: 74). Recently, Daniel Yacavone has made a similar statement, noting that 'films not only contain but *are* worlds' (2015: 39, emphasis in the original). For Yacavone, the film world 'constitutes a historical, trans-subjective event of artistic and cinematic truth' (ibid.: xv), the analysis of which requires the consideration of both the 'world-in' and the 'world-of' the film, where the former stands for film's 'fictional-represented reality' (ibid.: 31) and the latter designates 'the larger, multidimensional, and aesthetically realized' world of the film as artwork (ibid.: 3). Inspired by these remarks, in this sub-chapter I argue that the representation of theatre rehearsals in Charlie Kaufman's 2009 film *Synecdoche, New York* foregrounds the role of media as generators of fictional worlds and comments on our relationship with fictional worlds, as well as on the (often mimetic) relationship between fictional worlds and the reality on which they are dependent.

The capacity to construct fictional worlds is not the prerogative of one medium only, but the media's capacity of engendering worlds does differ. What these exact differences may consist of is, however, up for debate. Writing about the power of media to muster the 'image of "another life"', Bert O. States has suggestively distinguished between film and literature, on the one hand, and theatre on the other:

> I suppose most people think of their lives – if they have reveries in this vein at all – as being like films and novels rather than plays. These are the media, at once intimate and spacious, with almost unlimited power to imitate our experience of being present in the world: the daily texture of life, the 'around-ness' of space, the continuity (or the return or the lapse) of time, above all the shape we think of our life as accumulating (its crises, its ups and downs,

its chapters, the slow composition of its destiny), all given the dignity of significance by an imaginary orchestra or a sympathetic narrator (oneself, of course) who understands everything about us that the world has misunderstood. This is not the sort of 'other life' offered by the play. We are more apt to say that an evening or an experience was like a play (people 'create scenes' in restaurants, at parties, etc.) [. . .] Theater, especially since the advent of the novel, is by and large the form designed for the brief chronicle: the crisis, the turning point, the consequence of the act or the non-act. Theater is swift [. . .] (1987: 152–3)

The 'aroundness of space' afforded by the medium of film is also noted by Daniel Yacavone, via Gilles Deleuze: cinema 'does not just present images, it surrounds them with a world' (2015: xiii). Kaufman's theatre does not operate with the 'swiftness of condensation, of life raised to an intense power of temporal and spatial density' that States refers to (1987: 154), but instead stretches implausibly over a long period of time, as if to echo a line uttered in the film by the main character's wife: 'You act as if you have forever to figure it out.' The warehouses used in the film as theatre venues resemble massive sound stages, attempting a further blurring of the distinction between the two media. At the same time, Charlie Kaufman has suggested that his whole approach to making films has borrowed something from theatre:

> The thing you can do in theatre that you can't do in film is change it. And interact with the audience. That's what it has going for it, which is why I try to do that in film when I can, in sort of another way, having stuff be layered so that you can watch it again and feel like it's a different experience. (2008: 139)

Kaufman speaks of film aspiring towards the condition of a theatre performance, by soliciting multiple viewings on account of hidden delights. The very name of the film's main character (Caden Cotard) is layered, referencing both the Cotard syndrome, where a person believes s/he is already dead, and a character from Marcel Proust *Swann's Way*, but also functioning as an anagram of Acted Candor (Child 2010: 149). It has been noted that spectators of films written by Kaufman are expected to develop a 'moment-by-moment' vigilance (King 2009: 68) and the layering evidenced by *Synecdoche, New York* is one of the strategies deployed to encourage this type of engagement.

Partly because of its rather obscure title, the film struggled to find a US distributor after its 2008 Cannes premiere, and was eventually given a limited release through Sony's indie specialty division, Sony Pictures Classics (Hill 2011: 212). The films scripted by Charlie Kaufman are often discussed as examples of the phenomenon known as Indiewood, a type of cinema situated, both industrially and aesthetically, midway between and at the intersection of Hollywood product and indie fare. The film revolves around theatre director

Caden Cotard (Philip Seymour Hoffman), who at the beginning of the film works on a new staging of Arthur Miller's play *Death of a Salesman* for the Schenectady local theatre. Caden's family life is dysfunctional and his health a constant worry. His marriage to the miniature painter Adele (Catherine Keener) eventually comes apart when she announces her decision to move to Berlin with their daughter Olive (Sadie Goldstein) and her friend Maria (Jennifer Jason Leigh). After Adele's departure, Caden continues to attend therapy sessions with Dr Madeleine Gravis (Hope Davis), author of popular self-help books, and becomes more and more obsessed with his declining health. He attempts to romance Hazel (Samantha Morton), the box office girl at the theatre, but his efforts are compromised by lingering feelings for Adele. When he unexpectedly receives a MacArthur fellowship, he decides to use it for a theatre project meant to express his 'true self' and, to this purpose, he rents a massive warehouse in Manhattan's theatre district, working with an ever-expanding group of actors and constantly changing the script of the play, basing it ever more closely on his life. By the end of the film, the project will have spanned decades of work to no discernible finality. Caden marries Claire (Michelle Williams), the main actress in his theatre company, and they have a daughter, Ariel, but his new family life suffers from Caden's growing involvement in the theatre project and his concern for his first daughter Olive. He hires Hazel as a production assistant and a man named Sammy Barnathan (Tom Noonan), previously seen stalking Caden, to play him in the theatre production. Caden takes a part-time job as a cleaner in Adele's New York apartment, and when Claire finds out, she leaves him and backs out of the project. In Germany, a now adult Olive (Robin Weigert) is on her deathbed, after her full-body tattoo has become infected. Caden visits her and, just before she expires, he is made to apologise for his alleged homosexuality. Back on the theatre sets, Caden begins an affair with Tammy (Emily Watson), an actress hired to play Hazel, while Hazel herself dates Sammy, after her own marriage collapses. Caden realises that he is in love with Hazel and has been for years and kisses her on set, which prompts Sammy to commit suicide by jumping off a building. Caden spends the night at Hazel's perpetually burning house and wakes up to discover that Hazel has died of smoke inhalation. Millicent Weems (Dianne Wiest), initially cast as Adele's cleaning lady, swaps roles with Caden, becoming the de facto director of the play. The film ends with a very old Caden wandering around the abandoned sets of the warehouse after an unexplained disaster has left them in ruin. He chances upon an actress from his troupe and they converse for a while before Caden receives the final acting instruction from Millicent: 'Die!'

The fictional world of Caden's life and the fictional world of his play stand in a curious relation. Although they are both fictional in relation to the film spectator, within the economy of the film the former is supposed to function as an actual foil to the latter. However, the events in what we take to be Caden's actual world are sometimes far more extraordinary and implausible than their fictional counterparts. Moreover, *Synecdoche, New York* represents a particularly interesting example of a mix between things that have a clear anchorage in the 'real' world and things that are in breach of the rules governing the world as we know it. To use Marie-Laure Ryan's terms, the 'geography' and the 'inventory' (1991: 558–62) of the actual world of the film and those of the film spectator's reality system have several things in common. The fictional world of the film as a whole is inviting the viewer to activate references to real locations such as Schenectady, New York, Berlin, and to think of the universe of the film as comprehensible through a certain resemblance to and even partial identity with the actual world.

After a relatively prudent beginning, the fictional world soon goes haywire, amassing details that test the limits of a reality-sanctioned imagination, without entirely discontinuing the realist trend. Derek Hill has provided an explanation for this strategy: 'like the great storytellers of the weird and fantastic, Kaufman knows that the excursions into the surreal are only effective if as much imaginative fidelity is dedicated to realising the world of his characters [. . .] in concrete, resolutely naturalistic terms. It's got to be real ... before it gets unreal' (2008: 28). Another possible explanation for this quirky mix of different approaches comes from Geoff King, who argues that Indiewood films in general and Kaufman's films in particular often have it 'both ways', by both mobilising conventions and departing from them (2009: 53, 67). In keeping with this logic, *Synecdoche, New York* can be at once partly realistic and highly metafictional. Olive's flower tattoos, that wither and peel off like real flowers, Hazel's burning house, diaries and books that write themselves, the tight sandals that strap Madeleine's feet, biting into her flesh, the implausible story of the child prodigy Horace Azpiazu, these are just some of the elements that demand more than a routine acclimatisation to the film's reality. In many respects, the theatre world in the film is a much more controlled fictional environment than its frame world, Caden's actual world, an almost safer ground to tread, a distilled version of a chaotic subjectivity.

The three plays referenced in the film, Arthur Miller's *Death of a Salesman*, *Needleman in a Haystack*, the fictional play that Claire rehearses after she leaves Caden, and Caden's own untitled piece are all components of the same fictional world, although the former would constitute, in Terence Parsons's taxonomy of fictional objects (cited in Pavel 1986: 29), an 'immigrant object', of extra-fictional extraction, whereas the latter two would represent, in the same classification, objects that are 'native to the story'. *Needleman in a Haystack* appears to be a *mise en abyme* of Caden's own story. The imaginary play speaks of complexes, of lost potential, of a fun-less male character and a woman in his life who feels as if she has to move on. By the time *Needleman in a Haystack* is briefly introduced in the film, we have already witnessed Adele leaving Caden and Hazel complaining about him not being 'fun', as well as becoming familiarised with his enigmatic medical condition. Claire, up to this point portrayed in the film as the one who takes things too seriously, is suddenly cast as the 'fun loving girl', thus combining elements from both Adele and Hazel. Throughout the film, she oscillates between these two options: she starts by playing Hazel or someone like her in Caden's theatrical project and she ends up being a replacement for Adele and the mother of a substitute daughter in Caden's actual life, their family life a restaging of sorts of his family life with Adele and Olive.

The representation of theatre is initially handled in a realistic and humorous manner. The impression we get of Caden's staging of *Death of a Salesman*, especially in the light of the theatrical extravaganza to follow, is that of a modest theatrical success. There are lighting cues to supervise, accidents to prevent and actors to co-ordinate, but for the most part, the rehearsal process runs along comfortably scripted lines in a set that, for all its unpredictable failures, is tamed in time for the premiere. The device of having Linda and Willy Loman played by young actors operates as the main carrier of the play's themes and one that is sufficiently edgy to make the show popular with the critics. In the eve of the opening night, despite the fact that he still needs to explain the Brechtian dimension of the show to the actor playing Willy Loman, Caden handles him with kid gloves and tactfully concedes that the actor's attempt to 'crash differently, ambivalently' is indeed a noticeable and welcome addition to the scene. The set of *Death of a Salesman* has neither the spread nor the mimetic ambition of Caden's later project, but it manages nonetheless to evoke different locations through an arbitrary yet intelligible arrangement of decor (the transition into the outside of the Loman house is signalled by the frame of a door placed between the kitchen and the bedroom). In the scene of Willy's car crash, a wall placed on tracks sluggishly advances to create the collision, but, unable to perform properly during the rehearsals, becomes the very image of technological ineptitude, a caricature of theatre trying to emancipate itself from static decor.

In contrast with the plausible presentation, spatial restraint and held-back quality of this initial staging, the MacArthur funded project feels entirely unfettered and, after a certain point, impossible to square with criteria of real world believability. The more it strives for the imitation of life, the more implausible it becomes. Described by its fictional author as 'something big and true and tough', the project is of a radically mimetic nature: the theatrical sets, all developed inside what we discover towards the end of the movie to be three nested warehouses, closely replicate spaces in the outside world, and the actors on these ever-multiplying sets are constantly asked for lifelike renderings of even the smallest bits of business. As most critics have noted, the three nested warehouses generate a sense of infinite regress (David Smith 2011: 247; Evans 2014: 326), a sense of a representation representing itself ad infinitum. The nested warehouses could also be seen to correspond to a sense of layered self, of the type discussed by Andrew Filmer and Kate Rossmanith in their analysis of 'orientational metaphors' in theatre discourses (2011: 230). According to Filmer and Rossmanith, the manner in which theatre practitioners both manage the rehearsal spaces and speak about them evinces 'a figurative and literal mapping of rehearsal space and embodied self', in which both function as 'layered sites' to be 'accessed by penetrating a series of checkpoints', gradually surpassed in order to reveal a spatial core, 'a private, secret domain' (ibid.: 230–1). In other analogous formulations, the rehearsal is conceptualised as a 'series of concentric circles', where the 'outermost circle' represents the 'director's vision' and the innermost stands for the 'intimate space of the actor's imagination' (Susan Letzler Cole cited in Filmer and Rossmanith 2011: 231). The three nested warehouses could allude to a similar 'topography of self' (ibid.), especially since Caden refers to his theatre project as both a soaking in a communal bath and a plunge into his own depths. In one scene, we see Sammy playing Caden looking at a map of warehouse 1 for a way towards warehouse 2 and we subsequently follow Caden following Sammy on this trajectory of advancement towards a nested core, which further reinforces the sense of an assisted process of artistic self-examination that peels off layers of confusion to attain clarity and self-knowledge.

In support of the film's interest in the idea of mimesis or imitation and of the connection it establishes between theatre, truth and mimesis, one could invoke a whole tradition of philosophical thinking around these notions. Starting from the poststructuralist and deconstructionist critiques of mimesis, Jon Erickson has recently attempted to salvage the concept, by pointing out that these critiques often mistake 'the possible truthful or false *use* of mimesis (which in itself is neutral) for mimesis *as* something true or false in itself', proceeding to add that 'the representation of truth depends on the operation of mimesis, but the operation of mimesis need not be truthful' (2009: 22). Later in the argument, Erickson suggests that 'in its production of a possible (other) world', the theatrical manifests itself as 'a linguistic (or semiotic) idealism' (ibid.: 26). In this context, 'ideal' is taken to mean not the 'perfect corresponding representation of the world', as one might be tempted to think, but rather the very fact that theatre is 'removed from reality' and therefore 'cannot help but present an "ideal" image' (ibid.: 25). It is this type of idealism that Caden's project embodies despite his efforts to close the gap between representation and object of representation. In this respect, but coming at it via Erikson's discussion of mimesis in theatre, I concur with the general thrust of Richard Deming and David L. Smith's readings of the film. For Deming, what Caden unwittingly discovers is that 'To represent the world is to be flung outside of it' (2011: 206) and Smith reaches a similar verdict when he remarks that 'The representations by which we try to comprehend and lay claim to life [. . .] are the very things that alienate us from it' (2011: 243). This, for Smith, is partly what makes Kaufman 'a poet of disappointment' (ibid.: 239).

Caden strives to produce not only a comprehensive representation of real people in real situations, but also something more elusive, a truthful version of himself ('brutal truth' is the expression he uses). After seventeen years of continued rehearsing with no audience in view, the theatre director, confronted by his cast, spells out his artistic creed and working method as follows: 'I'm not excusing myself from this either. I will have someone play me, to delve into the murky, cowardly depths of my lonely, fucked up being. And he'll get notes too and those notes will correspond to the notes I truly receive every day from my god.' After this speech, we cut to a demiurgic image of Caden conferring order on his fictional world: he sits, his back turned to us, in silent rumination, writing at a desk covered with innumerable rows of notes, stretching as far as the eye can see. The notes are concise and poignant descriptions of acting instalments for each of the actors involved in the project. The myriad virtual situations that Caden conjures up in the notes might be taken to evoke what Esa Kirkkopelto has called 'the gift of nothing'. Elaborating on Philippe Lacoue-Labarthe's idea that 'theatre exemplifies general mimesis', Kirkkopelto has claimed that

> general mimesis, of which only humans are capable, does not imitate nature's productions but rather nature itself as a productive force, its way of withdrawing beneath all its manifestations. At the same time, *something else* appears, not a product of nature but a product of artistic, technical mimesis, a 'supplement'. What nature precisely cannot do is make a work of its own way of appearing. It cannot produce a product presenting its own production and appearing, it cannot *merely appear*. It would not need much to do so, but that something, the 'gift of nothing', is what human beings possess. (2014: 124–5)

By setting forth an action for each actor to imitate or find their way towards, Caden involves them in his own act of constructing a world, by enabling them to develop a relationship with that world, because as Esa Kirkkopelto argues, 'Theatre imitates what appears in action, its way of opening and intending a world' (2009: 233). On the other hand, Caden's act of self-inscription, of assuming a role in the work of fiction he is creating, turns the play into a world of extras swarming around him and a few lead actors, embodying his immediate entourage. 'No one, the film argues, can or will ever tell any story but his or her own' (Simerka and Weimer 2005: 93) – these words, written about *Adaptation*, a previous film scripted by Kaufman, equally apply to *Synecdoche, New York*. The comparison with *Adaptation* reveals further similarities: the writer in both films is a tragic figure who agonises in the process of writing and who, more or less reluctantly, accepts help from outside. The contrast between the fictional Susan Orlean and Charlie Kaufman in *Adaptation* – she writes 'efficiently and eloquently, while he struggles to produce words' (Hilderbrand 2004: 40) – is reprised in *Synecdoche, New York* with Adele and Caden. Adele is a successful miniature painter who is featured in a glossy magazine under the headline 'It's good to be Adele' and the quote 'When I look, I see. When I see, I paint. It's that simple'. For Caden, nothing is ever simple and nothing ever assumes definite shape: the titles in his play are changing all the time and so is the subject matter. Moreover, his numerous ailments contradict any sense of well-being. However, despite being blatantly insecure and neurotic, Caden is also undeterred in his efforts to construct a world and he manages, with only minimal displays of authority, to enlist and maintain the support of an enormous cast.

Caden and later on Sammy, one of the actors playing Caden, take rounds through the enormous sets, assessing the reality effect of the enterprise. The first of these professional rounds provides a glimpse into the interconnectedness of performances in Caden's gigantic theatre. The sequence of Caden overseeing rehearsals in the warehouse-cum-theatre laboratory is presented like a walk-in acting tutorial, the camera following Caden as he goes from one group of actors to the next, dispensing guidance and criticism. The clamorous inside of the warehouse is scattered with furniture units and populated by industrious actors. The script characterises this vast scene as made up of 'small squared-off "apartment" areas, with actors in each, going about their days' (Kaufman 2008: 67). The theatre roles have developed into something of a second life, experienced with a similar sense of days trailing along. We are only presented with a cross-section of this fictional universe, but the complexity of its organisation is already adumbrated. As soon as he finishes retouching one scene, Caden proceeds to the next one, the arrangement of the performances suggesting an assembly line of sorts. Sometimes the actors look at him and nod at the instructions; at other times they act as if he were not there, continuing to perform without any perceptible interruption. Occasionally Caden steps in character, playing himself, such as during the exchange with Claire who gets to air her frustration at a real-life situation transposed in fiction: 'Daddy doesn't live with us anymore, baby, he had to go find himself.' In the very first scene he is shown interacting with, a pair of actors are admonished by Caden for having forgotten that they are 'actors playing actors'. Within the play, they are supposed to film a TV drama, portraying a nurse and a doctor who are about to begin a love affair. To complicate their acting brief, Caden tells them that they are having an affair off set. As a result, the levels of fiction become temporarily tangled up both for the actors in the play and for us as spectators: off set for the TV drama means on set for the play and we are suddenly watching not only actors playing actors but actors playing actors playing actors in a TV drama within a play within a film.

The space occupied by the theatre sets steadily grows from this enormous rehearsing ground, partitioned into 'acting cells', to the all-encompassing warehouses. As the fictional universe expands, so do its solipsism and its obsession with mimetic accuracy. There is an increasing reliance in the play on Caden's own experience in the 'actual world'; indeed, the actual world in the film seems at times to serve no other purpose than the outsourcing of ideas and situations to the fictional world of the play.

We first see the theatrical venue (one of the warehouses, presumably the one that, by the end of the film, will incorporate the other two) at the end of a location-scouting episode. The sheer size of the place alerts us to its potential for eccentric use, but the information we are receiving plays down the idiosyncrasy of its appearance. The place, we are informed by a real estate agent in the film, is centrally located, in the heart of the theatre district and it is great for plays, having been used in the past to stage Shakespeare. Caden speaks of his theatre project as something that he wants to invite people to see, 'the sooner the better', but in practice, his play will be shut off from any external audience, allowing only a form of self-spectatorship. With this whole set of physical relations excluded, the theatre functions more as a sealed-off workshop, but its insularity is paradoxically coupled with an acute interest in reproducing the outside world. During one of his rounds on the theatre sets, Caden is seen handing a set of photographs of the façade of Adele's place to a worker who assures him that the new addition will be ready in a few days.

The thoroughgoing pursuit of truth and likeness ultimately undercuts the project, because, as Nelson Goodman remarks, the whole truth is 'a perverse and paralyzing policy for any worldmaker', as it is simply 'too much', 'too vast, variable, and clogged with trivia' (1978: 6). The warehouses are perpetual construction sites for the real, but this prodigious realist effort is revealed to be, like all fictional worlds, threatened by incompleteness. Writing about the indeterminacy of fictional worlds, Thomas Pavel has remarked that it is

> compensated for by the strength of our ontological commitments. We confidently regard our worlds as unified and coherent; we also treat them as

economical collections of beings, our fits of ontological prodigality notwithstanding. Since coherence and economy may not stand up to scrutiny, we most often start by refraining from close examination. The worlds we speak about, actual or fictional, neatly hide their deep fractures, and our language, our texts, appear for a while to be transparent media unproblematically leading to worlds. (1986: 73)

To quote Pavel again, 'in fiction, indeterminacy strikes at random' (ibid.: 107) and anything that is left unmentioned or unspecified (in the case of films, also not-shown, not indicated) can be considered a fissure in the system. When Caden notices that his love interest Hazel and Sammy are flirting on set, he questions her about it, only to find out that Derek, her husband in 'real' life, had left her. His reaction refers less to the situation in real life than to the consequences for the fictional world that duplicates it: 'I gotta let go of the actor playing Derek. What's his name?' Failure to follow up a lead once opened can be detrimental to the 'everything'-ness of the theatre project, but it is not the only shortcoming of such an inclusive agenda.

Theories of fictionality hold that 'fictional worlds are epistemologically accessible but physically inaccessible from the real world' (Ronen 1994: 93–4), and, by the same token, they exclude the possibility of 'cross-world killing, congratulating, handshaking and so forth' (Walton 1978: 17). However, as Herbert Blau has claimed, theatre has always trodden a fine line in this respect, by allowing a frail illusion that one might be able to tangibly access the fictional world from the place of spectating:

> Whatever else the considerable powers of film, it lacks the unnerving prospect that what doesn't touch *could*, and could *right there*, not just in the mind's eye. In the history of the theater, that has been a more or less alarming lived out possibility on both sides of the mirror, not only when the actors come off the stage to caress, belabour, or otherwise perform in the audience but when someone jumps onto the stage to punish Iago for the appalling and incomprehensible deception that is, when all is said and seen, the original sin of appearance – what the audience comes to see. (2010: 53–4)

Caden's fictional venture departs from the idea of conventional theatre spaces by proposing a very 'habitable' form and the game of mimetic reconstruction that the theatre director indulges in causes him to occasionally believe that he can access the inaccessible, touch the untouchable and thus become the victim of what Thomas Pavel would call 'ontological stress'. Pavel explains:

> Caused by difficulties of orientation among the complexities of modern ontological arrangements, this type of stress leads to the weakening of our adjustment to ontological landscapes. Its first victim was Don Quixote, unable to

distinguish actuality from fiction. Since ontological distinctions have become much more subtle and complex, users of contemporary ontological arrangements must travel between heterogeneous if not plainly hostile landscapes to which they are expected to adjust rapidly and only for short periods of time, not unlike modern city dwellers who cross long distances between work and home. (1986: 142)

This sense of ontological stress is in evidence when Caden takes over the scene in which Millicent as Ellen is preparing to enter a replica of Adele's flat and plays it as if it were the real flat, believing it to be so, his confusion accentuated by the memory of himself impersonating Ellen in order to gain access to the flat. To put it differently, what Caden believes for a brief moment is that, because of its deliberate, inbuilt likeness to the actual world of the movie, the fictional world of the play would also enjoy a special access to his real life and that it could, by virtue of this privilege, entrap the presence of loved and lost ones. A similar thing happens after Hazel's death: Caden changes the script into an act of private commemoration, trying to give shape to the afterlife of his lover and to revert to happier days ('I know how to do the play now. It will take place over the course of one day. And that day will be the day before you died. 'Twas the happiest day of my life.'). Towards the end, more firmly installed in the fictional world of his play than in his actual solitary life, Caden seems to be wandering in between worlds, drawn towards one or the other by the illusion of a voice (he thinks he hears Adele's voice in the onset reproduction of her apartment) or by the comforting sound of another (Millicent's acting instructions).

In *Synecdoche, New York*, the relation between the actual world of the characters and the fictional world of the play is not limited to a faithful reproduction of one within the other. Experiences in the actual world are altered (reinterpreted, and in some cases radicalised) by their restaging in the fictional world of the play. Let us consider, as an example, the scene of Caden coming home to Claire after cleaning Adele's flat. In the actual world, Claire is suspicious but chooses not to open an inquiry, whereas in the theatrical rewriting she is persistently and even aggressively inquisitive. Caden, played in the fictional version by Sammy, is equally transformed, from a meek and timorous character to a daring husband who gives earnest but hurtful answers. As Sammy discloses in the fictional world a truth pertaining to the actual world, Claire starts to address both the fictional Caden (Sammy) and the actual Caden present in the scene as director and eventually she completely steps out of the role in order to announce her decision to leave the project.

According to Lubomir Dolezel, 'Fictional worlds are accessible from the actual world only through semiotic channels' (1988: 484), the actor representing one such category of 'semiotic mediators' (ibid.: 485). I have already

Figure 3.1 Theatre imitating life – *Synecdoche, New York* (Charlie Kaufman, 2008, USA)

identified and discussed an instance where 'commuting' between two worlds led the actor/director to succumb to an ontological disorientation. In the scene under analysis, neither Sammy nor Claire suffer from delusions about the world they are supposed to inhabit at any one time, but they choose to manipulate their ability to switch between worlds in order to renegotiate their acting lot. Sammy wants to determine Caden to put more of himself in the play and Claire is using Sammy's interference as an opportunity to say her piece to Caden and extricate herself from a project that she no longer believes in. Placed between the episode of Caden's return home from Adele's flat and the stage version of this same moment, there is yet another rehearsal in which Claire acts as an undisciplined intercessor between worlds. During the rehearsal, Caden discreetly passes a note instructing Claire to think her character might be gay. Claire reads the note, disregards the instructions and defiantly rumples and throws away the piece of paper. The rehearsals seem to propose an infinitely permissive formula that assimilates all occurring disruptions. When Claire leaves the play, a replacement is quickly found through the secretarial solicitude of Hazel.

The real-life episode of Claire rehearsing for her new acting job (*Needleman in a Haystack*) is also restaged in Caden's fictional world, but the result is branded by Caden 'a lie'. The lie is a perspectival one. In the film's actual world, after moving out of the apartment, Caden is shown standing outside the building looking at Claire's windows as she paces the room rehearsing. In the initial theatrical representation, the structure copying the multi-storeyed apartment building where Claire lives is opened, onlooker-friendly. The preceding scenes, taking place in the replica of the apartment, have the same no-walls policy. Wanting to have his vision replicated on stage, Caden realises that, by keeping intact the open wall convention, he jeopardises the accuracy of perspective and, as a consequence, he has the section walled up. This directorial decision effectively seals him and the spectator out of the project.

Because the play never materialises into a show presented to an audience, the fictional world created by Caden's theatre is only accessed intermittently, during rehearsals. It is the medium of film that ultimately coagulates the fitful epiphanies of this fictional world. Caden's theatre is space-wise a facsimile of the real, a real that is in its turn a filmic construction. Theatre reproduces Caden's reality piecemeal and the replicas are noticeably enclosed by undeveloped, sketchy areas. It aims to incorporate the idea of a correct view, of a perspective that can be controlled and oriented. It is improvisational in perpetuity, changing titles, lines, sets and roles. It is also progressively unconcerned with the spectator. Intermediality plays itself out as a sustained shuttle between the sets and situations of the theatre pieces in the film and the sets and situations in the 'reality' in the likeness of which they are made. It relies for its realisation and impact on the complexities and ambiguities of set design. Although they strive for meticulous resemblance, the theatre sets are also established as artificial oases in a landscape of scaffolds. For all their inspiration from living counterparts, the theatre performances are signalled as such: they are interrupted, revised, rectified and generally in the making. There are moments in which the spectator can feel lost between worlds, but for the most part the film guides us to make the transition. Kept separate in the film, but not imperviously so, the fictional domain of the film and the world of the play-within-the-film are ingeniously connected, most strikingly at the level of the performances and of the spaces they employ, sometimes even share.

Part II

*Divided Attention:
Intermedial Performers and
their Split Audience*

The first part of this book has examined several ways in which films can encompass theatre performances or rehearsals, namely through *mise en abyme*, bracketing, alternation, repetition, as well as through more complex forms of embedding such as multiple framings and infinite regress structures. In the previous chapters, I connected these forms of embedding with questions of visuality and aurality and with the concepts of illusion, memory and artistic truth, as they relate to the two media under scrutiny. The second part of the book will look at various ways of articulating the relation between actor *qua* actor and audience, in films which represent or evoke theatre. Various modes of spectatorial address will be proposed in answer to the question: How are theatre performances seen, heard or discussed in film? Although my theoretical approach will remain eclectic, phenomenology will continue to play an important part. In what follows, I shall explain why this is the case and I shall briefly discuss several authors who have proven influential in the development of this section.

Used in conjunction with other types of film, drama and narrative theory, phenomenology as a theoretical lens continues to be pertinent for this book, partly because of the way in which theatre itself is often conceptualised. Writing about *auteurism* in contemporary theatre, Avra Sidiropoulou has noted 'theatre's inherent duality as a semiological/mimetic field and a phenomenological performing space' (2011: 8), but ideas such as this have not always commanded the attention they receive today. Rather, they are the result of a long and steady effort to shift emphasis from drama as literature to drama as a 'performance score', to use Phillip Zarrilli's expression (2004: 655). Erika Fischer-Lichte traces this effort back to the eighteenth century, when writers such as Diderot and Lessing started pointing out that the enactment of written drama required gestures, which constituted a different sign system than the linguistic one used in dramatic texts (2003: 145). However, as Fischer-Lichte rightly notes, in Diderot and Lessing's writings the actor's body is fundamentally a 'semiotic body', a sign- and meaning-producing body 'purged' of any traces of the actor's 'organic body' (ibid.: 148). For Fischer-Lichte, one has to wait until Georg Simmel's study 'On the philosophy of the actor' for an acknowledgement of the fact that the 'complete sensuous theatrical form' that a character takes on stage cannot be 'sketched in advance' by the playwright and that the differences in the performance of the same character are in no small measure due to the actors' 'different corporeality' (ibid.: 149–50). Once launched, this interest in embodiment granted 'the body a similar paradigmatic position as the text, instead of subsuming it under the paradigm of text', treating it as 'the condition underlying the possibility of each and every cultural activity' (ibid.: 151–2).

Erika Fischer-Lichte's distinction between the 'semiotic body' and the 'phenomenal body', the latter, according to her, never truly disappearing into the former (ibid.: 153), is encountered in different formulations in other authors as well, in Stanton B. Garner Jr. as the difference between the 'signifying body' and the 'body as it is lived' (1994: 45) and in Phillip Zarrilli as the notion of the actor's multiple bodies. Building on Drew Leder's work, Zarrilli distinguishes between no fewer than four 'modes of embodiment' (the 'surface body', the 'recessive body', the 'aesthetic inner bodymind' and the 'aesthetic outer body'), which are also modes of 'corporeal absence', in the sense that one tends to 'forget' them, to be only intermittently aware of them (2004: 655–7). In Zarrilli's typology, the surface body is an 'ecstatic' body which 'opens out' to the world, experiencing it through the senses (ibid.: 656–8). The recessive body is the 'visceral body', the body of blood and organs, which, like the surface body, only makes itself felt when one experiences 'pain or dysfunction' (ibid.: 659–60). The last two modes of embodiment pertain to what Zarrilli calls the 'non-ordinary, extra-daily lived body' (ibid.: 661). The aesthetic inner bodymind is the by-product of intense 'psychophysical practices or training regimes' which involve a laborious 'process of cultivation and attunement' of both mind and body. Zarrilli's examples vary from yoga and martial arts to theatre practices with a pronounced physical character, such as Meyerhold's biomechanics and Grotowski's experiments (ibid.: 661–3). By comparison, the aesthetic outer body, such as the body that emerges during a theatre performance, is a 'fictive body', inhabited by the actor but designed for and presented to the gaze of a spectator (ibid.: 664). Ultimately, Zarrilli concludes, the actor's body is a 'chiasmatic body' which modulates, interweaves and shifts between these four modes of embodiment (ibid.: 665). As some of the case studies in the chapters to follow will allow us to observe, Zarrilli's framework provides a useful reference point for those instances in which diegetic theatrical acting invites us to observe a layered corporeality, or for moments in which one mode of embodiment is shown to interfere with another. In representing theatre, film has often made of the histrionic body an object of fervent curiosity, an issue all the more interesting if we recall that one of the most frequently mentioned differences between theatre and film is precisely the physical presence or absence of the actor's body from the space of the spectator.

The phenomenological focus on embodiment does not only apply to the actor; it extends to the spectator as well, to the effect that theatre itself becomes conceptualised as an 'an intercorporeal space' (Parker-Starbuck 2014: 126). Stanton B. Garner Jr.'s work in particular is important in this regard, as he emphasises the 'bodied spatiality' of theatre, in a move to return 'both actor and spectator to the complexity of their environmental encounters' (1994: 13). Garner explains what he means by theatre's 'bodied spatiality' as follows:

> Theatrical space is 'bodied' in the sense of being comprised of bodies positioned within a perceptual field, but it is also 'bodied' in the more fundamental sense of 'bodied forth', oriented in terms of a body that exists not just as the object of perception, but as its originating site, its zero-point. To stage this body in space before the witness of other bodies is to engage the complex positionality of theatrical watching. (ibid.: 4)

For Garner, the theatrical environment is an inter-subjective arena which enables different perceptual experiences and levels to meet and intersect, to converge and diverge, and this understanding of the theatrical encounter assigns to the dramatic text the important function of laying out a 'specific discipline of body, stage and eye' (ibid.: 6–7). What the phenomenological perspective brings, according to Garner, is a shift from regarding the stage merely as a 'specular field' to treating it as a 'habitational field' (ibid.: 45). In order to illustrate this point, Garner begins with the example of an empty stage in front of an empty auditorium that he gradually populates. Adding first one spectator then several spectators to this virtual stage is tantamount to introducing 'variables of intersubjectivity and multiperspectivity' (ibid.: 46), but the most eventful addition is that of the actor on stage. Garner explains:

> With this appearance, the phenomenological parameters of both stage and spectatorship undergo complicated reorientation. On stage, what was oriented in relation to the gaze is now also oriented in relation to the body that inhabits its boundaries. Visual field now discloses, and must accommodate, a habitational field that constitutes a rival perceptual center. Within this internally divergent (or 'twinned' field), a drinking glass becomes both spectatorial object and object of handling for the performer who must encounter it as instrument or obstacle [. . .] (ibid.)

When representing theatre, film often pays attention to the actor's 'rival phenomenality' (ibid.: 47), to his/her experience of inhabiting the space of the stage, perhaps best illustrated in the chapters to follow by John Cassavetes's *Opening Night*.

It is also worth pointing out that scholars tend to distinguish between the way in which the 'theatrical apparatus as a "vision machine" operates in dramatic theatre as opposed to the so-called "postdramatic theatre"' (Bleeker 2008: 9–10). In an effective explanation of Hans-Thies Lehmann's ideas, Maaike Bleeker notes that in dramatic theatre, 'the dramatic structure functions as a framework that presents the audience with a perspective on what is there to be seen as a result of which the audience knows how to look and how to understand what it sees' (ibid.: 10), whereas in post-dramatic theatre, this orderly and purposeful dramatic structure is 'either deconstructed or rejected altogether', to the effect that 'elements of theatre performance lose their connection' with any discernible whole (ibid.: 11). These differences notwithstanding, the assumption underlying this distinction seems to be that theatre embodies intentionality, a hallmark of the phenomenological approach.

The way in which dramatic structures attempt to organise perception is complicated in films which represent theatre by what Vivian Sobchack has called the 'camera's projected and thus visible choice-making movements of attention' (2011: 437). To put it differently, in the films examined in this section, the 'game of orientation and positionality' (Garner 1994: 48) that theatre plays with its audience is significantly altered, exalted or frustrated, by the games of positionality played by the medium of film. Thus, the problem develops from being strictly and safely circumscribed within one medium to being considered in relation to two media and their interplay. The fourth chapter will look closely at various ways in which these games of orientation and positionality are played out in films in which the theatre audience has a diegetic presence. The fifth and final chapter will look at complications arising from the monologue's performative and spectatorial address.

CHAPTER FOUR

Spectatorship by Proxy meets Multimodal Performance

In an article on Marcel Carné's 1945 film *Les Enfants du Paradis/Children of Paradise*, Mirella Affron analyses the film's handling of the relationship between actor and audience in the following terms:

> Shot in close-up, from behind and silhouetted in the foreground of the lower third of the frame (replicating heads and necks in the preceding row which block one's vision of the stage), the surrogate audience forces the spectator in the movie house to adopt its point of view. What is achieved is the presence by proxy of the cinematic audience at the theatrical event. (1978: 47)

Affron equates the representation of perceptual impediments of the kind one might encounter in an actual theatrical space to a delegated experience of spectatorship. Starting from Affron's pithy aperçu, this chapter will focus on different modes of 'presence by proxy of the cinematic audience at the theatrical event', seeking to unpack the dynamic between the layered performance (film actors playing theatre actors playing fictional characters) and its dual spectatorial address (the film spectator and the vicarious theatre audience). The chapter will also account for the moments when the perspective afforded to the film spectator deviates from that of its surrogate, seeking to contextualise and explain the effects of this incongruity.

The interest in showing this type of spectatorial presence by proxy could be indicative of a desire to allude to cinema's original form of experience in the age of its 'relocation' to new spatial surroundings (Casetti 2009: 62). Francesco Casetti has referred to the 'attendance' form of filmic experience as 'the experience of a place, the experience of a situation and the experience of a world' (ibid.: 60). For Casetti, the movie theatre, as the initial defining 'habitat' of the filmic experience, occupies the 'middle ground' between a 'retreat' and an open place, enabling at once a form of imaginary *flânerie* and a sense of belonging, giving rise to a situation 'that is both real and unreal' and that has the unmistakable character of a 'collective rite' (ibid.). This foundational form of filmic experience, associated with both a 'residency' and a 'collectivity' (ibid.: 61), has enough in common with theatre attendance to be revisited indirectly whenever the viewing situation of the theatre spectator is represented in film. However, while both film and theatre spectatorship depend on a separation of spaces, when it comes to the depiction of a 'somewhere else' (McAuley 2010: 91), the stage is often considered more resiliently fictional than the screen, the latter more readily delivering the spectator 'into the arms of the other' (Rushton 2002: 117).

It is worth stating from the beginning that in their representation of theatre all three films analysed in this chapter (John Cassavetes's *Opening Night*, Eric Rohmer's *A Tale of Winter* and Manoel de Oliveira's *I'm Going Home*) operate with a highly conventional theatrical arrangement, described by Marco de Marinis as 'the "Italian" stage, the *boîte aux illusions* with its neat separation between a raised stage and the stalls, [. . .] laid out facing one another straight-on' (1987: 105). At stake in this arrangement are the frontality of the placement, a certain distance between the spectator and the performance, as well as the conditioning of the experience on the 'point of observation' (ibid.). Throughout the history of the medium, this type of spatial relationship between the playing area and the audience has been fruitfully challenged by both theatre theory and theatre design. Alternatives to the 'Italian stage' or the 'picture-frame stage', as it is also known, include the theatre-in-the-round and the environmental theatre (Pavis 1998: 351–2). At the end of the nineteenth century and the beginning of the twentieth, the Swiss stage designer Adolphe Appia, famous for his atmospheric lighting designs, dared his theatre contemporaries to imagine a 'cathedral of the future', an eminently adaptable space in which the presence of the spectator would be optional (Sidiropoulou 2011: 18–19). A host of subsequent theoreticians and practitioners, figures as diverse as Antonin Artaud and Ariane Mnouchkine, would dispense with the proscenium arch in their vision of what a theatre space should be. Previous chapters in this book have already showcased some variation in this respect, with the rehearsals in *The Jester*, *L'Amour fou* and *Synecdoche, New York* taking place in unconventional spaces, which either surrounded the performance or mobilised a more immersive engagement. Elsewhere, I have analysed a film (*Jesus of Montreal*) that used a mixture of site-specific theatre and promenade theatre to draw attention to the incongruities between the experience of the film spectator and that of the diegetic theatre audience (Sava 2010). In this chapter, although all three case studies are employing the same type of stage arrangement, the way in which the camera handles the theatrical relationship between audience and performer will vary, allowing us to observe distinct configurations of point of view and point of audition. These configurations can be broadly mapped onto the three phenomenal modes of the actor's presence conceptualised by Bert O. States.

Bert O. States has discussed the tripartite relationship between actor, character and audience not from the point of view of the physical placement of the audience relative to the performers, but rather in terms of the 'act of speech' that links them, where the act of speech is not confined to the actor's delivery of scripted or improvised lines, but is understood as the whole range of aspects involved in the performance of a role (1983: 360). States has proposed three pronominal modes that position the actor as speaker in relation to the spectator as listener and viewer: the self-expressive mode, the collaborative mode and the representational mode. As in the case of the actor's multiple bodies, these modes are not mutually exclusive, but rather variously modulated during a performance. To use States's words, 'the actor's relationship to the audience may shift "keys" during a performance' (ibid.), with the three modes forming a kind of 'perceptual synthesis' which allows them different degrees of relief at any one time (ibid.: 375).

In the self-expressive mode, the 'artist in the actor comes forth' through a display of virtuosity, a stylistic signature or a 'sub-theatrical' moment that enriches the role by revealing a 'slice of human behaviour that exists [. . .] for its own sake' (ibid.: 361–2). Both Gena Rowlands' Myrtle Gordon in *Opening Night* and Michel Piccoli's Gilbert Valence in *I'm Going Home* are in this sense blatantly self-expressive, not least because in the narrative context of their films they are presented as accomplished actors and this act of 'indexical elevation', to use a previously quoted expression, requires a suitable 'ostension' of theatrical skill. In the collaborative mode, the actor 'plays to the audience' and States offers as examples the comic aside and the monologue, both of which illustrate a form of complicity between the audience and the spectator (ibid.: 365). The disruptive improvisations of the actress in *Opening Night* are reaching out to the audience, and hence pertaining to this collaborative mode, but, as we shall see, they also trigger divergent responses from different categories of the audience. Centred as it is on cinematic monologues, the book's fifth chapter could, in a general sense, be considered a lengthy reflection on the collaborative mode. The final mode in States's typology is the representational mode, which is connected to what he calls 'theatre's endless mission [. . .] to be "about" something' (ibid.: 369), and which includes the actor's capacity to persuasively project and 'disappear' into a role, to 'deflect reference' (Rozik 2002). This mode will be especially emphasised with respect to Rohmer's *A Tale of Winter*, a film in which the issues of believability and faith, of *faire croire* (Greimas cited in De Marinis 1987: 101), loom large. This chapter will therefore combine the analysis of the spectators' perceptual perspective, as it is foregrounded by the selected films, with the examination of the fictional actors' negotiation of modes of embodiment and performative address.

SUBVERSIVE PERFORMANCES AND SONIC PERSPECTIVES IN *OPENING NIGHT*

The argument of this sub-chapter develops along two parallel lines. On the one hand, drawing on work by Josette Féral and Elena del Rio, I argue that *Opening Night* (John Cassavetes, 1977) makes a case for the disruptive nature of performance in theatre. On the other, I seek to demonstrate that the instances where the fictional actress in the film steps out of character generate a metaleptic effect for the inner-level audience (the spectators of the play) and that this inner-level audience is positioned for a different experience of the performed text from the film viewer's. I suggest that the film is both attempting to align the two experiences through camerawork and sound and separate them, by giving the film spectator an epistemic advantage over the diegetic theatre audience and by varying the camera angles and positions.

Metalepsis occurs when there is a crossing of the diegetic levels, an intrusion, for instance, of the extradiegetic into the diegetic or vice versa. In Gérard Genette's words, the boundary that metalepses overstep is 'a shifting but sacred frontier between two worlds, the world in which one tells, the world of which one tells' (1980: 5). Precisely because it disrupts something 'sacred' and important, it has been noted that metalepsis often results in a comic effect (Wolf 2003: 91), in a relaxation of the narrative tone. In *Opening Night* there is a palpable tension between abdicating to comedy and maintaining the underlying tragic quality. As we shall see, this clash has made critics feel uneasy about the ending of the opening night performance, which seems to be privileging the comic undercurrent to the detriment of the high-strung drama of the actress's struggle. I am suggesting that the use of metalepsis invites this type of mixed tone and that the comic undercurrent, while generally consistent with the collaborative mode of performance discussed by Bert O. States and amply exemplified in the film, also feeds into a destabilised theatrical form that is experienced as liberating by the performers.

In *Opening Night*, Gena Rowlands plays Myrtle Gordon, a theatre actress who in her turn plays Virginia, the main character in the fictional play *The Second Woman*, authored by the fictional playwright Sarah Goode (Joan Blondell). Throughout the film we witness a series of try-outs before the big opening night in New York, which concludes the film. Myrtle has a drinking problem and is in the habit of arriving late for her performances, minutes before the curtain is raised. Cast opposite her as Virginia's photographer husband Marty is Maurice (John Cassavetes), an actor with whom we understand Myrtle had an unhappy relationship. After one of the try-out shows, Myrtle is approached for an autograph by a young fan called Nancy (Laura Johnson) and Myrtle witnesses (or believes she has witnessed) the young woman's death in a car accident. She is disturbed by the accident, which does not seem to elicit much of a reaction from her entourage. Rejected by Maurice and increasingly lonely, she becomes dependent on late-night calls to the play's director, Manny Victor (Ben Gazzara). She starts displaying erratic behaviour in rehearsals and, driven by an outright dislike of the play, interferes with the text during the try-out shows in ever more radical ways. The theatre scenes are intercut with scenes of hallucination, in which Myrtle is visited by Nancy, the dead fan. Upon learning about it, Sarah suggests a séance with a spiritualist in the hope of reining in Myrtle's stage unpredictability, but the situation worsens when Myrtle hallucinates an attack from Nancy. Alarmed by Myrtle's self-inflicted violence, Sarah tries to have her replaced, but the show is too close to its opening night for any change of headline. In a final confrontation with Nancy's apparition, Myrtle symbolically kills her. During the opening night, the entire team is on edge, fearing a flop, after Myrtle arrives heavily inebriated. Efforts are made to invigorate the intoxicated actress and to conceal her unsteady movements. By the end of the show, Myrtle seems fully recovered and more daring than ever in her onstage exchange with Maurice, who joins her in what we suspect to be a spur-of-the-moment rewriting of the play's ending. To Sarah's dismay, the show receives a standing ovation and Myrtle is celebrated as the star of the show.

    Restoring the textual identity of the fictional play out of consecutive and ever more tampered-with performances is soon established as an impossibility, although traces of the 'original play' are retrievable. The various interferences with the text effected by the main actress during the performances are mixed with what appear to be occasional returns to the text. The temptation to separate the elements of the play into scripted and non-scripted is precluded by the overwhelming evidence of these interferences. Homay King has referred to this situation as a 'highly decentered' structure of enunciation in which 'we are never entirely certain who speaks [. . .]: the character Virginia, the actress Myrtle, the playwright Sarah (Joan Blondell), or ultimately the actress Gena Rowlands or the writer-director Cassavetes' (2004: 108). The opening night seems to retrospectively impart some sense of progression to our experience of the play. The scene of Virginia's visit to former husband Tony, played by Gus (John Tuell), which we see three times throughout the film, can be safely assumed to belong to the scripted play and occurs right at the beginning of the opening night performance, which would place the several scenes with second husband Marty in the succession of this initial scene. The play appears to offer snapshots from a failing marriage that keeps both partners captive and unable to meaningfully connect, mixed with a not-so-subtle concern with the ageing of the female body.

    In an interview with Michel Ciment included in the Optimum DVD release of the film, John Cassavetes confessed that he found the play 'too dull to write' and that, although the scenes we get to see on screen were longer in the initial script, the play was never developed beyond these scenes. Had he written more, he would have felt compelled, by his own admission, to make the scenes better. As it stands, with excised parts and severely altered sections, the play reads as a rather inconclusive piece. The difficulty experienced by Cassavetes in coming up with a 'bad play' was reportedly matched by the difficulty Gena Rowlands felt playing an actress who was not particularly committed to her role.

The film spectator is positioned in relation to the theatre action through both sound and camerawork. Several times throughout the film, the camera is placed in the theatre auditorium, with all the limitations of viewing that this emplacement entails, including a visual obstruction generated by the heads of theatre spectators seated in the rows that are intercalated between the camera and the stage. These observational circumstances are often mitigated or modified by either adjusting position through the use of slight pans and tilts, as in the beginning of the movie, or by skipping rows or 'jumping' on the stage, as in the later performances.

Raymond Carney has commented on the restlessness of the camerawork in *Opening Night*, by connecting it to what he believed to be the film's depiction of a bureaucratic dynamic within theatre that forces creativity into anguished states:

> The viewer of the film is circulated through plane after plane of limited perspective. There are views from in front of the stage, from on stage, from the wings, from the back of the theater, from outside the theater, from the perspective of an actor, from the perspective of the producer, from the perspective of the audience. We are made aware of layer after layer of personal perspective, theater technology, and commercial bureaucracy as we move through a series of disorientingly different and irreconcilable positions. (1985: 263)

For Thierry Jousse, the frequent changes in perspective in the film are part of a 'contrapuntal composition', meant to reveal the 'risks of performance' and topple 'the performance down from its pedestal' (cited in Kouvaros 2004: 140–1). Ivone Margulies concurs with the idea of a contrapuntal organisation in Cassavetes's films while at the same time underscoring their inherent theatricality: 'His free-form cinema is traversed by a clear dramatic design, as well as a theatrical space, a rift within his films between those who are on display and those who look on judging' (1998: 292). Reiterating a distinction drawn by Manny Farber and Patricia Patterson between 'dispersed movies' and 'boxed-in' movies, Margulies situates Cassavetes's films at the intersection of the two modes, a midway condition which she labels 'dispersed theater' (ibid.:

298–9). An alternative reading was proposed by Homay King, who sees in the style of the film an illustration of what Pier Paolo Pasolini called 'free indirect subjectivity' (2004: 107). For King, it is not only speech which undergoes a 'crisis of attribution' in the film, but also 'vision' and 'affect' (ibid.: 109). In this interpretive framework, the 'multiplicity of angles' is read as 'a sign of the impossibility of ever fully separating these ostensibly distinct points of view' (ibid.: 118).

The relationship between theatre and cinema in Cassavetes's films is also at the forefront of George Kouvaros's work, which understands it 'not as a series of historical and formal influences, but in terms of an idea of representation at its limit, neither simply taking place nor abandoned, but rather pushed along and placed in check by the physical processes and energies that are central to the act of staging' (2004: 122). Theatre is portrayed as a space of fluid relations and of deliberate disorientation, especially when animated by the flux of actors and stagehands after the performance. My own analysis will focus on what I consider to be the representation of an incongruity of experience between the theatre audience and the film spectator, as well as on the ways in which the individual performances interfere with the dramatic form.

Being placed in the auditorium is the closest the film viewer can get to the restrictive positioning of the theatre spectator. However, what the theatre spectator often lacks in terms of freedom of movement, s/he gains in sensorial range, in being able to hear without technological mediation. In a discussion of stage dialogue, Jean Chothia has remarked that 'much of the particular effect of drama derives from the gap between two ways of hearing, that of the interlocutor on stage and that of the audience, and from the audience's consciousness of the gap' (cited in Kozloff 2000: 16). To continue with Chothia's train of thought, in addition to being concomitant with the hearing happening on stage, the theatre audience's hearing completes and interprets the theatre speech. By contrast, the 'phenomenological absence of the actors from the filmgoers' space and reality' (ibid.) makes the filmgoers' hearing reliant on a recording technology. Interestingly enough, though, this technology can be used, as is the case with *Opening Night*, to create a sonic environment which incorporates sonic gradation and hearing impediments, to produce, in other words, an aural approximation of the theatrical environment.

The film could be said to break away from the standardised Hollywood practice of having a continuous sound track function as a 'satisfying and comfortable base from which the eyes can go flitting about, voyeuristically' (Altman 1992: 62). In this, it reactivates a debate concerning the intelligibility of dialogue versus the acoustic fidelity to the pro-filmic situation (ibid.: 59), a debate which was briefly touched upon in my analysis of *L'Amour fou*. From the very beginning of the film, when Myrtle enters the set and starts whispering to her dresser and a stagehand, the spectator is asked to prick up her ears. Although theatrical performances notoriously require actors to project their voice in order to be heard, in the film the sound level of the theatre performances is not uniformly conveyed, as they are heard, alternatively, from a perceptible remove (when the camera is in the auditorium), or from very close by (when the camera is on stage). The film spectator is 'seated' in the auditorium and because of this position, the laughter and noises of the diegetic theatre audience are heard closer than the voices on stage.

During the theatre performances, Cassavetes not only playfully varies the camera angle, he also varies the sonic perspective. The effect was deliberate. In the audio commentary of the Optimum DVD release of the film, Bo Harwood, in charge of both the sound and the musical score of *Opening Night*, singled out as one of the many challenges of the film's soundscape the creation of an 'ambiance of theater', down to the 'creaking floor'. During the first scene of the play as we initially see it performed, Myrtle as Virginia prepares to exit from the chaos of discordant reactions triggered by her visit to her former husband's home where she is confronted by the reality of a family she knew nothing about. As she goes through one of the doors on the set to collect her coat, the voices on the stage are for a brief moment heard slightly diminished. In the same scene performed later in the film, the loudness of the stage voices is kept loud as Myrtle appears to be reacting to one of the lines in the play uttered by the actress playing her ex-husband's wife ('What kind of a woman are you?') as if hearing it for the first time. When at the end of the scene she is 'expelled' from the fictional space of the stage and finds herself stranded in a backstage corridor, the audience's applause is aurally remote, its affecting force neutralised by the sonic distance. In all these cases, the point of audition is Myrtle's and the sound has been matched to the image. However, another important aspect is at stake here. Throughout the film, Myrtle is not only a character through which occasionally the film spectator exerts a type of aural focalisation, but also, and, perhaps more importantly, a character who listens. In a piece on 'sonic bodies' in *The Lives of Others*, Jennifer Barker has written of the actor's performance as a 'presence co-constituted against, around and alongside the spectator and the film itself' and of the actor who listens as not only a body who 'projects and performs' but also one who 'introjects and resounds' (2012: 252). For Barker, it is the act of listening that renders a place truly 'sonorous', contributing to what she calls the 'space of mutual reversibility' of the cinematic encounter (ibid.: 243). Myrtle's body is 'resounding' not only because as an actress she is shown in a state of alertness to on- and offstage cues, constantly interacting with and responding to other voices around her, but also because of a deeper search for a way of playing the role that takes her into a zone of intensified (inter)subjectivity (she tells Sarah

'I have this dead girl', where 'to have a dead girl' can be interpreted, among other things, as 'to be able to hear' a presence that no one else can).

Going back to the issue of the multiplicity of angles that the film adopts, many of them firmly lodged in the auditorium, I would like to propose that we think of them by dint of Josette Féral's insightful discussion of the differences between 'performance' as an art form and 'theatre'. Féral remarks that

> in contrast to performance, theatre cannot keep from setting up, stating, constructing, and giving points of view: the director's point of view, the author's towards the action, the actor's towards the stage, the spectator's towards the actor. There is a multiplicity of viewpoints and gazes, a 'density of signs' (to quote Barthes) setting up a thetic multiplicity absent from performance. (1982: 178)

Féral goes on to explain that while performance allows the 'flows of desire' to traverse the subject without being fixed, theatre, as a realm of the symbolic, 'inscribes the subject in the law and in theatrical codes' (ibid.). At one point during the film, Sarah explains to Myrtle what is expected of her ('All you have to do is say the lines clearly and with a degree of feeling and then Virginia will appear'), drawing out a neat, clear-cut trajectory of performance in complete subservience to the author's words in which the actor is denied any significant artistic input beside that of a straightforward, uninvolved delivery. It is against codes such as these that Myrtle can be said to rebel, through both an increasingly physical style of acting, culminating in the foot-shake at the end, and a metaleptic dismantling of the dramatic text she is meant to perform. The fact that the multiple viewpoints do have a constraining effect is visually intimated several times throughout the film, perhaps most strikingly in a shot that shows Manny looking through an open door at the inside of the theatre venue, where, in the distance, Myrtle is seen on stage, against the backdrop of Marty's oversized photos of elderly women. Compositionally, Myrtle is encased within the rectangle of the opened door, in what David Bordwell would call aperture framing, and visually dominated by the large foreground figure of the director.

The scene of Maurice and Myrtle rehearsing the moment when Marty slaps Virginia has been rightly singled out as important for an understanding of Myrtle's subsequent stage behaviour. After Maurice's first real try at a slap, Myrtle has a performative breakdown: when it is time for Maurice's second attempt, she falls to the ground before he even hits her and then, later, she bursts into laughter. Ivone Margulies interprets the moment as illustrating a 'liminal stage of existence', which she defines, using Turner, as consisting of the individual losing him-/herself 'in meaningless behavior, in anonymous, rankless play' (1998: 290). Myrtle's laughter can also be taken to signal the inauguration of a metaleptic attitude. The difficulty in connecting with the role, epitomised by the reaction to the stage slap (one could say that Sarah's play as a whole is for Myrtle a slap in the face), in conjunction with the death of the young fan (imagined or not, the film is slightly ambivalent on this score), act as a triggering factor for Myrtle's transgressive treatment of the script. The performances she will give after this rehearsal will challenge, a bit more each time, the text of the play, not by just changing the lines but by more broadly breaching the rules of the dramatic game.

Starting from Genette's work, theoreticians distinguish between different types of metalepsis (authorial, ontological, lectorial, rhetorical) (Fludernik 2003), and although the examples and the classifications may vary, metalepsis is widely understood as a device that exposes fictionality and confuses boundaries. Metalepsis is not written in the play nor is it a device to which the film as a whole subscribes, but Myrtle's actions make for a metaleptic agency. The 'violent streak', the 'aggression towards the subject' that Debra Malina sees as inherent in metalepsis (2002: 3), are prefigured in the film by the conflictual pairing of Myrtle and Sarah, on the one hand, and Myrtle and Nancy, on the other, the final violence on the text being preceded by Myrtle symbolically killing Nancy and by the aggressive verbal exchange between Sarah and Myrtle. What is also at stake in these conflictual pairings is a certain 'generationalism', a theme which is increasingly discussed in recent debates on postfeminism (Jermyn 2012: 2; Holmes and Jermyn 2015: 14) and which encapsulates the portrayal of the relationship between different generations of women as adversarial and competitive. Myrtle is caught between the younger Nancy and the older Sarah, equidistantly positioned in relation to both and unable to either regain or identify with aspects of their experience – she associates youth with emotions being 'close to the surface' and old age with menopausal and post-menopausal bodily transformations and symptoms (the 'hot flushes' that her character Virginia is experiencing in the play). That being said, the fact that Myrtle describes her obsession with Nancy as 'having a dead girl' could also indicate that the character is subjecting herself to a form of 'girling' (Jermyn 2012: 1).

When Myrtle and Maurice as Virginia and Marty reach the point of the slap during a try-out show, Myrtle falls to the ground just as in the rehearsals. The visual hindrance caused by the members of the audience seated between the camera and the stage is such that throughout most of the scene, while Myrtle is lying on the ground, we can only see a portion of her body and the blue patch of her bathrobe, a moving, throbbing, headless bodily mass that acts as a conduit for a diffuse, unscripted emotion. The film audience is given no indication of what the scripted roles would have sounded like; indeed, we can barely see Myrtle/Virginia, but we can judge by Maurice's

Figure 4.1 Vision obstructed – *Opening Night* (John Cassavetes, 1977, USA)

delay and bewilderment that she is not sticking to the written version of the role. Her performance is already out of bounds, textually insubordinate, surrendered to feeling. Myrtle allows her ecstatic body to take over, to dictate the course of events: one might surmise she lies down, because it feels good to lie down, especially in the context of a tense situation, where all eyes are on you. Maurice, on the other hand, stays in character, trying to save face for the theatrical audience. Although her intention is not entirely clear from the start, Myrtle decides during the performance to shed the role completely in an impromptu address to Maurice: 'Don't be afraid. I love you. You're a wonderful actor, Maurice. We must never forget this is only a play.' Maurice counters Myrtle's sustained recalcitrance with a disconcerting laughter directed at the audience. The lights on the stage go out on this line, in the sound of a round of applause, a sign that the theatre audience has not perceived the hijacking of the original text and instead has accepted the metalepsis as an authorial strategy, coming from either the playwright or the director. Myrtle's transgression is greeted with sarcasm after the show is over by Manny, the stage director: 'I think it is wonderful that you've told everyone Maurice is an actor. I mean no one would have known if you hadn't told them. And I think it's marvelous how you accurately described to them what they were watching: a play.'

The next represented performance takes us past the point of the slap to Marty saying to Virginia 'I'll be at the Beverly Hills Hotel' and exiting the scene. Left to her own devices, Myrtle once again stands in defiance of the scripted role and has Virginia engage in random bits of business: dropping the ashtray on the floor, giving mock answers on the phone or refusing to answer it altogether. The scripted visit of Virginia's ex-husband becomes an awkward situation in which Myrtle disappears behind a door, leaving the fate of the scene in the hands of the uninspired improviser Gus. Entreated to go back on stage, Myrtle re-enters the scene with a mischievous smile on her face, a sign for the film viewer that she is not done with interfering with the text. When an exasperated Manny drops the curtain on an unfinished scene, Myrtle generates yet another instance of crossed boundaries, by breaking the fourth wall. She requests the lifting of the curtain and proceeds to directly address the spectators in the auditorium about the humiliation of the hasty lowering of the curtain and about the passage of time ('Time is a killer, isn't it, folks?'). Once again, the film audience and the diegetic theatre audience are bound to perceive things differently. Because they are to be presumed unaware of the fact that Myrtle has been acting in a disruptive manner, the theatre spectators (an inner-level audience) have the option of seeing metalepsis as a phenomenon of the text (either inscribed in the play or introduced by the play's director), whereas for the film audience no such option is available, as we see what happens on stage through the filter of what preceded it offstage.

The opening night is the culmination of Myrtle's improvisational bravura. To quote Tom Charity: 'In rebelling against the naturalism of the stage ("the choking formality of the theatre", in Cassavetes's words), Myrtle has opened up a Pandora's box of irrationalities that no author can hope to control: not Myrtle, not Sarah, not even John Cassavetes' (2001: 160). On the opening night, as she arrives intoxicated and bruised, Myrtle is from the beginning caught in a network of gazes. Manny forbids a member of the theatre company from helping Myrtle reach her dressing room, which results in Myrtle leaning against walls and crawling and fainting her way to the dressing room where she crashes on a sofa. At this point, the playwright and the producer of the show are seen collectively looking down at her unresponsive body, assessing its ability to carry the performance. Later, sitting in the audience, they will form a particularly tense and anxious minority in an otherwise eager theatre crowd. The opening night begins with a delay, after the decision not to make an official announcement about Myrtle's incapacitated state. When her drunkenness causes Myrtle to faint, the other actors improvise around it, in a way that makes the bodily non-cooperation the means to a rechannelling of the stage activity. In order to appear, the fictive body of the character has to out-manoeuvre the actress's malfunctioning visceral and ecstatic bodies. Throughout the film, Myrtle is sustained by this agonistic approach; she literally makes things difficult for herself and for everyone around her, but this is, we feel, part of her creative process. In the scene of Myrtle's visit to Tony's home, the energy still gathers around the bullying ex-husband and his family and the enclosed nature of the setting creates a sense of domestic violence banging against the very walls of the enclosure. The camera is placed on the stage and at times what we grasp is simultaneously the performers acting on stage and the audience's reaction, which creates the sense of a scene being 'burst open' in front of an inspecting and relentless gaze and of the urgency of 'staying in the moment' as a performer. As a film audience, we enjoy all the advantages of insight into the intra-professional tensions of the theatre world as well as the emotions that come with it, as we watch Myrtle and perhaps also root for her to get through the ordeal. By comparison, the theatre audience is less privy to Myrtle's turmoil but has the fictional advantage of an uninterrupted performance and of a full grasp of the play's text, disrupted as it may be, a grasp denied to the film spectators.

As the stage director leaves the theatre for a drink in a nearby joint, the narrative also temporarily abandons the show. The next bit of performance that we see is the end of a scene heretofore excluded: Tony and Virginia embracing in the apartment vacated of the family drama previously witnessed. The scene works in a relation of symmetry with a behind-the-curtains scene of Myrtle being comforted by her dresser. The last instalment of the show is preceded by a shot of Myrtle, propped up by her dresser and a stagehand, traversing a featureless corridor linking her dressing room and the backstage area, and immersing herself in the darkness of the stage antechamber only to reemerge for the theatre spectators as Virginia. Judging by Sarah's discomfort and Manny's reactions in the audience, this last part is an ad-lib exchange between Myrtle and Maurice, freely improvising on the themes of the play, ageing and love, but also on the idea of acting as an 'invasion' by another being.

Although the opening night is described in the film as a success and the after party is experienced as a celebratory affair, many a critic has considered this resolution a letdown. Raymond Carney has described the final improvisation as 'humiliating' and 'embarrassing', adding that the 'cranky, improvised performance on stage in front of an indifferent audience is what makes *Opening Night* the darkest and most disturbing of his films' (1985: 270). Tom Charity has also given a rather critical assessment of the final segment of the movie, although considerably toned down by comparison: 'the presentation is exuberantly comic, and the *coup de grace* is as simple and straightforward as an old athletes "foot-shake", yet it's hard to feel this horseplay answers (or merits) the trauma Myrtle has put herself through' (2001: 162). George Kouvaros has refrained from directly evaluating the end of the film, emphasising instead the idea of the constant 'doubling and echoing' that happens between acting in life and acting in drama and the more general theme of ghosts and apparitions in Cassavetes's films (present in *Opening Night* in the figure of Nancy), which he likens to the 'physical blows to the heart, the fermata, heart stops, and incendiary images identified by Artaud in "Theatre and the Plague" that put the representation into question, a violent tearing of performative space by something singular, exorbitant and unaccountable' (2004: 147). Lisa Katzman is, by contrast, a favourable voice who notes that the end 'uses method acting technique as a redemptive force by positioning the tyranny of an obsession with youth not as a sexist problem, but as a metaphysical one, which stems from society's neurotic denial of death and aging' (1989: 39), an ending that she deems compatible with one of the aesthetic creeds associated with method acting, whereby the 'camera stalks the moment, subordinates everything – symmetry, balance, steadiness – to the moment' (ibid.: 35). In her reading, this moment, true carrier of 'emotional truth', is repressed for the most part and arrived at only in the end. For her part, Homay King has rejected the association of Cassavetes with method acting, pointing out that Cassavetes not only criticised the Stanislavskian method, but also developed a style of direction which was 'designed to subvert an interiorized or unidirectional model of performance' (2004: 111–12). What is evident across the range of the varying critical responses that I have briefly overviewed is that they all see the ending as bringing something different, be it a method-acting-styled way out of a performative situation that previously straitjacketed the actor, or a flimsy resolution to an excessively built-up emotional drama.

I would like to propose an interpretation of the ending using Josette Féral's distinction between performance and theatre filtered through Elena del Rio's notion of 'moving corporeality' (Del Rio 2008: 2). I am suggesting that Myrtle uses the freedoms afforded by performance to take the role apart and reconfigure it in a looser, lighter manner. As Féral argues, the chief aim of performance understood as an art form is 'to undo "competencies" (which are primarily theatrical). Performance readjusts these competencies and redistributes them in a desystematized arrangement' (1982: 179). The result, Féral goes on to add, is a 'deterritorialized gesturality' (ibid.). Myrtle's theatrical competencies, shown at work in the performances we see at the beginning of the film, when she does not yet infringe on the role, are downplayed or undermined from within. Féral interestingly writes of performance as an 'authorless, actorless, directorless infratheatricality' (ibid.: 178). It is this theatricality from underneath the layers of skill and convention that can be said to possess the two actors (and they do in fact talk of being 'killed' and 'invaded'). The stream of awkward jokes and physical gestures exchanged between Myrtle and Maurice is only loosely connected to the story, and it constitutes less a solution to the play and more a deconstruction of it.

The farcical disposition of both actors in the scene radically transforms what we can only assume to have been a very depressing ending (Myrtle had complained during the rehearsals about the lack of hope in the script) into a deliberately ludicrous wrap-up, in line with Myrtle's avowed intention of finding a way of playing the part where 'age doesn't make any difference'. The style of acting espoused by the two actors is more physical than anything we had witnessed up to that point. Using some of the mannerisms and tics that were on full display in her earlier film *A Woman Under the Influence* (John Cassavetes, 1974), Gena Rowlands clenches her fists, taps her fingers nervously, touches her forehead with her fingers, squints, scowls, shouts, in a panoply of gestures and facial expressions that are at odds with her previously tame performance. Her gesturality in the last scene is foreign to the play's corporeal instantiation up to this point. In other words, if we can still talk of a Virginia in the last scene, it is a very different Virginia from at the beginning of the show, a Virginia made strange. John Cassavetes as Maurice matches her level of slapstick with his own and he turns the nervous laughter he used in response to Myrtle's previous textual transgressions into an expressive pattern. Following Elena del Rio, one could argue that what we are witnessing is a demonstration of the powers of performance, performance as 'an affective and sensational *force* that disrupts, redirects and indeed affects narrative *form*' (2008: 15). Del Rio distinguishes between the 'organized body, slave to morality and representation' and the 'expressive body', which, through its 'creative capacity' and 'affective intensity' can acquire an ideologically subversive quality (ibid.: 16–17). Following this logic, the actors' bodies in the last scene of the opening night are disorganised bodies, bodies that are freely embracing their excess and their embarrassment, their discomposure and their randomness, and in the process are disabling the ideologically oppressive spectre of ageism which seems to permeate the fictional play they are (un)performing.

In this sub-chapter I have argued that John Cassavetes's approach to the representation of theatre in *Opening Night* is equally attuned to the relationship between the film spectator and the theatre audience and to the fictional actress's multiple interferences with the play and that this double-tiered attention is intermedial in nature. In the following case study, the use of the camerawork in the embedded theatre scene will be informed by a different understanding of theatricality in cinema.

CONSPICUOUS CAMERA AND UTOPIAN SPECTATORSHIP IN *A TALE OF WINTER*

Critical assessments of Rohmer's films seem to fall into one of two categories: a belief that they are 'all talk' or, alternatively, that they are 'so much more than talk'. For Leo Bersani and Ulysse Dutoit, in Rohmer's films 'Filmic material is produced by the talk that at once brings it into being and critically reflects upon it' (2009: 24) and the conversational aspect has ascendancy over the others to the extent that they believe it is difficult to produce an interpretation of the films that would not be reducible to a paraphrase of the films' dialogue. Together with the perceived neglect, or unusual employment, of cinematic devices, Rohmer's 'sophisticated *bavardage*' (ibid.) generates in the Bersani-Dutoit reading a verdict of theatricality:

> Rohmer's cinema seems to offer so little in the way of – cinema. With its interminable talk, its lengthy sequences in a single location, its spare use of background music, its relative indifference to such venerable cinematic techniques as shot/reverse shot, and the camera's apparent predilection for the person being addressed rather than the (presumably more expressive) face of the person talking – given all this, we might be excused for thinking that Rohmer has chosen the wrong medium, that his work is more theatrical than cinematic. (ibid.: 25)

Aimée Israel-Pelletier counteracts this line of argument with an interpretation building on Jacques Rancière's concept *phrase-image*, which boldly claims that 'Talking only *appears* to be the main attraction', when, in fact, the 'multi-layered experience of events' and the 'massive agitation and [. . .] instability positioned alongside the verbal sparring' are just as, if not more, important in the creation of the Rohmerian 'ambiance' (2005: 39–41). The characters' movement, analysed by Israel-Pelletier as 'a recurring *phrase-image*' (ibid.: 43), is also singled out by Derek Schilling, for whom the function of this 'connective tissue' is to provide a 'structural contrast to ubiquitous conversation' (2007: 107). Rohmer himself has been known to challenge the view that his films are theatrical or verbose, preferring the comparison to Balzac to the *marivaudage* the critics frequently identify in his work (Curchod and Rohmer 1992: 28), maintaining that music was a bigger influence on his movies than theatre (ibid.: 26), and that silent cinema was more important than sound cinema in his formative years (Petrie and Rohmer 1971: 40).

In what follows, I shall argue that in *A Tale of Winter* Rohmer conceives of theatre as a utopian space, where the main character finds a decision she has taken, which by worldly standards is unpragmatic, unrealistic but deeply felt, validated and reflected back to her in fictional form. At the same time, I shall scrutinise the way in which the play embedded in the film problematises the various means that arts use to make us believe or be affected by the stories they tell. The film can thus be said to revisit the venerable tradition of the *paragone*, the rivalry between arts, and the use of the camera supports an examination of the imbrication of showing and telling on which both theatre and film rely.

Rohmer's *A Tale of Winter* begins in silence and in the 'style of a photostory' (Giavarini 1992: 21, my translation) with the summer love affair of Félicie (Charlotte Véry) and Charles (Frédéric van den Driessche). After this season of love, they separate at a train station with the promise that they will meet on Charles's return from a trip abroad. When Charles asks for her address, Félicie experiences an unexplainable lapse and the name Levallois morphs into Courbevoie. After a five-year ellipsis, during which Félicie gives birth to Charles's daughter, Elise (Ava Loraschi), the story picks up at the moment when Félicie is supposed to choose between two lovers, Maxence (Michel Voletti), the owner of a beauty parlour, and Loïc (Hervé Furic), a librarian. She breaks up with Loïc and moves with Maxence to Nevers, believing it to be the right decision, but, on a similar impulse, she returns to Paris after a brief period in the provinces. She visits Loïc, they spend an evening at the theatre, seeing a staging of William Shakespeare's *The Winter's Tale*, and on their way back, Félicie shares with Loïc her feeling of renewed faithfulness to the absent Charles, which Loïc compares with Pascal's wager. The film ends with the blissful, fortuitous reunion of Félicie and Charles on a Parisian bus and a subsequent visit to Félicie's mother.

Shakespeare's *The Winter Tale* ends in such a striking manner that critics have often felt inclined to privilege the last scene over the rest. It is therefore no surprise that Rohmer would choose a fragment from the play's ending to include in the film. During this last scene, the King of Sicilia, Leontes, visits the court lady Paulina, who is rumoured to possess a statue closely resembling Leontes' wife, Hermione, long thought dead. Leontes had lost both his wife and his son after wrongfully accusing Hermione of being the mistress of his friend Polixenes. His newborn daughter Perdita was sent away following the two tragic 'deaths'. After sixteen years, a contrite Leontes, reunited with Perdita and reconciled with Polixenes, is accompanied by them on his visit to Paulina, who pretends to use white magic in order to bring to life the queen's statue. The play ends with Leontes expressing gratitude for the vivifying act.

For most reviewers, Rohmer's choice of scene is explicable through the correspondence it establishes between the ending of the play and the ending of the film. The relation of the film with the play has been mostly interpreted as a deliberate 'misreading' (Ennis 1996: 318), tailored 'to suit the confidence of Félicie' (Strick 1993: 44) and to foretell the reunion with Charles. This interpretation has been significantly complicated by Stanley Cavell, who has produced a subtle analysis of the film's 'various ingestions, both huge and tiny, of Shakespeare's play' (2004: 432). Cavell treats Rohmer as a thinker who uses the camera as his 'organ of thought' (ibid.) and argues that Rohmer is 'serious about' Shakespeare's play, to such an extent that 'he cannot avoid the maximum theatrical stake of Shakespeare's structure, namely to consider whether the statue's being replaced by life holds, or "works", theatrically, whether the audience is given enough motive to stay with the moment' (ibid.: 429). He identifies and elaborates on a series of 'transfigurations' operating within the film, each 'lend[ing] a new cast to Shakespeare's texture', namely the transfigurations 'of Loïc out of Paulina, of Félicie out of Hermione and Leontes as well as out of Perdita, of the girlchild Elise out of the dead boy-child Mamillius' (ibid.: 435), establishing a link between Félicie's 'strangeness to the world' and Leontes's 'extravagant and lethal strangeness' (ibid.: 426). For the purposes of my own analysis, I want to retain and develop Cavell's suggestion that *A Tale of Winter* contains 'a declaration of film's competition with theater' (ibid.: 424). He spells out the grounds of this competition by actually juxtaposing the photograph and the statue:

> Let us ask: What is the difference proposed in Rohmer's film between a photograph's being replaced by life and a statue's coming to life? One might answer that it is the difference between the wondering whether you know that a person exists, is alive, and wondering whether you know the person's identity. The statue is not a reminder, it is not dispensable, in this granting of life, it has a (virtual) life of its own. The dispensability of the photograph is declared when Charles says that he recognised Felicie even though he had no photograph of her. But is the photograph dispensable when, as in the case of the child, it is all she has as proof of her father's identity? (ibid.: 436)

Cavell refers here to a photograph of Charles that Félicie keeps in her apartment, the means through which her young child is acquainted with her father. The photograph stands metonymically for the indexicality of film, because it is film which, according to Cavell, 'animates' still photographs, the 'death masks of time' (ibid.). Theatre is connected in Cavell's argument with 'religion' (the animated statue) and is deemed to achieve its own brand of resurrection through 'metempsychosis, the replacement in a body of another soul' (ibid.: 437), a process to which we have referred elsewhere, via Zarrilli, as the emergence of a 'fictive body'. The ontological scrutiny of several media via the concept of resurrection allows him to establish a link between the film and the play: 'In both *The Winter's Tale* and *A Tale of Winter*, the relation of art or image to reality is portrayed, or recaptured, as miraculous, specifically as resurrection' (ibid.: 436). The way in which Cavell organises his argument makes it possible for him to pull together different threads (photography, sculpture, theatre and film as media, Shakespeare's play and Rohmer's film).

I shall begin my own analysis by focusing on the scene of the resurrected statue from *The Winter's Tale*, quoted almost entirely in *A Tale of Winter*. I propose that we think of this pivotal scene as informative of the film's inter-artial strategies, and as mobilising a whole history of comparative aesthetic thought. In the first part of the analysis, my aim will be to shed light on this complexity of signification, with the assistance of a body of literature which has puzzled over the final scene of the play. I shall then deal with the ways in which the scene is represented, witnessed and discussed in the film.

The play's last scene has been variously described by critics as a 'thoroughly unshakespearian theatrical shock tactic' (Gurr 1983: 420) and 'a sophisticated confidence trick' (Meek 2006: 406). The readers of the play are let in on Paulina's ruse: a stage direction reads 'Paulina draws a curtain and reveals Hermione standing like a statue' (Shakespeare 2007: 764). The theatregoers are also likely to favour the rational explanation of the event (Hermione did not die but stayed in hiding for sixteen years) over the magical explanation. The rational explanation is nevertheless not without its ambiguities; indeed, it does not make much more sense than the magic account. Leonard Barkan has drawn attention to this implausibility:

> Either Hermione died and was resurrected in marble, or else she spent sixteen years in a garden-shed on the grounds of her husband's palace, a solitude broken only by daily visits from her protectress – or jailer? – Paulina, all the while that this same worthy lady was encouraging Leontes into deeper paroxysms of grief over having in effect killed his wife. (1981: 640)

Shakespeare prepares us for the ambivalence of the play's ending. The words used by the Third Gentleman to describe Hermione's statue in the play's penultimate scene are 'a piece many years in doing and now newly performed by that rare Italian master, Julio Romano' (Shakespeare 2007: 762). The notion of a performed statue suggests at once immobility and movement, stasis and transformation. According to Barkan, because it collapses the boundary between life and art, theatre and sculpture, Hermione's 'dramatic statue' should be interpreted as 'Shakespeare's fulfilment of the paragone, one of his most intricate essays in artistic self-consciousness' (1981: 661). This *paragone*, the contest between sister arts invoked by Barkan, ultimately declares Shakespeare's own art winning, an 'art of four-dimensional sculpture', of 'statues coming to life' (ibid.: 662, 664). This victory is achieved through a stratagem, by temporarily equating drama with life, before exposing all arts as fictions. To quote Richard Meek, 'In the theater, we watch actors representing characters who talk and move like real people, but we are not watching "nature" or "reality" in any simple sense' (2006: 402). What Shakespeare does through an 'overloading of art – and levels of mimesis' is to '[create] enough confusion to make some critics write about Hermione as if she were a real person' (ibid.: 403). In Meek's reading, the penultimate scene of the play is complementing the scene of the resurrected statue, in that it foregrounds the issue of measuring showing against telling, and thus scrutinises 'the relationship between narrative and drama' (ibid.: 395).

This penultimate scene consists of the conversation between the three gentlemen and Autolycus, describing the reunion of Leontes, Polixenes and Perdita. The Third Gentleman's account starts with a narrative guarantee: 'That which you hear you'll swear you see, there is such unity in the proofs' (Shakespeare 2007: 400). This promise and the terms in which it is formulated indicate that the Third Gentleman is engaging in a specific type of description, a description characterised by *enargeia*. This rhetorical notion, the cornerstone of Meek's analysis, was commonly employed both in ancient literary criticism and during the Renaissance to refer to a vivid account, which creates an effect of visual presence and expresses a desire for 'a primal, linguistic plenitude' (Paul Julian Smith cited in Sharpling 2002: 174). For Meek, Shakespeare's use of *enargeia* in the gentlemen's conversation is meant to argue that 'narrative can do things that "showing" alone cannot' (2006: 398), and, in combination with the last scene, it demonstrates 'the ability of art both to accurately counterfeit life and to hoodwink us' (ibid.: 405). Starting from Samuel Johnson's critical response to Shakespeare's shift in narrational mode from showing to telling in this penultimate scene and using Elaine Scarry's distinction between 'immediate perception, delayed perception, and mimetic perception', William Gruber has argued that the scene in question is a 'cleverly ironic' 'artistic sleight-of-hand', replacing 'immediate' perception with 'mimetic perception', inviting 'spectators to think of their own role as both viewers *and* listeners', but also raising 'two questions regarding dramatic composition that are central to every playwright' (2010: 2–4). In Gruber's view, the two questions are: '(1) How to choose which events of a life to dramatize on stage, and which to express only in retrospect, by recitation? (2) How to establish and maintain a productive relationship between enactment and narrative in theatre?' (ibid.: 4). While these problems could be raised, with equal interest, in relation to film, what Rohmer's film does is, more interestingly, to raise them in relation to both media.

During the stage show, just like Kieślowski's Véronique and Almodóvar's Manuela, Rohmer's Félicie is marked out for special scrutiny. The few cutaways from the stage are, without fail, shots of Félicie in the audience. There is a static shot that places her within the audience next to Loïc, then a dolly-in that brings us closer, inviting us to note her riveted attention. At the moment of the statue's resurrection, in a medium shot, she takes Loïc's hand into her own, holding it close to her chest, visibly moved (she later confesses that at that point she 'almost screamed'). When the queen addresses her daughter Perdita, wanting to know how she managed to find her way back to the court, Félicie is in tears and the close-up excludes all else from our field of vision. Interspersed throughout the theatre scene, Félicie's reaction shots arrange themselves clearly along an upward trajectory of emotion. At the same time, I would argue, these shots compose the image of a 'utopian performative', as defined by Jill Dolan:

> Utopian performatives describe small but profound moments in which performance calls the attention of the audience in a way that lifts everyone slightly above the present, into a hopeful feeling of what the world might be like if every moment of our lives were as emotionally voluminous, generous, aesthetically striking, and intersubjectively intense. (2005: 5)

Although Dolan's use of the word is more political than the context of this film allows, I would contend that the concept encapsulates well the significance of the play for Félicie and the way in which, to quote Dolan again, performance becomes 'a doing' (ibid.), providing 'an affective vision of how the world might be better' (ibid.: 6). Félicie feels empowered to hope and wait for a reunion with Charles, having had the vision of a similar, but more fantastic reunion in the play. This is a vision of a private world made better, a world in which life arranges things in such a manner as to engineer improbable events in the name of love and hope.

The theatre scene appears to have been filmed with a particular objective in mind. Rohmer has stated that he wanted 'the presence of the camera to be felt, like it would be in the television coverage of a play' and that, to this end, he worked with two cameras and he kept in things he would have otherwise edited out, such as 'transition shots, reframing shots, shots where the camera passes from one character to another, without showing the character who speaks' (Curchod and Rohmer 1992: 27, my translation). The result, according to Rohmer, was a theatricality stemming from an 'excess of "filmicity"' ('La théâtralité provient, si j'ose dire, d'un excès de "cinématographicité"') (ibid.). Ignored by critics, Rohmer's statement is useful in a number of ways. Not only is it a throwback to an earlier discussion in this book, adding to the panoply of meanings of theatricality, but also, more significantly for the present case study, it helps elucidate the representational means in use in the theatre scene.

The film supports Rohmer's claims. The theatre scene is never filmed in long shot. The most inclusive framing of the scene falls somewhere between a full shot and a *plan américain*. Instead, the scene mostly unfolds as a succession of medium shots, close-ups and the occasional medium long shot, the latter used mainly for small groups of characters. It not only preserves what Rohmer says he would normally have discarded (shots capturing random movement on stage), it also shuns the overall image, splitting it into a series of moving and talking busts and heads.

The characters in the scene are surrounded by statues, and both the staging and the shooting capitalise on this proximity between people and sculptures, reinforcing the sculpture–theatre–film *paragone*. In one shot, Paulina (Danièle Lebrun) stands in front of a statue, blocking it almost completely from view, and the shoulders of the statue, barely visible behind Paulina's shoulders, look as if they were part of an attempt to trace the contours of the human figure, an attempt to draw around it. The position of the camera enables this effect of superimposition, which is dependent upon a temporarily fixed point in space. The camera fastens our eyes on this coincidence of placement at the same time as it reveals it. In yet another shot, Paulina stands next to the 'statue' of Hermione (Diane Lepvrier) and the interval between them allows us to observe a statue of Venus Pudica in the background. The arrangement suggests a ranking of reality effect. In this case, Hermione stands for her own imitation, in an inversion of the mimetic relation. Through her almost monochromatic appearance and frozen mien, Hermione resembles a statue and is supposed to efficiently pass for one at the beginning of the scene, while the veracity of details (the red lips, the blood in the veins, the 'fixture of her eye') betrays an indwelling difference, that Paulina tries in vain to explain away as fresh paint and excellent craftsmanship.

The gaze of the enraptured king, ever more intrusive, ever more daring, determines Paulina to orchestrate the final revelation, 'shap[ing] the passionate desires of the participants into an artful verbal ritual', during which 'speech gradually imbues the statue with life' (Neely 1975: 335). For Carol Neely, therein lies the import of the play: 'language may corrupt and divide feeling and seeing, but may also clarify and reconcile them' (ibid.: 321). On the other hand, as Leonard Barkan has remarked, the fact that 'the couple

Figure 4.2 Human statues – *A Tale of Winter* (Eric Rohmer, 1992, France)

can meet as statue and speechless viewer' is meant to 'purify the disasters of speech' (1981: 659), the speech-triggered and speech-enhanced tragedies of the first three acts of the play. Silence and stillness only characterise the brief segment of the presumed resurrection, when the king and his suite are themselves forming a statuary group of sorts, bound as they are by Paulina's request for immobility. The rest of the scene is spent talking about the statue, in what represents an encomium dedicated to both an impossibly accomplished work of sculpture and to the unrivalled qualities of the presumed dead but aesthetically reanimated queen.

After the first few gestures synchronised with the sounds of the flute, played so that she can awaken, the queen is seen traversing the space separating her from a now frightened Leontes (Roger Dumas). Paulina sets the king at ease and the royal couple join their hands in a tender clasp, as the king utters 'If this be magic let it be an art lawful as eating'. Hermione embraces him and the camera then pans leftwards to meet Polixenes (Daniel Tarrare), who advances from the back of the scene to the front. Facing the spectators, he succinctly describes the scene we had just left: 'She embraces him. She hangs about his neck. If she pertain to life, let her speak too.' In Shakespeare's play, the lines are said in turn by Camillo and Polixenes, but in the film's version of the scene, it is only Polixenes who recites these lines, a modification which focuses the description. The descriptive telling witnessed in this scene could be considered a remnant of the three gentlemen's conversation. As a follow-up, and in a symmetrical address, Paulina announces the last stage in the life-restoring spell, the regaining of speech. Polixenes's retelling of the reunion that we were also, for a moment, allowed to see on screen ('she embraces', 'she hangs about his neck') promotes a type of complementarity between showing and telling which the film will be consistent in supporting and which affirms the plurimediality of film and theatre compared to the monomedial capabilities of sculpture, painting or poetry, the usual competitors in the Renaissance *paragone*. The film both hints at a history of aesthetic jealousy between media and undertakes to settle it, by giving the two endeavours (showing and telling) separate but interdependent roles in the representation of an event.

A case in point is Félicie's meditation in the Nevers cathedral. Félicie's experience in the cathedral is both shown and told, even told twice. During the argument with Maxence, she uses the conclusion of the experience to justify the break-up and the return to Paris. Later in the film, after the evening at the theatre, she has a conversation with Loïc, in which she expands the account of her experience in Nevers. In the film, Félicie lets herself be persuaded by Elise to enter the cathedral and look at the Nativity. While her little daughter is observing the miniature set-up of the Nativity, Félicie retreats to a chair in the nave and, in her turn, contemplates the grander set-up of the cathedral's interior. The scene has attracted the attention of critics because it is one of the very few moments in the film when music is used. Music is also heard diegetically in the theatre scene, which has prompted analyses that match the two occurrences. The use of music by itself was enough to garner scholarly attention, because Rohmer is known for what David Heinemann calls 'a stylistic asceticism and the elimination of the director's personal presence, achieved through the paring away of editorializing devices such as non-diegetic music, unmotivated camera movements, ostentatious camera placement, and pictorialism' (2000: 50). Although the scene of the resurrected statue could be used as a counter-example to Heinemann's statement, it generally holds true as a succinct description of Rohmer's style.

The cathedral scene is effective in its rendition of a woman's face as it is visited by thoughts, as it visualises these thoughts. Félicie is filmed in close-up as she beholds an invisible thought and her expression suggests the unexpected surge of an idea against what appears to be initially, if not lack of application, at least a drifting thought process. As she tries to hold on to the invisible thought and steer this thought in her mind, Félicie bites her lips and settles into a mid-air stare. For all her delicate performance of the moment, the scene would leave us wondering about the nature of the visiting thought, were it not for the extradiegetic use of the same tune as in the opening the film. Even though this all-important clue takes the viewer back in time, achieving an effect of sudden inner display, it does not translate fully into words. Rohmer seems to be particularly interested in this matter, the verbal account of an event or an emotion, succeeding the showing of that event or emotion.

Rohmer has Félicie talk about the moment twice. During the argument with Maxence, immediately following the contemplative moment, Félicie begins to indirectly explain the significance of the moment. The thought turns out to have been as much a decision ('I can't live with a man that I am not mad about'), as a powerful impression of clarity. She emphasises the fact that she has seen the decision, as opposed to having understood it, and that, following this logic, Maxence could not understand her decision because he did not see it. Seeing yields a special kind of authorisation, one that turns the seer into the sole guardian of an unverified but potent and seemingly incontrovertible personal truth. Interestingly enough, the *paragone* discourse often establishes a hierarchy of senses in which sight is usually endowed with 'special dignity and priority' (Summers 1987: 39). As David Summers points out, for many ancient and Renaissance authors, 'Not only is sight reason-like, but reason is sight-like' (ibid.: 40). In the film, sight, while preserving and even consolidating its 'special dignity', seems to be hailed by Félicie as different from reason. The way she tells it, inner seeing allowed her to take a step back from her own thoughts, as it were, and evaluate them. In the process, her reasoning acquires a hard-hitting quality, unable any more to consent to half measures and middle-of-the-road attitudes. From a privileged position, Félicie imparts her visual revelation first to Maxence, then to Loïc. In this respect, she is like Shakespeare's Paulina, enunciating a belief and overseeing its transmission. As Félicie herself remarks, both Maxence and Loïc are uncharacteristically submissive when faced with her decisions, and, one might add, just as governable as the miracle-seeking Leontes in relation to Paulina. The connection between the theatre performance and the cathedral scene, already adumbrated by the musical motif, is confirmed by the conversation between Félicie and Loïc, in which there is an effortless transition from discussing the faith-awakening moment in the play to recounting the analogous moment in the cathedral.

Loïc first advertises the play to Félicie as 'rocambolesque' (far-fetched, fantastic) and, right after the performance, he reiterates his reservations, declaring himself bothered by the play's 'ambiguity' and calling it 'implausible'. His misgivings specifically revolve around the issue of the queen's reanimated statue, an issue that Félicie seems to have no qualms about and that she dispatches with the word 'faith' ('Faith brings her to life'). If we recall Bert O. States's typology of the actor's phenomenal modes, it is the representational mode with its achievement of 'theatre "magic"' (1983: 370) that Félicie is referencing here, not only in terms of her own reaction to the play, but also in terms of the fictional characters' reaction to Paulina's 'theatre', her careful orchestration of the resurrection effect. At this point, Félicie initiates the account of her visit to the cathedral ('I'll tell you something that will startle you. Yesterday I prayed in a church.'). The prosy details that Félicie provides closely and accurately corroborate the prior visual representation: 'I had sort of a row with Maxence. Something he said hurt me. I went out to get it off my mind. We passed the cathedral, Elise wanted to see the Nativity. Mum told her about God, and set up a Nativity at home. So we went in. While she looked, I sat on a chair.' The sequence in which they are recounted abides by the order in which we first witnessed them. She confesses to suddenly seeing everything clearly, and when asked about what she saw, she answers:

> It's hard to say. I didn't think, I saw my thoughts (*j'ai vu ma pensée*). All my reasoning on whether to leave or not came in a flash. And I saw it, I saw what I had to do, and saw I was right [. . .] Before, I'd tried to choose, then I saw there was no choice. I didn't have to choose something I didn't want. See? I know it sounds trite, but suddenly it became obvious. It's hard to explain [. . .] In that second that was so full of things, I saw I was alone in the world: it was up to me to act and not be pushed around by anyone or anything.

Not unlike the three gentlemen in Shakespeare's play, whose sentiments are 'very much those of [the] "you had to be there"' variety, but whose 'desire to tell is overwhelming' nonetheless (Meek 2006: 398), Félicie admits that her experience, on account of being private, is also, to a certain extent, unnarratable. What she has to tell is 'hard to say', 'hard to explain', yet she does not seem to want to leave it at that, determined to find words for the pregnant moment of her story. What she manages in her account is to verbally circle around this event, emphasising her visual involvement. The film offers a collection of such descriptions and retellings. We are made aware of the Courbevoie–Levallois lapse the moment it happens, as Rohmer draws our attention to the fact that the name inscribed in Charles's notebook does not match the name in the bus itinerary display. The skilful visualisation is then supplemented in the film by Félicie giving a detailed account of her mistake to Maxence. Félicie also discusses her reactions to the play and Maxence and Loïc's reactions to the break-up, despite the fact that the film viewer has already witnessed these reactions. Beyond the extra narrative and character information that these retellings happen to add to the 'original' showing, they are also significant in relation to Polixenes's description of Leontes and Hermione's embrace, a description given on stage simultaneously and alongside the actual embrace and preferred to it by the film camera. Although some may argue, and indeed have argued, that Rohmer manifests a marked predilection for dialogue, and that almost nothing of importance happens in his film without subsequently being told or discussed, I am more inclined to see this combination of showing and telling, usually occurring in this order, as an unmasking of the plurimediality of film, a medium poised between the two possibilities, just like theatre. There is a layering to the problem as well: the fragment of theatre shows and tells of a reunion, whereas the film that incorporates it not only shows and tells of its own reunions, but also intensifies and orients theatre's showing. Furthermore, through the deliberate carelessness of the transition and reframing shots mentioned by Rohmer, left in when they could easily have been debarred, the film is underlining the fact that it is in the process of showing and that the object of this showing is a differently mediated event. Usually acting as a consortium of sorts in representation, showing and telling seem endlessly permutational. What is ultimately at stake in the relationship between showing and telling when it comes to theatre-in-film is the highlighting of the multimodal nature of the two media, of their different, non-conflicting possibilities of staging meaning.

EXIT THE ACTOR: RESTRAINED PERFORMANCES AND THE VIEW FROM THE WINGS IN *I'M GOING HOME*

Randal Johnson has called Manoel de Oliveira's 2001 film *Vou para casa/ Je rentre à la maison/I'm Going Home* 'perhaps his lightest and most accessible film' (2007: 114). Although the assessment is certainly not inaccurate, it does little to prepare the viewer for the richness of the film. It is true, however, that, featuring, like many of Oliveira's other films, a 'montage of texts' (Lavin 2008: 52, my translation), a selection made in this case by Oliveira's literary consultant Jacques Parsi (Ciment and Herpe 2001: 9), *I'm Going Home* is not as obdurate an example of what critics have called the director's 'refusal of naturalism' (ibid.: 155). This refusal of naturalism, sometimes associated with a 'naivety of decor' (Lardeau et al. 1988: 21, my translation), is considered by Mathias Lavin a key element in understanding the use of theatre in Oliveira's films. Lavin begins his analysis of the 'theatrical metaphor' in Oliveira's work by considering the director's own view of the relationship between theatre and life and noting that theatre functions in his films as the ultimate 'expression of the mimetic act' (2008: 154–6, my translation). The connection between theatre and life resides, for Oliveira, in the use of convention. Since our behaviour is subject to conventions, life is in his words 'already a representation of itself', a kind of 'pre-theatre', and, as such, the very condition of possibility of theatre (Lardeau et al. 1988: 85, my translation). In its turn, theatre is at its most authentic ('le théâtre en soi, le vrai théâtre') when it manifests itself as something 'terribly austere and harsh', like a 'testimony in the court of justice' (ibid.). In light of these comments, the theatrical mise-en-scène of his films can be and has been read as a strategy of exposing the generalised, inescapable artificiality of all arts and of life in general. However, this is not going to be my approach in this piece. Instead, as in the immediately preceding case studies, I shall be interested in how the diegetic theatre articulates the relationship between 'someone seeing and what is seen' (Bleeker 2008: 2) and how in its turn, the film camera intervenes in this perceptual field with its own orientation, with a view to arguing that the film sets up a complex relationship between theatrical speech, a distanced mode of viewing and what Carl Plantinga has called 'the scene of empathy' (1999: 239).

Critics have mostly interpreted *I'm Going Home* through the lens of its representation of old age, which is undoubtedly central to the film's concerns (Oliveira himself was in his nineties at the time of the film's production and release). According to Patrice Blouin, *I'm Going Home* draws 'a portrait of the actor as an old man', a story of 'great sufferings and small vexations' (2001: 72–3). Dave Kehr comments that it is 'an impossibly delicate, indirect film about the least delicate of subjects: mortality', about life as 'a series of reductions and denials' (2002: 18). Similarly, for Núria Casado-Gual, the film depicts the main character's 'progressive alienation as a categorized "old man"' (2014: 210). Oliveira himself has stated that he intended to convey the idea of an undeserved tragedy befalling an actor of moral and professional integrity, to explore the notion that we are not masters of our own fate (Ciment and Herpe 2001: 8–9).

The film begins with a lengthy fragment of a theatre performance (Eugène Ionesco's *Le Roi se meurt/Exit the King*), watched impatiently from the wings by three men, one of whom is the actor's agent, while the other two are unnamed and credited as the agent's friends. At the end of the performance, the main character, Gilbert Valence (Michel Piccoli), who played the king on stage, is taken aside by his agent and told the tragic news of the death of his wife, daughter and son-in-law. This makes him the sole guardian of his grandson. The story picks up 'some time later', the indeterminate parenthesis serving as an indication of the kind of indifference to temporality that accompanies mourning. From this point of re-entry into the actor's story, the canvas unfurls of an unhurried routine existence that proves at the end to have been a long preparation for a discreet exit. Gilbert watches his grandson play, takes long walks, buys an expensive pair of shoes, is robbed of these shoes during one of his promenades, and continues working for the theatre, playing Prospero in William Shakespeare's *The Tempest*. As Casado-Gual rightfully points out, 'Even if Le Roi and Prospero are powerful symbols of dispossession at a literary level, in the theatrical world they are signs of prestige for mature performers, and they enable a positive use of agedness on the stage' (2014: 209). Gilbert therefore is initially portrayed as a highly respected actor who can have his choice of roles and who tackles difficult and prestigious parts. We subsequently see him decline an offer to act in a TV series, but deciding to accept the role of a younger character, Buck Mulligan, in a French–American adaptation of James Joyce's *Ulysses*. Gilbert has a humiliating first day of rehearsals, during which he is corrected several times by the American director of the adaptation (John Malkovich) and sent home to study the part. During the second round of rehearsals, which proves even more disastrous than the first, he stops abruptly, announcing that he will go home to rest. At home, he goes upstairs to lie down and the film ends with an enigmatic, prolonged shot of Gilbert's grandson silently watching him. In Dave Kehr's poetic words, we can assume that 'He goes gently, not into the good night but into the warm sunshine of a Paris afternoon' (2002: 18). In Ionesco's *Exit the King* Queen Marguerite warns the four-hundred-year-old king Berenger that he is going to die 'at the end of the show' (Ionesco 1963: 26), and even if the film does not explicitly encourage any meta-reflections on its own time running out, the actor's return home is equated with an exit from the story and from the world.

The longest theatre segment in the film (some thirteen minutes including the curtain call) is the Eugène Ionesco segment, a fragment from his 1962 play *Exit the King*. The segment is actually composed of two separate extracts from the play. The longer section is a tragicomic exchange between the dying king and his diminished entourage, emblematic of the King's denial of his own mortality, stitched together with a shorter extract from the concluding part of the play during which Queen Marguerite, left alone with the King, manages to guide his last steps, remove invisible burdens and instruct her husband to give himself up to death one finger at a time. This is a rather enigmatic ending, showing a training session in accepting death, likened by Ionesco to a Tibetan death rite (Barranger 1975: 504). According to Susan Letzler Cole, the whole play is built around an ambivalence, an interplay of opposites: 'Ionesco's play is energized by the attempt to make fun of, or have fun with, all the things that tragedy takes seriously: in that sense, it is an anti-tragedy. It mocks the protagonist's resistance to dying just as it mocks the attempt of the living to cling to some meaningful bond with the dead' (1991: 86). Inspired perhaps by Ionesco's conflation of the two terms – 'It seems to me that the comic is tragic and that the tragedy of man is pure derision' (cited in Cole 1991: 85) – Oliveira has his character experience, alongside a shattering tragedy, a series of embarrassments, both trivial and more consequential, not so much or not only in order to convey Gilbert's increasing 'fragility as an old man' (Casado-Gual 2014: 209), but also to underscore the absurd juxtaposition of frivolity and seriousness, self-regard and self-abandonment, that combine to make the 'insubstantial pageant' of a lived life.

The playwright's stage directions for the closing of the play require the realisation of a complicated dramatic illusion that the filmmaker seems to have chosen to forgo. In the play, Queen Marguerite's exit on the left gives way to the 'disappearance of the windows, the doors and the walls, the King and the throne', the latter part of the process taking the form of a fade into mist (Ionesco 1963: 93). This exit left of the stage is represented only partially in the film, when Queen Marguerite (Catherine Deneuve) comes into the stage wings, entering the frame from the left. Her entrance, whereby she joins the three messengers and the other actors, is the last link in a network of character movements and camera positions that Oliveira composes around this theatrical performance, which will form the focus of the following section.

Oliveira's film manages to juggle different types of spectatorship and their corresponding perspectives: a generally compliant audience 'chained' to the theatre seats, competent at cueing in laughter and applause during the shows, whose reactions we see a few times and whose perspective is given not in the sense in which it was in *Opening Night* but in a more disembodied way, the involuntary audience made up of the messengers who have no choice but to follow the show to its end, and the film audience who can amalgamate these different perspectives.

The three messengers embody a type of spectatorship on the move. Their first appearance occurs in the theatre boxes, whence they proceed to the corridor encircling the auditorium and leading into the wings of the stage. The next time we encounter these restless spectators, they are in the wings and the stage is situated to the right. The eldest messenger is seated while the other two are striding through the room; he will continue to wait in the wings while the others will resume their perambulation. The two will eventually return to this stage-adjoining space, their entrance revealing the spatial orientation of a wooden mannequin, a dressing screen and a shelves unit, our main landmarks in the layout of the wing. Although the location remains the same throughout these movements, Oliveira places his camera both on the side of the mannequin and the dressing screen and on the opposite side, to the effect that the characters have sometimes to look rightward for the stage and at other times leftward. This inconsistency creates, in spite of the otherwise static use of the camera, a sense of filmic 'agitation' around the theatre performance.

Mathias Lavin notes the 'structuring separation' between stage and auditorium in the film's theatre performances (2008: 174) and, more generally, the importance that the gaze has in creating a pattern of alternation (ibid.: 173) and introducing a 'gap' ('écart') and a shift ('déplacement') between the view from the position of the theatre audience and the view from the wings.

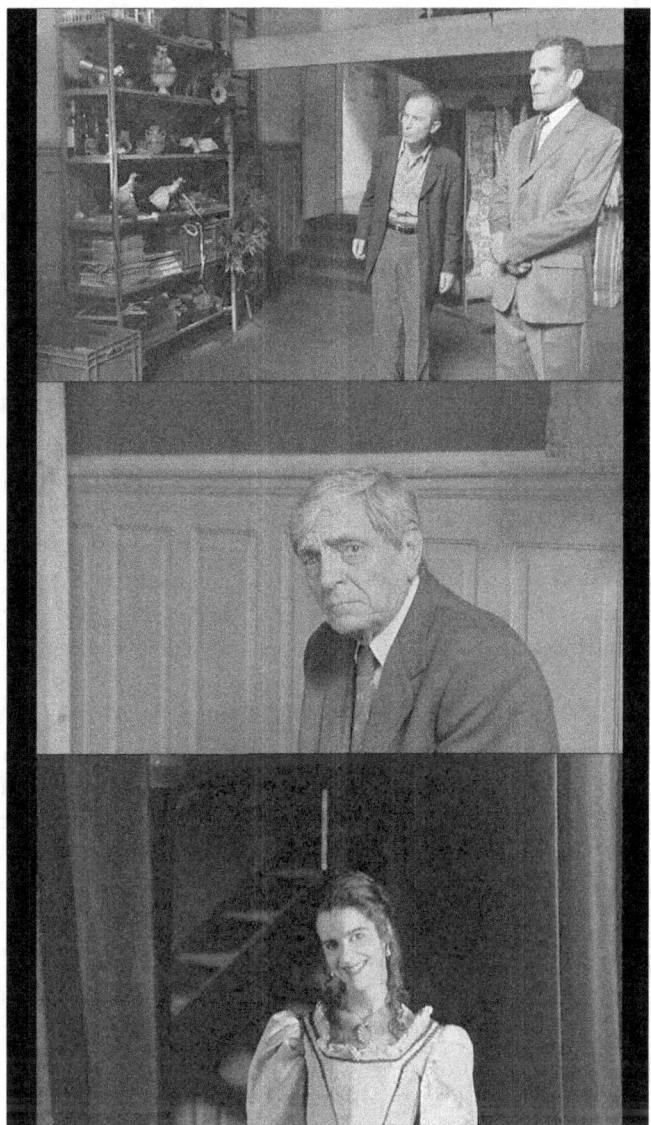

Figure 4.3 Viewers from the wings – *I'm Going Home* (Manoel de Oliveira, 2001, France, Portugal)

He also remarks the parallel development that takes place in the wings with the disquieting arrival of the messengers, which results in the maturation of the 'hypothesis' of a drama into its 'enunciation' (ibid.: 174). In terms of the theatrical stagings in the film, the 'sundry', 'worn-out' decors and costumes lead him to conclude the existence of a 'distance' between the 'idea of theatre' and the 'singularity of the shows' (ibid.: 173; all translations mine). Although his comments are judicious, they are also brief and are, in this sense, an impatient reading that does little to account for the duration and the specifics of the theatrical performances. Although the accumulation of tension in the wings is important in narrative terms, its narrative weight should not override all other considerations. The first segment of theatre is not only significant as a performance that needs to be patiently sat through. There is a deliberate tension between the immediately intelligible arrangement of figures and props on the stage and the way in which the surrounding spaces are somewhat disarranged by editing and varying camera positions. The eager circulation taking place at the peripheries of the stage and the spectating attention that it carries with it confirm the impenetrability of the theatrical event, its wondrous independence, but at the same time invite us to reflect on what it means to see something through a particular perspective, on the differences between a seemingly disembodied perspective and an embodied one.

In her book on visuality in theatre, Maaike Bleeker reprises Hans-Thies Lehmann's comparison between drama and perspective, suggesting that, similarly to the way in which the pictorial perspective creates the sense of an 'objectively given world' (2008: 14), 'the aesthetic logic of the dramatic theatre presents the audience with a stable and detached point of view, allowing spectators to project themselves into the onstage world', which 'simultaneously brings spectators closer to the world onstage, while creating a distance from their bodies as the loci of their looking' (ibid.: 15). Bleeker develops her thought in dialogue not just with Lehmann but also with Barbara Freedman, for whom 'Theatricality evokes an uncanny sense that the given to be seen has the power both to position us and displace us', in the sense that, although ascribed a position, the viewer as a seeing subject does not necessarily have to identify with that position (ibid.: 9). In *I'm Going Home*, the frontal shots of the stage, of which there are several, can be said to epitomise this 'stable and detached point of view' that is equally situating and displacing the spectator.

The mise-en-scène of the theatre performances in Oliveira's film attempts only the slightest orientation of the theatre spectator's seeing. In the case of the first performance, the sparse group of actors moves slowly and sporadically, a little at a time, one of the characters (the guard, played by Ricardo Trêpa) remaining quasi-immobile. The scarcity of movement and the rigidity of the spatial allocation are distorted (in Sarah Bay-Cheng's sense of the word, detailed in Chapter 1 of this book) by the presence of the film camera, which at times chooses to break up the group of actors in sub-groups of two or three and then recompose the unity of the ensemble with views from the wings or from the auditorium. Although all but one of the figures are standing, the stage is composed as a rather narrow seating area. Oliveira's take on the 'vaguely dilapidated, vaguely Gothic' Throne Room imagined by Ionesco (1963: 9) replaces the Gothic design with the slanted ruin of a classical entablature painted on the backdrop. The decor is for the most part a variation on the 'chair' theme. The main throne complete with a canopy, the smaller throne next to it, the child's chair and the wheelchair are used only by the enfeebled king, who first collapses on the queen's throne, later delivers a long speech on the small chair and ends the play on the main throne. For Susan Letzler Cole, the king's 'repeated falling and rising to his feet' represent the '*reductio ad absurdum* of the rise and fall of kings as well as a slapstick version of the conflicting impulses within the tragic protagonist' (1991: 86). The king's wobbly movements are at all times overseen by his entourage, a group that exists in a tight co-ordination of reactions. When the king sits down on the small chair, his back to the audience, the figures surrounding him (on one side, the two queens, played by Catherine Deneuve and Leonor Silveira, and the maid, Juliette (Leonor Baldaque), on the other, the doctor, played by Jean-Michel Arnold) arrange themselves in a succession of profiles turned towards the king, from either side. This is the main type of perceptual orientation encouraged by the first theatrical staging: a synchronous orchestration of character behaviour that does not leave the theatre spectator in doubt about where s/he should look.

Although a sense of focus is achieved, this type of theatrical composition has an altogether different effect from a point of view. As Daphna Ben Chaim notes, the relationship between the dramatic representation and the 'perceptual activity of the spectator' does not lend itself to a point-of-view type of arrangement:

> When the actor steps upstage center, the audience tends to notice him, but the movement does not necessarily express a particular orientation to the fictional character or to the play as a whole. Although various directorial decisions can force (or encourage) the viewer to focus on particular characters or activities onstage, it is difficult to control the various physical elements in the theatre to enforce a point of view toward the work [. . .] (1981: 65)

Chaim refers here to point of view as orientation of the play's fictional world and of the viewer's relation to it, and not in the more general sense of the different creative constraints and theatrical codes used in its staging, as was the case with Josette Féral's distinction between performance and theatre, referenced in my analysis of *Opening Night*. A similar point is made by Anne Ubersfeld, who remarks that in theatre we do not have 'the sort of dissection of the image perceived by a single glance, the sort of framing and cutting up into shots that, in cinema, lead the viewer by the hand' (cited in Gaudreault 2009: 84) and that consequently the theatre spectator 'must frame and organize his or her perception, must remember' (ibid.: 85), whereas the film medium operates with what André Gaudreault calls 'an intermediary gaze' (ibid.).

Film is far more adept at conveying point of view. The messengers are often expectantly observing the performance and there are several shots of the stage from the wings, not always strictly point-of-view shots but aligned with the messengers nonetheless. When the agent and one of his friends return in the wings, they immediately start watching the actors towards the left of the frame and the next shot is that of the stage as it would appear from the wings. The initial disposition of the actors on stage slightly reshuffles, as if in response to the presence of the spectating messengers. At one point the actress played by Catherine Deneuve takes a few steps, briefly addresses the guard and then slightly gyrates, to face the wings. In her turn, Juliette directs her snide comment about the king's embalmment towards the messengers. The camera then returns to the wings, this time to register the elder messenger in the position of the beholder, and lingers a while on his anguished face before turning to the mannequin. The image of the mannequin is joined with the king's stutter, at the precise point of transition from one section of the play to the next, after which the elder messenger is seen joining his two friends.

The eyeline match structure that interconnects the three messengers, by beginning with the agent and one of his friends looking at the stage, revealing the performance from the wings and subsequently presenting it as the object of the third messenger's gaze, manages a subtle reassignment of perspective. The camera dwells on the reaction of the elder messenger at the moment in the play when the king says that he does not want to be a corpse, burned, buried or thrown to the vultures, but would take instead a warm embrace. While these lines are uttered, the elder messenger sits slightly hunched over, looking at the stage then downward at the floor then glancing away at the mannequin, lips pursed as if suppressing tears, his shoulders seen rising and falling in a sigh. The shot calls to mind 'the scene of empathy' conceptualised by Carl Plantinga as a scene in which 'we see a character's face, typically in close-up, either for a single shot of a long duration or as an element of a point-of-view structure', where the 'prolonged concentration on the character's face' serves to 'elicit empathetic emotions in the spectator', allowing him/her to 'catch' the emotion of the character (1999: 239, 243). As Plantinga argues, the significance of the scene of empathy goes beyond the mere function of communicating the emotion of the character to enabling the emotion to become 'contagious', to spread to the spectator (ibid.: 248–9). For this empathetic response to occur, several conditions need to be met, such as the provision of sufficient narrative context (ibid.: 251), the effective integration of the scene in the film's 'moral and ideological project' (ibid.: 253) and the establishing of a degree of 'affective congruence between narrative context, character engagement, various uses of film style and technique, and the psychological impressions and responses they generate' (ibid.). The scene of empathy is a fairly conventional technique, but, given Oliveira's modernist credentials, the use of the device in the film is not as straightforward as it might seem.

Let us consider, for instance, the issue of narrative context. The messenger's empathetic response is dependent on his ability to correlate the acted emotions of a fictive body (Gilbert playing the dying king and the emotions triggered by his imminent death) with the anticipated emotion of the tragic disclosure to follow (the death of the actor's family). This ability anchors the emotions to the extent that the messenger appears 'under-distanced', as Chaim would say, a spectator who feels too much. However, as film spectators, we are asked to watch a scene of empathy before we are given the information that would allow us to make the same connections, and although the emoting face of the elder messenger creates a sense of emotional foreknowledge, we are insufficiently equipped from an epistemic point of view. Moreover, if we take into account the film's later narrative developments and strategies, the use of the scene of empathy appears even more unconventional. At various points throughout the narrative, the film denies us access to facial expressions. In one of its most striking scenes, Gilbert and his agent are conversing in a café. Gilbert is very pleased with the pair of expensive shoes he bought, shoes he will be robbed of before the evening is over, and during the conversation, instead of capturing the faces of the two conversing friends, the camera is kept for a good few minutes at the level of their feet. The agent's suggestion that Gilbert seek female company to alleviate his solitude, the actor's increasing annoyance with the suggestion and his slip into a mock-declamatory mode towards the end of the exchange, are not shown through a focus on the faces, but by paying attention to the characters' feet and their occasional movements. This deliberate avoidance of facial expressiveness stands at odds with the previously described scene of empathy.

In the second theatrical performance of the film, the staged text consists of a fragment from *The Tempest*'s Act IV, Scene One, containing Prospero's oft-quoted revels speech followed by a dialogue between Prospero and Ariel about Caliban, Stephano and Trinculo and their mutinous plans against the magician. The play is replete with performances, as the spirits led by Ariel are asked several times by Prospero to enact masques and 'tricks' (Shakespeare 2007: 38). The vanishing banquet, described by Sebastian as a 'living drollery' (ibid.: 35), is one such trick, another being the wedding masque of Act IV. The wedding masque is performed by spirits native to the island, who, in the play, take the shape of nymphs and reapers summoned by Iris and joined in a 'graceful dance' to celebrate a 'contract of true love' (ibid.: 40). Although in the play Ferdinand talks of a 'majestic vision', the staging we see in the film limits the realisation of this vision to a set of underwhelming blue veils hovering above the heads of the actors for a few instants in the sounds of a violin score. The decor is minimal and, one could speculate, requiring little if any modification, given the fact that the dramatic events take place for the most part on Prospero's island. Just as in the first performance, the stage arrangement is conventional, with the auditorium directly facing the stage. This type of stage design has inspired Oliveira to declare that theatre is truly operating with an 'angle/reverse angle' logic – 'Le théâtre use de l'authentique champ/contrechamp' (cited in Lardeau et al. 1988: 87). The staging emphasises the elevation of the stage in relation to the auditorium by having an oversized trapezoidal sandbox placed on the stage, thus creating an enclosure within the already existing one. In the brief shot that reveals this spatial layout, the perceptual impediment created by the raised frontal curb and the depth of stage visually enhanced by the diagonal borders make for a mix of obstruction and visual draw. Yet, during most of the performance the camera shuns the observational particularities resulting from the creation of the island on stage and the degree of visual accessibility possible within the context of a theatrical space, insisting on a mid-shot of Valence during the revels speech which could be described, paraphrasing Edward Branigan, as an 'ideal' view 'from nowhere' in the theatre (1984: 4). As in the first theatre performance, the wings are not inert neighbouring spaces. The actress playing Miranda (Leonor Baldaque), after exiting the stage, lingers in the wings, trying to catch Valence's gaze. His muted annoyance with her infatuation temporarily detaches him from the role. This micro-reaction disconnecting the actor from the energy of his performance is noticed by Miranda and, through her, by the film spectator but conceivably remains undetectable by the theatre spectators in the auditorium.

If we depart from the assumption that the theatre spectator's relation to the play is defined partially by his/her ability to notice the changing 'ranking of all its partial texts – the spoken text, the gestural text, the scenery, music, sound effects' (De Marinis 1987: 37), then one might be inclined to suggest that in *I'm Going Home* both the theatre and the film spectator are encouraged to interact with the theatre performances mostly at the level of the spoken word. Oliveira's views about films incorporating or adapting pre-existent texts seem to prescribe precisely such a logocentric staging. With regard to one of his earlier films, *Amor de Perdição/Ill-fated Love* (1978), Oliveira remarked that the presence and the body of the actor are generally the commanding element in a performance and that, for this reason, they can easily distract the attention of the spectator from the text (Oliveira in Lardeau et al.: 100). Oliveira went on to suggest that an actor given to gestural restraint, to immobility even, can counteract this potential for distraction of the figure, causing the attention of the spectator to revert to the text (ibid.). Jared Rapfogel came to a similar conclusion when he remarked that 'In Oliveira's hands, each text is not a starting point but an inviolable element' that actors are encouraged to deliver 'stripped of melodrama, expressiveness, or affect' (2008: 15).

The revels speech has Gilbert as Prospero advance closer to the auditorium (even closer to the camera), occupying a position from which his gaze pans from left to right and back again. He occasionally makes a half-turn towards Ferdinand to whom he initially addresses the speech, again positioning himself ambiguously as a lone figure who thinks aloud and at the same time as someone who is never too far removed from the company of others, be they humans or spirits. As the actor pauses for words, his hands seem to decipher an invisible score, accompanying the leisurely delivery with gestures that give an extra sense of its flow, its accents and its temporary halts. In keeping with Oliveira's distrust of movement in performance, in this particular instance the actor's gestures are not distracting the spectator from following the speech as they are designed to draw attention to its phrasing and punctuation. My analysis of the rigid composition of the first theatre staging in the film can equally be read in support of this view.

Oliveira has been quoted saying that 'if cinema is movement, it is thanks to the speech. It is the sound which is movement, not the image' (Lardeau et al. 1988: 73, my translation). In another interview, while pleading for 'slow' films, he proposed that 'speech is an image', an idea that Oliveira arrived at via a Molière statement: 'La parole est faite pour expliquer la pensée, mais elle est en même temps le portrait de la pensée'/'Speech is meant to explain thought/thinking, but it is at the same time the portrait of thought' (Ciment and Herpe 2001: 12, my translation). If, for Oliveira, visuality is already contained in speech, what results is an unsettling of the very notion of spectatorship for both theatre and film. On the basis of the previously analysed extracts, it is safe to suggest that Oliveira's filmmaking practice demonstrates a propensity to emphasise an underlying verbality which sets in motion the actors in the theatre and the complex networks of gazes around them. This is also consistent with Oliveira's idea of a 'return to theatre' that he justifies as a reaction to a cinema that has become 'too technical', a return that would allow cinema to function as 'our modern theatre' (Lardeau et al. 1988: 88, my translation).

Precisely because of the centrality of speech, the film emphasises, even outside and beyond the theatre performances, the listening dimension of spectating. During the first rehearsal for the Ulysses project, soon after his entry into the scene as Buck Mulligan, Gilbert Valence is relegated to the off-camera space from where only his voice will make its way to the film spectator. Valence is reduced to a voice. He receives no instructions about his movements within the scene, or about the use of gestures; the only elements that are constantly under painful scrutiny are his intonation and his mastery of the lines. The film director, played by John Malkovich, corrects Gilbert's 'I told the milk woman to come after eight' with 'I told her to come after eight', and when the mistake is repeated during the second rehearsal, the rectification is reiterated as well. Blatantly miscast as a younger and vociferous character, the actor is dealing simultaneously with a failing memory and with problems of linguistic adjustment. An ill-starred performance to begin with, his rendition hobbles with barely remembered lines that cause the director to grimace or intervene. Gilbert literally does not sound the part. The director's attention is fastidiously analysing the sound of the performance, its progression, constantly comparing it with his own representation of how the text should be read, with a desired vocality. Oliveira uses the scene of empathy again, but in reverse compared with the previous instance. The fictional director's face is presented in a medium close-up as he listens to Gilbert's performance and the shot is prolonged: we see him blinking repeatedly and skin-picking at his fingers, clear signs of discomfort and unease. Our empathy, I would argue, is, however, not aligned with John Malkovich's character but with the old actor struggling with his lines off-screen.

To conclude, in this sub-chapter I have argued that in *I'm Going Home*, the film spectator and her theatre proxies are coming together through their shared attention to sound. The film uses and at the same time questions the scene of empathy, underscoring the function of the spoken word as the prime mover of the theatre and film performances.

CHAPTER FIVE

Cinematic Monologues and their Spectatorial Address

The previous chapter examined different forms of correlation between the audience's experience and the actors' performative address, by drawing on theories of performance, spectatorship and theatre phenomenology. The present chapter will expand the reflection on the relation between performer and spectator to include a theatrical and literary device that has found its way into cinema as well, namely the monologue. In this chapter, I shall consider several broadly understood forms of monologue that serve different purposes and are to be understood within different traditions and contexts (the Brechtian tradition, the ekphrastic tradition, the solo performance and verbatim theatre). At the same time, I shall attempt to connect the different understandings of monologue with recent scholarship on direct address in cinema.

The reason I mentioned that the monologues selected for this chapter are broadly understood as such is because the term 'monologue', like most frequently used terms, is not easy to disentangle. Patrice Pavis, for instance, defines it as 'a speech by a character to himself' and differentiates it from soliloquy, which for him is 'addressed directly to an interlocutor who does not speak' (1998: 218). However, for many other scholars, the reverse seems to be true. For others still, the soliloquy is a variety of monologue (Baldick 2001: 161). It would appear that there is also a degree of interchangeability as regards how the two terms have been used so far. Since the discussion of my case studies will in fact draw insight from this distinction as well as from features that are discussed in relation to both terms, I shall briefly pause to consider in more detail how they have been understood, addressing further terminological complications as they arise.

The soliloquy is generally conceptualised as a form of self-address or self-talk, which often also entails a type of dialogism. Carol MacKay traces it back to Saint Augustine and defines it as 'solitary speech', a speech which, originally at least, could 'merge into prayer or an internal series of thoughts' (1987: 1). MacKay is also keen to point out that, even as a matter of literary and dramatic convention, speaking aloud to oneself has been perceived as 'somehow unnatural' and that consequently it was not uncommon for it to be accompanied by an explanation or apology, or for soliloquists to be presented as 'self-conscious and fearful of being overheard' (ibid.). The issue of the naturalisation of the device, be it monologue or soliloquy, is especially important for film, a medium in the theory of which issues of verisimilitude and plausibility often rank high. The dialogic aspect of the dramatic soliloquy manifests itself when the character 'gives voice to two or more distinct emotions' (Hirsh 2012: 312) or deliberates between the terms of an inner conflict, whereas in philosophy, the soliloquy is treated as a 'rational dialogue (or dialogue with Reason) in which questions are asked and answers given within the mind of a single person' (Stock 2010: 1). For Saint Augustine, whom most accounts credit with the invention of the term, the aim of the soliloquy is to attain self-knowledge (ibid.: 6), which puts us on the right path to understand the use of the soliloquy as a form of articulating the self.

The presence of 'dialogic traits' has been noted with regard to monologue as well, for instance by Patrice Pavis, who reprises Émile Benveniste's understanding of monologue as 'internalized dialogue', carried out between 'a speaking I and a listening I' (1998: 218). A recent study on the contemporary American monologue provides a useful historical context around the development of the device and its resurgence in recent times, reviewing a wide range of cognate forms and sub-types from the expository speeches of ancient tragedies, through Shakespeare's soliloquies and Eugene O'Neill's 'thought asides' to Samuel Beckett's reworking of the 'monodrama' (Paterson 2015: 13–37). In delineating this context, Eddie Paterson notes that while 'in linguistic terms monologic speech is both univocal and monophonic', in reality 'solo speech is far more likely to exist in a complicated relationship with dialogue' and that, as a piece of sustained speech that allows 'a single voice to assert itself', the monologue is a 'seductive type of speech' (ibid.: 13). This is worth keeping in mind especially since, in the case of performers such as Spalding Gray, the inner dialogism of the monologues has often led to the positing of a split subject.

In terms of its address, the monologue is generally understood to be aimed at a spectator and as taking him/her as 'an accomplice and a watcher/hearer' but also involving more generally the 'world of which it speaks': 'the whole stage becomes the monologuist's discursive partner' (Pavis 1998: 219). This complicated reach, at once targeted and inclusive, isolating and collaborative, makes the monologue an unsettling element to incorporate in any medium and genre. There are also medium-specific complications: the direct address of the monologue has different phenomenological implications in film and theatre. As Stanton B. Garner Jr. notes,

> although a character/actor in a film may stare directly at the camera and hence 'at' the spectator, in the absence of a live performer such a gaze is never

in any genuine sense reciprocal, though we may laugh at the sleight of hand that may pretend that this is so [. . .] Despite the insulating 'otherness' of dramatic fiction, the dynamics of theatrical watching are much more complex. The performer/character's gaze, like the body's living presence that it asserts, exceeds the containing parameters of representational space and confronts the audience's gaze with an intersubjectivity that represents a potential or actual 'catastrophe' in terms of spectatorial detachment. (1994: 49)

Garner alludes here to the frequent association between the breaking of the fourth wall and the distanciation of the spectator, complicating the matter by proposing that the body of the performer in theatre, as a 'sign that looks back' (ibid.), can undermine this distanciation. The issue of the differences between filmic direct address and theatrical direct address has also been raised by Tom Brown: 'In contrast with live theatre, whose actors are fully present to its spectators and in which interaction (or inter-acknowledgment, at least) is sometimes expected/encouraged and/or a convention, a film performance was recorded in a place and a time removed from the moment of its spectating' (2012: xii). Brown does not restrict the use of the direct address to direct verbal communication, of which the monologue is an important type, and some of the forms of direct address he analyses are in fact silent (the characters merely looking at the camera as if in acknowledgement of the film spectator). His book is an important contribution to the understanding of the device in cinema, especially as it concerns a type of direct address that 'intensifies' the film viewer's 'relationship with the fiction' rather than weakens it (ibid.: x). Relevant to the scope and interests of this chapter is his insistence that 'direct address can create a peculiarly intimate link between performer/character and audience *at the same time* as helping to open up a kind of critical distance in the characterisation' (ibid.: 117, emphasis in the original).

The notion of spectatorial address has also been discussed by Richard Rushton in his take on Michael Fried's (1980) famous distinction between absorption and theatricality, between works of art which appear to be oblivious of the presence of the spectator and those which are conscious of their status as objects to be looked at. Rushton (2004) connects Fried's distinction with another pair of similarly positioned concepts, namely voyeurism and exhibitionism, seeking to foreground their complementarity. For Rushton, absorption and theatricality are neither as straightforward nor as easy to separate as they might initially seem. Using examples culled from classical cinema, Rushton shows that its mode of viewing is

> one which establishes a tense dialectic between the spectator's seeking of the film, that is, *the spectator's absorptive pull into the film*, and the film's seeking of the spectator, the film's attempt to 'present' itself to the spectator, in other words, its *theatricality*. (Rushton 2004: 234, emphasis in the original)

Building on Brown and Rushton's dialectics of intimacy and critical distance, absorption and theatricality, the present chapter will unravel at the core of the analysed monologues a number of similar dialectical tensions, between interruption and continuity (*The Travelling Players*), representation and misrepresentation (*My Dinner with André*), improvisational freedom and fixity (Spalding Gray's performance films), individual focus and collective re-enactment (*The Arbor*). The chapter will probe the complexities of various forms of monologue in cinema, by analysing them in their narrative contexts and through the formal strategies they employ to position the film spectator in relation to the monologue's purveyor.

THE TRAVELLING PLAYERS AND THE HISTORICAL MONOLOGUE

Theo Angelopoulos's film *O Thiassos/The Travelling Players* (1975) is sometimes grouped together with *Days of '36* (1973), *The Hunters* (1977) and *Megalexandros* (1980) to form the director's 'historical tetralogy'. Interestingly enough, the eponymous travelling players also make a brief appearance in Angelopoulos's *Landscape in the Mist* (1988), but, as Les Roberts argues, in this later film they are 'ravaged by time' and engaging in a 'cacophony of monologues' (2005: 334), their function emblematic and self-referential, but their presence ultimately undeveloped. Although part of a cycle of films, *The Travelling Players* also stands out through its sustained interest in theatre. Critical estimates of the film have proposed plural forms of detection and analysis of the employment of theatre in the film, some obvious, others more studied, but all pointing to the existence of a rich texture of references. The inevitable starting point for all of these readings is constituted by the most explicit instances of embedded theatre, namely the fragments from Spyros Peresiadis's pastoral drama *Golfo the Shepherdess*, the myth of the Atrides referenced in the names and the relationships between the characters, and the theatrical masks and costumes. Before zooming in on the use of monologue in the film, some clarification of the heavily theatricalised ambiance of the film is in order.

The film begins in 1952, with a group of actors arriving in Aegion, during the political campaign leading to the election of Field Marshall Papagos as the Prime Minister of Greece. As we follow the actors walking down the main street, the time frame subtly changes to 1939, when the same theatre company, in a larger formula, arrived in Aegion during the regime of another self-proclaimed 'Saviour of the Nation', General Metaxas. The segment of time between these two right-wing dictatorships is the interval of the film's story, which charts the journey of the actors through an embattled and impoverished Greece. In the course of these thirteen years, the troupe gradually loses some of its most prominent members. The head of the travelling players, Agamemnon (Stratos Pachis), is executed by a firing squad, after a fellow actor, the pro-fascist Aegisthus (Vangelis Kazan), informs the Gestapo that he was hiding an Englishman. The film's Elektra (Eva Kotamanidou) conspires with her brother Orestes (Petros Zarkadis) to kill Aegisthus and their unfaithful mother Clytemnestra (Aliki Georgoulis), during a performance of the pastoral drama. Orestes, a communist sympathiser and guerrilla fighter in the anti-fascist resistance movement, is eventually captured and put to death. However, despite these losses, the company also has mechanisms of regeneration and the film ends with the son of Elektra's sister Chrysothemis (Maria Vassiliou) making his debut in *Golfo the Shepherdess* as Tassos, a role consecutively held by Agamemnon, Orestes, Orestes's friend, Pylades (Kyriakos Katrivanos), and Aegisthus.

According to Marina Kotzamani, *Golfo the Shepherdess* was a staple of 'the repertory of the *boulokia*, itinerant popular theatre companies active until the 1950s in Greece' (2009: 26). The play has the added value of being somewhat of a landmark in Greek film culture. It was its adaptation that resulted in 'the first full-length Greek feature film [...] produced in 1914 and first exhibited in January 1915' (Langman 2000: 196). In the context of *The Travelling Players*, *Golfo the Shepherdess* is generally interpreted as a mystifying object, vehicle of a 'reactionary ideology' (Demopoulos and Liappas 2001: 20), sitting in an uneasy relationship with the rest of the story, an 'outdated drama', projecting the 'smooth image, deprived of perspective, of an archaic Greece, captured at a standstill, outside history' (Rollet 1993: 18, my translation), in marked contrast with the way in which the plot of the film is at all times framed by historical events pertaining to the troubled interval 1939–52.

For most exegetes, the fact that the performance of the play is 'stopped, hectored, harassed or violently interrupted' (Wilmington 1997: 62) is indicative of the merciless intrusion of history upon the lives of the actors. According to Linda Myrsiades, the performance is 'violated because the world rejects idylls' (2000: 140). The film's spaces, the streets, the squares, the tracts of land are often astir with commotion. There are marches, demonstrations, assemblies of all kinds, which engulf or intersect the movement of the actors, who are often seen joining the crowds or being rescued by them. At other times, we are surprised to suddenly discover one of the actors in the crowds. At a political demonstration taking place in a square, the military forces open fire on the participants and, as a result, the crowd scatters in all directions, leaving behind several bodies. Having feigned its injury, one of these bodies comes back to life, only to reveal itself as the accordionist of the theatre company. Wherever they turn, the actors are confronted with the signs of an unstable political landscape, an ever-changing and always eventful backdrop to their itinerancy. The challenged theatre company regroups each time around the production of *Golfo*, as if to guard and pass on a legacy of resilience.

Angelopoulos has stated that, considered against this volatile historical background, 'the play itself gains another dimension. Let's take, for example, one line from the play: "Are we being watched?" This doesn't have anything to do with the popular drama anymore; it refers to the actors themselves, the characters of the film' (Demopoulos and Liappas 2001: 20). This type of parallelism exists, in one form or another, in almost all my case studies. In *The Travelling Players*, it is combined, most interestingly, with examples of divergence between the play and the story of the actors. At the beginning of the play, Tassos describes an idyllic landscape with 'peaks drenched in sunlight', singing nightingales and partridges bathing in the streams. Even if the pastoral play ends in tragedy, the setting is, at least initially, favourable to the young love, in stark opposition to the constantly inimical weather that characterises the atmosphere of the film. Furthermore, the play seems to subscribe to one of the defining features of the pastoral genre, 'the ideal of otium' (Alpers 1982: 437). When he meets Golfo, Tassos tells her that she should not be afraid of prying looks, as the clouds surround them 'like a blanket thrown from heaven to shield us from malicious gossip and indiscreet eyes'. No such heavenly blanket is afforded to the actors. They are seen hiding in the streets, trying not to get caught in the line of fire, and they are almost gunned down in the middle of the night. When they arrive in Aegion (in 1939 and again in 1952), they confess to being tired ('We hadn't slept for two days'). Under constant military threat of one kind or another, the Greece they are familiar with could not be more different from the 'locus amoenus' of the pastoral.

Aeschylus's *Oresteia* provides the basic scheme of family relations that turns the ensemble of actors into a group progressively eroded by different forms of disloyalty, but it is also an echo of classical Greece and of a different kind of theatre, counterposed to both the pastoral production and to the more modern interventions in the film (especially Brechtian theatre). Andrew Horton (1997) also traces in the film the triple influence of Greek blues (*rebetika* music), Greek popular theatre (*Karaghiozis* shadow puppet theatre) and Greek vaudeville (*epitheorisis*). The influence of *rebetika* translates for Horton in the 'motionless and expressionless' manner of the characters (ibid.: 49–50). The influence of Karaghiozis seems to be a more diffuse effect, found both at a thematic level and in the 'visual framing':

> In *The Travelling Players* the line of the players standing in bright backlight at the tavern window doing their little preview song and dance is a direct reminder of the warm-up dance tune played at the beginning of every Karaghiozis presentation [. . .] There is one other characteristic at the heart of what Karaghiozis represents for Greeks, and that is the capacity to endure.

> Angelopoulos shares this spirit. Sometimes Karaghiozis wins, and just as often he is tricked and cheated and beaten himself. But he goes on. Similarly, the 'framing' shot of the players in *The Travelling Players* standing, suitcases in hand, at the railroad station, but at two completely different time periods, suggests that they too keep on playing and keep on travelling. (ibid.: 52–3)

The *Yaxebore* preview song, mentioned by Horton, is witnessed in its full glory early on, but the film also interferes with its performances by removing them from conventional spaces and placing them in alternative arenas (the beach, the mountains). The outbursts of song in the film have generally been read as signs of renewed bonding, as declarations of togetherness in the face of adversity, but they are also the reaffirmation of a status, despite the fact that at times the audience appears to be absent. As Linda Myrsiades has noted, preview songs are consistent with what is known of the Greek theatre of the 1940s, when regional travelling troupes, occasionally facing animosity, would take care 'to announce themselves before they entered an unfamiliar town', trying to 'gauge its relative friendliness or hostility, typically offering a town, as indeed Angelopoulos's troupe does, free samples of its skits and songs' (2000: 137). Initially performed in the film by a large ensemble in suitable attire and in front of an audience, the song is later reprised by a diminished troupe, performed in ordinary clothes and for no immediately perceivable audience in a wintry and mountainous setting. The actors are starving and their performance is brought to a sudden halt by the sight of male corpses hanged from a tree. The actors led by Aegisthus and Clytemnestra start off from assigned positions, three pairs following one another, but as they descend on the sinuous mountain path, making their way through a visibly ruined village, they move in and out of their arrangement, a gambolling and vivacious suite. Even if they do not seem to be watched, the song they are performing still preserves the attributes of a theatrical enticement. The concerted effort is hyperbolically jubilant and in open disregard of the hostile season and the reigning insentience. Originally designed to lure the audience out of its hiding places, when stripped of its effects, the song can be seen to draw attention to the eminently adjustable character of the performance. The reprise of *Yaxebore* is also similar in kind to other non-theatrical public manifestations. Later in the film, the decapitated heads of two communist rebels are held up for display by a soldier in a military jeep driving through a village and the grim spectacle is complete with a similar dancing and music-making retinue. This similarity suggests that at least from a formal point of view, the promotion of the play through an independent musical number is closely related to the agitated political life of the Greek provinces through which the actors are passing, as if they were both fuelled by the same drive.

The unconventional rendition of the preview song is not the only instance when the actors are seen performing outside a 'proper' theatrical context. At least twice during the film, they are asked to identify themselves as actors in what I shall call an 'evidential performance'. During the German night raid which results in the capture and killing of Agamemnon, the search for the Englishman they were suspected of hiding takes the form of a screen test of sorts for the actors. Each in his/her turn is required to go on stage and recite lines from the play. This brief demonstration need not constitute an example of good acting, as what is at stake is not an assessment of craftsmanship. Instead, the purpose of the raid is to identify in the actors' midst a non-native incapable of producing, upon request, a random, memorised fragment. Geared towards a fast acquittal, the performance is equated with an act of unstrained recollection. Within this narrow compass, the actors opt for different ways of discharging the duty: they perform the request in a bland, inexpressive way (Chrysothemis, Aegisthus), they become effortlessly histrionic (Clytemnestra) or they use the words of the play to incriminate and defy the Nazis (Elektra, the elder actor). Interestingly enough, the scene of the raid is inaugurated by an example of 'real' life acting. Aegisthus, the Nazis' informant, lets them in while the others are asleep. He then resumes his position on the floor, lying next to one of his fellow actors, pretending to be awoken and surprised by their intrusion.

The second evidential performance occurs on a beach, as the actors cross paths with a group of British soldiers. After inspecting their luggage and correctly reading the costume clues, the English officer urges them to act, a demand that turns into insistence when the soldiers join in. As a result, the play is performed out of a suitcase. The loss of troupe members causes the roles to be redistributed among the remaining actors. The accordionist, initially in charge with the dramatic exordium and the epilogue, takes over the role of Tassos's father and he also, quite literally, brings the curtain down at the end of the performance. The few theatrical conventions that are still kept in place (the scenic backdrop and the curtain) are manipulated in daylight by the actors doubling as stagehands. The backdrop of a stream coursing down is held up in front of the sea, and the performance is thus thrice handicapped (the actors have to play more than one role, they are not wearing their costumes and the natural setting overpowers the effect of the decor). The unusual circumstances surrounding the performance seem to exempt the actors from a fastidious impersonation. As he kneels down in front of a dying Tassos, played by Aegisthus, the elder actor already carries the accordion that he will use to conclude the scene, as a different character. The result is a performance which looks fast-tracked and rudimentary, unable to realise all of its effects. Given the linguistic barrier between the Greek actors and the

British soldiers and the lack of staging amenities, the play seems to rely on its elementary appeal, on its easily communicable events. The ending, showing three characters fallen to the ground, either dead or in extreme grief, seems to 'translate' particularly well. The scene also illustrates what Angelopoulos described as one of his chief strategies in the film: 'Certain acts and events are repeated all through the film and given more than one sense' (Demopoulos and Liappas 2001: 37). Thus, the fictional death of Tassos and Golfo on the improvised stage coincides with the actual death of a British soldier, gunned down while watching the performance. The evidential performances foreground theatre as something to be displayed or succinctly demonstrated. In the first example, the German raid, we are dealing with an aberration of the function of the performance, with theatre used as an identity check, instrumentalised. In the case of the beach performance, the 'on demand' nature of its occurrence and the unconventional space in which it has to happen seem to operate in a subtractive way, merging the roles and filtering out the unmanageable elements.

An important strand of theatricality in the film is the Brechtian aesthetic, favoured in their analyses by reviewers such as Isabelle Jordan and Susan Tarr, but also acknowledged by Angelopoulos himself: 'What I was trying to achieve is a kind of Brechtian epic, where no psychological interpretation is necessary' (Demopoulos and Liappas 2001: 18). Isabelle Jordan is equally categorical: '*The Travelling Players* is an epic film just like Brecht's non-Aristotelian theatre is an epic theatre' (1975: 15, my translation). She then goes on to isolate the three characteristics that warrant this verdict. First of all, the film 'refers to known events at the same time as it emphasises particular events', meaning that the template provided by the ancient tragedy divests the plot of 'anecdotal surprise' (ibid.: 16), but a certain measure of specificity is ensured all the same by the historical events, which remind us that the 'conflict is not personal but political' (ibid.: 17). Furthermore, the film is 'gestural' and it 'practises the interruption of action, arousing the interest of the public through astonishment' (ibid.: 15). The last two characteristics are discussed together, following the example of Walter Benjamin, who posited that gestures are best remembered when interrupted. For Jordan, this function of interruption devolves upon the 'frontally framed monologue' ('monologue frontal') (ibid.: 19; all translations mine). Similarly, Susan Tarr and Hans Proppe identify in the film a 'dialectic of historical continuity', relying on three main devices: 'time shifts within one sequence', 'the interruption of the players' performance by history' and 'the use of soliloquies' (1976: 5), these combined strategies placing Angelopoulos, according to the authors, in the company of Brecht, Piscator, Vertov and Godard, who similarly create a sense of 'critical distance for the audience while engaging them as participants at the cognitive level' (ibid.: 6). In addition to these Brechtian effects and influences, Angelos Koutsourakis (2015) has traced the importance of Brecht's notion of *Fabel* understood as 'collective narrative' in both *The Travelling Players* and more broadly in Angelopoulos's political phase (1970–80).

David Bordwell also situates Angelopoulos in the company of 'politicized modernists' (2005: 156), but he does so by exploring the director's use of de-dramatisation techniques such as inexpressive shots and *temps morts* as part of his 'long shot long take aesthetic'. Bordwell provides a compelling inventory of staging techniques employed by Angelopoulos, including centring, aperture framing, three-quarter dorsality and planimetric imagery, arguing that the director was a veritable 'synthesiser' of modernist filmmaking (2005: 140–85). However, despite the noted allegiance to the de-dramatisation tradition, Bordwell argues that Angelopoulos never opted for the kind of 'emotional neutrality' one might encounter in the works of some of the other political modernists: 'even in his "Brechtian" days', Bordwell remarks, 'Angelopoulos gave his work a strong emotional overlay' (1997: 24). For his part, Angelos Koutsourakis (2015) has argued that Brecht himself was not entirely and not straightforwardly opposed to emotions, but rather interested in foregrounding and mobilising their social dimensions. Bordwell is not the only one to argue that Angelopoulos's cinema brings a Brechtian approach with a difference. Linda Myrsiades remarks that 'sliding in and out of character in the monologues both deepens the role in an act of self-reflexivity and flattens it as it loses its existential reality, giving the film character a prismatic quality as if perceived from more than one angle at the same time' (2000: 143). It will be this variation from the Brechtian norm that will interest me in the section to follow.

In analysing the monologues, I do not wish to take issue with the Brechtian interpretation; indeed, I believe it to be essential in understanding the presence of monologues in the film. At the level of their content, the three monologues (Agamemnon's address about his arrival in Greece in 1922 from Asia Minor, Elektra's recollection of the 1944 Battle of Athens and Pylades' account of his time in prison) are all, in a Brechtian sense, 'history lessons', albeit delivered in the guise of personal memories. Beyond acknowledging the Brechtian imprint of the monologues, what I intend to do is to explore in more detail how this theatrical device functions within the film at the level of spectatorial address. To use Michael Fried's terms, absorption and theatricality find themselves mixed in Angelopoulos's film, as the spectator experiences a pull between awareness of artificiality and immersive engagement. What a closer analysis of the monologues reveals is that care has been taken to mitigate somewhat the strangeness of the device, to prepare the spectator for the peculiar semantic regime of the monologue. At the same time, while

Figure 5.1 The three monologues in *The Travelling Players* (Theo Angelopoulos, 1975, Greece)

critics are quick to associate the monologue with frontality and interruption, I intend to show that neither of these terms is straightforwardly illustrated in the film's monologues, and that while there is frontality and there is interruption, the way in which they have been arrived at, usually ignored by critics, is just as interesting as the function they perform in the film.

I would like to begin by considering the following statement made by Deborah R. Geis:

> At the heart of the paradoxical quality of the monologue is its simultaneous focusing and interruption of stage action; it forces the spectators to imagine things they cannot see yet is accompanied by the invisible exhortation that they 'see' the speaker as a character in (or at least in the context of) the onstage action they have been witnessing up to that point. It inevitably involves, then, the redirection of the audience's attention. (1993: 13)

The monologue offers verbal access to an experience of a different kind and situated at a different level, but it concomitantly asks to be accommodated within the narrative from which it branched out. The monologue's function of interruption has been extensively commented upon, following the Brechtian route. What is equally intriguing is the manner in which the monologue also preserves a semblance of continuity with the narrative, ensuring the possibility for the character to be 'taken back' into it. To illustrate this curious relation of the monologues with the developing story, the never entirely abdicated position within a narrative, I shall privilege the transitions in and out of the monologues.

The first monologue takes place in a train coach. Agamemnon slowly tears himself away from his sleeping or distracted companions, who will remain for the whole duration of the monologue non-responsive in relation to him, although at times absorbed in some minor activity (smoking, looking out of the window). In the shot preceding the extended monologue, the camera pulls in on Aegisthus, as he stops outside a tavern, having moved away from the group of actors. The shot is the conclusion of a scene in which Aegisthus, after the first in a series of betrayals, is confronted (musically) by his peers and temporarily ostracised from the troupe. The character has his back to the camera and the following shot, after the cut, takes off from a similar viewing position: we see a soldier traversing the coach, his back to the camera, moving away from it. These shots cultivate a sense of being present in a scene and looking in without being noticed; it is this feeling of not being noticed that the monologue will disrupt. In the train coach, the camerawork is suitably jittery. Agamemnon seems at first just as unmindful of the camera/spectator as the rest of his companions. He casts, however, several barely noticeable, split-second glances towards the camera: an initial probing from the corner of the eye across the train coach as if to test a potentially interested audience, followed by a similarly quick look in the same direction before he finally arranges his hat and stands up, as if to casually, non-purposively, stretch his legs. It is a brief but effective courtship, an invitation to monologue. As he begins to approach the camera, he passes Aegisthus, who dozes through the journey. Aegisthus awakens, sensing Agamemnon's movement, and gives him an annoyed look before returning to his drowsiness. It is the only time during the scene that Agamemnon provokes any reaction from his fellow travellers, one that is short-lived and without consequences. Around this moment, he seems to be crossing an invisible line into a space which is mysteriously coextensive with the space of the sleepy actors but which elicits no reactions and no acknowledgement from them.

In the film the space that the character finds for his confession is a niche that is claimed from the space and time occupied by the other characters and yet somehow also fictionally insulated from them. When Agamemnon sits down, the camera responds by tilting down, as if adjusting from looking up at Agamemnon to looking at him as he takes a seat nearby. During the monologue, Agamemnon alternates between gazing intently at the camera/the spectator and staring into mid-air, between momentary self-absorption and re-engagement with the spectator. At one point, a second military official enters the coach, the expectation being that he will traverse it, thus exposing the artifice of Agamemnon's monologic space, contesting the possibility of a wilful and reversible exit from the dialogic space of the others. Instead, this private corner seems only to be inspected from afar, from the unfocused area of narrative onwardness. The actors pass idle minutes while Agamemnon's monologue flows in a parallel stream of time. The story told by Agamemnon is a sweeping glance over an indefinite period (finding work as a refugee, searching 'heaven and earth' for his lost family and never finding it). The next thing we see after the monologue ends is the actors' arrival at the train station, a scene that reabsorbs Agamemnon into the fictional universe from which he temporarily parted, reuniting him with his other family.

In contrast with the gradual advent of the first monologue, Elektra's discourse is more abrupt. At the beginning of the monologue, we find her on the ground near a river, after being gang-raped by the fascists. Her robe and her bruised face still link her to the events of the preceding night. She rises to her feet suddenly, as if listening to a prompt or aware that the camera has started rolling. She dusts herself off and, for a few moments, the camera functions as a restorative mirror. She ties the cord of the dressing-gown around her waist, pulls a handkerchief from her sleeve and starts methodically wiping her face. The monologue begins as she is still engaged in these private gestures of grooming. She then crosses her arms across the chest, a defensive pose, and 'settles' into the story. As she recounts the events of the thirty-three days of the Battle of Athens, Elektra is certainly not devoid of emotion. The episode of the boy with a bugle, wounded but of fate unknown, appears, for instance, to be more difficult to tell than the others.

For Andrew Horton, through the monologue, Elektra goes 'from victim to a woman historian' (1997: 115). Her personal trauma (the rape) is assimilated into the grander narrative of historical turmoil and the emotions associated with it elided in favour of moral outrage and collective suffering. The sense of unbearable repetition, of an action with no end in sight, informs both the representation of the rape (Elektra's repetitively defensive line 'in the mountains' during the prolonged rape scene) and Elektra's account of the Battle of Athens ('they kept firing at us from the pediments', 'they fired at us a second time', 'we took to the streets again', 'on the way back we were attacked again').

Pylades' monologue is delivered upon his return from detention after signing, under torture, a denunciation of the political left. The experience of confinement from which he extricated himself visually 'follows' him, invoked by the cast shadow of the window frame on the wall which forms the background of the monologue, shadow that resembles a set of prison bars. The monologue is narratively cued in by Elektra's question ('Did you sign?'). The answer comes in the form of a long monologue, uttered for the most part with averted eyes until the very last moment, when the delayed eye contact with the camera is finally established. Up until this point, Pylades hesitatingly angles between a profile position and frontality. It is a choreography of intermediary positions: frontality is achieved at the point of release from a painful confession, but there are previous tentative movements towards this liberating position. The monologue is characterised by a kind of spatial awkwardness to match the character's feeling of shame, an unsteady address that proceeds by infinitesimal changes of angle.

Each time, the monologue employs the same characters as the story from which it branches out, but these characters talk more and with a kind of impetus and self-possession that are lacking from their daily interactions, where their attitudes are far more opaque. At the same time, the characters are also in some way 'beside' themselves, outside of their own experience on which they comment. The monologues are also lodged in the same or similar sets, but they inhabit these sets ambiguously and peripherally, as if they were occurring before a curtain or against a backdrop of indifferent motion. Unlike 'psychological soliloquies' which effect a 'temporary transportation of the audience and character from staged or visible space into the imagined, nondirectly perceivable, linguistically commanded space of the psyche' (Geis 1993: 16), the monologues in *The Travelling Players*, although still to a certain extent providing a view into a past experience, an experience that is revisited for the spectators, are also, perhaps more significantly, functioning as abstract, cerebral links between the characters and the historical events that surround them. The viewer is invited to listen to the speaking subject but at the same time to maintain him/her anchored in the story from which s/he has temporarily taken leave of absence, which makes for a complex mode of address.

'SOMETHING TO DO WITH LIVING': *MY DINNER WITH ANDRÉ* AND THE EKPHRASTIC DUOLOGUE

Louis Malle's 1981 film *My Dinner with André* consists of a lengthy dialogue between the eponymous André and his friend Wally and, as such, does not lend itself to a discussion of monologues in the strictest sense. However, for most of its running time, the film unfurls as a de facto monologue. The main protagonist in *My Dinner with André* and its monologist extraordinaire is the theatre director André Gregory, 'a kind of pioneer potentate of the theater of the weird' (Brenner 1981: 36), whose relatively short-lived but famous theatre company, *The Manhattan Project*, had its heyday in the 1960s. The productions staged by the company courted controversy and were 'pronounced genius and fraud, often at the same time' (ibid.: 37). His dinner companion and partner in conversation is the playwright and actor Wallace Shawn, whose first play (*Our Late Night*) Gregory had directed with the Manhattan Project (Tesich et al. 1981: 29). Louis Malle, chosen to direct the script, coached Shawn and Gregory to become the characters we see on screen. In 1994, the director collaborated with them for a second time, in the Chekhov adaptation *Vanya on 42nd Street*. A third big screen collaboration between Shawn and Gregory, a film based on Henrik Ibsen's play *A Master Builder*, was directed by Jonathan Demme and released in 2013.

In *My Dinner with André*, Gregory and Shawn are playing themselves or, more accurately, playing characters who speak like them but are not quite them. As Shawn has explained, the film script was only obliquely self-referential:

> The actual script has nothing to do with any conversation we've ever had, though it's almost entirely made out of conversations. When Andre says something in the script, he really did say that to me. But each half of a sentence is attached to another half of a sentence from months later. It's a confection. It looks like Andre and me, but it isn't really us – we're characters. (Tesich et al. 1981: 30)

According to Shawn, in the taped conversations they recorded over several months, conversations that formed the basis of the film, he and Gregory spoke without 'emotional colouration' and, when Malle advised them to become 'heated' in the film, to 'speed up' their speech, the suggestion felt 'forced and theatrical' (1982: 120). Even though theatricality seems not to have been a desirable effect as far as Shawn was concerned, Malle had the idea of using theatre as a training ground for the shooting of the much-rewritten and much-rehearsed dialogue and the script was first performed as a play at the Theatre Upstairs (Royal Court) in London, in November 1980. Although at the time one critic was hoping for 'a longer theatrical life' of the script

(Billington 1993: 162), it was always meant to reach the screen and in 1981 it eventually did.

For the better part of the dinner conversation that gives the film its title, Wally's role is confined to providing a steady supply of questions for André, whose wordiness requires only the slightest prodding and elicits at times a minimal show of interest. By the end of the evening Wally comes out of his shell and we get to witness a more balanced exchange. However, it remains the case that the bulk of the film is taken up by the recital of André's eccentric adventures, the equivalent of an extended monologue addressed to both Wally and the film audience. As spectators, we hear of André's involvement in Jerzy Grotowski's paratheatrical happenings, his fortuitous encounter with a Buddhist monk, Kozan, whom he wanted to cast in a staging of Antoine de Saint-Exupéry's *The Little Prince*, a disappointing trip to India, a stay with an eco-friendly community in the Scottish village of Findhorn and perhaps his most radical experience, being buried alive on Halloween at a property in Long Island. The recital of these adventures is followed by an indictment of life lived as if in a trance and by a plea for a life of awareness and clarity. Once able to reform ways of seeing and feeling, theatre is found to be severely irrelevant to and disconnected from the crisis of the contemporary world. Wally counters André's pessimism with a paean to the little joys of life, to the electric blanket that stands for all the hard-earned comfort and pleasure that we can still experience.

Despite being a confection 'written to the dot' (French 1993: 137), cut and revised numerous times, the film's dinner conversation struck some scholars as a plausibly conveyed verbal exchange. Conceptualising what he called the 'rhetorical conversation' as 'a narrative episode in which a conflict over opposing moral viewpoints re-unites the agents with their own moral histories, with the moral traditions of which they are part' (Frentz 1999: 291), Thomas Frentz looked no further than the film for an illustration of his model and even remarked on the providential finding:

> Conversations – rhetorical ones included – are difficult to pin down. No sooner are they enacted than they evaporate, leaving barely a trace of their existence... Fortunately, a memorable rhetorical conversation has not only been preserved, but it also comes to us in the highly accessible form of a film entitled *My Dinner with Andre*. (1999: 295)

Sarah Kozloff has issued a general warning about such trusting attitudes, advising that 'linguists who use film dialogue as accurate case studies of everyday conversation are operating on mistaken assumptions' (2000: 19). Allowing, as we must, that this is indeed a fair criticism that one could make of Frentz's enterprise, his analysis is nonetheless an insightful elucidation of the structure of the film's conversation which he interprets as a friendly contest between two 'incomplete moral selves', which get 'reassembled' in the process (ibid.: 296–9).

The film's considerable reliance on dialogue has not been unanimously applauded by the critics. Michel Chion objected to the 'televisual style' evinced by the film, remarking that 'the lasting impression is that of a mechanical use of a convention on a visual and aural material which does not offer any interesting "resistance"' (1983: 51). The critical literature alternately marshals terms like 'theatrical', 'televisual', 'cinematic' into the discussion of the film's aesthetic. Bruce Kawin and Nathan C. Southern are both exponents of an approach which asks for a rethinking of the cinematic, on the basis of the achievements of this particular film. For Kawin, *My Dinner with André* reminds us of a forgotten potential:

> The tyranny of the 'cinematic' (in the reduced sense of doing only what only film can do: spectacles, cutaways, documentation, visualizations of mental and emotional states, etc.) has cut film off from the fascinations of the mundane and of language, from the resources of sitting around a fire – even if that be the arc-light of a projector – and telling a good story. *My Dinner with Andre* not only contains many wonderful and well-told stories but also vindicates and revitalizes the conditions of their telling. (1981–2: 63)

For Southern, this revitalisation is due, in no small part, to the uncommon sources of inspiration Gregory and Shawn drew on, namely 'the radio dramas of their childhood, and the work and teachings of the surrealists' (2006: 209), which resulted in the consistent and subliminally effective use of an 'imagistic dialogue' (ibid.: 210).

In contradistinction to these approaches, my analysis of the film will treat portions of the dialogue, primarily André's description of his participation in a Grotowskian experiment known as a 'beehive', as ekphrastic monologue. Ekphrasis is often discussed as an example of 'intermedial evocation', whereby the effects of a heteromedial work are produced through homomedial means (Wolf 2005: 255). James Cisneros has suggested that it might be instructive to think of ekphrasis as a 'precursor' to intermediality: 'Both figures hover around the interface of text and image, both situate the media in an inter- and trans-disciplinary space, and both carry a reflexive delay in their respective movements' (2007: 21). In my reading of the film, I shall apply aspects of the concept of ekphrasis to *My Dinner with André* while acknowledging that the concept is both useful and restrictive for the purposes of this analysis. Variously defined as the 'verbal re-creation of visual elements' (Yacobi 1995: 600), as 'an exact description meant, to a certain degree, to evoke and substitute' the artwork itself (Kibédi Varga cited in Yacobi 1995: 608), or as 'the verbal representation of graphic representation' (Heffernan 1991: 299), ekphrasis is sometimes stretched to mean description in general, but it is most commonly understood, in the tradition of Lessing, as the conversion of a 'spatial art' (painting or sculpture) into a temporal expression (the verbal medium, be it poetry or storytelling). In a recent study on the relationship between painting, novel and film, Laura Eidt has expanded the use of the term to film, noting that 'Filmic ekphrasis allows the viewer to compare the filmic representation or enactment of the art work with the actual work itself, thus creating a synthesis of the two images in the viewer's mind' (2008: 19). Eidt seems to render the definition of ekphrasis a bit too broad for comfort, noting that 'ekphrasis need not be purely verbal' and bringing it in line with the notion of 'transmedialisation' (ibid.). While I generally agree that if one wants to apply the term 'ekphrasis' to the medium of film, one cannot afford to restrict it to the 'purely verbal', I would like to retain an emphasis on the verbal in my use of the word in the context of *My Dinner with André*. What makes the study of ekphrasis pertinent in the context of a reflection on modes of spectatorial address is the fact that ekphrasis is by its very nature 'oriented' towards an audience, for whom it strives to create visual effects through verbal means (ibid.).

One of the valuable insights of the literature on ekphrasis into the very condition of ekphrasis, which can be used as a legitimate line of inquiry for intermedial evocation in general, is 'the inseparability of representation and misrepresentation' (Heffernan 1991: 307). This is specifically the case for more conventional instances of ekphrasis (literature describing visual works) because 'it releases the narrative impulse that graphical art typically checks' (ibid.: 304) and, in doing so, it 'overrides – and hence misrepresents – the reality of what can be experienced in a single instant' (ibid.: 307). In what follows, I intend to explore the dialectic between representation and misrepresentation in *My Dinner with André*, seeking to demonstrate that the film proposes its own version of this ekphrastic dialectic. To this end, I shall mostly concentrate on the description of the Grotowskian beehive which occurs some fifteen minutes into the film.

The film begins and ends with Wally's voice-over, a preface and an afterword to the dinner with his friend which forms a substantial middle. Wally enters late into the discussion launched by Gregory, but he does so from an antithetical ideological position. The polarisation and final reconciliation that occur during the dialogue have been interpreted elsewhere and my analysis will not attempt to re-examine these issues other than in passing. Instead, I shall attentively scrutinise the monologic moments in the dialogue when theatre and (para)theatrical experiments are being mentioned, described, contemplated, compared, evaluated and used as evidence.

The first reference to theatre in *My Dinner with André* is an approximately ten-minute story told by André about his involvement in the experiments carried out by the Polish theatre director and theoretician Jerzy Grotowski. The second half of this story is devoted to the description of a specific experiment, a so-called beehive. André shares his initial puzzlement regarding what a beehive is and the somewhat circular answer he received from Grotowski himself: 'a beehive is at eight o'clock a hundred strangers come into a room [. . .] and whatever happens is a beehive'. I shall analyse the evocation of the beehive by, first of all, comparing it to descriptions of similar experiments conducted by Grotowski's Theatre Laboratory, namely the beehives pertaining to the 'Mountain with a Pillar of Flame' project in July 1975, recounted by Richard Mennen, and the 'structured events' within the 'Tree of People' project, happening in January 1979 and again in January 1980, related by Robert Findlay. I shall pay close attention to the mise-en-scène of the beehive evoked by the film, to the ways in which André choreographs the event for us and conveys the participants' arrangement, movement and interaction, as well as their perception of the temporal dimension of the event. I shall conclude this section by linking the beehive with other Grotowskian ideas that permeate André's discourse and by elucidating the combination of representation and misrepresentation that I announced to be at the core of the intermedial evocation.

There are many overlaps and at least one significant difference between the beehive described by Gregory and the experiments attended by Mennen and Findlay. An obvious procedural commonality is the use of singing and dancing as triggers of the collective event. In the film, André tells of how he was entrusted by Grotowski with leading a beehive and how one of the first things he did was to choose a theme song, 'one of the most beautiful songs of St. Francis': 'I decided that when the people arrived for the beehive that our group would already be there singing this song.' His plans are said to have worked because 'after a while they were, whatever it was, a hundred and something people who were all singing this beautiful song together, and we sang it over and over again'.

Richard Mennen's *Ul* (another word for the beehive) is set in motion by a similar initiative:

> We just sat there for a long time – a long, long time. And then somebody began something like humming and that went on for a long time – and this very slowly built up to where everybody was humming or singing or making sounds. Then everybody got up and started dancing and milling around and dancing and then – BOOM – they came running in with flaming torches – this was obviously planned – and started running around the room. (1975: 63)

There is a similar sense in Gregory's account of things progressing slowly, of prodigality with time, of repeated action that gradually draws everyone in. The intended result in Grotowski's experiments was, as Findlay states, a 'temporary culture' (1980: 353) where people 'play off one another' as they would in jazz (ibid.: 352), a culture of alertness to the presence of the other and of maximised responsiveness. Hence, the second feature held in common – the emphasis placed on the 'physical and vocal contacts' (ibid.) between participants. Mennen remembers a moment during the beehive when participants were licking honey off each other's hands and an instance when his own hair was being rubbed with wheat by a fellow resident experimentalist (1975: 64). Findlay talks about bodies piling together (1980: 352) and André recalls his hands vibrating in unison with a girl's hands, a girl with whom he then shared a sobbing embrace. Thirdly, the experiments in all three accounts seem to toy with the idea of an excess or an extreme that the participants feel they must attempt or approach, an element of risk that they welcome. André puts his hands in the flames, whereas Mennen tells the story of a beehive happening prior to the one he joined in which 'there was fire on the floor and people were jumping and rolling through the fire' (1975: 64).

The discrepancies between the three different descriptions can be located, on the one hand, in the way in which they perceive the relation between theatre and paratheatrical activity, and, on the other, at the level of the envisioned structure or lack thereof of the experiments. For Mennen, the change of paradigm in the Theatre Laboratory from the 'poor theatre' to the 'paratheatre' meant that, as Grotowski himself declared, the 'notion of theatre' was completely jettisoned and 'what remained was a notion of meeting' (1975: 60). Therefore, when participants would report an impression of the paratheatrical experiment being just 'another kind of theatre' (ibid.: 65), the observation would function as an indication of a let-down. Findlay, who participated in several paratheatrical projects, occurring one year apart, noted 'a more precise structuring of the work' from one year to the next but opted to interpret it not as a 'return to theatricality', but rather as 'an extension of the theatrical dimensions inherent in paratheatrical work' (1980: 355). As for André, he does not seem to regard the similarity between theatre and the experimental workshops as a problem at all. In relation to both the forest experiments which follow the beehive and the beehive itself, he remarks unapologetically that what happened there was 'just like in the theatre', or 'something like a theatrical improvisation', only self-oriented.

That brings us to the second divergence, the problem of the events' structure. Findlay recognises that the experiments had a 'frame' that one needed to accept for the experiment to function, but considers that what rules did exist were the result of a 'non-verbalized', 'intuitional agreement' (1980: 351) and that real choices were possible and were made as part of the game. In Mennen's account, things get more complicated. He detects at least two types of beehives: a beehive whose structure was 'very out front' and a beehive which, despite being 'all planned', was nonetheless 'trying to convey that it wasn't, that it was happening spontaneously' (1975: 64). While acknowledging the high-mindedness of the overall project, its ambition 'to set up a field of disorientation within the environment which would stimulate doubts about identity and challenge expectations vis-à-vis relationships with others', Mennen believes that the 'real reciprocal choice, which Grotowski has always insisted is a sine qua non of paratheatrical experiments', was actually missing from the experiments (ibid.: 65–6). Furthermore, he finds that 'Other than walking into the room, or deciding to sing, no choices were made, nor did there seem to be a good base from which to make any' (ibid.: 65).

Interestingly enough, André's evocation of the beehive acknowledges the existence of 'a pre-determined sequence' in the experiments the least. In his depiction of the beehive, he privileges words and syntagms which express and enhance the sense of unpredictability, of lack of premeditation: 'suddenly' (in different contexts: 'I suddenly grabbed this teddy bear', 'a hundred and forty or thirty people suddenly exploded', 'suddenly our hands began vibrating'), 'before I knew it', 'Grotowski and I found ourselves sitting opposite each other'. Despite being the appointed leader of the beehive, he has us believe there were things which constantly escaped his notice, which he was unsure of, which he did not anticipate, which did not work. He portrays himself as someone who tried to maintain some control over the proceedings, but who was always taken by surprise, not least by his own reactions. Even when the events and the elements he describes are experimental ingredients which we can find in both Mennen's and Findlay's accounts (the American Indian dance, the clockwise and counter-clockwise movements, the fire, the chanting), they are in no way signalled as stock ideas of the Theatre Laboratory.

In any description of a scene, one of the main challenges is what W. J. M. Levelt calls 'the speaker's linearization problem' (cited in Fowler 1991: 29), namely the need to decide upon a selection of elements and upon their order. Additionally, according to D. P. Fowler, 'the speaker's solution of the linearization problem necessarily imposes a point of view' (ibid.). Once again, André's evocation of the beehive proves to be a gratifying example to consider. After describing in some detail the setting of another set of experiments in which he partook, a Polish forest with huge trees, tiny castle and great stone slab, an enumeration which Nathan Southern rightfully discusses as an example of a 'surrealistic size contrast' (2006: 211), André leaves the setting of the beehive curiously undescribed. We learn that the idea of the experiment came to André 'a night or two before we were supposed to go off to the country', so presumably while still in the city, but nothing else after that in terms of the location and temporal frame of the beehive. As listeners to his account, we are more than once slightly confused, 'stranded' in a room without qualities, tentatively counting the hours (an hour of preliminary singing before an hour-long excitement involving a teddy bear, followed by a succession of sub-events which ends 'hours later'). The order in the conversation is from the outset reversed. Although it precedes the forest experiments, the evocation of the beehive comes after the account of these experiments.

As for the participants, we know from André's description of their subsequent work in Poland that they were people gathered at his special request ('forty women' and some 'very interesting men', none of them speaking English but all of them playing an instrument). During the evocation, the people in the group are demoted to an indistinct mass; they react as one, 'exploding' or 'weaving through the room' in 'hypnotic dance'. Our only visual aid in the effort to imagine the geography of the room and its frenzied occupation consists of André's gestural output. Stowing away one's valuables, throwing a teddy bear up in the air, moving clockwise and counter-clockwise, forming and then breaking away from a tight little circle of dancers, sitting opposite each other in the middle of a room, all these different acts, movements and positions are both verbalised and accompanied by sign-language.

In the account, the beehive gradually organises itself into 'six or seven different things going on at once', six or seven interconnected improvisations. While we are hearing about this development, about this veritable 'human kaleidoscope', André is drawing up an invisible graph, mapping things out in thin air. He is in fact creating a double-tiered story: a frame of words for a virtual canvas. André himself encourages the pictorial analogy: he describes the outburst happening after he decides to use a teddy bear brought in by one of the participants as similar in effect to a 'Jackson Pollock painting'. This is an example of what Tamar Yacobi calls 'a generalized reference', a 'departicularized allusion' which is narratively more 'maneuverable' than a particularised reference (1995: 633). The listener is not asked to think of a specific Pollock painting, but rather to activate 'mental schemata', which, at least in Shawn's case, are presumed to exist. Such generalised references, albeit non-pictorial, are quite frequent in the film, in various degrees of departicularisation: William Blake, Moby Dick, Martin Buber, to name but a few.

During the conversation, the camera moves from a close-up of André to a more inclusive framing as the story progresses. Most of the time, the camera sits behind Wally, looking over his shoulder at Andre, but occasionally it moves behind André, to register Wally's reaction, capturing, for instance, the moment when he is startled by André showing him the throwing of the teddy bear.

Figure 5.2 The ekphrasis of paratheatre – *My Dinner with André* (Louis Malle, 1981, USA)

The teddy bear and the unexpected role it plays in energising the group can be read as a parable of sorts of the object being interposed between subjects (André Gregory and Jerzy Grotowski). In a discussion of stage objects, Alice Rayner explains: 'From a purely linguistic standpoint, the word object stands for any "thing" that is thrown (-jected) in front (ob), suggesting not simply the thingliness of objects but their position in relation to a subject, like an obstacle or an object of study' (2006b: 49). The teddy bear is thrown back and forth between Gregory and Grotowski, who also pretend to feed it at the breast. The experiment expresses at this point a fascination with movement, physicality and agency, mixed with an interest in primal behaviour.

Although these interpretations can be advanced about the teddy bear fragment, it also seems to function as a parody of paratheatre and as a humorous moment. If we think of the Aristotelian definition of drama as an imitation of an action, the experiment appears to be, again, 'like theatre'. The trifling nature of the teddy bear game, which nonetheless manages to rouse the participants to explosive action, can be contrasted to André's *The Bacchae* project, a story that he tells later in the film. As a young director at Yale, André wanted to propose a staging of extreme literalism that would have shocked the audience into examining reality anew:

> My impulse – when Pentheus has been killed by his mother and the furies, and they pull the tree back and they tie him to the tree and fling him into the air, and he flies through space and he's killed and they rip him to shreds and, I guess, cut off his head – my impulse was that the thing to do was to get a head, from the New Haven morgue, and pass it around the audience. You know, I wanted Agave to bring on a real head, and that this head should be passed around the audience so that somehow people realize that this stuff was real, see, that it was real stuff.

This gruesome 'object of study' was meant to force the subjects to stare reality in the eye, meant to bring them back 'in contact' with it. The Bacchae project fleshes out Wally's postulate about the mission of theatre and it represents one of the points of convergence between the two ways of seeing the world (Wally's and André's). It is significant that in giving this example, André creates again a vivid account. The quick succession of verbs, linked through the copulative conjunction, achieves the sense of an unstoppable, tragic chain of events unleashed by Pentheus's act of transgression. Moreover, André is shown to have always been interested in the setting loose of impulses, the maenadic dance being very similar to the 'hypnotic dance' of the beehive.

Theatre comes up all the time during the dinner conversation, as does the more general issue of role-playing in social contexts. Wally mentions the play *The Violets Are Blue* and the time he had to perform in a cat costume for a stage version of *The Master and Margarita* and André references the past achievements of Edward Gordon Craig, Eleonora Duse and Bertolt Brecht, in order to produce a diagnosis of contemporary theatre. Theatre furnishes the testing ground for the ideas exchanged by the two friends; it is what the characters depart from and what they come back to. This network of explicit references sustains the evocation of theatre, which is an altogether different operation.

To go back to the definition of intermedial evocation, a work that resorts to this device is supposed to use the medium in which it is realised in order to convey the effects of another medium, in the way ekphrasis re-creates with words a painting or a sculpture. How, if at all, can we apply this notion to film in general and to *My Dinner with André* in particular? My answer would be that, if we adhere to the above-cited definition, the film medium evokes theatre by selecting among its numerous capabilities, by, in a sense, ignoring or downplaying some of its potential and over-emphasising the rest. Werner Wolf makes it clear in his definition that evocation does not involve 'heteromedial quotation' (2005: 255). Film can easily and proficiently reproduce, and, half-jokingly, Wallace Shawn was aware of this alluring, but ultimately detrimental possibility when he wrote, in an article about the search for a suitable director for the film, that he was looking for someone who 'would not get nervous at the last moment and start throwing in flashbacks' (1982: 119). The media traditionally associated with ekphrasis are usually bound by their respective limits but they also find specific strengths in these limits. As Murray Krieger points out, words 'are not – and happily are not – pictures' (1992: 2), and in their turn, pictures have their own way of signifying, the two being situated by critics on opposite sides of the temporal/spatial divide.

Film mobilises both words and images and because it can simply show pictures, moving pictures at that, it can also theoretically dispense with verbal evocation. Why does *My Dinner with André* not forgo this device? Why does it not just show us the paratheatrical experiments in a flashback? Obvious difficulties would arise with the idea of real people playing themselves, or playing characters who resemble them closely, but even with these difficulties in sight, the question, I believe, is still relevant. Malle's answer would be 'A movie can be anything' (French 1993: 137), something that he actually said in an interview in response to the sceptics who doubted the film would work as the 'mammoth conversation-piece' (Frey 2004: 20) that it ended up being. A movie can indeed be anything, including an extended verbal evocation of another medium, with no other role for the sets, the camerawork and editing than to best frame the dialogue, to create 'a realistic ambience', 'while at the same time not allowing the ambience to destroy the intense concentration on conversation' (Shawn 1982: 120).

There is yet another possible explanation for the film's over-indulgence in dialogue, more specifically, for its use of verbal evocation. In the periodisation of the Grotowskian theatre activities, the paratheatre phase (1969–78), also known as the 'Theatre of Participation', is the second phase, following the 'Theatre of Productions', partially overlapping with the 'Theatre of Sources' and preceding the 'Objective Drama' and the 'Ritual Arts' phases (Osiński et al. 1991: 95). It is a phenomenon which, although proclaiming the renunciation of theatre proper, found its rightful place in the history of the medium. The later phases of Grotowski's experimentation aimed to reveal and even practise the so-called 'pre-differentiation Art', a type of art that is contiguous with ritual and better understood as a 'way of knowledge' (ibid.: 96). The formulation is interesting, all the more so since one could argue that intermediality theory deals mostly with 'post-differentiation' art. Marvin Carlson discusses Grotowski's work, alongside the productions of Chaikin, Schechner and the Living Theatre, as 'performances that emphasize physical stimulus and de-emphasize text and narrative' (1993: 500). In Carlson's overview of the theories of theatre that were popular in the interval 1965–80, the interval when the paratheatrical experiments described by André took place, one theory in particular stands out as germane to this analysis: Jean-François Lyotard's idea of a 'theatre of energies rather than signs', subsequently reprised and elaborated by Régis Durand. In Carlson's account of this theory, 'The alternative to a theatre "smothered by conversation" is not necessarily a theatre of gestures and cries, as Artaud thought, but rather a "theatre of impulses and intensities the movements and variations of which are experienced"' (ibid.: 504).

In its relentless vitality, the beehive can be considered emblematic of this 'theatre of impulses and intensities'. Incidentally, the word 'impulse' also crops up in André's account. I would argue that in *My Dinner with André* the medium of film becomes the arena for a seemingly impossible encounter between the theatre of conversation and the theatre of energies and impulses, bringing together these two unlikely bedfellows. Grotowski's paratheatrical experiments were often founded on a tacit interdiction against speaking. There is therefore an intrinsic representational clash between André's wordiness and the non-verbal nature of the event he describes. The previously mentioned dialectic between representation and misrepresentation is another way of formulating this clash: on the one hand, the forward thrust of the discourse is a good match for the chain of actions constituting the beehive, as temporality matches temporality, but on the other hand, there is a fundamental irony about using inflated language to describe an initiative that is designed to go against or do without language. André's speech attempts to describe not only the visuality and aurality of the beehive, but also its tactility. When André uses gestures to convey the spatiality of the beehive, its configuration, the words, feared to misrepresent, are supplemented by visual signs.

According to Robert Findlay, the Grotowskian experiments were meant to create 'a third realm – a realm that is neither art on the one hand nor life on the other but rather something else that partakes of both without really being either' (1980: 353). One could argue that the film harbours a similar aspiration, to create a third realm, in which the theatre of conversation and the theatre of impulses are hosted and made to communicate through the medium of film.

SPALDING GRAY AND THE AUTOBIOGRAPHICAL MONOLOGUE

In the preface to a collection of his early monologues published in 1986 and quoted in the artist's journals, Spalding Gray recounted how at the end of the 1960s he attended the Open Theater Workshop run by Joyce Aaron and Joseph Chaikin. One of the workshop exercises asked the participants to improvise a personal story in as fast a manner as possible. The exercise was a test in both quick delivery and the ability to conjure up, process and perform biographical material with little room for thought. The way in which the exercise was set up allowed for the possibility that the participants would occasionally draw a blank, in which case they were encouraged to try word association while regrouping. Gray did not make use of this allowance and instead found himself able to produce extempore a richly detailed account. To quote him, 'when it was my turn I experienced a memory film, a series of rather mundane events that had occurred during the previous week. I had no trouble editing or selecting which materials to use as I spoke. The images came into my mind in vivid frames and I was able to describe it all in perfect detail' (Gray and Casey 2011: 25). His reasoning bears some resemblance to Henri Bergson's famous claim that 'the mechanism of our ordinary knowledge is of a cinematographical kind' (cited in Olkowski 2014: 77), but lacks the broad philosophical sweep of the Bergsonian dictum and functions instead as a work formula within the context of a specific practice.

Spalding Gray's autofictional turnaround continued to be swift throughout his career. He subsequently came back to the idea of the memory film more than a decade later in an interview with Steve Capra. Asked about the nature of the audience's involvement in his autobiographical monologues, he expanded on the analogy to accommodate the activity of the spectator. In his staged, well-crafted confessions, he went on to explain, 'I'm describing a film that I'm seeing – I'm describing my memory. I have an inner scene of that event – I'm seeing it as I tell it. It's a kind of *mind theatre*. I think when the audience can tune to it is when they also begin to do their own seeing' (Capra 2004: 114, emphasis in the original). These statements point to the foundational role that film plays in the genesis of the theatrical monologues. In this subchapter, I shall treat Gray's autobiographical monologue as an endeavour that, while intimately wedded to the medium of theatre, is at the same time intermedial by design and hence requires the audience to draw on a number of media for a full appraisal of its effects. As Eddie Paterson notes, Spalding Gray's 'autobiographical and confessional performances are seminal examples of the flourishing of the monologue genre in the United States during the latter years of the twentieth century' (2015: 53) and, as such, unavoidable landmarks for this chapter's preoccupations. At the time of their release, the films were generally regarded as little more than faithful recordings of Gray's theatrical monologues. Richard McKim remarked, for instance, that *Swimming to Cambodia* offered 'a dramatic showdown between two art forms rooted at opposite ends of cultural history' and that, ultimately, 'the drama lies in the authority with which the older art remains in command throughout' (1987: 41–2). Rather than being a mere afterthought, confined to the function of preserving Gray's monologic performances, the two films that I shall be looking at, Jonathan Demme's *Swimming to Cambodia* (1987) and Nick Broomfield's

Monster in a Box (1992), reveal a more complex media overlay, and in what follows, I intend to restore a sense of complexity to the relation between film and theatre as evidenced by selected scenes from the two films.

Spalding Gray first performed the monologue *Swimming to Cambodia* in December 1983 at the Performing Garage, an Off-Off-Broadway theatre in New York, shortly after completing a small part in the film *The Killing Fields*, directed by Ronald Jaffe. Fine-tuned over the course of nearly two hundred performances (Gray 1985: xv), the monologue documented Gray's three-month stay in Thailand during the shooting of the film and offered a compelling mix of personal stories, historical asides and humorous glimpses into the expat adventures of the crew, earning Gray an Obie Award. Initially performed in two parts amounting to more than four hours of material, the monologue was eventually pared down to an 85-minute film version theatrically released in 1987 and widely acknowledged as a watershed moment in Gray's career, despite the fact that by that point he had been performing monologues on stage for roughly two decades. After the 1988 *Terrors of Pleasure*, produced by HBO, 1992 marked the release of Nick Broomfield's *Monster in a Box*, a filmed monologue which chronicled yet another artistic project, this time a novel entitled *Impossible Vacation*, featured as a conspicuous prop in the film. As was the case with *Swimming to Cambodia*, the account of an agonising creative process was interspersed with digressive episodes in which Gray told of an interview project entitled *LA other*, a fact-finding trip to Nicaragua, sponsored by Columbia Pictures, as well as of touring Russia with *Swimming to Cambodia* and of his involvement with a staging of Thornton Wilder's *Our Town*. Both films were made during the very productive personal and professional partnership with Renée Shafransky, who acted as the producer of the films and was managing Gray's career at the time. Shafransky is the interlocutor of choice in both *Swimming to Cambodia* and *Monster in a Box*, the co-subject in this phase of Gray's lifelong commitment to the autobiographical form. In an interview with Richard Schechner, Gray acknowledged Shafransky's essential role and credited her contribution to the monologues: 'We lived our life almost like two characters, I would tell stories about our life together and that would make the monologue. So in a way Renée was a cowriter because I would often be quoting her' (Schechner 2002: 164). The blurred boundary between actor and role that Gray alludes to here is not without its complications, because, as Jon Erickson has argued, Spalding Gray 'mystified in the very act of self-revelation' (2009: 32).

While Gray seemed happy to settle in the autobiographical monologue, which he found eminently suited for his needs, he was also acutely aware of the affordances of the different media and never ceased to move between them. The greatest advantage in using the theatre monologue form was its inherent pliancy and openness, its capacity to incorporate change and allow itself to be shaped by it, but equally tempting was the arresting of the flow, be it in print or on film. To use Gray's words again, 'The memories would appear to me as if on a wheel and to set them in print would be to stop the wheel but to speak them in different order each night would be to be free to spin the wheel until the right combination came up' (Gray and Casey 2011: 179). Between this freedom to 'spin the wheel' and what he calls in a journal entry from 1981 'my wanting to hold things still so I can look at them forever' (ibid.: 99), the choice was never clearly made. The spinning of the wheel was from the beginning assisted by all manner of technology and media. Tape recorded for revision purposes, the performances were also constantly accompanied by notebooks that together with the tapes tell the story of these constant amendments in search of the right combination. The film versions would typically occur towards the end of the performance rounds and the temptation therefore is to think that their role was to 'embalm' performance, to preserve it once it has ceased to grow and renew itself. The statements which prefaced this section indicate, however, that film was not only last to intervene, but also first on the author's mind, to the effect that in Gray's account the stage monologues appeared to be a kind of ekphrasis of the memory film, at once evoking and substituting it. The theatrical form, in other words, was set in motion by a filmic way of seeing.

This film–theatre–film conceptual concatenation can be further complicated by adding the influence of radio (Schechner 2002: 156), through the centrality and evocative nature of the voice, and stand-up comedy, through the sense of timing (Stone 2015: 159) but also by virtue of what Miriam Chirico has called the comedians' 'observational distance from their *experiencing self*' (2016: 23, emphasis in the original). Michael Bliss and Christina Banks have pointed out the mesmerising quality of the sound in the monologues: 'The problem that a famous Zen meditation aide poses is, "What is the sound of one hand clapping?" A similar kind of meditationlike focusing effect occurs when we watch *Swimming to Cambodia*, which concentrates our attention to the sound of one man rapping' (1996: 76). What emerges is the idea of a hybridised, ultra-mediated form, caught in a compulsive cycle of doing and undoing but which offers a spellbinding experience for the spectator. Although to some extent it could be argued that the two films perform a function of 'transcription', in the sense employed by Susan Sontag in her essay 'Film and Theater' (1966: 25), and that their use of filmic devices is for the most part unobtrusive and subordinated to the autobiographical enterprise, it is nonetheless significant that certain elements of the theatrical performance are either enhanced or supplemented in a way that will be discussed in the sections to follow.

The notion of the autobiographical split has become common currency in writings on the topic of autobiography and the manner in which it is usually discussed involves a division between the speaking/writing self and the self who is spoken/written. Philippe Lejeune, for instance, remarks that 'Every speaker bears within him two polarities, that of sender and receiver', functioning 'by virtue of this schism' (1977: 30). Autobiography stages this communicative division, allowing the narrating self to take stock of its own multiplicity, a multiplicity which encompasses past and present selves in dialogue with each other but also the productive interstices between the self as narrator and the self as protagonist. William Demastes has convincingly argued that in Gray's case we are dealing with a triangulation, between Gray 'the observer of events', who collects the material, 'Gray the artist' who shapes the material, endowing it with irony and critical edge, and Gray 'the naïve performer' who is seemingly unaware of this layering (1989: 86). Following on from his points, one could argue that the original memory film is complicated, at times corrupted, not only by the different levels of transcription but by the different Grays subverting one another. Either way, the heterogeneity and opaqueness discussed by Parret (2011) as constitutive of the autobiographical subject appear to be exacerbated in Gray's case and the films foreground this dramatic multiplicity of selves.

Some eight minutes into *Swimming to Cambodia*, Gray recounts a substance-induced episode that occurred during Renée's visit to Thailand, during which, after smoking a Thai stick, he began to experience an ever weirder and darker succession of apparitions. The hallucination starts with a stainless steel counter that becomes the site of a troubling clash of energies, as a pile of body waste meets a floating mass of pastel energy. One might be tempted to see in this imagery Gray's tongue-in-cheek version of Lautréamont's dissecting table, only less fortuitous, as Gray the hallucinator, impersonated by Gray the performer, knows what his vision represents, namely positive and negative vibes. At this stage, the hallucination takes the form of a metacognitive experience during which the hallucinating protagonist tries to use the knowledge of what he is (mis)perceiving to bring about specific effects. As the monologue progresses, he considers tugging at the invisible, mental strings that tie him to these competing fields of energy but the thought of being rid of the energies and left with the stainless steel counter, an image of sterility and impenetrability, of the anaesthetised mind, is enough to stop him in his tracks. It is at this point that the hallucinating Gray seems to be transported to the next phase of the hallucination, as the stainless steel counter morphs into a gold-leaf tunnel with the gold leaves functioning like the blades of an iris mechanism. In this context, the gold leaves are referring to the potent form of marijuana under the spell of which Gray experiences his head trip, again

Figure 5.3 Pull and counter-pull – *Swimming to Cambodia* (Jonathan Demme, 1987, USA)

reinforcing the metacognitive aspect of his hallucination. Gray the observer channelled by Gray the monologuist is seized by a growing sense of anxiety and he feels pulled through this tunnel towards the centre of the earth. As he describes this irresistible pull, the camera back-tracks and the rhythmical jolts in the soundtrack, the intermittent shading cast by the ceiling fan in the otherwise minimal set, Gray's frantic hand gestures and his keyed-up state combine to create a whirl of sensation for the audience, who experiences the sudden distance from Gray as a counter-pull. The camera then regains its proximity to the performer as Gray, eyebrows tensely arched, lets out a series of quasi-ritualistic shouts meant to convey to the audience the effect of the accelerated parting of the blades. Throughout this performed delirium, the assortment of filmic devices are deployed to allow Gray's remembered self-perception during a powerful sensory illusion to reverberate across the distance separating him from the film viewer, distance which goes from constricted to expanded to constricted again in the span of seconds.

Managing to wrest himself away from this overpowering fantasy, Gray the observer takes a moment to reassess his situation, only to confess that at the time he had no idea where he was or where Renée had gone and the only sense he could make of his surroundings was the feeling he was in 'a demented Wallace Stevens poem with food poisoning' (Gray 1985: 8). Wallace Stevens is referenced in several of Gray's works. *Sex and Death to the Age 14* briefly mentions the search for the poet's house in Hartford and in *Impossible Vacation*, Gray singles out 'The Idea of Order at Key West' as his favourite Wallace Stevens poem (Gray 1992: 64). The latter can give us some insight into the significance of the Stevens reference in the context of *Swimming to Cambodia*. The narrative premise of the poem is the narrator/speaker and a friend/companion crossing paths with a woman who sings as she walks along a shore. The juxtaposition of the human voice and the primeval ocean roar enable, according to Helen Vendler, a reflection on the 'Wordsworthian orders of mind and world' which are found to be 'exquisitely fitted and yet subtly uneasy with each other', with the former granted a higher 'magnitude' of power than the latter (1984: 68). The oft-quoted line 'Oh! Blessed rage for order' reads as a consecration of the command of poetry over the natural world, a celebration of the human ability to, in the words of the poem, 'arrange' and 'deepen' the night through imagination. The woman's song has been interpreted as 'an act of solipsistic creativity' (Rotella cited in Bloom 2003: 67), an orderly, transformative effort that shapes an indifferent, chaotic world. For a storyteller compulsively prone to the artistic re-organisation of experience such as Gray, the poem may well have seemed as the ultimate validation of his own endeavour. One could hypothesise that the feeling of inhabiting an unspecified Stevens poem during the hallucination bespeaks a similar impulse to stage a rarefied meeting of opposites (the rage and the order, the poetic and the demented) to that which we have seen at work in the clash of energies.

As he experiences an extreme physical disorientation, Gray the observer notices in the distance what he surmises to be a group of Thai girl scouts dancing around a bonfire, an alluring vision that he feels tempted to join in the hope he will be brought 'back in time'. Gray the raconteur hastens to reassure the audience that the circle of girls he briefly caught sight of was 'not a hallucination', thus creating a breach in the discourse through which the audience momentarily perceives the workings of Gray the ironist. Interestingly but perhaps not surprisingly given the arguably more inert format, the line is missing from the published version (Gray 1985: 8), which curtails for the reader the play of different voices to which the spectator is privy in the film.

Moreover, in the film, the evocation of the dancing Thai girls is accompanied by recorded giggles, which, by virtue of being recorded and intermittently used, appear spectral and distanciated, further calling into question the status of the images evoked by Gray.

What follows in Gray's account is an episode of vomiting in which, after staggering like a 'drunken teenager' to an isolated corner of the beach, he becomes violently sick. He covers the ejected matter with sand, only to trigger yet another disturbing hallucination. His sand-covered vomit assumes the shape of a black mask which attaches itself to Gray's face. As he continues to frantically conceal the traces of his sickness, Gray unwittingly puts together a sand corpse, a sand double which stares at him from the abyss of contemplated death. When he brings to life this episode in his monologue, Gray is shown bending over the pages of his notebook, which adds another level of meaning, an ironic insert hinting that the monologue too is expelled material, vomit on a page.

Gray's performance notebooks, archived at the Harry Ransom Center of the University of Texas at Austin, provide an illuminating glimpse into Gray's approach to the monologue form. In one of these notebooks, the first hallucination segment of his *Swimming to Cambodia* monologue, which has been the focus of this analysis, is broken down in a series of key words in upper-case letters, listed one below the other, in the following order:

> Stainless steel counter
> Gold-leaf
> Wallace Stevens
> Thai girl scouts
> Stagering [*sic*]
> Vomit-cover-mask
> Corpse
> 'What's wrong hon?'
> Carried me out
> Big scene in the movie

Distance markers on a trajectory of self-disclosure, the key words were meant to guide Gray in and out of a scene, with the last set of verbal aids in the enumeration above referring to the moment when Renée, absent from and oblivious to Gray's morbid hallucination, rejoins him and is puzzled to find him unwell. The segment wraps up with a reminder of the unfortunate timing of the hallucination, occurring as it did the day before Gray's 'big scene' in *The Killing Fields*. The notebooks with their minimal verbal scaffolding seem to corroborate the way in which Gray himself explained his method, by likening the memory work involved in each of his performances to 'bushwhacking', to hacking one's 'way up the hill each night' (Schechner 2002: 166), each performance presenting itself as a renewed challenge to forge a pathway and self-edit in sparingly charted territory.

Beyond what can be noticed about the structure of each of these segments, Demastes suggests that there is a broader logic at work in the monologues, with Gray 'introducing an event or a key phrase and then repeating what has become familiar at a slightly later point, making the tale something that the audience feels it owns' (2008: 121). This becomes apparent if we briefly compare the first hallucination which I described in detail with the one recounted in the film one hour after the first and leading to Gray's much coveted 'perfect moment', swimming in the Indian Ocean and overcoming his intense drowning anxiety to eventually feel of a piece with the ocean. Both triggered by a few mild tokes of a Thai stick, the hallucinations develop at a breakneck speed and although escalating speed is something that regularly occurs throughout the monologue, it is in connection with the hallucinations that Gray makes a point of self-reflectively underlining for the audience what it felt like to experience the rush of these uncontrollable sensations and thoughts and to subsequently try to convey them. The tunnel hallucination is brought to a halt by Gray confessing that he could not 'stand the speed of it any longer'. Similarly, in the later hallucination, reaching the point when Gray the observer fears that his friend Ivan has been engulfed by a rip tide, Gray the performer tells the audience he 'can't even speak as fast as the images went'. Gray the seemingly naïve performer reveals himself as someone who finds it difficult being in lockstep with his experiencing self, an anxious self which constantly overtakes him and makes him play catch-up. The spectator is caught in a similar cycle of having to keep up with the intensified rhythm and then loosen up when the tension eases. Gray the self-reflexive artist is also involved insofar as we perceive a knowing intent to speed up delivery in order to match the fast editing of the memory film. This explicit concern with speed chimes with a more general attitude towards time that is foregrounded in the hallucinations, namely a fluctuating feeling of being outside time, back in time, of there being no time and of fear anchoring one in time ('I'm back in time, I'm back in fear'). Gray's description of his immersion in the perfect moment as a 'smiling ear-to-ear pumpkin head perceiver', floating up and down the waves and feeling boundless and 'blended with the ocean' (Gray 1985: 80), calls to mind the famous exchange between Sigmund Freud and Romain Rolland regarding the so-called 'oceanic feeling' ('la sensation océanique'), understood as a 'mystical experience of oneness with the world' and interpreted by Freud as a regressive pattern, suggestive of the union between mother and child (Parsons 1999: 4).

Throughout these gut-wrenching performances, Gray maintains his privileged position at the centre of the frame even if camera angles tend to vary with frontality in the tunnel episode being replaced by a slightly angled vision in the subsequent episode. This centrality of the subject is important because it brings to mind questions of perceptual discernibility and conceptual address. Reflecting on what he calls the 'malady of scopophilia' in Gray's work, Marc Silverstein once remarked:

> Performance allows him to position himself as a spectacular subject, not merely soliciting the audience's gaze but controlling the audience by surveying and fixing them in his own field of vision; an act that should – if not able to effect the impossible transformation of the stage into a private space – accentuate the distance between stage and auditorium, the distance Gray needs to protect himself from 'the overexposure and transparence of the world which traverses him' (133). (2007: 117)

Silverstein's characterisation of Gray's positioning as both controlling and shielding is consonant with Laurie Stone's remark that the 'power position in comedy' is 'the place of no power, where the teller is stripped of protection and keeps investigating uncertainty' (2015: 156–7). Occasionally, Gray lashes out from this defensive positioning, getting close to the mike and shouting at the unsuspecting audience; at other times he approaches the mike as if in confidence, willing to share some whispered secret. This unremitting ebb and flow of energy keeps the audience on its toes, transfixed and with nowhere to hide. The turning of the head to the right and left indicates a temporary impersonation of a different character, engaged in conversation with Gray the observer. Integral to the issue of his positioning in relation to the audience is Gray's use of the main element of set design in his performances, the table, which he clarifies in several interviews. A 'housing' and a 'shell' (Kammer 1986), for Gray, the table and the imperative to sit behind it during the performance are meant to engender 'a steady state' in contradistinction to the movement across the stage which 'creates time' (Capra 2004: 115). According to Gray, this self-imposed stasis, this steadiness of physical arrangement enables the audience to add its own contribution to the 'collective memory' that the room (presumably the being together in a room) generates (ibid.).

Monster in a Box has its share of anxiety-ridden incidents, perhaps none more memorable than a hypochondria episode unfolding in public which subsequently triggers a longer spell of AIDS hysteria. Invited to see Cher's (then) new movie *Moonstruck*, Gray was set to meet Renée at the Museum of Modern Art where the film was to be screened. Having arrived earlier than Gray at their meeting place, Renée goes to warm up in the New York Public Library where she chances upon some images of AIDS-related rashes, one of which looks suspiciously similar to her own. Renée had noticed a few days prior what she initially thought to be an innocuous spider bite but the rash quickly turned into what Gray calls in the monologue 'fluorescent blue shingles crawling up her thigh', impossible to square with the idea of a spider bite. Before being told about the images glimpsed in the library, Gray sees Renée approaching him and senses there is something wrong, because she 'has that face', the expression of which he correctly decodes as 'something's happened and I don't want to know about it'. As Gray clinically observes his mounting trepidation, the film cues the audience on his rapidly deteriorating state, by introducing heartbeat sound effects, which are quickly supplanted by the ominous strings and percussion sounds of the score written by Laurie Anderson. The camera starts creeping closer to Gray from a long shot vantage point to a medium close-up. Gray gradually becomes less articulate as he convinces himself that a former lover, Judy, had passed on the virus to him. He starts barking uncontrollably as the fear of AIDS takes over and Gray the performer impersonates both Renée's response and the split at the heart of his own:

> I just went, 'Oh! U . . . Oh! What library? Um, René . . . You're Renée, right? I'm Spalding. Um, wait a minute. Um.' (Denial.) 'Uh wait! Now why did we come to New York City for Thanksgiving? What was that? Whose idea – was that?' (Denial.) And my feet began to sweat. I've never wanted to disappear from a place more in my life.
> [. . .]
> So we go in to try to forget about it for a little bit, and I'm sitting, trying to get into the movie, but every time I see Cher, I don't see Cher. I see instead the face of that sleazy, sexy, stage-door-Judy – with the very questionable sex and drug habits – that I went home with one night after a show. A long time ago. *But not long enough ago!* And every time I see that face I start barking like a dog.
> [. . .]
> And Renée says, 'Spald, stop it. Now we're going to have to leave. MacNeil Lehrer is behind you taking notes.'
> I turn around and there he is – I don't know which one – but he's there! And he's taking notes! (1991: 32–4)

The disjunctive interventions of the different Grays, the neurotic Gray unable to keep his anxiety in check, Gray the open conduit who delivers yet another energetic and spasmodic performance and Gray the ironic commentator who sees the initial stammer and confusion for what it is ('Denial') are once again on display, additionally thematised by the reference to Robert MacNeil and Jim Lehrer, the PBS duo, between whose members Gray is unable to distinguish ('I don't know which one, but he's there'). This lack of proper identification matches the confusion of the subject who experiences its split in the process of storytelling. As the words and emotions precipitate, the music follows suit, brought to an almost unbearable level of intensity.

Interestingly also, the medium of film evokes itself as the act of watching a movie is conveyed through the flicker effect on Gray's face, aided by the tight framing and by Gray's backlit silhouette within the surrounding darkness.

Philip Auslander has borrowed the term 'autopathography' from G. Thomas Couser, a term designating 'autobiographical accounts of illness, injury, or disability' (2005: 163) in order to argue, with examples drawn from *Gray's Anatomy* and *It's a Slippery Slope*, that in Gray's case the written autopathography functions differently from the performed autopathography, with the former reading as a type of comedy and the latter practised as a form of therapy (ibid.: 164). In a passage from *It's a Slippery Slope*, a monologue that some have deemed to be the 'metaconfession' of a 'serial confessor' (Terry 2006: 222), Gray tells of how on some nights he would scream in the streets of New York, only to have his screams echoed by other passers-by, to the point where what began as an episode of 'real panic' would be 'turned into a performance' (Auslander 2005: 171). According to Auslander, 'the presence and reaction of an audience', be it an 'accidental audience' like the regular passers-by, enable Gray to 'perceive the symptoms of his mental illness' from a different perspective and as a spectator himself (ibid.). A similar process is at work in the episode from *Monster in a Box*, where, in the midst of his breakdown, Gray becomes aware of the staring gazes directed at him, not only from MacNeil/Lehrer but also from Cher and her entourage. After his neurosis comes under the repeated scrutiny of celebrities, which turns him into an unwitting performer and an even more reluctant spectator of his own disorder, Gray facetiously declares himself temporarily cured: 'what is amazing is that everytime I see that I am being looked at by a celebrity, I'm no longer afraid of death or dying, which is something weird, I haven't been able to analyse that one yet'. Having to perform the breakdown after the fact on a stage places Gray in the situation of artistically malingering, of harnessing the derangement, of giving it a flow and a structure. It also functions as a vivid reminder that, as Adam Phillips has remarked, 'madness is often deemed to be theatrical in a way that sanity is not' to the effect that madness appears to test 'the limits of theatre' or expose 'something about theatricality, about the impulse behind it, about what it's driving at' (2012: 176–7).

Gray's performed unravelling within what amounts to a parodic, multi-layered and intrinsically deconstructed monologic form, invites an actively engaged viewer/listener, a form of interaction that Gray himself has described as 'dancing with the audience' (Capra 2004: 114). In the last case study of the book, I shall explore another example of performed self-narrative, this time in the context of verbatim theatre.

The Arbor AND THE Unreliable Monologue

Clio Barnard's 2010 film *The Arbor* combines fragments of archival footage from TV documentaries, lip-synched audio interviews that assume the form of a series of monologues and an open-air theatre staging, in order to produce an intermedial reflection on the intersection between document and artistic experiment. In this sub-chapter I shall use Nathan Stucky's notion of 'natural performance' and Erica Nagel's 'aesthetic of neighborliness' to elucidate the manner in which a technique borrowed from verbatim theatre, the performed interview, contributes to the complex (self-)representation of a working-class family. Centred on the figure of the British playwright Andrea Dunbar, the film owes its title to a play written by Dunbar, when she was a teenager living on the Buttershaw council estate in Bradford in the late 1970s, a play which in its turn bears the name of the street where Dunbar lived (Brafferton Arbor). The play was submitted to the Young Writers' Festival and was picked out by the Royal Court Theatre's artistic director, Max Stafford-Clark, who staged the first, one-act version of the play in the Theatre Upstairs, and then commissioned Andrea to write a second act for a run on the main stage of the Royal Court in a more ambitious programming, alongside established names (Stafford-Clark 2000: 3). The full-length version was first performed on 24 June 1980 (Dunbar 1980).

At the time, the Royal Court Theatre was already gaining a reputation as London's foremost 'writers' theatre', one with an orientation towards female playwrights to boot – in 1975 Caryl Churchill was the first woman to have a residency at the Royal Court, after the same theatre produced her play *Owners* in 1972 (Wandor 2000: 60; Reinelt 2009: 19). Stafford-Clark's tenure as artistic director at the Royal Court Theatre (1979–93) has been recognised for its 'championing of work by women', with Churchill as well as Andrea Dunbar, Timberlake Wertenbaker and Louise Page adduced as examples of playwrights to whom he lent his support (Radosavljević 2013: 104). Max Stafford-Clark's commitment to new writing is very much in evidence in Dunbar's case. Not only did he guide the transition of *The Arbor* from a school exercise written in green ink to a full-blown theatrical text (Stafford-Clark 2000: 1), but he also staged Dunbar's second and better-known play, *Rita, Sue and Bob Too*.

Duška Radosavljević credits Stafford-Clark with implementing influential 'ensemble-work principles' in play development (2013: 104), during his involvement with the Joint Stock company (1974–9), a theatre group which he co-founded with David Hare, William Gaskill and David Aukin. The Joint Stock method of play writing entailed a research period followed by an interval during which the dramatist would draft the play, in its turn followed by rehearsals, and one of the effects of the increased immersion of the playwright in the processes of the theatre company was that the resulting texts and performances would be endowed with what Radosavljević calls a 'kinaesthetic intelligence' (ibid.: 105). The idea of kinaesthetic intelligence as one of the objectives of the playwright's participation in the rehearsals is consistent with Stafford-Clark's own account of his collaboration with Andrea Dunbar on *The Arbor*. According to Stafford-Clark, Dunbar was invited to attend the rehearsals of her play at the Royal Court Theatre and would intervene during the rehearsals precisely to provide correctives of movement and expression when she felt that the performance deviated from her recollections, which closely informed the text: 'her comments were apt and incisive: "He weren't sitting down, he were standing up when he said that", she would say. Or, "She didn't laugh then, but she did laugh when she said that"' (2000: 3). This painstaking attention to the details of remembered behaviour has led some to speculate that Dunbar's plays were 'quite possibly verbatim accounts of what actually happened to her' (Radosavljević 2013: 137), although strictly speaking Dunbar is not considered a representative of verbatim theatre. As Will Hammond and Dan Steward have pointed out, the term 'verbatim theatre' designates more a 'technique' than a 'form' and refers to the process whereby 'the words of real people are recorded or transcribed by a dramatist' or 'appropriated from existing records' and subsequently 'edited, arranged or recontextualised to form a dramatic presentation, in which actors take on the characters of the real individuals whose words are being used' (2008: 9). This type of theatre inspired Clio Barnard to use interviews as one of the narrative strands in her film, but Barnard practises both a form of intense attention to the characters' self-representation and a radical questioning of their testimonies, in a way that will be clarified throughout this analysis.

Dunbar died of a brain hemorrhage when she was 29, after collapsing in a local pub. Clio Barnard's debut feature *The Arbor* revives the story of the troubled British playwright but it also brings into focus the equally tragic fate of her eldest daughter, Lorraine, tracking her brush with prostitution, descent into drug addiction and imprisonment following the death of her son Harris, who ingested methadone in circumstances yet to be clarified. Different readings of the film are in broad agreement about the meaning of such a juxtaposition: Beth Johnson writes of a 'destructive pattern of addiction' that is linked to 'spaces and places of social exclusion' (2016: 284), whereas Cecília Mello focuses on the film's editing to argue that what is at play is a sense of 'an almost genetic or deterministic history of violence and abuse' (2016: 120). The two intertwined stories, Andrea's and Lorraine's, are reconstructed through snippets of documentary footage and audio interviews conducted with members of the Dunbar family, with close acquaintances and neighbours, chief among them Dunbar's children, Lorraine (Manjinder Virk) and her half-siblings Lisa (Christine Bottomley) and Andrew (Matthew McNulty), their one time foster parents Steve Saul (Neil Dudgeon) and Ann Hamilton (Monica Dolan), Pamela (Kathryn Pogson) and David Dunbar (Jonathan Jaynes), Andrea's sister and brother, and Jimmy 'the Wig' (George Castigan), one of Andrea's partners and father of her youngest child. In addition to the use of interviews and archival footage, which make direct reference to Dunbar, there is a further level of intertextuality evident in the casting: Pamela's words are delivered by Kathryn Pogson, who played the main role (the Girl) in the original staging of *The Arbor*, Jimmy's role is taken on by George Costigan, the actor who played Bob in the 1986 Alan Clarke film adaptation of Dunbar's second play, and the Girl in the open-air theatre performance is played by Natalie Ganvin, who was discovered during an audition held at a school on the Buttershaw estate (Hickling 2010).

The incorporation of different kinds of archival and documentary material and the reliance on the resonances that these pre-existent texts possess have long been the staple of what is variously called 'documentary theatre', 'theatre of fact', 'theatre of witness', 'nonfiction theatre', 'tribunal theatre' and 'verbatim theatre', subsumed by Carol Martin (2013) under the more comprehensive term 'theatre of the real', which allows for subtle differences between sub-types such as verbatim theatre (drawing on oral testimonies) and tribunal theatre (drawing on written records) to exist under an encompassing conceptual umbrella. Martin situates this contemporary mode of theatre creation and practice at the intersection between the 'technological postmodern' and 'oral-theatre culture' (2006: 9), thus drawing attention to the use of technologies of recording in the preservation and transmission of oral testimonies. She also notes that the 'theatre of the real' usually consists of an 'assemblage of selected verbatim texts that are also often collectively devised', which fundamentally challenges the role of the playwright (2010: 3). In other words, the lasting and growing popularity of the 'theatre of the real' is connected with changing attitudes towards authorship and with the proliferation and widespread use of technologies of recording, which in many respects align it with postmodern culture. Ryan Claycomb operates with an alternative term to designate similar practices, namely 'staged oral history', shifting attention from the preoccupation with an inescapably mediated and ultimately elusive reality which is primarily at stake in the expression 'theatre of the real' to the 'polyphonic', fragmentary and constructed aspects of documentary theatre (2003: 97). Max Stafford-Clark, associated with what has been termed a 'quasi-verbatim' methodology, whereby actors would interview real people and take notes but would not mechanically record the interviews (Paget cited in Radosavljević 2013: 136) and affiliated with Barnard's project not only by virtue of having his opinions featured in the film but also as director of Robin Soans's verbatim play *A State Affair*, which the film quotes, has proposed that another effect of verbatim theatre is a sense of displayed rawness: 'It's like cooking a meal but the meat is left raw, like a steak tartar' (Hammond and Steward 2008: 51).

Clio Barnard has stated that she was aiming for the opposite effect to that of documentary theatre, namely widening the 'gap between reality and representation' and 'deliberately making you aware of the illusion rather than trying to collapse it or make it smaller' (James 2010: 26). However, this appears to be an underestimation of what documentary theatre itself, at its most interesting, can achieve. While acknowledging that the term 'documentary theatre' is problematic, Carol Martin notes that some forms of documentary theatre do rise to the occasion by 'complicating and interrogating archival truth' (2006: 12). Without needing or wanting to propose a blanket evaluation of documentary theatre, I would suggest that it actively engages with notions of memory, evidence and testimony, which goes some way towards explaining its appeal for a project such as Barnard's. The filmmaker seems to have been generally aware of the interpretive possibilities inherent in the genre when she chose to use in the film the technique of lip-synched audio interviews. The technique brings to the fore the sound–image split constitutive of the dual-track film medium and thus invites a reflection on the very nature of sound in cinema. This strategy, which most critics regard as a Brecht-inspired distanciation device and which Richard Porton rather noncommittally labels 'an audacious formal decision' which 'might be viewed as either ingenious or perverse' (2011: 12), could also be seen to offer an almost literal illustration of Rick Altman's suggestive likening of sound in film with a ventriloquist who, 'by moving his dummy (the image) in time with the words he secretly speaks, creates the illusion that the words are produced by the dummy/image whereas, in fact, the dummy/image is actually created in order to disguise the source of the sound' (1980: 67). For Lib Taylor, what the technique achieves is to 'physicalise' the 'distinction between actor and character' through the 'separation of voice and body' (2013: 375). This 'performed dislocation' is in Taylor's view supplemented by 'the critical displacement present in the bodily performance', such as the one exemplified by casting the actor Danny Webb to impersonate both Max Stafford-Clark and the father in the autobiographical play (ibid.).

Barnard had previously experimented with this technique in the arguably less effective short *Random Acts of Intimacy*. Transplanted into film, the verbatim technique as employed by Barnard trades on an expressive disjunction between the recorded voice and the performing body, which lends itself to the act of hosting the voice. What we see and hear on screen is at the same time presumed to be to some extent adhering to biographical fact, but also composite, deflected and incongruous. Chris Mirto has remarked in relation to documentary theatre that it often confronts us with the paradox of 'the voice and body being together and separate at the same time' (cited in Martin 2006: 10). In *The Arbor*, while the actors' aim was presumably never to conceal the lip-synching technique altogether, their mastery of the speech flow is nonetheless sufficiently convincing to generate at least an intermittent suspension of disbelief and this skilful achievement working at two opposite levels chimes with Mirto's statement. Manjinder Virk, the actress playing Lorraine, compared the effort required by the role to 'circular breathing' and to 'learning a piece of music', perfected through repeated listening, and described the process as technical at first and then moving on to a phase of constructing 'emotional context' around the lines, more akin to traditional actorly work (Olsen 2011; Wood 2011).

In addition to the interpretations outlined thus far, I would like to suggest that the lip-synching technique could also be fruitfully analysed using Nathan Stucky's concept of 'natural performance'. Stucky has defined natural performance as a dramatic 're/performance' of 'naturally occurring', 'first-order performance events' (1993: 169–75). His interest lies in the type of everyday performativity that characterises, for instance, ordinary conversations, as well as in the imitation of this everyday performativity that occurs when situations 'happening in the ordinary course of things' (ibid.: 175) are then re-performed in an artistic context. Stucky goes on to explain that, in order to successfully 'outer' the complexity of another person's speech, their 'living text', the performer needs to engage in 'acts of kinetic understanding' and pay attention to 'paralinguistic cues', such as intonation and any other elements pertaining broadly to that person's manner of speaking (ibid.: 172). The notion of 'kinetic understanding' returns us to an earlier point made in this sub-chapter, concerning the 'kinaesthetic intelligence' of the Joint Stock method and of Andrea Dunbar's own observations during rehearsals, proving a certain consistency of approach across various theatre cultures when it comes to the meeting between documentary and drama. Stucky developed the concept of 'natural performance' primarily with reference to documentary theatre and to the ideas of one of its prominent practitioners in the USA, Anna Deavere Smith, who explained her method of embodying someone else's voice as finding a way to 'wear' their words (ibid.). In order to elucidate the 'acts of kinetic understanding' of speech showcased by *The Arbor*, in what follows I shall concentrate on two moments in the film when the characters' monologues are staged with them facing or looking out of a window.

The first moment I shall analyse is a rare example of discursive convergence in the film, whereby four interlinked monologues seem to support one view, namely that the Dunbar siblings felt nurtured by Steve Saul and Ann Hamilton, both during their mother's short life and afterwards. The moment follows various assessments of Jim's role in the children's lives during his six-year relationship with Andrea Dunbar. These assessments are delivered by Lorraine, Lisa, David Dunbar, Andrea's sister Pamela, and Ann, the latter two recounting how he would regularly drop the children off, especially Lorraine and Lisa, either with one of Andrea's sisters or at the bus stop, so that they could catch a ride to Buttershaw estate. Steve and Ann, living as they did across the road from Jim, often found themselves taking in the unminded children and offering them moments of respite and joy in an otherwise deeply dysfunctional caregiving environment. Lorraine's monologue begins immediately after Ann's own intervention, as a voice-over superimposed on a shot of Ann and Steve, with Ann turning her gaze away from the camera to briefly but lovingly glance at Steve as he rejoins her in the doorway of their house. This image of marital stability and relaxed togetherness, quickly followed by a shot of Jim closing the bonnet of his car, establishes them as the affectionate, healthy alternative for the children to Andrea Dunbar's serial miscalculations when choosing a partner. At a later point in the film, Jim is seen wiping grease off his hands, another shortcut to his characterisation as someone more absorbed by personal interests than by child rearing. As Lorraine remembers the time during her childhood when, together with her siblings, she would wave at Ann from the window of Jim's house, what the film viewer in her turn sees is a low angle shot taken from outside a red-brick house of the three grown-up Dunbar siblings approaching two white-framed windows, in a slowly choreographed movement, illustrative of what Beth Johnson has called the film's 'spectral stylisation' (2016: 287). In addition to the abstract, distanciating quality of the three children being replaced in the re-enactment by their adult versions, the shot reinforces Lorraine's isolation as her approach is slightly delayed compared to that of her siblings and receding by at least a step, as she stands by a window alone, separated from Andrew and Lisa who neatly and symmetrically occupy the space demarcated by two panes of the same window. The connotation of entrapment is unmistakable for all three, but Lorraine is more marginalised by her solitary framing. As Alison Peirse has argued, Lorraine is also marked as different through her mixed race and her speech, as she drops fewer vowels than Lisa, whose 'very broad West Yorkshire accent' is less clear than Lorraine's (2016: 62). As we then cut to each of the three Dunbar siblings consecutively delivering their brief monologues, only Lorraine and Lisa maintain their framing by the window, this time in a profile view medium shot, near a white curtain which starts gently billowing as Lisa's monologue trails off. The picture they are both painting of their time with Steve and Ann is one of utopian abundance and availability, as evidenced by the references to 'lovely food', 'loads of areas to play', 'loads of toys' in Lorraine's account and the sense of an open-door approach, of boundless hospitality with seemingly no expiration date in Lisa's monologue, conveyed and reinforced through the use of the adverbs 'always', 'every day' and 'all the time'. Although both produce a rose-coloured vision of warm, freely given care, there is a slightly different tone to these reminiscences. Lorraine's account begins with an expression of wonder that such an unmitigatedly generous arrangement would come to pass in the first place – she speculates, rather implausibly, that Ann must have thought the kids crazy and, her voice rising in bemusement, she admits to not remembering how the visits started. Pain is what seems to underlie her wistfulness, as the kindness she remembers is a paradise briefly known and quickly lost. She looks out of the window, then briefly at the camera, unsmiling and with a slightly furrowed brow. The enumeration of the things she enjoyed at Steve and Ann's is left unfinished, hanging in mid-air, and, before we cut to the next shot of Lisa we see Lorraine mouth open, gazing out of the window and slightly upwards, as if in search of an answer to an unformulated question or in sudden realisation of something that was evident all along. Lisa's monologue starts as prelap, preceding the cut to a graphically matched shot of her positioned identically by the window and mirroring the profile followed by frontal address pattern we previously saw with Lorraine. As a point of difference, however, Lisa holds the audience's gaze longer than Lorraine and this corresponds to a spike in self-confidence we hear in her discourse: rather than be in awe of Steve and Ann's benevolence, like Lorraine, Lisa frames it as the type of thing families normally do and family is what she considers the couple to be, even in the absence of blood ties: 'with my eyes, I class them as my family anyway, so . . .' While Lorraine's previous monologue had an unremitting gravitas about it, Lisa smiles to herself as she reminisces, at one point tilts her head to the right and generally comes across as more dynamic, more self-assured and at ease with kindness being shown to her, rather than as someone for whom kindness is an almost miraculous exception. Since the audio interviews were conducted separately, it is a feat of editing that there is such an audio-visual flow to these brief monologues in the film.

In contradistinction to the graphically matched shots of Lorraine and Lisa by the window, Andrew Dunbar is framed in a long shot in a living-room, sharing a leather sofa with, one assumes, his very young daughter towards whom he glances a couple of times during his monologue. As he speaks, corroborating Lisa's remarks by saying that Steve and Ann are like his 'mum and dad', 'always there' for him, playing 'a very big part' in his life, he fiddles with a pen while his daughter doodles on a sheet of paper and the impression is that the monologue has interrupted a moment of shared activity and emotional

Figure 5.4 The monologue at the window – *The Arbor* (Clio Barnard, 2010, UK)

bonding between the two. On the right-hand side of the shot we see a pile of toys, visually echoing the reference to 'loads of toys' in Lorraine's monologue. This, combined with the fact that Andrew is shown in the company of a small child, close by and paying attention, works to establish a link between Ann and Steve's parenting style and Andrew's own approach to fatherhood. The following monologue closes the loop, by returning us to Lorraine, who, this time around is in a changed location. Barnard has stated that she wanted the production design to contribute to the sense of authenticity: 'In terms of the production design, those were the environments where I had interviewed people, and what you would understand about somebody from those environments' (Damon Smith 2011). Elsewhere, she clarified that she met Lorraine at the 'drug rehabilitation unit of a prison in Surrey' (Hickling 2010), which situates the next monologue on what appears to be the set of the unit's bathroom at nighttime. The adult Lorraine's childish, red-trimmed, fruit and flower print white pyjamas serve not only to infantilise her appearance but to also place her into the psychic orbit of the lovelorn child she once was, forever in need of notice and words of encouragement. Remembering Ann and Steve's prediction that she would grow up to be 'such a pretty young lady', Lorraine once again displays the scrunched-up brow indicative of her legacy of diffidence, as she tries to contain an ever-widening smile of delight, glancing by turns at the camera and away from it (downwards, sideways, upwards at the ceiling), in a performance consistent with an attempt to come out of one's shell to embrace a modicum of positivity and acceptance.

As Carol Martin has argued, in documentary theatre, and by extension in films working in its manner, 'glances, gestures, body language, the felt experience of space, and the proximity of bodies', and one might add to this enumeration Stucky's 'acts of kinetic understanding' that animate a speech, while being the very elements which turn 'the archive into repertory', are also things that fall 'outside the archive' and, hence, are 'created by actors and directors according to their own rules of admissibility' (2006: 11). It is at this level, of nuanced and variegated embodied interpretations of absent, archived people, that I would locate one of the main achievements of the film. By using the figure of the woman at the window as a reiterated staging option, Barnard mobilises an expressive arsenal of longing which has been famously used and analysed in other contexts as well. Julianne Pidduck, writing about the use of the figure in the 1990s Austen adaptations, has persuasively connected this 'gendered structure of feeling' with a 'spatiotemporal economy of physical and sexual constraint', seeing it as the expression of 'a lingering quality of anticipation, a poignant desire' (1998: 382). While the gendering of the figure is still female in *The Arbor* and its general association with an expression of yearning is also maintained, the inflections of this image in the film are, as one might expect, significantly different from those delineated by Pidduck in relation to the Austen adaptations. One of the most striking uses of the figure occurs within minutes of the sequence of monologues I have just analysed, as part of a longer scene in which Lorraine recounts an initially happy childhood memory, of her father coming to visit her unannounced and bearing gifts. Lorraine's account is laced with anger as she remembers her mother, in a racially motivated gesture, ripping the velvet dresses with frills she received from her Pakistani father. As the camera cuts from a long shot of the young Lorraine happily dancing in her new garments on the roof of her father's car against the backdrop of the grim looking city sprawling in the distance to an indoor close-up shot of the grown-up Lorraine by the white-curtained window, the monologue acts as a sound bridge between the two, while the background sound changes from the lively Indian music to the tune of which the young Lorraine was seen cheerily swaying to eerie wind-like sounds. Unlike the cluttered interiors of the Regency era, contrasted in Pidduck's analysis with the lush, expansive natural spaces on the threshold of which the figure at the window is desiringly poised, the indoor spaces of *The Arbor* are often sparsely decorated or framed and lit in such a manner as to preclude anything but the broadest contours from being clearly discernible. This de-emphasises the importance of the present setting and privileges the overpowering hold of fantasy and of remembered past on the characters. As Lorraine reaches the point in her monologue when she tells of her father's broken promise to return every weekend, the editing of the film takes us from the close-up shot of Lorraine's face by the window to an over-the-shoulder shot of her patting her hair in a preening gesture while looking out of the window with her back to the camera. As she touches her hair, a rack focus blurs this micro-gesture and redirects our attention to the white curtain through which we notice, together with Lorraine, a shadowy silhouette quickly crossing the screen space behind the curtain, the rushed footsteps in the soundtrack completing this image of thwarted expectation. The scene ends with a medium long shot of Lorraine in contre-jour at the window, her back to the camera, engulfed in the bleakness of her surroundings, her abandonment now a stark visual certainty. The figure at the window is in this case a powerful visualisation of the psychic nexus that Adam Phillips has eloquently written about, namely the frustrating relationship between 'the lived and unlived life', between the 'life that we wish for and the one that we practise, the one that never happens and the one that keeps happening' (2012: xvii). In the preceding examples, another form of doubleness was at stake in the same figure, that between the present we choose to construct for ourselves and the past that informs it in ever complex and abstruse ways.

The relationship between the past and the present in *The Arbor* is not always staged through the type of overlapping accounts that I analysed in the brief monologues about Steve and Ann's role in the lives of the Dunbar children. More often than not, what we witness are subtle and not so subtle forms of contradiction in the interviews Barnard gathered for her project, which perturb any notion of accessible truth. This is also a thorny issue in documentary theatre. Stephen Bottoms had underlined the importance of textual reflexivity for a successful treatment of non-fictional materials on stage. Rightfully reacting against a simplistic view of documentary theatre that associates it with realism, Bottoms warned against an unexamined use of documents, pointing out its inherent peril, namely that 'such plays can too easily become disingenuous exercises in the presentation of "truth", failing (or refusing?) to acknowledge their own highly selective manipulation of opinion and rhetoric' (2006: 57–8). In his view, precisely because 'the term "verbatim theatre" tends to fetishize the notion that we are getting things "word for word", straight from the mouths of those "involved"', there is a need for these plays and their performances 'to foreground their own processes of representation in order to acknowledge the problem and encourage audiences to adopt an actively critical perspective on the events depicted' (ibid.: 59). Clio Barnard was mindful of these challenges when she decided to use the verbatim technique in *The Arbor*. One of the very first conceptual moves of the film is to establish the inconclusiveness of its central testimonies. To do it so early and so forthrightly is to admit that ultimately the events represented in the film cannot be fully authenticated, that they exist in a web of contestation and uncertainty which forever unsettles their claim to biographical truth. This atmosphere of epistemic mistrust is introduced at the same time as the device of the lip-synched direct address.

Max Stafford-Clark has written about his first impression of the neighbourhood in the following terms:

> A pack of abandoned and feral dogs roamed the centre of Brafferton Arbor, the crescent on which Andrea lived. The pastoral name was misleading: it

was bleak. Some houses were boarded up, and some gardens were a tangled mess of grass and weeds often featuring rusty bits of car engine mounted on breeze blocks. Like the occasional battered caravan that also blossomed in some garden, they were dreams of escape – hopeless male fantasies doomed to remain forever in a state of incompletion. (2000: 1)

Barnard's film also chooses to begin with a shot of stray dogs roaming about, a powerful symbol of dereliction and dashed hopes. This gives us an early glimpse into the situation from which Dunbar's characters emerged. The image of the overgrown grass, on the other hand, is used more lyrically in the film, with Andrea Dunbar shown in footage introduced later in the film fondly remembering how she would 'duck down' in grass as a child to hide from her parents and Lorraine's own memory of her father's visit starting with a shot of uncut grass used by the neighbourhood kids to play hide and seek. Its use is consonant with poetic realism, in the vein of which Barnard worked in her later film *The Selfish Giant*. After the grassy shots of the housing estate, we see Lorraine and Lisa in a visual re-creation of a childhood memory. The story in its two conflicting versions is carried by the real voices of Lorraine and Lisa, while their impersonators are either roaming the house, or facing us directly to deliver the testimony. In Lorraine's account, she was the one who once set fire to the bedroom to keep her younger brother and sister warm, as the house was severely under-heated. In Lisa's version, Lorraine was playing with matches and the mattress in the bedroom accidentally caught fire. The accounts offer equally different explanations for why the children were locked in the room when the fire started and had to be rescued from their confinement. According to Lorraine, Andrea had made a habit out of locking her kids in the bedroom, by removing the door handle. The way Lisa remembers it, she was the one who unscrewed the door handle with a knife. Throughout the film, these viewpoints will be maintained, with little variation: Lorraine's testimony is an unremitting 'J'accuse!' directed at her mother, whereas Lisa comes across as an apologist for parental neglect. Lisa and Lorraine are our and each other's unreliable witnesses. In their memory reports, they offer minimal reciprocal validation and even when the same details feature in their accounts (such as the missing door handle), the underlying logic of organisation of these details is fundamentally different. The disparity of the testimonies which were supposed to anchor the representation firmly in the real offsets Andrea Dunbar's statements about her own work, quoted later in the film: 'you write what's said. You don't lie. If you write about something that's happened, you're not gonna lie and say, "It didn't happen", when it did all the time.' Dunbar's naturalistic creed and, in the words of Max Stafford-Clark, her 'gift of total recall' (2000: 3) are skilfully and subtly contrasted with her daughters' grasping at straws for a shred of truth.

Dunbar's plays have generally been discussed in the context of the representation of the 'new poor', 'a burgeoning underclass created by the Conservative government's liberalisation of markets and employment legislation' (Jones 2008: 454) in the Thatcher era (1979–90). This social category is often discriminated against and associated in the political discourse of the right with the tendency to drop out from the labour force, with drug consumption and antisocial behaviour. The play *The Arbor*, which is partially featured in the film, is unambiguously autobiographical: while the main character is referred to throughout the play as the Girl, in several bits of dialogue, she explicitly identifies herself as Andrea Dunbar, born on 22 May 1961, which leaves us no room for doubt about where the inspiration for the character came from. The first act of the play tells of an unexpected pregnancy ending in miscarriage and the theme carries over in the second act which sees the Girl in a mixed-race relationship with a Pakistani man, Yousaf, a character based on Lorraine's real-life father. The Girl falls pregnant again and while this time round the pregnancy does not end with a miscarriage, it does bring about an equally distressing denouement, with the Girl seeking refuge from her increasingly violent partner in a shelter for battered women. An interesting dimension of the play is the way in which it interweaves the private story of the Girl and her misfortunes with the life of the neighbourhood. The family arguments occasionally spill over into the street and there is often something discordant, boisterous, happening in the street that distracts from and interferes with the characters' actions. By staging *The Arbor* on the Buttershaw estate and combining it with lip-synched re-enactments, Clio Barnard doesn't just manage to create 'an artfully crafted mosaic' (Porton 2011: 12), but she also returns and reinscribes the play and the figure of the playwright within the fabric of her community. The onlookers featured in the film are the current residents of the council estate and almost all the theatre scenes are framed with an audience in the background. The actors playing members of Dunbar's family in the film are sometimes seen infiltrating this real-world audience, which is in keeping with the film's consistent strategy of probing the boundaries between fact and fiction. The decor of the outdoor staging is minimal: a sofa and an armchair stand for a living-room, a set of discarded or torn car seats metonymically replace a vehicle and the actors are either populating this decor or casually performing a walkabout. Furthermore, the stamina of the performances and the sheer energy of the scenes manage to convey what a critic has called the 'naughty Northern naturalism' (Ann McFerran cited in Jones 2008: 454) of Dunbar's style.

For Simon Jones, the reception of Dunbar's works in the period when she was active and the type of publicity she was given, underscoring her working-class credentials and her 'raw talent', evince problematic aspects, as they imply a concern with locating an 'aura' of authenticity (2008: 454). Moreover, he points out that her plays exemplified a 'voyeuristic (and safely distanced)' perspective on poverty, which did little to raise 'consciousness' regarding the issues facing the 'new poor' (ibid.). I argue that the effort of reclaiming Dunbar's largely forgotten work carried out by Clio Barnard manages to steer clear of these ideological pitfalls, not only through the lip-synched monologues but also through what Erica Nagel has called 'an aesthetic of neighborliness' (2007). Writing about community-based theatre, Nagel borrowed the term 'neighborliness' from anthropologist Mary Savage (1988) to refer to a type of artistic practice whereby the artist would enter an 'alliance' with the community, that would energise the community, and would commit to represent the 'group's understanding of its own circumstances' (2007: 159). Community-based theatre of the type envisaged by Nagel often adopts 'multivocality' and 'contradictory viewpoints' (ibid.) in order to re-create a sense of collectivity and, as my analysis has already shown, contradiction is showcased in the film's central testimonies. Although arguably concentrated mostly on Dunbar's family and her immediate entourage, Barnard's film nevertheless treats them as members of a specific community, affected by the issues facing that community, and it also allows other members of the same group to appear, to be made visible within the spaces fictionalised by Dunbar, gesturing towards including the community at large in the network of testimonies that are woven around the elusive figure of the playwright.

The fact that Barnard emphasised the community's self-representation rather than going down a self-reflexive path has kept the focus squarely on Dunbar, her background and her divisive legacy, mitigating the potential blind spots resulting from Barnard's class positioning, as a middle-class filmmaker tackling working-class subjects. In this respect, it would be instructive to briefly consider the film in relation to Moisés Kaufman's verbatim play *The Laramie Project* (2000), which was turned into a film commissioned by HBO and first shown in 2002 at the Sundance Film Festival. The play revolves around the 1998 murder of the gay college student Matthew Shepard in the town of Laramie, Wyoming, and is the result of several visits that the members of the New York City-based theatre company The Tectonic Theater Project made to the town shortly after the murder. During these visits, the actors of the theatre company established and headed by Kaufman gathered '400 hours of taped interviews' with residents of Laramie, 'people who did and did not know Shepard, gay and straight, law enforcement officers, bar patrons, university staff and students, and healthcare personnel' (Baglia and Foster 2005: 2009), as well as kept journals, fragments of which were used in the play alongside the interviews to document the actors' own mixed and evolving reactions to the experience. Although both premiered at independent film festivals (*The Arbor* at Tribeca) and both have their roots in verbatim theatre, the films differ greatly in their approach to the subject matter. Produced and distributed by HBO, the subsidiary of the media conglomerate Time Warner, *The Laramie Project* used well-known Hollywood actors to impersonate the people of Laramie and took advantage of the commercial synergies of the media giant in competition with a rival project on the same topic broadcast on NBC, leading Jay Baglia and Elissa Foster to argue that the corporate handling of the filmed version of the play amounted to a 'commodification of Shepard's murder' (2005: 137). By contrast, *The Arbor* was financed by the London-based arts organisation Artangel, used little-known actors and was aimed at an arthouse audience. The difference that is most pertinent to this analysis, however, is the attitude towards the figure of the interviewer. *The Laramie Project* filters much of what is recounted through the eyes of the interviewing actors, whose experience, for all its misgivings, is self-referentially foregrounded in the film and to a lesser, but still significant, degree in the play. Jill Dolan has claimed the following:

> Although its motives are sympathetic and benign, the play positions the people of Laramie as specimens to be amiably studied by an audience that's presumed to be from New York (like the performers) or from other sophisticated urban centers. The project proceeds from the perspective of outsiders *for* outsiders, with the danger of condescension to the local using such a technique involves. (2005: 117)

Dolan goes on to argue that by mobilising this outsider perspective, which includes but is not restricted to a certain 'urban naiveté about "country ways"' (ibid.), the play 'inadvertently exoticizes Laramie – sometimes belittling it and sometimes romanticizing it' (ibid.: 118). There were similar risks attached to Barnard's own outsider perspective, namely that the Arbor community would end up treated as incomprehensibly but alluringly alien to the interviewer, reduced to a series of stereotypical aspects or blatantly distorted by the observer's lens. Yet, Barnard manages to circumvent these risks, in the first instance by her complete self-effacement as an interviewer. Although the verbatim texts included in the film originated as interviews, the interview set-up is not preserved as such in *The Arbor* re-enactments and the characters' answers are presented as seemingly unsolicited monologues. Although any representation is inescapably produced from a vantage point and that vantage point is bound to show in some ways, Barnard, committed as she appears in *The Arbor* to the 'aesthetic of neighborliness' with its intrinsic 'multivocality', effectively avoids any homogeneity of attitude towards the social issues to which she draws attention, by setting the different voices from within the community alongside and at times against one another. Barnard has recounted how Lisa made her a Sunday roast when she went to visit her, noting that she was keen to convey in the film the idea of the 'functioning domestic life' (Damon Smith 2011) that Lisa wanted to project. It was not only off-camera that Lisa presented herself as well-adjusted and responsible, but also in several of her interventions in the film. Lorraine's joyful recollection of the time when, upon being released from prison, she got pregnant with Harris is followed and undercut by a story told by Lisa of an incident that occurred around the same time, when she discovered in a bag left behind at her house by Lorraine a kitchen spoon with traces of heroin on it and a dirty needle, an incident which angered her. Another time, Lisa is heard deploring the fact that Lorraine did not have any milk in the house while raising an infant. Nicolas Rapold has judiciously observed that Lisa comes across as 'self-righteous' (2011: 69), but the effect is also one of a community that is not reduced to any one behaviour or world view, but rather portrayed with different shades. As represented in the film, the community embodies, through its various members, a whole spectrum of understanding, judgement, tolerance, and ability to cope with adversity.

The film's generic blur (documentary–fiction–adaptation), its effective combination of two forms of theatre (verbatim monologue and street theatre) and its disjunctive partnering of sound and image qualify it as perhaps the most experimental case discussed in this book and, as such, a fitting note on which to conclude.

Epilogue

In an article published in 2007, Jacques Aumont set out to answer the question 'Can film be an act of theory?'. Towards the end of his demonstration, after weighing different possibilities and allowing that film can 'speculate', but only 'about the conditions of an experience related to the film experience' (2007: 211, my translation), Aumont proposed that film is better understood as 'a poetic act' than as an act of theory (ibid.: 208).

By way of concluding this book, in what follows I want to both retain Aumont's idea of film as a poetic act and complicate his qualified rejection of the notion of film as an act of theoretical speculation, by adding two other voices into the mix. In her reflection on the newly emergent field of performance philosophy, Laura Cull, building on a similar position articulated by Robert Sinnerbrink with regard to cinematic thinking as a form of aesthetic disclosure, has recently suggested that 'performance can be understood as doing its own kind of philosophical work, without it being illustrative of concepts or arguments already outlined by "traditional" philosophy' (2014: 24–5). Later in the same argument, she would add provocatively: 'perhaps we might equally conclude that performance is at its most philosophical (in its own way) precisely at those points when it resists our attempts, not only to paraphrase it, but even to think it at all' (ibid.: 30). In 1949, in an essay entitled 'The Meaning of a Literary Idea', the American critic Lionel Trilling remarked that in poetry, 'whenever we put two emotions into juxtaposition we have what we can properly call an idea', proceeding to explain that the 'force of such an idea depends upon the force of the two emotions which are brought to confront each other, and also, of course, upon the way the confrontation is contrived' (1964: 283). In his view, poems, just like syllogisms, functioned as 'developing series' and the value of any such development was to be assessed according to the 'interest of its several stages' (ibid.). By allowing that performance (and film, by the same token) can philosophise, Cull is not bringing performance within the fold of philosophy, nor is she equating the two, but rather gesturing towards a more flexible understanding of what it means to think that establishes a mutually replenishing relationship between the two. Similarly, in his elegant statement, Trilling is reacting against compartmentalised reasoning, by inviting us to think of two usually opposing terms (emotions and ideas) as flowing into one another and developing in analogous ways.

I share Cull and Trilling's general sentiment, as my ambition and hopes for this book have been to place film and theatre in dialogue with one another in a way that expands understanding and appreciation of both. My case studies invite us to reflect on what film 'thinks' of theatre and how this thinking is formally carried out. It is at this point that I would like to return to Aumont's notion of film as a poetic act. The subtitle of this book contains the word 'poetics' in recognition of the nature of the questions I am asking and striving to address. As Jason Mittell has stated, 'the guiding question for poetics looking at a cultural text [. . .] is "how does this text work?"' (2015: 4). Bold claims have been made regarding both theatre and film. Chiel Kattenbelt has referred to theatre as 'the paradigm of all arts, and a hypermedium that incorporates all arts and media' (2006: 29), and in her book on cinema and intermediality Ágnes Pethő has argued that one of the persistent questions in the literature on film mediality has been: 'Is film (even in its traditional form) an "intermedium", a "composite" medium, in other words perhaps the ultimate "mixed" or "hybrid" medium that combines all kinds of media in its texture of signification?' (2011: 28). With the realisation that theatre is not just another object of representation in film but a medium of similar complexity and richness comes the need to understand how these representations 'work' in a formal sense, an understanding which is what this book has attempted to provide.

Part I of the book was concerned with examining in depth various ways of formally arraying theatre for a film audience and the effects that correspond to these diverse modes of embedment. In the process of exploring these formal arrangements (*mise en abyme*, bracketing, repetition, alternation, infinite regress structures and multiple framings), my analysis also teased out concepts that have proven resilient in the discussion of the two media (such as illusion, memory, fictional worlds, artistic truth) and reflected on their different medial articulations. Part II shifted emphasis towards considering how films that represent, evoke or record theatre negotiate the dynamic between spectators and performers, given the layered aspect of embedded representations and the phenomenological differences between the two media. This has led me to consider not only issues of point of view and point of audition, but also the imbrication of showing and telling in and between the two media. A separate chapter was dedicated to the complexities of monologic address in films which both explicitly and implicitly reference theatre. Although each case study constructs its own argument, they jointly contribute to an understanding of the versatility of the film medium in accommodating representations of theatre performances or rehearsals, in 'thinking' about theatre.

The case studies which have given texture to my argument were chosen because, without exception and without diminution, they made the representation of theatre the locus of an elaborate commentary on the interaction between the two media. All, in different ways, can be considered formal experiments. The earliest case study discussed in this book was Jacques Rivette's 1969 film *L'Amour fou*. For a study that uses intermediality as a guiding concept, the 1960s represent a meaningful, non-arbitrary starting point. It was in 1966 that Dick Higgins borrowed the term 'intermedium' from Samuel Taylor Coleridge to designate a 'conceptual fusion' of media (Zurbrugg 2004: 201) and to refer to objects and events, such as the ready-made and the happening, which, in his view, did not 'conform to the pure media' (Higgins [1966] 2002: 30) and were the negation of the 'precious object of any kind' (ibid.: 29). Higgins was reacting against a 'compartmentalised approach', which he felt was out of step with the changes he was seeing around him, changes he over-optimistically interpreted as 'the dawn of a classless society' (ibid.: 29). For Higgins, therefore, positioning oneself between media was first and foremost a political act. This is also evident in his views about traditional, 'proscenium theatre', which he saw as an 'outgrowth of seventeenth-century ideals of social order' and which he believed would be fundamentally challenged by the removal of the 'performance–audience separation', brought about by the happening as an intermedium (ibid.: 30–1). In this context, it is worth noting that, as several scholars have noted, the theatrical practices and set-ups that are represented in films are often of a traditionalist type. Jacques Gerstenkorn has remarked on the 'conventional, academic *mises en scène*' with which theatre is more often than not equated in films (1994: 16) and Alain Ménil has similarly written of the 'theatre of the cinephile' as a 'an aesthetic monster' that exists solely in cinemas (1998: 72). While this is certainly not the case for all the films discussed in this book, it happens often enough to warrant a mention.

The growing awareness of the exciting possibilities of challenging and intersecting media was consistent with the general 'aesthetic and social radicalism' of the 1960s (James 1989: 4), a period that saw the flourishing of a multitude of alternative practices, ranging from 'medium-specific, reflective filmmaking' to the 'filmless films' of the so-called 'expanded cinema' (Walley 2003: 16–17). Although I cannot claim that the films analysed in this book partake of a similar aesthetic and political insurrectionism, a post-1960s corpus was deliberately chosen because at this later date the attention that film accords theatre can no longer be explained away as the attempt of a newer medium to gain legitimacy by referencing an older and more venerable rival, the default explanation for earlier instances of both film adaptations of plays and filmic representations of theatre. If we were to use a cultural capital/taste formation paradigm, of the kind developed by Pierre Bourdieu, the representation of theatre in film could be viewed as having an upmarket appeal, but beyond this sociological lens, the representation of theatre can be underwritten by many different interests, having little or nothing to do with legitimacy and/or cultural prestige.

A compelling explanation for cinema's fascination with theatre at this later date has been offered by András Bálint Kovács in his book *Screening Modernism*. Writing about European art cinema in the interval 1950–80, Kovács distinguishes between several styles: minimalist, naturalist, ornamental and theatrical. Noting that modern ornamental films promote the cult of primitivism and 'represent the world of traditional mythologies as a hidden or unconscious mental structure underlying the cool, alienated and technological surface of the modern world' (2007: 182), Kovács finds that these types of films 'may have theater as a cultural referential background' (ibid.: 175), as is the case with Theo Angelopoulos's *The Travelling Players*, in which he detects a mixture of ornamentalism and minimalism. Understandably, however, he reserves his lengthier observations about theatre in modern cinema for his discussion of the theatrical style.

Kovács associates theatricality in modern cinema with the artificiality of either acting or mise-en-scène and briefly discusses a number of filmmakers deemed to have forged theatrical styles in cinema, chief among them Alain Resnais, Jean-Marie Straub and Danièle Huillet , R. W. Fassbinder and Hans Jürgen Syberberg and, to a lesser extent, directors such as Jean-Luc Godard, insofar as they have been influenced by Bertolt Brecht. Following in the footsteps of Pascal Bonitzer and Jacques Aumount, Kovács argues that the turn to theatricality and, through theatricality, to a form of abstraction was a response to a crisis of authenticity in modern cinema, signalling its desire for renewal (ibid.: 200–1). At the same time, he is careful to distinguish this modern quest for renewal through theatre from the postmodern use of theatre by directors such as Peter Greenaway, which serves the purpose not of a 'regeneration', but of a 'deconstruction' (ibid.: 202).

Béatrice Picon-Vallin has suggested that it is the 'multimedia climate' which brought film and theatre closer together (2001b: 193). She has formulated a number of hypotheses regarding film's formal and representational interest in the more 'artisanal' art of theatre, including a reaction against the 'technological multiplication of methods of reproduction and of surfaces of inscriptions (screens)', a desire to articulate a 'discourse of resistance' fuelled by what Pasolini called 'the revolutionary force of the past' or a fascination of an 'ethical' nature with theatre's working methods (ibid.: 193, translations mine). Picon-Vallin connects this newer phase in the relationship between film and theatre with changes that have occurred in the media landscape.

Epilogue

Although this book has not explicitly asked what it is about the filmic representations of theatre that appeals to filmmakers and scholars alike, I would like to add another potential rationale for the appeal of filmic representations of theatre, a rationale that bears some similarity both to Picon-Vallin's views and to Paul Young's discussion of the way in which Hollywood responded to the rising threat of media such as radio, television and internet, by mounting 'an institutional defense of classical form, address and spectatorship' (2006: xxviii). For Young, this institutional defence took the form of a body of film work grouped under the label 'media fantasy films', which expressed the anxieties and hopes surrounding the new media and thus engaged in a discursive negotiation of media identities and meanings. Whereas Young's book is concerned with how Hollywood envisioned the media future, this book has looked at how an alternative mode of film practice, the arthouse film, envisioned the media past, by repositioning the film medium in relation to theatre, in what might seem a retrograde media fantasy. This calls to mind Marshall McLuhan's concept of the 'rear-view mirror', whereby 'we move into the future with our sight on the past' (Levinson 1999: 15). Film's attachment to theatre could perhaps be seen as a form of coping with the uncertainties of the (digital) future.

Bibliography

Acevedo-Muñoz, Ernesto (2003), 'The Body and Spain: Pedro Almodóvar's *All About My Mother*', *Quarterly Review of Film and Video*, 21:1, 25–38.
Affron, Mirella (1978), '*Les Enfants du Paradis*: Play of Genres', *Cinema Journal*, 18:1, Autumn, 45–52.
Ailloud-Nicholas, Catherine (2003), '"Prenons une chaise" dans tous les sens ... du terme: de l'objet textuel à l'objet scénique', in Christine Hamon-Sirejols and Anne Surgers (eds), *Théâtre: espace sonore, espace visuel*, Lyon: Presses Universitaires de Lyon, 243–58.
Allen, Richard (1993), 'Representation, Illusion, and the Cinema', *Cinema Journal*, 32:2, Winter, 21–48.
Allen, Richard (1995), *Projecting Illusion: Film Spectatorship and the Impression of Reality*, Cambridge: Cambridge University Press.
Allen, Richard (1998), 'Film Spectatorship: A Reply to Murray Smith', *The Journal of Aesthetics and Art Criticism*, 56:1, 61–3.
Allinson, Mark (2005), '*Todo sobre mi madre/All About My Mother* (Pedro Almodóvar, Spain, 1999)', in Alberto Mira (ed.), *The Cinema of Spain and Portugal*, London and New York: Wallflower Press, 229–36.
Alpers, Paul (1982), 'What Is Pastoral?', *Critical Inquiry*, 8:3, Spring, 437–60.
Altman, Rick (1980), 'Moving Lips: Cinema as Ventriloquism', *Yale French Studies*, 60, 67–79.
Altman, Rick (1992), 'Sound Space', in Rick Altman (ed.), *Sound Theory Sound Practice*, New York, London: Routledge, 46–64.
Arroyo, José (1999), '*Todo sobre mi madre*', *Sight and Sound*, 9:9, 40.
Aumont, Jacques, Jean-Louis Comolli, Jean Narboni and Sylvie Pierre (1977), 'Time Overflowing: Interview with Jacques Rivette', trans. Amy Gateff, in Jonathan Rosenbaum (ed.), *Rivette: Texts and Interviews*, London: BFI, 9–38.
Aumont, Jacques (2007), 'Un film, peut-il être un acte de théorie?', *Cinémas: Revue d'Etudes Cinématographiques*, 17:2/3, Spring, 193–211.
Auslander, Philip (2005), 'Performance as Therapy: Spalding Gray's Autopathographic Monologues', in Carrie Sandahl and Philip Auslander (eds), *Bodies in Commotion: Disability and Performance*, Ann Arbor: University of Michigan Press, 163–74.
Baglia, Jay and Elissa Foster (2005), 'Performing the "Really" Real: Cultural Criticism, Representation, and Commodification in *The Laramie Project*', *Journal of Dramatic Theory and Criticism*, 19:2, 127–45.
Baker-White, Robert (1999), *The Text in Play: Representations of Rehearsal in Modern Drama*, Lewisburg: Bucknell University Press.
Baldick, Chris (2001), *The Concise Oxford Dictionary of Literary Terms*, Oxford: Oxford University Press.
Ballesteros, Isolina (2009), 'Performing Identities in the Cinema of Pedro Almodóvar', in

Brad Epps and Despina Kakoudaki (eds), *All About Almodóvar*, Minneapolis: University of Minnesota Press, 71–100.

Bardèche, Marie-Laure (1999), *Le principe de répétition: Littérature et modernité*, Paris, Montréal: L'Harmattan.

Barkan, Leonard (1981), '"Living Sculptures": Ovid, Michelangelo, and the *Winter's Tale*', *ELH*, 48:4, Winter, 639–67.

Barker, Jennifer M. (2012), 'Sonic Bodies: Listening as Acting', in Aaron Taylor (ed.), *Theorizing Film Acting*, New York and London: Routledge, 243–55.

Barnes, Betsy K. (1995), 'Discourse Particles in French Conversation: (eh) ben, bon and enfin', *The French Review*, 68:5, 813–21.

Barranger, M. S. (1975), 'Death as Initiation in "Exit the King"', *Educational Theatre Journal*, 27:4, December, 504–7.

Barthes, Roland (1976), 'The Dolls of Bunraku', trans. David Savran, *Diacritics*, 6:4, 44–7.

Bay-Cheng, Sarah (2007), 'Theatre Squared: Theatre History in the Age of Media', *Theatre Topics*, 17:1, March, 37–50.

Bazin, André (1967), *What Is Cinema? Volume I*, trans. Hugh Gray, Berkeley, Los Angeles and London: University of California Press.

Bellour, Raymond (1979), 'Cine-Repetitions', *Screen*, 20:2, Summer, 65–72.

Belting, Hans (2005), 'Image, Medium, Body: A New Approach to Iconology', *Critical Inquiry*, 31:2, Winter, 302–19.

Bersani, Leo and Ulysse Dutoit (2004), *Forms of Being: Cinema, Aesthetics and Subjectivity*, London: BFI.

Bersani, Leo and Ulysse Dutoit (2009), 'Rohmer's Salon', *Film Quarterly*, 63:1, Fall, 23–35.

Billington, Michael (1993), *One Night Stands: A Critic's View of Modern British Theatre*, London: Nick Hern Books.

Blau, Herbert (2010), 'The Most Concealed Object', in Jane Collins and Andrew Nisbet (eds), *Theatre and Performance Design: A Reader in Scenography*, London and New York: Routledge, 51–5.

Bleeker, Maaike (2008), *Visuality in the Theatre: The Locus of Looking*, Basingstoke: Palgrave Macmillan.

Bliss, Michael and Christina Banks (1996), *What Goes Around Comes Around: The Films of Jonathan Demme*, Carbondale and Edwardsville: Southern Illinois University Press.

Bloom, Harold (ed.) (2003), *Wallace Stevens: Bloom's Major Poets*, Philadelphia: Chelsea House.

Blouin, Patrice (2001), 'Fin de partie', *Cahiers du cinéma*, 560, September, 72–4.

Bollas, Christopher (1993), *Being a Character: Psychoanalysis and Self Experience*, London and New York: Routledge.

Bolter, Jay David and Richard Grusin (2000), *Remediation: Understanding New Media*, Cambridge, MA and London: MIT Press.

Bolton, Christopher A. (2002), 'From Wooden Cyborgs to Celluloid Souls: Mechanical Bodies in Anime and Japanese Puppet Theater', *positions: asia critique*, 10:3, 729–71.

Bordwell, David (1997), 'Modernism, Minimalism, Melancholy: Angelopoulos and Visual Style', in Andrew Horton (ed.), *The Last Modernist: The Films of Theo Angelopoulos*, Trowbridge: Flicks Books, 11–26.

Bordwell, David (2005), *Figures Traced in Light: On Cinematic Staging*, Berkeley, Los Angeles and London: University of California Press.

Bory, Jean-Louis (1968), '*L'Amour fou* de Jacques Rivette', *Le Nouvel Observateur*, 21/10, Revue de presse numérisée, La Bibliothèque du Film, Cinémathèque Française, Paris.

Bottoms, Stephen (2006), 'Putting the Document into Documentary: An Unwelcome Corrective?', *TDR*, 50:3, Autumn, 56–68.
Branigan, Edward (1984), *Point of View in the Cinema: A Theory of Narration and Subjectivity in Classical Film*, Berlin, New York and Amsterdam: Mouton.
Branigan, Edward (2006), *Projecting a Camera: Language-Games in Film Theory*, New York and London: Routledge.
Brecht, Bertolt (2014), *Brecht on Theatre*, ed. Marc Silberman, Steve Giles and Tom Kuhn, trans. Jack Davis, Romy Fursland, Steve Giles, Victoria Hill, Kristopher Imbrigotta, Marc Silberman and John Willett, London: Bloomsbury.
Brenner, Marie (1981), 'My Conversation with André', *New York Magazine*, 19 October, 36–40.
Brewster, Ben and Lea Jacobs (1997), *Theatre to Cinema: Stage Pictorialism and the Early Feature Film*, Oxford: Oxford University Press.
Brown, Tom (2012), *Breaking the Fourth Wall: Direct Address in the Cinema*, Edinburgh: Edinburgh University Press.
Burnham, Douglas and Martin Jesinghausen (2010), *Nietzsche's Thus Spoke Zarathustra: An Edinburgh Philosophical Guide*, Edinburgh: Edinburgh University Press.
Burns, Elizabeth (1972), *Theatricality: A Study of Convention in the Theatre and in Social Life*, London: Longman.
Cahir, Linda Costanzo (1994), 'The Artful Rerouting of *A Streetcar Named Desire*', *Literature Film Quarterly*, 22:2, 72–7.
Capra, Steve (2004), *Theater Voices: Conversations on the Stage*, Lanham: Scarecrow Press.
Cardullo, Bert (ed.) (2012), *Stage and Screen: Adaptation Theory from 1916 to 2000*, London: Continuum.
Carlson, Marvin (1993), *Theories of the Theatre: A Historical and Critical Survey, from the Greeks to the Present*, Ithaca: Cornell University Press.
Carlson, Marvin (2003), *The Haunted Stage: The Theatre as Memory Machine*, Ann Arbor: University of Michigan Press.
Carney, Raymond (1985), *American Dreaming: The Films of John Cassavetes and the American Experience*, Berkeley, Los Angeles and London: University of California Press.
Carroll, Noël (1982), 'The Future of Allusion: Hollywood in the Seventies (and Beyond)', *October*, 20, 51–81.
Carroll, Noël (2003), *Engaging the Moving Image*, New Haven and London: Yale University Press.
Casado-Gual, Núria (2014), 'Old Tropes through New Lenses: Representing the Older Actor in Manoel de Oliveira's *I'm Going Home* and Roger Michell's *Venus*', *Quarterly Review of Film and Video*, 32:3, 208–15.
Casetti, Francesco (2009), 'Filmic Experience', trans. Dafne Calgaro and Victoria Duckett, *Screen*, 50:1, 56–66.
Casey, Edward (2000), *Remembering: A Phenomenological Study*, Bloomington and Indianapolis: Indiana University Press.
Cavell, Stanley (1979), *The World Viewed: Reflections on the Ontology of Film*, Cambridge, MA and London: Harvard University Press.
Cavell, Stanley (2004), *Cities of Words: Pedagogical Letters on a Register of the Moral Life*, Cambridge, MA and London: The Belknap Press of Harvard University Press.
Caws, Mary Ann (1989), *The Art of Interference: Stressed Readings in Verbal and Visual Texts*, Cambridge: Polity Press.
Chaim, Daphna Ben (1981), *Distance in the Theatre: The Aesthetics of Audience Response*, Ann Arbor, Michigan: UMI Research Press.
Charity, Tom (2001), *John Cassavetes: Lifeworks*, London: Omnibus Press.

Chazal, Robert (1969), '"L'Amour fou": une passionnante expérience', *France-soir*, 29/01, Revue de presse numérisée, La Bibliothèque du Film, Cinémathèque Française, Paris.
Chevrie, Marc (n.d.), 'Les aventures de la fiction: "Mais le lendemain matin . . ."', in *Jacques Rivette: La Règle du Jeu*, Turin: Centre Culturel Français de Turin, Museo Nazionale del Cinema di Torino, 133–7.
Child, Doreen Alexander (2010), *Charlie Kaufman: Confessions of an Original Mind*, Santa Barbara: Praeger.
Chion, Michel (1983), 'Bouvard et Pécuchet dînent à New York', *Cahiers du cinéma*, 346, April, 50–1.
Chion, Michel (1994), *Audio-Vision: Sound on Screen*, ed. and trans. Claudia Gorbman, New York: Columbia University Press.
Chion, Michel (1999), *The Voice in Cinema*, ed. and trans. Claudia Gorbman, New York: Columbia University Press.
Chion, Michel (2009), *Film, a Sound Art*, trans. Claudia Gorbman, New York: Columbia University Press.
Chirico, Miriam (2016), 'Performed Authenticity: Narrating the Self in the Comic Monologues of David Sedaris, John Leguizamo, and Spalding Gray', *Studies in American Humor*, 2:1, 22–46.
Ciment, Michel and Noë Herpe (2001), 'Ce qui nous reste, c'est la mémoire: Entretien Manoel de Oliveira', *Positif*, 487, September, 8–12.
Ciment, Michel and Stéphane Goudet (2003), 'Entretien Takeshi Kitano: Au coeur de l'amour, la mort n'est jamais loin', *Positif*, 506, April, 15–19.
Cisneros, James (2007), 'Remains To Be Seen: Intermediality, Ekphrasis, and Institution', in Marion Froger and Jürgen E. Müller (eds), *Intermedialité et socialité: Histoire et géographie d'un concept*, Münster: Nodus Publikationen, 15–28.
Claycomb, Ryan (2003), '(Ch)oral history: Documentary Theatre, the Communal Subject and Progressive Politics', *Journal of Dramatic Theory and Criticism*, 17:2, 95–122.
Coates, Paul (2008), 'On the Dialectics of Filmic Colors (in general) and Red (in particular): *Three Colors: Red*, *Red Desert*, *Cries and Whispers*, and *The Double Life of Véronique*', *Film Criticism*, 32:3, 2–23.
Cole, Susan Letzler (1991), *The Absent One: Mourning Ritual, Tragedy, and the Performance of Ambivalence*, University Park: Penn State University Press.
Collard, Christophe (2014), 'Mediaturgy's Troubled Tensions with Adaptation: Convergence or Divergence?', *Adaptation*, 7:3, 265–74.
Conkie, Rob (2012), 'Rehearsal: The Pleasures of the Flesh', *Shakespeare Bulletin*, 30:4, 411–29.
Corrigan, Mary Ann (1997), 'Realism and Theatricalism in *A Streetcar Named Desire*', in Robert A. Martin (ed.), *Critical Essays on Tennessee Williams*, New York: G. K. Hall, 83–93.
Coste, Didier and John Pier (2009), 'Narrative Levels', in Peter Hühn, John Pier, Wolf Schmid and Jörg Schönert (eds), *Handbook of Narratology*, Berlin, New York: Walter de Gruyter, 295–308.
Cull, Laura (2014), 'Performance Philosophy – Staging a New Field', in Laura Cull and Alice Lagaay (eds), *Encounters in Performance Philosophy*, Basingstoke: Palgrave Macmillan, 15–38.
Curchod, Olivier and Eric Rohmer (1992), 'Coïncidences: Entretien avec Eric Rohmer par Olivier Curchod', *Positif*, 372, February, 24–30.
Dällenbach, Lucien [1977] (1989), *The Mirror in the Text*, trans. Jeremy Whiteley with Emma Hughes, Cambridge: Polity Press.
Daney, Serge (1982), 'Revoir *L'Amour fou*', *Libération*, 22/08, Revue de presse numérisée, La Bibliothèque du Film, Cinémathèque Française, Paris.

Daussois, Guy (1969), 'L'Amour fou', *Populaire*, 31/01, Revue de presse numérisée, La Bibliothèque du Film, Cinémathèque Française, Paris.
Demastes, William W. (1989), 'Spalding Gray's *Swimming to Cambodia* and the Evolution of an Ironic Presence', *Theatre Journal*, 41:1, March, 75–94.
Demastes, William W. (2008), *Spalding Gray's America*, New York: Limelight.
Deming, Richard (2011), 'Living a Part: *Synecdoche, New York*, Metaphor, and the Problem of Skepticism', in David LaRocca (ed.), *The Philosophy of Charlie Kaufman*, Lexington: University Press of Kentucky, 193–207.
Demopoulos, Michel and Frida Liappas (2001), 'A Journey through Greek Landscape and History: *The Travelling Players*', in Dan Fainaru (ed.), *Theo Angelopoulos Interviews*, Jackson: University Press of Mississippi, 16–22.
Deschamps, Hélène (2001), *Jacques Rivette: théâtre, amour, cinema*, Paris: L'Harmattan.
D'Lugo, Marvin (2002), 'The Geopolitical Aesthetic in Recent Spanish Films', *Post Script*, 21:2, Winter, <http://www.freepatentsonline.com/article/PostScript/94061530.thml> (last accessed 11 October 2012).
Doane, Mary Ann (1980), 'The Voice in the Cinema: The Articulation of Body and Space', *Yale French Studies*, 60, 33–50.
Doane, Mary Ann (2007), 'The Indexical and the Concept of Medium Specificity', *Differences: A Journal of Feminist Cultural Studies*, 18:1, 128–52.
Dolan, Jill (2005), *Utopia in Performance: Finding Hope at the Theater*, Ann Arbor: University of Michigan Press.
Dolezel, Lubomir (1988), 'Mimesis and Possible Worlds', *Poetics Today*, 9: 3, 475–96.
Dunbar, Andrea (1980), *The Arbor*, London: Pluto Press.
Dupeyron, Georges (1969), 'L'Amour fou', *Europe*, 1/06, Revue de presse numérisée, La Bibliothèque du Film, Cinémathèque Française, Paris.
Durand, Régis (1997), 'The Disposition of the Voice', in Timothy Murray (ed.), *Mimesis, Masochism, and Mime: The Politics of Theatricality in Contemporary French Thought*, Ann Arbor: University of Michigan Press, 301–10.
Eidt, Laura M. Sager (2008), *Writing and Filming the Painting: Ekphrasis in Literature and Film*, Amsterdam, New York: Rodopi.
Elleström, Lars (2010), 'The Modalities of Media: A Model for Understanding Intermedial Relations', in Lars Elleström (ed.), *Media Borders, Multimodality and Intermediality*, Basingstoke: Palgrave Macmillan, 11–48.
Elliott, Kamilla (2014), 'Rethinking Formal–Cultural and Textual–Contextual Divides in Adaptation Studies', *Literature Film Quarterly*, 42:3, 576–93.
Elsaesser, Thomas (1991), 'Tales of Sound and Fury: Observations on the Family Melodrama', in Marcia Landy (ed.), *Imitations of Life: A Reader of Film & Television Melodrama*, Detroit: Wayne State University Press, 68–91.
Elsaesser, Thomas and Malte Hagener (2010), *Film theory: An Introduction Through the Senses*, New York and London: Routledge.
Elster, Jon (1999), *Alchemies of the Mind: Rationality and the Emotions*, Cambridge: Cambridge University Press.
Ennis, Tom (1996), 'Textual Interplay: The Case of Rohmer's *Ma nuit chez Maud* and *Conte d'hiver*', *French Cultural Studies*, 7, 309–19.
Erickson, Jon (2009), 'On Mimesis (and Truth) in Performance', *Journal of Dramatic Theory and Criticism*, 23:2, Spring, 21–37.
Erll, Astrid (2011), *Memory in Culture*, trans. Sara B. Young, Basingstoke: Palgrave Macmillan.

Evans, Joel (2014), 'Figuring the Global: on Charlie Kaufman's *Synecdoche, New York*', *New Review of Film and Television Studies*, 12:4, 321–38.

Favorini, Attilio (2008), *Memory in Play: From Aeschylus to Sam Shepherd*, New York: Palgrave Macmillan.

Felleman, Susan (2006), *Art in the Cinematic Imagination*, Austin: University of Texas Press.

Féral, Josette (1982), 'Performance and Theatricality: The Subject Demystified', trans. Terese Lyons, *Modern Drama*, 25:1, Spring, 170–81.

Féral, Josette (2002), 'Theatricality: The Specificity of Theatrical Language', trans. Ronald P. Bermingham, *SubStance*, 31:2/3, 94–108.

Filmer, Andrew and Kate Rossmanith (2011), 'Space and Actor Formation', *Theatre Research International*, 36:3, 228–39.

Findlay, Robert (1980), 'Grotowski's "Cultural Explorations Bordering on Art, Especially Theatre"', *Theatre Journal*, 32:3, October, 349–56.

Fischer-Lichte, Erika (2003), 'Embodiment – From Page to Stage: The Dramatic Figure', in Christine Hamon-Sirejols and Anne Surgers (eds), *Théâtre: espace sonore, espace visuel*, Lyon: Presses Universitaires de Lyon, 145–55.

Fleche, Anne (1995), 'When a Door Is a Jar, or Out in the Theatre: Tennessee Williams and Queer Space', *Theatre Journal*, 47:2, May, 253–67.

Fludernik, Monika (2003), 'Scene Shift, Metalepsis, and the Metaleptic Mode', *Style*, 37:4, <http://findarticles.com/p/articles/mi_m2342/is_4_37/ai_n6344005/> (last accessed 5 November 2011).

Fowler, D. P. (1991), 'Narrate and Describe: The Problem of Ekphrasis', *The Journal of Roman Studies*, 81, 25–35.

Frappat, Hélène (2001), *Jacques Rivette, secret compris*, Paris: Cahiers du Cinéma.

French, Philip (ed.) (1993), *Malle on Malle*, London: Faber & Faber.

Frentz, Thomas S. (1999), 'Rhetorical Conversation, Time and Moral Action', in Jean Louis Lucaites, Celeste Michelle Condit and Sally Caudill (eds), *Contemporary Rhetorical Theory: A Reader*, New York: The Guilford Press, 288–99.

Frey, Hugo (2004), *Louis Malle*, Manchester and New York: Manchester University Press.

Fried, Michael (1980), *Absorption and Theatricality: Painting and Beholder in the Age of Diderot*, Chicago: Chicago University Press.

Froger, Marion (2007), 'Introduction: Appareil et intermédialité', in Jean-Louis Déotte, Marion Froger and Silvestra Mariniello (eds), *Appareil et intermédialité*, Paris: L'Harmattan, 5–15.

Füredy, Viveca (1989), 'A Structural Model for Phenomena with Embedding in Literature and Other Arts', *Poetics Today*, 10:4, Winter, 745–69.

Gaggi, Silvio (1986), 'Sculpture, Theater, and Art Performance: Notes on the Convergence of the Arts', *Leonardo*, 19:1, 45–52.

Garner Jr., Stanton B. (1994), *Bodied Spaces: Phenomenology and Performance in Contemporary Drama*, Ithaca and London: Cornell University Press.

Gaudreault, André (2000), 'The Diversity of Cinematographic Connections in the Intermedial Context of the Turn of the 20th Century', in Simon Popple and Vanessa Toulmin (eds), *Visual Delights: Essays on the Popular and Projected Image in the 19th Century*, Trowbridge: Flicks Books, 8–15.

Gaudreault, André and Philippe Marion (2005), 'The Neo-Institutionalization of Cinema as a New Medium', in Simon Popple and Vanessa Toulmin (eds), *Visual Delights Two: Exhibition and Reception*, Eastleigh: John Libbey, 87–95.

Gaudreault, André (2009), *From Plato to Lumière: Narration and Monstration in Literature and*

Cinema, trans. Timothy Barnard, Toronto, Buffalo and London: University of Toronto Press.

Geis, Deborah R. (1993), *Postmodern Theatric(k)s: Monologue in Contemporary American Drama*, Ann Arbor: University of Michigan Press.

Genette, Gérard (1980), *Narrative Discourse: An Essay in Method*, trans. Jane E. Lewin, Ithaca, New York: Cornell University Press.

Genette, Gérard (1997), *Palimpsests: Literature in the Second Degree*, trans. Channa Newman and Claude Doubinsky, Lincoln and London: University of Nebraska Press.

Gerow, Aaron (2007), *Kitano Takeshi*, London: BFI.

Gerstenkorn, Jacques (1994), 'Lever de rideau', in Christine Hamon-Sirejols, Jacques Gerstenkorn and André Gardies (eds), *Cinéma et théâtralité*, Lyon: Cahiers du Gritec, Aléas, 13–18.

Giavarini, Laurence (1992), 'Les Vies de Félicie', *Cahiers du cinéma*, 452, February, 20–2.

Gibson, Andrew (2001), '"And the Wind Wheezing Through That Organ Once in a While": Voice, Narrative, Film', *New Literary History*, 32:3, Summer, 639–57.

Goffman, Erving (1986), *Frame Analysis: An Essay on the Organization of Experience*, Boston: Northeastern University.

Goodman, Nelson (1978), *Ways of Worldmaking*, Hassocks: Harvester.

Gorfinkel, Elena (2005), 'The Future of Anachronism: Todd Haynes and the Magnificent Andersons', in Marijke de Valck and Malte Hagener (eds), *Cinephilia: Movies, Love and Memory*, Amsterdam: Amsterdam University Press, 153–67.

Gray, Spalding (1982), 'Interview', *Alive: The New Performance Magazine*, November/December, 19–21.

Gray, Spalding (1985), *Swimming to Cambodia*, New York: Theatre Communications Group.

Gray, Spalding (1991), *Monster in a Box*, London, Sydney and Auckland: Pan.

Gray, Spalding (1992), *Impossible Vacation*, New York: Vintage.

Gray, Spalding and Nell Casey (ed.) (2011), *The Journals of Spalding Gray*, New York: Alfred A. Knopf.

Green, Eugène (2010), 'All the World's a Stage', *Sight & Sound*, 20:11, 14.

Gruber, William (2010), *Offstage Space, Narrative, and the Theatre of the Imagination*, New York: Palgrave.

Gurr, Andrew (1983), 'The Bear, the Statue, and Hysteria in *The Winter's Tale*', *Shakespeare Quarterly*, 34:4, Winter, 420–5.

Gussow, Mel (2000), 'Off- and Off-Off Broadway', in Don B. Wilmeth and Christopher Bigsy (eds), *The Cambridge History of American Theatre Volume III: Post-World War II to the 1990s*, Cambridge: Cambridge University Press, 196–223.

Haltof, Marek (2004), *The Cinema of Krzysztof Kieślowski: Variations on Destiny and Chance*, London and New York: Wallflower Press.

Hamilton, James R. (1982), '"Illusion" and the Distrust of Theatre', *The Journal of Aesthetics and Art Criticism*, 41:1, Fall, 39–50.

Hammond, Will and Dan Steward (eds) (2008), *Verbatim Verbatim: Contemporary Documentary Theatre*, London: Oberon.

Hamon-Sirejols, Christine, Jacques Gerstenkorn and André Gardies (eds) (1994), *Cinéma et théâtralité*, Lyon: Cahiers du Gritec, Aléas.

Hawker, Rosemary (2009), 'Idiom Post-medium: Richter Painting Photography', *Oxford Art Journal*, 32:2, 263–80.

Heath, Stephen (1981), *Questions of Cinema*, Bloomington: Indiana University Press.

Heffernan, James A. W. (1991), 'Ekphrasis and Representation', *New Literary History*, 22:2, Spring, 297–316.
Heine, Steven (1994), 'Tragedy and Salvation in the Floating World: Chikamatsu's Double Suicide Drama as Millenarian Discourse', *The Journal of Asian Studies*, 53:2, May, 367–93.
Heinemann, David (2000), 'Reinventing Romance: Eric Rohmer's *Tales of the Four Seasons*: Freedom, Faith, and the Search for the Grail', *Film Comment*, 36:6, November/December, 50–4.
Helman, Alicja (1999), 'Women in Kieślowski's Late Films', in Paul Coates (ed.), *Lucid Dreams: The Films of Krzysztof Kieślowski*, Trowbridge: Flicks Books, 116–35.
Hickling, Alfred (2010), 'Back to Bradford: Andrea Dunbar Remembered on film', *The Guardian*, 12 April, <https://www.theguardian.com/film/2010/apr/12/theatre> (last accessed 10 April 2018).
Higgins, Dick [1966] (2002), 'Intermedia', in Randall Packer and Ken Jordan (eds), *Multimedia: From Wagner to Virtual Reality*, New York and London: Norton, 27–32.
Hilderbrand, Lucas (2004), '*Adaptation*', *Film Quarterly*, 58:1, Autumn, 36–43.
Hill, Derek (2008), *Charlie Kaufman and Hollywood's Merry Band of Pranksters, Fabulists and Dreamers: An Excursion into the American New Wave*, Herts: Kamera Books.
Hill, Derek (2011), '"There's No More Watching": Artifice and Meaning in *Synecdoche, New York* and *Adaptation*', in David LaRocca (ed.), *The Philosophy of Charlie Kaufman*, Lexington: University Press of Kentucky, 208–23.
Hironaga, Shuzaburo (1976), *The Bunraku Handbook: A Comprehensive Guide to Japan's Unique Puppet Theatre with Synopses of All Popular Plays*, Tokyo: Maison des Arts.
Hirsh, James (2012), 'Dialogic Self-address in Shakespeare's Plays', *Shakespeare*, 8:3, 312–27.
Holmes, Su and Deborah Jermyn (2015), 'Here, There and Nowhere: Ageing, Gender and Celebrity Studies', in Deborah Jermyn and Su Holmes (eds), *Women, Celebrity and Cultures of Ageing*, Basingstoke: Palgrave Macmillan, 11–24.
Horton, Andrew (1997), *Theo Angelopoulos: A Cinema of Contemplation*, Princeton: Princeton University Press.
Hurt, James (ed.) (1974), *Focus on Film and Theatre*, Englewood Cliffs, London: Prentice Hall.
Hutcheon, Linda (1980), *Narcissistic Narrative: The Metafictional Paradox*, Waterloo Ontario: Wilfrid Laurier University Press.
Hyers, Conrad (1996), *The Spirituality of Comedy: Comic Heroism in a Tragic World*, New Brunswick, NJ: Transaction.
Ibáñez, Juan Carlos (2013), 'Memory, Politics, and the Post-Transition in Almodóvar's Cinema', in Marvin D'Lugo and Kathleen M. Vernon (eds), *A Companion to Pedro Almodóvar*, Chichester: John Wiley, 153–75.
Insdorf, Annette (1999), *Double Lives, Second Chances: The Cinema of Krzysztof Kieślowski*, New York: Miramax.
Ionesco, Eugene (1963), *Plays – Volume V*, trans. Donald Watson, London: John Calder.
Israel-Pelletier, Aimée (2005), 'Godard, Rohmer, and Rancière's "Phrase-Image"', *SubStance*, 34:3, 33–46.
Jackson, Russell (2013), *Theatres on Film: How the Cinema Imagines the Stage*, Manchester: Manchester University Press.
James, David E. (1989), *Allegories of Cinema: American Film in the Sixties*, Princeton: Princeton University Press.
James, Nick (2010), 'Clio, Andrea and Lorraine Too', *Sight and Sound*, 20:11, November, 25–6.
Janik, Vicky K. (1998), 'Introduction', in Vicky K. Janik (ed.), *Fools and Jesters in Literature, Art,*

and History: A Bio-Bibliographical Sourcebook, Westport, CT and London: Greenwood Press, 1–22.

Jermyn, Deborah (2012), '"Get a Life, Ladies. Your Old One Is Not Coming Back": Ageing, Ageism and the Lifespan of Female Celebrity', *Celebrity Studies*, 3:1, 1–12.

Johnson, Beth (2016), 'Art Cinema and *The Arbor*: Tape-recorded Testimony, Film Art and Feminism', *Journal of British Cinema and Television*, 13:2, 278–91.

Johnson, Randal (2007), *Manoel de Oliveira*, Urbana and Chicago: University of Illinois Press.

Jones, Simon (2008), 'New Theatre for New Times: Decentralisation, Innovation and Pluralism, 1975–2000', in Baz Kershaw (ed.), *The Cambridge History of British Theatre*, Cambridge: Cambridge University Press, 448–69.

Jones, Stanleigh H. (2013), 'Introduction', in *Bunraku Puppet Theatre: Honor, Vengeance, and Love in Four Plays of the 18th and 19th Centuries*, Honolulu: University of Hawaii Press, 1–9.

Jordan, Isabelle (1975), 'Pour un cinéma épique', *Positif*, 174, October, 15–22.

Kakutani, Michiko (2007), 'Ingmar Bergman: Summing Up a Life in Film', in Raphael Shargel (ed.), *Ingmar Bergman Interviews*, Jackson: University of Mississippi, 156–70.

Kalin, Jesse (2003), *The Films of Ingmar Bergman*, Cambridge: Cambridge University Press.

Kammer, Karry (1986), 'Spalding Gray by Karry Kammer', *Bomb*, 17, Fall, <http://bombmagazine.org/article/833/spalding-gray> (last accessed 14 August 2017).

Kaplin, Stephen (1999), 'A Puppet Tree: A Model for the Field of Puppet Theatre', *The Drama Review*, 43:3, Autumn, 28–35.

Kattenbelt, Chiel (2006), 'Theatre as the Art of the Performer and the Stage of Intermediality', in Freda Chapple and Chiel Kattenbelt (eds), *Intermediality in Theatre and Performance*, Amsterdam, New York: Rodopi, 29–39.

Katzman, Lisa (1989), '*Opening Night*: Moment by Moment', *Film Comment*, 25:3, 1989, 34–9.

Kaufman, Charlie (2008), *Synecdoche, New York: The Shooting Script*, New York: New Market Press.

Kaufman, Helena and Anna Klobucka (1997), 'Politics and Culture in Postrevolutionary Portugal', in Helena Kaufman and Anna Klobucka (eds), *After the Revolution: Twenty Years of Portuguese Literature, 1974–1994*, Lewisburg: Bucknell University Press, 13–30.

Kawin, Bruce F. (1972), *Telling It Again and Again: Repetition in Literature and Film*, Ithaca and London: Cornell University Press.

Kawin, Bruce (1981–2), '*My Dinner with André*', *Film Quarterly*, 35:2, Winter, 61–3.

Keene, Donald (1990), *Major Plays of Chikamatsu*, New York: Columbia University Press.

Kehr, Dave (2002), 'Distributor Wanted: "I'm Going Home"', *Film Comment*, 38:1, January, 18.

Kickasola, Joseph G. (2004), *The Films of Krzysztof Kieślowski: The Liminal Image*, New York, London: Continuum.

Kilbourn, Russell J. A. (2010), *Cinema, Memory, Modernity: The Representation of Memory from the Art Film to Transnational Cinema*, New York and London: Routledge.

Kim, Ji-Hoon (2009), 'The Post-medium Condition and the Explosion of Cinema', *Screen*, 50:1, Spring, 114–23.

Kimbrough, Andrew M. (2011), *Dramatic Theories of Voice in the Twentieth Century*, Amherst, New York: Cambria Press.

Kinder, Marsha (2004), 'Reinventing the Motherland: Almodóvar's Brain-Dead Trilogy', *Film Quarterly*, 58:2, Winter, 9–25.

Kinder, Marsha (2013), 'Re-envoicements and Reverberations in Almodóvar's Macro-Melodrama', in Marvin D'Lugo and Kathleen M. Vernon (eds), *A Companion to Pedro Almodóvar*, Chichester: John Wiley, 281–303.

King, Geoff (2009), *Indiewood, USA: Where Hollywood Meets Independent Cinema*, London, New York: I. B. Tauris.
King, Homay (2004), 'Free Indirect Affect in Cassavetes' *Opening Night* and *Faces*', *Camera Obscura*, 56, 19:2, 105–39.
Kirkkopelto, Esa (2009), 'The Question of the Scene: On the Philosophical Foundations of Theatrical Anthropocentrism', *Theatre Research International*, 34:3, 230–42.
Kirkkopelto, Esa (2014) 'The Most Mimetic Animal: An Attempt to Deconstruct the Actor's Body', in Laura Cull and Alice Lagaay (eds), *Encounters in Performance Philosophy*, Basingstoke and New York: Palgrave Macmillan, 121–44.
Knopf, Robert (ed.) (2005), *Theater and Film: A Comparative Anthology*, New Haven and London: Yale University Press.
Kolin, Philip C. (2000), *Williams: A Streetcar Named Desire*, Cambridge: Cambridge University Press.
Kotzamani, Marina (2009), 'Athens in the Twenty First Century', *PAJ: A Journal of Performance and Art*, 31:2, May, 12–44.
Koutsourakis, Angelos (2015), 'The *Gestus* of Showing: Brecht, Tableaux and Early Cinema in Angelopoulos' Political Period (1970–1980)', in Angelos Koutsourakis and Mark Steven (eds), *The Cinema of Theo Angelopoulos* [Kindle book], Edinburgh: Edinburgh University Press.
Kouvaros, George (2004), *Where Does It Happen? John Cassavetes and the Cinema at Breaking Point*, Minneapolis/London: University of Minnesota Press.
Kovács, András Bálint (2007), *Screening Modernism: European Art Cinema 1950–1980*, Chicago and London: University of Chicago Press.
Kozloff, Sarah (1988), *Invisible Storytellers: Voice-Over Narration in American Fiction Film*, Berkeley, Los Angeles and London: University of California Press.
Kozloff, Sarah (2000), *Overhearing Film Dialogue*, Berkeley, Los Angeles: University of California Press.
Krauss, Rosalind E. (1999), *'A Voyage on the North Sea': Art in the Age of the Post-medium Condition*, London: Thames & Hudson.
Krauss, Rosalind E. (2010), *Perpetual Inventory*, Cambridge, MA and London: MIT Press.
Krieger, Murray (1992), *Ekphrasis: The Illusion of the Natural Sign*, Baltimore and London: The Johns Hopkins University Press.
Kulezic-Wilson, Danijela (2015), *The Musicality of Narrative Film*, Basingstoke: Palgrave Macmillan.
Lagerroth, Ulla-Britta (2008), 'Musicalisation of the Stage: Ingmar Bergman Performing Shakespeare', in Maaret Koskinen (ed.), *Ingmar Bergman Revisited: Performance, Cinema and the Arts*, London and New York: Wallflower Press, 35–50.
Lalanne, Jean-Marc (1999), 'La Nouvelle Eve', *Cahiers du cinéma*, 535, May, 34–5.
Langman, Larry (2000), *Destination Hollywood: The Influence of Europeans on American Filmmaking*, Jefferson: McFarland.
Lardeau, Yann, Philippe Tancelin and Jacques Parsi (1988), *Manoel de Oliveira*, Paris: Editions Dis, Voir.
Lavin, Mathias (2008), *Le cinéma selon Manoel de Oliveira*, Rennes: Presses universitaires de Rennes.
Lawlor, Patricia M. (1985), 'Lautréamont, Modernism and the Function of Mise en Abyme', *The French Review*, 58:6, May, 827–34.
Lawrence, Amy (1991), *Echo and Narcissus: Women's Voices in Classical Hollywood Cinema*, Berkeley, Los Angeles and Oxford: University of California Press.

Lejeune, Philippe (1977), 'Autobiography in the Third Person', trans. Annette Tomarken and Edward Tomarken, *New Literary History*, 9:1, 27–50.

Lemière, Jacques (2008), '"Faire un contrepoint à l'éloquence grandiose D'Herculano": *O Bobo*, de José Álvaro de Morais (1979–1987)', in Anabela Dinis Branco de Oliveira et al. (eds), *Diálogos lusófonos: Literatura e cinema (Literatura, cinema e multiculturalismo no mundo lusófono 2006–2007)*, Braga: Centro de Estudos em Letras Universidade de Trás-os-Montes e Alto Douro, 135–49, <http://www.utad.pt/vPT/Area2/investigar/CEL/CelCollections/Documents/CEL_Cultura_1.pdf> (last accessed 29 October 2015).

Levinson, Paul (1999), *Digital McLuhan: A Guide to the Information Millennium*, London and New York: Routledge.

Livingston, Paisley (2003), 'Nested Art', *The Journal of Aesthetics and Art Criticism*, 61:3, Summer, 233–45.

Loiselle, André and Jeremy Maron (2012), 'Introduction', in André Loiselle and Jeremy Maron (eds), *Stages of Reality: Theatricality in Cinema*, Toronto, Buffalo and London: University of Toronto Press, 3–10.

Lorca, Federico Garcia (1997), *Four Major Plays*, trans. John Edmunds, Oxford: Oxford University Press.

Lunenfeld, Peter (2001), *Snap to Grid: A User's Guide to Digital Arts, Media, and Cultures*, Cambridge, MA and London: MIT Press.

MacKay, Carol Hanbery (1987), *Soliloquy in Nineteenth-Century Fiction*, London: Macmillan.

Maddison, Stephen (2000), 'All About Women: Pedro Almodóvar and the Heterosocial Dynamic', *Textual Practice*, 14:2, 265–84.

Malina, Debra (2002), *Breaking the Frame: Metalepsis and the Construction of the Subject*, Columbus: Ohio State University Press.

Malkin, Jeanette R. (1999), *Memory-Theater and Postmodern Drama*, Ann Arbor: University of Michigan Press.

Mann, Karen (2002), 'Kieslowski's Narrative Conscience: Physical Time and Mental Space', *Quarterly Review of Film & Video*, 19:4, 343–53.

Mannone, Jane (1999), 'Des castelets et des marionettes, ou le théâtre en réduction au cinéma', in René Prédal (ed.), *Le théâtre à l'écran*, CinémAction, 93, Condé-sur-Noireau: Corlet, 205–11.

Margulies, Ivone (1998), 'John Cassavetes: Amateur Director', in Jon Lewis (ed.), *The New American Cinema*, Durham and London: Duke University Press, 275–306.

Mariniello, Silvestra (2011), 'L'intermédialité: un concept polymorphe', in Célia Vieira and Isabel Rio Novo (eds), *Inter Media: Littérature, cinéma et intermédialité*, Paris: L'Harmattan, 11–30.

Marker, Lise-Lone and Frederick J. Marker (1982), 'Talking About Theater: A Conversation with Ingmar Bergman', in *Ingmar Bergman: Four Decades in the Theater*, Cambridge: Cambridge University Press, 5–30.

Martin, Carol (2006), 'Bodies of Evidence', *TDR*, 50:3, Autumn, 8–15.

Martin, Carol (2010), 'Introduction', in Carol Martin (ed.), *Dramaturgy of the Real on the World Stage*, Basingstoke: Palgrave Macmillan, 1–14.

Martin, Carol (2013), *Theatre of the Real*, London: Palgrave Macmillan.

Martin-Márquez, Susan (2004), 'Pedro Almodóvar's Maternal Transplants: From *Matador* to *All About My Mother*', *Bulletin of Hispanic Studies*, 81:4, 497–509.

Maurer, Monika (2000), *The Pocket Essential Krzysztof Kieślowski*, Herts: Pocket Essentials.

Mazars, Pierre (1969), '*L'Amour fou*', *Le Figaro*, 23/01, Revue de presse numérisée, La Bibliothèque du Film, Cinémathèque Française, Paris.

McAuley, Gay (2008), 'Not Magic but Work: Rehearsal and the Production of Meaning', *Theatre Research International*, 33:3, 276–88.

McAuley, Gay (2010), 'A Taxonomy of Spatial Function', in Jane Collins and Andrew Nisbet (eds), *Theatre and Performance Design: A Reader in Scenography*, London and New York: Routledge, 89–94.

McConachie, Bruce (2008), *Engaging Audiences: A Cognitive Approach to Spectating in the Theatre*, Basingstoke and New York: Palgrave Macmillan.

McKim, Richard (1987), 'Swimming to Cambodia', *Cineaste*, 15:4, 41–3.

McDonald, Keiko I. (1994) *Japanese Classical Theater in Films*, Rutherford, Madison and Teaneck: Fairleigh Dickinson University Press.

Meek, Richard (2006), 'Ekphrasis in *The Rape of Lucrece* and *The Winter's Tale*', *SEL Studies in English Literature 1500–1900*, 46:2, Spring, 389–414.

Mello, Cecília (2016), 'Art and Reality in *The Arbor* (2010)', *Acta Univ. Sapientiae*, 12, 115–28.

Mendes, João Maria (2011), 'A obra longa e breve de José Ávaro Morais', *Novas & velhas tendências no cinema português contemporâneo*, <http://www.crossmediaplatform.ciac.pt/downloads/multimedia/texto/34/anexos/aobralongaebrevedejoslvaromorais.pdf> (last accessed 29 October 2015).

Ménil, Alain (1998), 'Mesure pour mesure: Théâtre et cinéma chez Jacques Rivette', *Etudes cinématographiques*, 63, Paris, Caen: Lettres Modernes Minard, 67–96.

Mennen, Richard (1975), 'Jerzy Grotowski's Paratheatrical Projects', *TDR*, 19:4, December, 58–69.

Mittell, Jason (2015), *Complex TV: The Poetics of Contemporary Television Storytelling*, New York: New York University Press.

Monaco, James (1976), *The New Wave: Truffaut, Godard, Chabrol, Rohmer, Rivette*, New York: Oxford University Press.

Montano, Alicia G. (2004), 'Almost All About Almodóvar', in Paula Willoquet-Maricondi (ed.), *Pedro Almodóvar: Interviews*, Jackson: University Press of Mississippi, 130–8.

Morrey, Douglas and Alison Smith (2009), *Jacques Rivette* (Manchester and New York: Manchester University Press.

Morrissette, Bruce (1975), 'Post-Modern Generative Fiction: Novel and Film', *Critical Inquiry*, 2:2, Winter, 253–62.

Mullarkey, John (2009), *Refractions of Reality: Philosophy and the Moving Image*, Basingstoke: Palgrave Macmillan.

Müller, Jurgen E. (2010), 'Intermediality Revisited: Some Reflections about Basic Principles of this *Axe de pertinence*', in Lars Ellestrӧm (ed.), *Media Borders, Multimodality and Intermediality*, Basingstoke: Palgrave Macmillan, 237–52.

Mulvey, Laura (2006), *Death 24X a Second: Stillness and the Moving Image*, London: Reaktion.

Musser, Charles (2004), 'Towards a History of Theatrical Culture: Imagining an Integrated History of Stage and Screen', in John Fullerton (ed.), *Screen Culture: History and Textuality*, Eastleigh: John Libbey, 3–19.

Myrsiades, Linda (2000), 'Theatrical Metaphors in Theodoros Angelopoulos's *The Traveling Players*', *Journal of Modern Greek Studies*, 18, 135–49.

Nagel, Erica (2007), 'An Aesthetic of Neighborliness: Possibilities for Integrating Community-Based Practices into Documentary Theatre', *Theatre Topics*, 17:2, 153–68.

Nagib, Lúcia (2014), 'The Politics of Impurity', in Lúcia Nagib and Anne Jerslev (eds), *Impure Cinema: Intermedial and Intercultural Approaches to Film*, London, New York: I. B. Tauris, 21–39.

Nagler, Lili (2003), 'Singling Out the Double: Objectivity, Subjectivity and Alterity in Kieslowski's *The Double Life of Véronique*', *Post Script*, XXII: 3, 8–20.

Naremore, James (1988), *Acting in the Cinema*, Berkeley, Los Angeles and London: University of California Press.

Neely, Carol Thomas (1975), 'The Winter's Tale: The Triumph of Speech', *SEL Studies in English Literature, 1500–1900*, 15:2, Spring, 321–38.

Neupert, Richard (1995), *The End: Narration and Closure in the Cinema*, Detroit: Wayne State University Press.

Neve, Brian (2009), *Elia Kazan: The Cinema of an American Outsider*, London: I. B. Tauris.

Nicoll, Allardyce (1936), *Film and Theatre*, London, Bombay and Sydney: Harrap.

Nora, Pierre (1989), 'Between Memory and History: Les Lieux de Mémoire', trans. Marc Roudebush, *Representations*, 26, 7–24.

Olkowski, Dorothea (2014), 'Henri Bergson', in Felicity Colman (ed.), *Film, Theory and Philosophy: The Key Thinkers*, London and New York: Routledge, 71–80.

Olsen, Mark (2011), 'Indie Focus: "The Arbor" Puts Words in Actors' Mouths', *Los Angeles Times*, 8 May, <http://articles.latimes.com/2011/may/08/entertainment/la-ca-indie-focus-20110508> (last accessed 11 March 2017).

O'Rawe, Des (2007), 'Inviolable Attachments: Takeshi Kitano's *Dolls*', *Screening the Past*, 21, July, http://tlweb.latrobe.edu.au/humanities/screeningthepast/21/takeshi-kitano-dolls.html (last accessed 17 September 2015).

Osiński, Zbigniew, Ann Herron and Halina Filipowicz (1991), 'Grotowski Blazes the Trails: From Objective Drama to Ritual Arts', *TDR*, 35:1, Spring, 95–112.

Parker-Starbuck, Jennifer (2014), 'The Spectator and Her Double: Seeing Performance through the Eyes of Another', *Theatre Topics*, 24:2, 125–36.

Parret, Herman (2011), '"Ma Vie" comme effet de discourse', *La Licorne: Revue de langue et de littérature françaises*, 14, <http://licorne.edel.univ-poitiers.fr/document.php?id=5085> (last accessed 9 July 2015).

Parshall, Peter F. (2012), *Altman and After: Multiple Narratives in Film*, Lanham, Toronto and Plymouth: Scarecrow Press.

Parsons, William B. (1999), *The Enigma of the Oceanic Feeling: Revisioning the Psychoanalytic Theory of Mysticism*, New York, Oxford: Oxford University Press.

Paterson, Eddie (2015), *The Contemporary American Monologue*, London: Bloomsbury.

Pavel, Thomas G. (1986), *Fictional worlds*, Cambridge, MA and London: Harvard University Press.

Pavis, Patrice and Elena Biller-Lappin (1981), 'Problems of a Semiology of Theatrical Gesture', *Poetics Today*, 2:3, Spring, 65–93.

Pavis, Patrice (1998), *Dictionary of the Theatre: Terms, Concepts, and Analysis*, trans. Christine Shantz, Toronto and Buffalo: University of Toronto Press.

Pavis, Patrice (2003), *Analyzing Performance: Theater, Dance, and Film*, trans. David Williams, Ann Arbor: University of Michigan Press.

Pavis, Patrice (2008), 'On Faithfulness: The Difficulties Experienced by the Text/Performance Couple', *Theatre Research International*, 33:2, 117–26.

Peirse, Alison (2016), 'Speaking for Herself: Andrea Dunbar and Bradford on Film', *Journal for Cultural Research*, 20:1, 60–72.

Pethő, Ágnes (2011), *Cinema and Intermediality: The Passion for the In-between*, Newcastle upon Tyne: Cambridge Scholars Publishing.

Petrie, Graham and Eric Rohmer (1971), 'Eric Rohmer: An Interview', *Film Quarterly*, 24:4, Summer, 34–41.

Pfister, Manfred [1977] (1993) *The Theory and Analysis of Drama*, trans. John Halliday, Cambridge: Cambridge University Press.

Phillips, Adam (2012), *Missing Out: In Praise of the Unlived Life*, London: Hamish Hamilton.
Picon-Vallin, Béatrice (ed.) (2001a), *Le Film de théâtre*, Paris: CNRS éditions.
Picon-Vallin, Béatrice (2001b), 'Passages, Interférences, Hybridations: Le Film de théâtre', *Theatre Research International*, 26:2, 190–8.
Pidduck, Julianne (1998), 'Of Windows and Country Walks: Frames of Space and Movement in 1990s Austen Adaptations', *Screen*, 39:4, 381–400.
Pierre, Sylvie (1968), 'Le dur désir de durer', *Cahiers du cinéma*, 204, September, 55.
Pierre, Sylvie (1969), '*L'Amour fou*', in 'Liste des films sortis en exclusivité à Paris', *Cahiers du cinéma*, 209, February, 62.
Piris, Paul (2014), 'The Co-Presence and Ontological Ambiguity of the Puppet', in Dassia N. Posner, Claudia Orenstein and John Bell (eds), *The Routledge Companion to Puppetry and Material Performance*, London and New York: Routledge, 30–42.
Plantinga, Carl (1999), 'The Scene of Empathy and the Human Face on Film', in Carl Plantinga and Greg M. Smith (eds), *Passionate Views: Film, Cognition and Emotion*, Baltimore and London: The Johns Hopkins University Press, 239–55.
Ponsoldt, James (2008), 'The Play's the Thing', *Filmmaker Magazine*, <http://filmmakermagazine.com/archives/issues/fall2008/synecdoche.php> (last accessed 20 November 2016).
Porton, Richard (2011), 'Documentary Cinema and Reality Hunger', *Cineaste*, 36:3, Summer, 10–14.
Posner, Dassia N. (2014), 'Contemporary Investigations and Hybridizations' (Introduction to Part III), in Dassia N. Posner, Claudia Orenstein and John Bell (eds), *The Routledge Companion to Puppetry and Material Performance*, London and New York: Routledge, 225–7.
Prédal, René (ed.) (1999), *Le théâtre à l'écran*, CinémAction 93, Condé-sur-Noireau: Editions Corlet.
Puchner, Martin (2014), 'The Problem of the Ground: Martin Heidegger and Site-Specific Performance', in Laura Cull and Alice Lagaay (eds), *Encounters in Performance Philosophy*, Basingstoke: Palgrave Macmillan, 65–86.
Rabine, Henry (1969), '*L'Amour fou*', *La Croix*, 21/01, Revue de presse numérisée, La Bibliothèque du Film, Cinémathèque Française, Paris.
Radosavljević, Duška (2013), *Theatre-Making: Interplay Between Text and Performance in the 21st Century*, Basingstoke: Palgrave Macmillan.
Radstone, Susannah (ed.) (2000), *Memory and Methodology*, Oxford: Berg.
Radstone, Susannah and Katharine Hodkin (eds) (2003), *Regimes of Memory*, London and New York: Routledge.
Rajewsky, Irina O. (2005), 'Intermediality, Intertextuality, and Remediation: A Literary Perspective on Intermediality', *Intermédialités*, 6, 43–64.
Rapfogel, Jared (2008), 'A Steady Gaze: The Films of Manoel de Oliveira', *Cineaste*, 33:3, Summer, 14–17.
Rapold, Nicolas (2011), 'Review: The Arbor', *Film Comment*, 47:2, March/April, 68–9.
Rayner, Alice (1994), *To Act, To Do, To Perform: Drama and the Phenomenology of Action*, Ann Arbor: University of Michigan Press.
Rayner, Alice (2006a), *Ghosts: Death's Double and the Phenomena of Theatre*, Minneapolis and London: University of Minnesota Press.
Rayner, Alice (2006b), 'Presenting Objects, Presenting Things', in David Krasner and David Z. Saltz (eds), *Staging Philosophy: Intersections of Theater, Performance and Philosophy*, Ann Arbor: University of Michigan Press, 180–99.
Redmond, Sean (2013), *The Cinema of Takeshi Kitano: Flowering Blood*, London and New York: Wallflower Press.

Reinelt, Janelle (2009), 'On Feminist and Sexual Politics', in Elaine Aston and Elin Diamond (eds), *The Cambridge Companion to Caryl Churchill*, Cambridge: Cambridge University Press, 18–35.

Replogle, Carol (1969), 'Not Parody, Not Burlesque: The Play within the Play in *Hamlet*', *Modern Philology*, 67:2, November, 150–9.

Rhodie, Sam (2015), *Film Modernism*, Manchester: Manchester University Press.

Rimmon-Kenan, Shlomith (1980), 'The Paradoxical Status of Repetition', *Poetics Today*, 1:4, Summer, 151–9.

Rivette, Jacques and Marilù Parolini (n.d.), 'Scénario: *L'Amour fou*' (unpublished manuscript, La Bibliothèque du Film, Cinémathèque Française, Paris).

Roberts, David (2007), 'The Play within the Play and the Closure of Representation', in Gerhard Fischer and Bernhard Greiner (eds), *The Play within the Play: The Performance of Meta-Theatre and Self-Reflection*, Amsterdam, New York: Rodopi, 37–46.

Roberts, Les (2005), 'Non-places in the Mist: Mapping the Spatial Turn in Theo Angelopoulos's Peripatetic Modernism', in Wendy Ellen Everett and Axel Goodbody (eds), *Revisiting Space: Space and Place in European Cinema*, Oxford: Peter Lang, 325–44.

Rollet, Sylvie (1993), '*Le voyage des comédiens*: L'histoire est-elle une comédie?', *Positif*, 383, January, 51–4.

Romney, Jonathan (1992), '*The Double Life of Véronique*', *Sight and Sound*, 2:11, March, 43.

Romney, Jonathan (2003), '*Dolls*', *Sight and Sound*, 13:6, June, 42.

Romney, Jonathan (2011), '*The Double Life of Véronique*: Through the Looking Glass', <https://www.criterion.com/current/posts/457-the-double-life-of-veronique-through-the-looking-glass> (last accessed 21 June 2016).

Ron, Moshe (1987), 'The Restricted Abyss: Nine Problems in the Theory of Mise en Abyme', *Poetics Today*, 8:2, 417–38.

Ronen, Ruth (1994), *Possible Worlds in Literary Theory*, Cambridge: Cambridge University Press.

Rossmanith, Kate (2008), 'Traditions and Training in Rehearsal Practice', *Australasian Drama Studies*, 53, 141–52.

Rozik, Eli (2002), 'Acting: The Quintessence of Theatricality', *SubStance*, 31:2/3, 110–24.

Rozik, Eli (2005), 'Back to "cinema is filmed theatre"', *Semiotica*, 157:1–4, 169–85.

Rugg, Linda Haverty (2014), *Self-Projection: The Director's Image in Art Cinema*, Minneapolis and London: University of Minnesota Press.

Rushton, Richard (2002), 'Cinema's Double: Some Reflections on Metz', *Screen*, 43:2, Summer, 107–18.

Rushton, Richard (2004), 'Early, Classical and Modern Cinema: Absorption and Theatricality', *Screen*, 45:3, Autumn, 226–44.

Rushton, Richard (2011), *The Reality of Film: Theories of Filmic Reality*, Manchester and New York: Manchester University Press.

Rutter, Carol Chillington (2001), *Enter the Body: Women and Representation on Shakespeare's Stage*, London and New York: Routledge.

Ryan, Marie-Laure (1991), 'Possible Worlds and Accessibility Relations: A Semantic Typology of Fiction', *Poetics Today*, 12:3, Autumn, 553–76.

Ryan, Marie-Laure (2005), 'Media and Narrative', in David Herman, Manfred Jahn and Marie-Laure Ryan (eds), *The Routledge Encyclopedia of Narrative Theory*, London: Routledge, 288–92.

Sava, Laura (2010), 'The Problem of Film–Theatre Intermediality in *Jesus of Montreal*', *Excursions*, 1:1, June, 102–22, <https://www.excursions-journal.org.uk/index.php?journal=excursions&page=article&op=view&path%5B%5D=5&path%5B%5D=58> (last accessed 29 August 2015).

Sava, Laura (2011), 'Théâtre du Soleil Meets the Cinema: Acting and Mask Work in Ariane Mnouchkine's *Molière*', *Screening the Past*, 31, <http://www.screeningthepast.com/2011/08/theatre-du-soleil-meets-the-cinema-acting-and-mask-work-in-ariane-mnouchkine%E2%80%99s-moliere-2/> (last accessed 3 May 2015).

Savage, Mary C. (1988), 'Can Ethnographic Narrative Be a Neighborly Act?', *Anthropology & Education Quarterly*, 19:1, 3–19.

Schechner, Richard [1988] (2005), *Performance Theory*, New York and London: Routledge.

Schechner, Richard (2002), 'My Art in Life: Interviewing Spalding Gray', *TDR*, 46:4, Winter, 154–74.

Schilling, Derek (2007), *Eric Rohmer*, Manchester: Manchester University Press.

Schneider, Rebecca (2006), 'Intermediality, Infelicity, and Scholarship on the Slip', *Theatre Survey*, 47:2, November, 253–60.

Schröter, Jens (2011), 'Discourses and Models of Intermediality', *CLCWeb: Comparative Literature and Culture*, 13:3, <http://docs.lib.purdue.edu/clcweb/vol13/iss3/3> (last accessed 9 March 2015).

Schwartz, Bruce D., Theodora Skipitares, Julie Taymor and C. Lee Jenner (1983), 'Interview: Working with Puppets', *Performing Arts Journal*, 7:1, 103–16.

Sellier, Geneviève (2008), *Masculine Singular: French New Wave Cinema*, trans. Kristin Ross, Durham and London: Duke University Press.

Seznec, Alain (1972), 'The Uses of *enfin* in Racine's "Andromaque"', *The French Review*, 4, Spring, 61–4.

Shail, Andrew (2010), 'Intermediality: Disciplinary Flux or Formalist Retrenchment?', *Early Popular Visual Culture*, 8:1, 3–15.

Shakespeare, William (2007), *The Complete Works*, ed. Jonathan Bate and Eric Rasmussen, Basingstoke: Macmillan, Royal Shakespeare Company.

Sharpling, Gerard Paul (2002), 'Towards a Rhetoric of Experience: The Role of *Enargeia* in the Essays of Montaigne', *Rhetorica: A Journal of the History of Rhetoric*, 20:2, Spring, 173–92.

Shawn, Wallace (1982), 'Some Notes on Louis Malle and *My Dinner with André*', *Sight and Sound*, 51, 118–20.

Shelley, Percy Bysshe (1993), *Selected Poems*, New York: Dover.

Shotter, John (1993), *Conversational Realities: Constructing Life Through Language*, London, Thousand Oaks and New Delhi: Sage.

Sidiropoulou, Avra (2011), *Authoring Performance: The Director in Contemporary Theatre*, New York: Palgrave Macmillan.

Silverstein, Marc (2007), '"Eyes Full to the Point of Bursting": Spalding Gray and the Malady of Scopophilia', *Critique*, 48:2, Winter, 114–36.

Simerka, Barbara and Christopher B. Weimer (2005), 'Duplicitous Diegesis: *Don Quijote* and Charlie Kaufman's *Adaptation*', *Hispania*, 88:1, March, 91–100.

Smith, Damon (2011), 'Clio Barnard: *The Arbor*', *Filmmaker Magazine*, 27 April, <https://filmmakermagazine.com/23471-clio-barnard-the-arbor/> (last accessed 3 May 2017).

Smith, David L. (2011), 'Synecdoche, In Part', in David LaRocca (ed.), *The Philosophy of Charlie Kaufman*, Lexington: University Press of Kentucky, 239–53.

Smith, Gennelle (2013), 'Duplicated and Duplicitous Self-configurings in Kaufman's *Adaptation* (2002)', in Judith Buchanan (ed.), *The Writer on Film: Screening Literary Authorship*, Basingstoke: Palgrave Macmillan, 164–77.

Smith, Murray (1995), 'Film Spectatorship and the Institution of Fiction', *The Journal of Aesthetics and Art Criticism*, 53:2, Spring, 113–27.

Smith, Murray (1998), 'Regarding Film Spectatorship: A Reply to Richard Allen', *The Journal of Aesthetics and Art Criticism*, 56:1, 63–5.
Smith, Murray (2006), 'My Dinner with Noël; or, Can We Forget the Medium?', *Film Studies*, 8, Summer, 140–8.
Smith, Paul Julian (1998), *The Theatre of Garcia Lorca: Text, Performance, Psychoanalysis*, Cambridge: Cambridge University Press.
Smith, Paul Julian (2000), *Desire Unlimited: The Cinema of Pedro Almodóvar*, London and New York: Verso.
Sobchack, Vivian (1992), *The Address of the Eye: A Phenomenology of Film Experience*, Princeton: Princeton University Press.
Sobchack, Vivian (2011), 'Phenomenology', in Paisley Livingston and Carl Plantinga (eds), *The Routledge Companion to Philosophy and Film*, London and New York: Routledge, 435–45.
Sofer, Andrew (2003), *The Stage Life of Props*, Ann Arbor: University of Michigan Press.
Sontag, Susan (1966), 'Film and Theatre', *Tulane Drama Review*, 11:1, 24–37.
Sontag, Susan [1983] (2013), 'A Note on Bunraku', in Susan Sontag, *Where the Stress Falls*, Penguin: Kindle Edition, 130–3.
Southern, Nathan C., with Jacques Weissgerber (2006), *The Films of Louis Malle: A Critical Analysis*, Jefferson, NC and London: McFarland.
Stafford-Clark, Max (2000), 'Introduction', in Andrea Dunbar, *Rita, Sue and Bob Too*/Robin Soans, *A State Affair*, London: Methuen, 1–10.
Stam, Robert (1992), *Reflexivity in Film and Literature: From Don Quixote to Jean-Luc Godard*, New York: Columbia University Press.
States, Bert O. (1983), 'The Actor's Presence: Three Phenomenal Modes', *Theatre Journal*, 35:3, October, 359–75.
States, Bert O. (1987), *Great Reckonings in Little Rooms: On the Phenomenology of Theater*, Berkeley, Los Angeles and London: University of California Press.
States, Bert O. (1996), 'Performance as Metaphor', *Theatre Journal*, 48:1, 1–26.
Stern, Lesley and George Kouvaros (1999), 'Introduction: Descriptive Acts', in Lesley Stern and George Kouvaros (eds), *Falling for You: Essays on Cinema and Performance*, Sydney: Power Publications, 1–35.
Stern, Lesley (2001), 'Paths That Wind through the Thicket of Things', *Critical Inquiry*, 28:1, Autumn, 317–54.
Stock, Brian (2010), *Augustine's Inner Dialogue: The Philosophical Soliloquy in Late Antiquity*, Cambridge: Cambridge University Press.
Stok, Danusia (ed.) (1993), *Kieślowski on Kieślowski*, London and Boston: Faber & Faber.
Stone, Laurie (2015), 'The Time of His Life: Spalding Gray', in Joan Hawkins (ed.), *Downtown Film and TV Culture 1975–2001*, Bristol and Chicago, USA: Intellect, 147–66.
Strauss, Frédéric (ed.) (1994), *Almodóvar on Almodóvar*, London: Faber & Faber.
Strick, Philip (1993), '*Conte d'hiver (A Winter's Tale)*', *Sight and Sound*, 3:1, January, 44.
Stucky, Nathan (1993), 'Toward an Aesthetics of Natural Performance', *Text and Performance Quarterly*, 13, 168–80.
Summers, David (1987), *The Judgement of Sense: Renaissance Naturalism and the Rise of Aesthetics*, Cambridge: Cambridge University Press.
Tarr, Susan and Hans Proppe (1976), '*The Travelling Players*: A Modern Greek Masterpiece', *Jump Cut*, 10/11, January, 5–6.
Taylor, Lib (2013), 'Voice, Body and the Transmission of the Real in Documentary Theatre', *Contemporary Theatre Review*, 23:3, 368–79.

Terry, David P. (2006), 'Once Blind, Now Seeing: Problematics of Confessional Performance', *Text and Performance Quarterly*, 26:3, 209–28.

Tesich, Steve, Wallace Shawn, David Mamet, John Guare, Michael Weller and Michael Earley (1981), 'Playwrights Making Movies', *Performing Arts Journal*, 5:3, 20–53.

Thomas, François (n.d.), 'Les Films "Parallèles": Musique et sons directs', in *Jacques Rivette: La Règle du Jeu*, Turin: Centre Culturel Français de Turin, Museo Nazionale del Cinema di Torino, 165–9.

Tillis, Steve (1996), 'The Actor Occluded: Puppet Theatre and Acting Theory', *Theatre Topics*, 6:2, September, 109–19.

Törnqvist, Egil (2003), *Bergman's Muses: Aesthetic Versatility in Film, Theatre, Television and Radio*, Jefferson: McFarland.

Trilling, Lionel (1964), *The Liberal Imagination: Essays on Literature and Society*, London: Secker & Warburg.

Uricchio, William (2004), 'Re-discovering the Challenge of Textual Instability: New Media's Lessons for Old Media Historians', in John Fullerton (ed.), *Screen Culture: History and Textuality*, Eastleigh: John Libbey, 161–8.

Vendler, Helen (1984), *Wallace Stevens: Words Chosen Out of Desire*, Cambridge, MA and London: Harvard University Press.

Villeneuve, Johanne (2007), 'L'oralité, l'intermédialité et la question de l'appareil de la technique et des enchantements', in Jean-Louis Déotte, Marion Froger and Silvestra Mariniello (eds), *Appareil et intermédialité*, Paris: L'Harmattan, 207–22.

Waller, Gregory A. (1983), *The Stage/Screen Debate: A Study in Popular Aesthetics*, New York and London: Garland.

Walley, Jonathan (2003), 'The Material of Film and the Idea of Cinema: Contrasting Practices in Sixties and Seventies Avant-Garde Film', *October*, 13, Winter, 15–30.

Walton, Kendall L. (1978), 'How Remote Are Fictional Worlds from the Real World?', *The Journal of Aesthetics and Art Criticism*, 37:1, Autumn, 11–23.

Wandor, Michelene (2000), 'Women Playwrights and the Challenge Of Feminism in the 1970s', in Elaine Aston and Janelle Reinelt (eds), *The Cambridge Companion to Modern British Women Playwrights*, Cambridge: Cambridge University Press, 53–68.

Weber, Samuel (2004), *Theatricality as a Medium*, New York: Fordham University Press.

Wexman, Virginia Wright (1980), 'The Rhetoric of Cinematic Improvisation', *Cinema Journal*, 20:1, Autumn, 29–41.

Wiles, Mary M. (2012) *Jacques Rivette*, Urbana, Chicago and Springfield: University of Illinois Press.

Williams, Jeffrey (2004), *Theory and the Novel: Narrative Reflexivity in the British Tradition*, Cambridge: Cambridge University Press.

Williams, Tennessee (1959), *A Streetcar Named Desire and The Glass Menagerie*, ed. E. Martin Browne, Harmondsworth: Penguin.

Wilmington, Michael (1997), 'Theo Angelopoulos: Landscape, Players, Mist', in Andrew Horton (ed.), *The Last Modernist: The Films of Theo Angelopoulos*, Trowbridge: Flicks Books, 57–68.

Wilson, Emma (2000), *Memory and Survival: The French Cinema of Krzysztof Kieślowski*, Leeds: Modern Humanities Research Association and Maney Publishing.

Wilson, George M. (2011), *Seeing Fictions in Film: The Epistemology of Movies*, Oxford: Oxford University Press.

Wojcik, Pamela Robertson (2006), 'The Sound of Film Acting', *Journal of Film and Video*, 58:1/2, Spring/Summer, 71–83.

Wolf, Werner (2002), 'Towards a Functional Analysis of Intermediality: The Case of Twentieth Century Musicalized Fiction', in Erik Hedling and Ulla-Britta Lagerroth (eds), *Cultural Functions of Intermedial Exploration*, Amsterdam and New York: Rodopi, 15–34.

Wolf, Werner (2003), 'Metalepsis as a Transgeneric and Transmedial Phenomenon: A Case Study of the Possibilities of "Exporting" Narratological Concepts', in Jan Christopher Meister, Tom Kindt and Wilhelm Shernus (eds), *Narratology Beyond Literary Criticism: Mediality, Disciplinarity*, Berlin: Walter de Gruyter, 83–107.

Wolf, Werner (2005), 'Intermediality', in David Herman, Manfred Jahn and Marie-Laure Ryan (eds), *The Routledge Encyclopedia of Narrative Theory*, London: Routledge, 252–6.

Wolf, Werner (2006), 'Introduction: Frames, Framings and Framing Borders in Literature and Other Media', in Werner Wolf, Walter Bernhart (eds), *Framing Borders in Literature and Other Media (Studies in Intermediality 1)*, Amsterdam, New York: Rodopi, 1–40.

Wolf, Werner (2008), 'The Relevance of Mediality and Intermediality to Academic Studies of English Literature', in Martin Heusser, Andreas Fischer and Andreas H. Jucker (eds), *Mediality/Intermediality*, Tübingen: Gunter Narr Verlag, 15–43.

Wolf, Werner (2009), 'Metareference across Media: The Concept, Its Transmedial Potentials and Problems, Main Forms and Functions', in Werner Wolf (ed.), *Metareference Across Media: Theory and Case Studies*, Amsterdam, New York: Rodopi, 1–85.

Wolf, Werner (2013), 'Aesthetic Illusion', in Werner Wolf, Walter Bernhardt and Andreas Mahler (eds), *Immersion and Distance: Aesthetic Illusion in Literature and Other Media* (Studies in Intermediality 6), New York and Amsterdam: Rodopi, 1–63.

Wood, Jason (2011), 'The Arbor: Interview with Clio Barnard', <http://www.electricsheepmagazine.co.uk/features/2011/03/02/the-arbor-interview-with-clio-barnard/> (last accessed 6 October 2016).

Wood, Robin (1981), 'Narrative Pleasure: Two Films of Jacques Rivette', *Film Quarterly*, 35:1, Autumn, 2–12.

Yacavone, Daniel (2015), *Film Worlds: A Philosophical Aesthetics of Cinema*, New York: Columbia University Press.

Yacobi, Tamar (1995), 'Pictorial Models and Narrative Ekphrasis', *Poetics Today*, 16:4, Winter, 599–649.

Young, Paul (2006), *The Cinema Dreams Its Rivals: Media Fantasy Films from Radio to the Internet*, Minneapolis and London: University of Minnesota Press.

Zarrilli, Phillip B. (2004), 'Toward a Phenomenological Model of the Actor's Embodied Modes of Experience', *Theatre Journal*, 56:4, December, 653–66.

Žižek, Slavoj (2001), *The Fright of Real Tears: Krzysztof Kieślowski between Theory and Post-Theory*, London: BFI.

Zurbrugg, Nicholas (ed.) (2004), *Art, Performance, Media: 31 Interviews*, Minneapolis and London: University of Minnesota Press.

Index

Aaron, Joyce, 182
Adaptation (Kaufman, 2002), 107
Affron, Mirella, 119
Ailloud-Nicolas, Catherine, 4
All About Eve (Mankiewicz, 1950), 72, 73
All About My Mother/Todo sobre mi madre (Almodóvar, 1999), 12, 22, 53, 71–83
Allen, Richard, 10, 25
Almodóvar, Pedro, 57, 71, 72, 74–6, 79, 80
Altman, Rick, 197
Amalric, Mathieu, 18
Amour fou, L'/Mad Love (Rivette, 1969), 12 22, 84, 85, 86–100
Andromaque (Racine), 84, 89, 91, 92–4, 98–9
Angelopoulos, Theo, 162, 165, 166
Anouilh, Jean, 18
apparatus, 23, 34, 35, 55–6, 85, 87, 118
Appia, Adolphe, 120
Arbor, The (Barnard, 2010), 12, 194–208
Arroyo, José, 72
Artaud, Antonin, 120
audience, 12, 21, 34, 68, 119–20
    and actors, 120–1
    and Bunraku, 46
    and Gray, 193
    and *I'm Going Home*, 148–50, 151–2, 154–6
    and monologue, 158–9, 166–7
    and *Opening Night*, 124, 125–6
    and puppet theatre, 23–4
Augustine, Saint, 157, 158
Aukin, David, 194
Aumont, Jacques, 209, 210, 212
Auslander, Philip, 193

Baker-White, Robert, 84–5
Bal, Mieke, 30
Banks, Christina, 185
Bardèche, Marie-Laure, 79
Barkan, Leonard, 137–8, 140–1
Barker, Jennifer, 126

Barnard, Clio, 195, 196–8, 201, 202, 203, 204
    and community, 206, 207–8
Barnes, Betsy, 94
Barthes, Roland, 39, 44
Bay-Cheng, Sarah, 44, 45, 47, 48, 49–50
Bazin, André, 12n1, 45
Beckett, Samuel, 158
    Rockaby, 38
beehive, 175–8, 182
Bellour, Raymond, 54
Belting, Hans, 64
Bene, Carmelo
    Our Lady of the Turks, 58
Bergman, Ingmar, 1–3, 4, 5, 6
Bergson, Henri, 183
Bersani, Leo, 73, 134
Blau, Herbert, 109
Bleeker, Maaike, 118, 150
Bliss, Michael, 185
Blood Wedding/Bodas de Sangre (Lorca), 72, 82–3
Bollas, Christopher, 65
Bolter, Jay, 13n3
Bonitzer, Pascal, 212
Bordwell, David, 166
Bottoms, Stephen, 203
Bourdieu, Pierre, 212
bracketing, 12, 39–40, 51–2
Branigan, Edward, 21, 53
Brecht, Bertolt, 67, 68, 70, 165–6, 197, 212
    Short Organum for Theatre, 26
Brewster, Ben, 10
Brown, Tom, 159
Bunraku, 39–40, 41–52

Carlson, Marvin, 53, 181–2
Carney, Raymond, 124, 132
Carroll, Noël, 51–2, 54
    Engaging Cinema, 8
Casado-Gual, Núria, 146–7
Casetti, Francesco, 119

Casey, Edward, 63–4, 65
Cassavetes, John, 123–4, 126, 132, 133
Cavell, Stanley, 10, 136–7
Caws, Mary Ann, 5
Chaikin, Joseph, 182
Chaim, Daphna Ben, 151, 153
Charity, Tom, 132
Cher Antoine/Dear Antoine (Anouilh), 18
Chikamatsu Monzaemon, 39, 42–4
Chikamatsu's 'Love in Osaka' (Uchida, 1959), 41
Chion, Michel, 35–6, 53, 61, 68, 173
Chothia, Jean, 125
Churchill, Caryl, 194
Cisneros, James, 173
Claudel, Paul, 48
Claycomb, Ryan, 196
Coates, Paul, 31
Cole, Susan Letzler, 147–8, 151
Conkie, Rob, 98
Courier for Hell, The (Meido no hikyaku) (Chikamatsu Monzaemon), 39, 42, 43–4, 47, 51
Cull, Laura, 209, 210

Dällenbach, Lucien, 34–5
Daney, Serge, 93
Days of '36 (Angelopoulos, 1973), 160
Death of a Salesman (Miller), 102, 103, 104–7
Del Rio, Elena, 122, 132, 133
Deleuze, Gilles, 24–5, 101
Delvaux, André, 57
Demastes, William, 186, 190
Deming, Richard, 106
Déotte, Jean-Louis, 56
Derrida, Jacques, 5, 68
Deschamps, Hélène, 92–3, 97
dialogism, 157, 158, 172–3
Diderot, Denis, 115–16
direct address *see* monologues; soliloquies
distortion, 44, 45, 46–50
D'Lugo, Marvin, 82
Doane, Mary Ann, 77, 80, 81
documentary theatre, 196, 197, 198, 203
Dolan, Jill, 139, 207
Dolls (Kitano, 2002), 12, 22, 23, 26–7, 39–52
Double Life of Véronique, The (Kieślowski, 1991), 12, 22, 23, 26–39
double vision, 23–4
Dunbar, Andrea, 194, 195–6, 199, 203–6
Durand, Régis, 56–7, 78, 182
Dutoit, Ulysse, 73, 134

Eidt, Laura, 174
ekphrasis, 173–4, 180–1
Elleström, Lars, 13n3–4
Elliott, Kamilla, 7
Elsaesser, Thomas, 21
Elster, Jon, 92
embedment, 12, 17–19, 59–60; *see also* bracketing; *mise en abyme*
Enfants du Paradis, Les/Children of Paradise (Carné, 1945), 119
Erickson, Jon, 105–6
Eurydice (Anouilh), 18
Exit the King/Le Roi se meurt (Ionesco), 146–8, 150–3

Fanny and Alexander (Bergman, 1982), 1–3, 4
Fassbinder, R. W., 212
Favorini, Attilio, 54
Felleman, Susan, 19–20
Féral, Josette, 3, 122, 127, 132–3
fictional worlds, 86, 100, 102–3, 106, 108–10, 112
(figurative) occlusion, 27, 36, 38, 48, 53
Filmer, Andrew, 86, 96–7, 105
Findlay, Robert, 175, 176–7, 182
Fischer-Lichte, Erika, 115–16
Fleche, Anne, 75
Fowler, D. P., 177
framing, 3–4, 12, 18–19, 21
 and *A Tale of Winter*, 139–40
 and *Dolls*, 39–40, 44, 48–9, 52
 and *I'm Going Home*, 151–2
 and *The Jester*, 62–3
 and sound, 53
Frappat, Hélène, 93
Freedman, Barbara, 150
Frentz, Thomas, 172–3
Fried, Michael, 159, 166
Fuente, Leonardo de la, 27

Gaggi, Silvio, 38
Gang of Four/La Bande des quatre (Rivette, 1989), 88
Garner, Stanton B., Jr., 116, 117, 158–9
Gaskill, William, 194
Gaudreault, André, 8
gaze, 40, 44, 49–50, 62–3
Geis, Deborah R., 168
Genette, Gérard, 122
Gerow, Aaron, 39–40, 41, 50
Gerstenkorn, Jacques, 211
 Cinéma et théâtralité, 11
gesture, 46–7, 97, 133, 165

Gibson, Andrew, 68–9
Gide, André, 28
Godard, Jean-Luc, 212
Goffman, Erving, 3–4
Golfo the Shepherdess (Peresiadis), 160, 161–2, 164–5
Gorfinkel, Elena, 54
Gray, Spalding, 158, 182–93
Green, Eugène, 57, 60
Greenaway, Peter, 7, 212
Gregory, André, 171, 172, 173, 174–80, 181–2
Grotowski, Jerzy, 116, 172, 174, 175–9, 181, 182
Gruber, William, 138–9
Grusin, Richard, 13n3

Haciendo Lorca/Performing Lorca (Pasqual), 79, 82–3
Hagener, Malte, 21
Handke, Peter, 4
Hare, David, 194
Harwood, Bo, 126
Heath, Stephen, 49
Heine, Steven, 42
Heinemann, David, 142
Henson, Jim, 29
Herculano, Alexandre
  O Bobo (The Jester), 58, 67
Higgins, Dick, 211
Horton, Andrew, 162–3, 169–70
Hunters, The (Angelopoulos, 1977), 160
Hutcheon, Linda, 32

Ibáñez, Juan Carlos, 79
Idziak, Sławomir, 31
Ill-fated Love/Amor de Perdição (Oliveira, 1978), 154–5
illusion, 12, 23, 24–6
I'm Going Home (De Oliveira, 2001), 12, 120, 121, 145–56
Impossible Vacation (Gray), 184, 188
Indiewood, 101, 103
Insdorf, Annete, 38–9
intermediality, 6–9, 11–12, 13n3, 14n5, 56, 211; *see also* ekphrasis; *paragone*
Ionesco, Eugène, 147
Israel-Pelletier, Aimée, 134

Jacob, Irène, 27, 32
Jacobs, Lea, 10
Jester, The/O Bobo (Morais, 1987), 12, 22, 53, 57–71

Jesus of Montreal (Arcand, 1989), 120
Johnson, Beth, 195, 199
Johnson, Randal, 145
Joint Stock company, 194–5
Jones, Simon, 205–6
Jordan, Isabelle, 165
Jousse, Thierry, 124

Kabuki theatre, 41, 42
Kalfon, Jean-Pierre, 88
Kaplin, Stephen, 31
Kattenbelt, Chiel, 210
Katzman, Lisa, 132
Kaufman, Charlie, 86, 87, 101
Kaufman, Moisés, 206–7
Kawin, Bruce, 73–4, 80, 173
Kazan, Elia, 74–5, 76
Keene, Donald, 43
Kickasola, Joseph, 27
Kieślowski, Krzysztof, 23, 26, 29, 36–7
Kilbourn, Russell, 54
Killing Fields, The (Jaffe, 1984), 184, 189
Kimbrough, Andrew, 24
Kinder, Marsha, 72
King, Geoff, 103
King, Homay, 123, 125, 132
Kirkkopelto, Esa, 106
Kitano, Takeshi, 23, 26, 39, 50
Kolin, Philip, 75, 76
Kornatowska, Maria, 26
Kotzamani, Marina, 161
Koutsourakis, Angelos, 166
Kouvaros, George, 5, 125, 132
Kovács, András Bálint
  Screening Modernism, 212
Kozloff, Sarah, 68, 172
Krauss, Rosalind, 8, 54
Krieger, Murray, 181
Kulezic-Wilson, Danijela
  Musicality of Narrative Film, The, 50

Labarthe, André S., 89, 94–5
Lagerroth, Ulla-Britta, 6
Lalanne, Jean-Marc, 72
Landscape in the Mist (Angelopoulos, 1988), 160
Laramie Project, The (Kaufman), 206–7
Lavin, Mathias, 145, 148–9
Lawlor, Patricia, 28
Lefebvre, Henri, 96
Lehmann, Hans-Thies, 150
Lejeune, Philippe, 186

Lemière, Jacques, 58
Lessing, Gotthold, 115–16
Levelt, W. J. M., 177
lip-synching, 71, 80–1, 197–8
Livingston, Paisley, 19, 20, 95–6
Lorca, Federico García, 82–3
Love on the Ground/L'Amour par terre (Rivette, 1984), 88
Lyotard, Jean-François, 182

McConachie, Bruce, 24
MacKay, Carol, 157–8
McKim, Richard, 183
McLuhan, Marshall, 213
Maddison, Stephen, 76
Malkin, Jeanette, 53
Malle, Louis, 171, 181
Manhattan Project, The, 171
Mann, Karen, 38–9
Margulies, Ivone, 124–5, 127
Marinis, Marco de, 120
Marion, Philippe, 8
Martin, Carol, 196, 197, 201
Martin-Márquez, Susan, 71, 73
Master Builder, A (Demme, 2013), 171
Mazars, Pierre, 93–4
Meek, Richard, 138
Megalexandros (Angelopoulos, 1980), 160
Mello, Cecília, 195
memory, 12, 53–5
   and *All About My Mother*, 71
   and Gray, 183, 185, 189–90
   and *The Jester*, 60–2, 63–6
Ménil, Alain, 211
Meninas, Las (Vélazquez), 35
Mennen, Richard, 175–6, 177
metalepsis, 122, 127–31
mimesis, 105–6
Mirto, Chris, 198
mise en abyme, 12, 20
   and *Double Life of Véronique, The*, 27, 28–30, 32–6, 38–9
   and *Synecdoche, New York*, 103–4
Mittell, Jason, 210
Mnouchkine, Ariane, 120
Molière, ou la vie d'un honnête homme (Mnouchkine, 1978), 13n2
Monaco, James, 88
monologues, 12, 157–60
   and *The Arbor*, 198–201, 202–3, 204, 207–8
   and autobiographical, 182–93

   and *My Dinner with André*, 171, 172, 173–4, 175–8
   and *The Travelling Players*, 165–70
Monster in a Box (Broomfield, 1992), 12, 183–4, 191–3
Moonstruck (Jewison, 1987), 191, 193
Morais, José Álvaro, 57–9, 67
Morrey, Douglas, 98
Morrissette, Bruce, 33
Mozos, Manuel, 57
Mullarkey, John, 5
Müller, Jürgen, 7
Mulvey, Laura, 6
Music for Chameleons (Capote), 72
Musser, Charles, 10
My Dinner with André (Malle, 1981), 12, 171–82
Myrsiades, Linda, 161, 163, 166

Nagel, Erica, 194, 206
Nagib, Lúcia, 7–8
Naremore, James, 6
   Acting in Cinema, 3
Neely, Carol, 140
nesting, 19–20, 95–6
Neupert, Richard, 51, 52
Noh theatre, 41
Nora, Pierre, 59

Ogier, Bulle, 88
Oliveira, Manoel de, 145–6, 154–5
O'Neill, Eugene, 158
Open Theater Workshop, 182–3
Opening Night (Cassavetes, 1977), 12, 71, 80, 120, 121, 122–34
O'Rawe, Des, 40, 41–2
Oresteia (Aeschylus), 162
ostension, 19, 96, 121
Out 1: Noli Me Tangere (Rivette, 1971), 88, 93

Paech, Joachim, 7
Page, Louise, 194
paragone, 135, 138, 140, 142, 143
paratheatre, 176, 178–9, 181–2
Parolini, Marilù, 90, 92
Pasqual, Lluis, 82, 83
Paterson, Eddie, 158, 183
Pavel, Thomas, 100, 108–10
Pavis, Patrice, 47, 70, 157, 158
performance, 9–10, 44–5, 209–10
   and evidential, 164–5
   and natural, 198
   and *Opening Night*, 132–4

Pethő, Ágnes, 7, 9, 24, 210
phenomenology, 7, 55, 63–4, 115–17
Phillips, Adam, 193
Piccoli, Michel, 121
Picon-Vallin, Béatrice, 212, 213
Pidduck, Julianne, 202
Pierre, Sylvie, 87
Pirandello, Luigi, 89
Piris, Paul, 23, 25, 46
Platinga, Carl, 152–3
Ponsoldt, James, 85
Porton, Richard, 197
Posner, Dassia, 23–4
Puchner, Martin, 46
puppet theatre, 12, 23–4, 25, 26
    and *Dolls*, 39–40, 41–2
    and *Double Life of Véronique, The*, 27–8, 29–38, 39
    and *Karaghiozis*, 162–3
    see also Bunraku

Radosavljević, Duška, 194–5
Rajewsky, Irina O., 14n5
Rancière, Jacques, 68
Random Acts of Intimacy (Barnard, 2002), 197–8
Rapfogel, Jared, 155
Rapold, Nicolas, 208
Rayner, Alice, 55–6, 61, 66, 74, 77–8, 179
Redmond, Sean, 26, 41, 50
reflexivity, 19–20
rehearsals, 84–6
    and *I'm Going Home*, 147, 156
    and *The Jester*, 59–60, 69–70
    and *L'Amour fou*, 88–9, 91–2, 94–5, 96–100
    and *Opening Night*, 127–8
    and *Synecdoche, New York*, 101–12
Rejas, Miguel, 72
repetition, 12, 53, 54, 73–4
Replogle, Carol, 32, 33
Resnais, Alain, 18–19, 212
Rhodie, Sam, 88, 99
Rita, Sue and Bob Too (Dunbar), 194
Rivette, Jacques, 86, 87, 88, 90–3, 97–8
Roach, Joseph, 98
Roberts, David, 34
Roberts, Les, 160
Rohmer, Eric, 134–5, 136, 139–40, 142, 143, 145
Romney, Jonathan, 32, 41
Ron, Moshe, 28, 30
Rossmanith, Kate, 86, 96–7, 105

Roth, Cecilia, 79
Rowlands, Gena, 121, 122, 124, 133
Royal Court Theatre, 171, 194, 195
Rozik, Eli, 4, 10
Rugg, Linda Haverty, 87
Rushton, Richard, 24–5, 159–60
Rutter, Carol Chillington, 5

Schechner, Richard, 4, 184
Schilling, Derek, 134–5
Schröter, Jens, 9
Schwartz, Bruce, 29, 36–8
Selfish Giant, The (Barnard, 2013), 204
Sellier, Geneviève, 90
Sex and Death to the Age 14 (Gray), 188
Seznec, Alain, 92
Shafransky, Renée, 184, 188, 189, 191–2
Shail, Andrew, 14n5
Shakespeare, William, 32, 137–8, 158
Shawn, Wallace, 171, 172, 173, 174–5, 180–1
Sidiropoulou, Avra, 115
Silverstein, Marc, 191
Simmel, Georg, 115–16
Sinnerbrink, Robert, 209
Smith, Alison, 98
Smith, Anna Deavere, 198
Smith, David L., 106
Smith, Murray, 8, 19, 25
Sobchack, Vivian, 64, 118
Sofer, Andrew, 4
soliloquies, 157–8
sonic perspective, 125–7
Sontag, Susan, 12n1, 54, 185
    and Bunraku, 45, 47–8, 49
Southern, Nathan C., 173, 177
spectators *see* audience
speech, 155–6; *see also* monologues
Spielmann, Yvonne, 7
Stafford-Clark, Max, 194, 195, 196–7, 197, 203–4
staging, 9–10, 44–5, 46, 120
    and *The Arbor*, 201–3, 205
    and *I'm Going Home*, 149–51, 154
    and *The Travelling Players*, 166
Stam, Robert, 20
State Affair, A (Soans), 197
States, Bert O., 2, 4–5, 100–1, 120–1
Stern, Lesley, 5, 64–5
Stevens, Wallace, 187–8
Stone, Laurie, 191
Straub, Jean-Marie, 212
Streetcar Named Desire, A (Williams), 57, 71, 72–3, 74–7, 78–82

Streiff, David, 57–8
Stucky, Nathan, 194, 198
Swimming to Cambodia (Demme, 1987), 12, 183–4, 185, 186–91
Syberberg, Hans-Jürgen, 57, 212
Synecdoche, New York (Kaufman, 2008), 12, 22, 84, 85, 86–7, 100–12

Tarr, Susan, 165
Taylor, Lib, 197
Tempest, The (Shakespeare), 146–7, 153–6
theatre
    and *All About My Mother*, 71, 72
    and audience, 119–20
    and Bergman, 1, 2–3
    and community-based, 206
    and embedment, 17–19
    and film, 9–11, 14n5–6, 20, 210–13
    and framing, 3–4
    and ghostliness, 55
    and Gray, 182–3, 185
    and Greece, 162–3
    and Grotowski, 175–9, 181
    and illusion, 26
    and Japan, 41–3
    and memory, 53–4, 60
    and *My Dinner with André*, 171–2, 179–82
    and narration, 67, 68, 69–70
    and Oliveira, 145–6
    and *Opening Night*, 123–5, 128–32
    and playwrights, 194–5
    and props, 4–5
    and spatiality, 12n1
    and time, 77–8
    and verbatim, 196–8, 203
    see also *A Streetcar Named Desire*; *Andromaque*; *Exit the King*; *Golfo the Shepherdess*; performance; puppet theatre; rehearsals; *Tempest, The*; *Winter's Tale, The*
Theatre Laboratory, 175–9
'theatre of the real', 196
theatricality, 2–5, 11, 17, 39, 46, 133–4, 140, 159, 160, 165, 171, 193, 212
Thomas, François, 93
Tillis, Steve, 27, 36, 38

Travelling Players, The/O Thiassos (Angelopoulos, 1975), 12, 160–70, 212
Trilling, Lionel, 209–10

Ubersfeld, Anne, 151–2
Uricchio, William, 6

Vanya on 42nd Street (Malle, 1994), 171
Vendler, Helen, 188
verbatim theatre, 157, 193–4, 195, 196–8, 203
Villeneuve, Johanne, 56, 64
Virk, Manjinder, 198
Vitez, Antoine, 86
voice, 12, 56–7, 68–9
    and *All About My Mother*, 71, 72–3, 78, 80–1, 83
    and *The Jester*, 61, 66–7, 69–71
    see also speech
Vous n'avez encore rien vu/You Ain't Seen Nothin' Yet (Resnais, 2012), 18–19

Waller, Gregory A., 14n6
Weber, Samuel, 3
Wertenbaker, Timberlake, 194
Wiles, Mary, 89
Williams, Jeffrey, 52
Williams, Tennessee, 75
Wilson, Emma, 28, 34
Wilson, George M., 10
Winter's Tale, The (Shakespeare), 135–41, 143–5
Wittgenstein, Ludwig, 21
Wojcik, Pamela Robertson, 68
Wolf, Werner, 14n5, 32, 180
Woman Under the Influence, A (Cassavetes, 1974), 133
Wood, Robin, 88

Yacavone, Daniel, 100, 101
Yacobi, Tamar, 178
Young, Paul, 213

Zarrilli, Phillip, 115, 116
Žižek, Slavoj, 28

EU representative:
Easy Access System Europe
Mustamäe tee 50, 10621 Tallinn, Estonia
Gpsr.requests@easproject.com

www.ingramcontent.com/pod-product-compliance
Lightning Source LLC
Chambersburg PA
CBHW071836230426
43671CB00012B/1978